Myths and Hero Tales

A Cross-Cultural Guide to Literature for Children and Young Adults

Alethea K. Helbig and Agnes Regan Perkins

Greenwood Press
Westport, Connecticut • London

Library of Congress Cataloging-in-Publication Data

Helbig, Alethea.
 Myths and hero tales : a cross-cultural guide to literature for
children and young adults / Alethea K. Helbig and Agnes Regan
Perkins.
 p. cm.
 Includes bibliographical references and indexes.
 ISBN 0–313–29935–8 (alk. paper)
 1. Mythology—Juvenile literature—Abstracts. 2. Mythology—
Juvenile literature—Indexes. I. Perkins, Agnes. II. Title.
 BL313.H45 1997
 016.3982—DC21 97–8778

British Library Cataloguing in Publication Data is available.

Library of Congress Catalog Card Number: 97–8778
ISBN: 0–313–29935–8

First published in 1997

Greenwood Press, 88 Post Road West, Westport, CT 06881
An imprint of Greenwood Publishing Group, Inc.

Printed in the United States of America

The paper used in this book complies with the
Permanent Paper Standard issued by the National
Information Standards Organization (Z39.48–1984).

10 9 8 7 6 5 4 3 2 1

Contents

Preface   vii

Index of Writers, Book Titles, and Stories   1

The Guide: Annotated Bibliographical Entries   51

Index of Stories by Types   171
    Table of Contents of Types   171
    List of Stories by Types   172

Index of Cultures   237

Index of Characters, Places, and Other Significant Items   243

Index of Book Titles by Grade Levels   273

Index of Book Titles   279

Index of Illustrators   285

Standard Books of Myths and Hero Tales   287

Preface

Myths and Hero Tales: A Cross-Cultural Guide for Children and Young Adults is designed to direct teachers and students to some of the best stories in world literature, as well as to facilitate studies in comparative mythology and in-depth research of a geographical area or culture. It contains entries on 189 books of retellings of myths and hero tales both ancient and modern from around the world, published from 1985 through 1996, suitable for use by and with young people from mid-elementary school through high school. Alto-gether, 1,455 stories are represented. The entries, which consist of brief, crit-ical reviews of the books arranged in alphabetical order by writer, appear in the Guide. Supplementing the Guide are seven indexes—writer; type of story; culture; characters, places, and other significant items; grade level; title; and illustrator—all of which are keyed to entries in the Guide. The book concludes with a bibliography of retellings that were published earlier and have come to be considered important standard works.

Some books in *Myths and Hero Tales* contain stories from a single culture or people; others are anthologies that offer selections from a variety of cultures. Individual stories range from a dozen lines to book-length narratives. Some books are highly illustrated, while others contain only texts. When they seem appropriate for the intended audience, picture books have been included.

Myths and hero tales are among the most imaginative and mind-stretching narratives available for young readers. They belong to the vast body of liter-ature known as oral tradition, which also includes folk tales, fables, proverbs, and such information as weather saws and recipes—sayings and stories that for the most part antedate writing and were passed along by word of mouth, in many instances for hundreds of years before they were set down. While some of these stories now exist only in writing, some continue in oral tradition, and many coexist in both oral and written form.

Although myths and hero tales are often considered to be one genre, the term *myth* also including *hero tale*, they are really two distinct literary forms. While the types may be intermingled in a particular story, each form serves its own purpose. Of the two, myths are thought to be the older—the world's earliest literature. They go back to the beginnings of human existence in postulating in story form answers to fundamental questions about life and the natural world. How did the earth come to be? How did human beings originate? Where did the gods come from, and what are they like? What is the relationship between gods and humans? What do gods expect of humans? And humans of their gods? Why are there certain facts of existence, like fire, floods, food, nations, war, beauty, love, hatred, and death? Why are there mountains, seas, rivers, trees, and flowers—such features of landscape and terrain? Where do we go when we die? Will the world always be as it is, or will it end? If so, how? When? Are there other worlds now? Will another world follow upon this one?

Early humans answered such vital questions in terms of what they knew and understood, connecting the answers with the divine order—with those powerful, superhuman beings called gods. The concerns addressed in these old stories are still pertinent, although some of the answers may seem naive to moderns. The basic insights embodied in the myths, however, remain relevant, and the beliefs the stories reflect deserve respect, as do the best truths of all people at all times.

Gods are at the center of the myths. The action in myths occurs in early and far-off times, before the earth became as it is today. Hero tales, on the other hand, are more likely to take place in the world as we know it. They feature the great men and women of the human race, those whose exploits were related for countless generations, also passed along by word of mouth. While gods may appear in the hero tales, and indeed they often do to help or hinder events, it is the hero, man or woman, who remains the focus. Heroes may be the offspring of gods, but they are almost always partly human, and thus they represent the heights to which humans may aspire, as well as the depths to which they may descend. As such, the heroes are highly symbolic figures.

Hero stories, which may be subdivided into such categories as epics, sagas, romances, and legends, are narratives that are longer and more complex in structure than myths. Like myths, hero tales are finely honed literary creations, nonessentials having long ago been pared away through myriads of tellings, so that what remains reflects the heart of the culture, those values to which the heroes in performing their brave deeds dedicate themselves.

As university teachers of literature for more than twenty-five years each, we have taught classes specifically in mythology and hero tale to college students, most of whom are prospective teachers. Alethea Helbig has also taught Native American Indian literature, which includes oral tradition, and the Bible as literature and has published a scholarly study of the Ojibwa figure of oral tradition, Nanabozhoo. We are well aware of the difficulty both teachers and students have in finding appropriate retellings of myths and hero tales for literary enjoyment and comparative study. We are concerned with the importance of quality in literature for young readers. Retellings from oral tradition should be both true to the culture and to the story details of the originals and also be attractive stylistically.

We find a wide variation in the skill with which the writers have handled their material, even given the range in intended audience. Some retellers have stayed very close to the originals, while others have added plot incidents, description, characters, dialogue, and even motivation, an aspect that is conspicuously absent in oral tradition where narrative, not psychological speculation, receives the emphasis. Other writers reduce intriguing stories to a mere precis of the action, destroying much of the drama and force.

Some retellers have scrupulously indicated what materials they have followed, even in picture books, a practice that should be applauded. Others have neglected to do so, an omission particularly significant in books aimed at those older readers in whom respect for sources should be standard and encouraged. High school students especially should develop a solid appreciation for sources and documentation. As a help to both teachers and students, we have pointed out in the entries of the Guide where sources are omitted or misused.

Although retellers do not always acknowledge their sources as they should, we find that increasingly they are looking to cultures less well known for stories to retell. For example, some narratives from Tibet, Siberia, and even the Russian Altaic, a culture some linguists do not accept as distinct, are represented in *Myths and Hero Tales*, although most books published in this twelve-year period still draw from largely familiar cultures. Publishers have issued a few eclectic anthologies of world myths with wide, if often superficial, coverage—overloaded with names, lacking in narrative impact, and conveying little sense of the culture—and a number of much more detailed collections focusing on regional areas or cultural groups. From the Native American Indian and Sub-Saharan African traditions come many beautiful single-story picture books, collections for middle-grade children, and scholarly works for more sophisticated readers. Publishers have, however, put out few extended hero tales giving the depth and understanding of such earlier works as Rosemary Sutcliff's *The Hound of Ulster* and Joseph Gaer's *The Adventures of Rama*. Nor have there been many collections of Greek and Norse myths and hero tales of the caliber of Edith Hamilton's *Mythology* and Dorothy Hosford's *Thunder of the Gods*. As a general rule, however, the variety of stories available, particularly for the elementary and middle-grade range, is greater than ever and well beyond the number available at mid century.

We have added a list of classic and standard books of mythology and hero tales published before 1985 and still readily available. The list is not intended to be definitive, but anyone wanting a well-written, comprehensive retelling of the best-known stories for their enjoyment or against which to judge newer works can find one on the list.

A word should be said about the arrangement of *Myths and Hero Tales*.

Since we are aware that different readers have different needs, we have provided a number of indexes to facilitate their research. The Index of Writers, Book Titles, and Stories gives an overview of the contents. Since all indexes are keyed to entries in this Guide, it appears next. For those readers who wish to locate particular types of stories (e.g., origin of humans, flood stories, trickster tales), there is the Index of Stories by Types. Other readers will be interested in exploring stories from a particular culture or geographical area, or wish to pursue a specific figure or concept (e.g., Medea, Maui, Dreamtime), or want books for a certain grade level. These indexes appear in order, followed by indexes of book titles and illustrators and the selective bibliography of standard works.

The Index of Writers, Book Titles, and Stories lists not only writers and names of books, but also the general culture area (e.g., British Isles, Japan, Native America), the sort of book (anthology, collection, single story), and the stories within the book that can be classified as myth or hero tale. The number of stories listed does not necessarily reflect the full contents of the book, since some anthologies and collections also contain folk tales, fiction, poetry, memoirs, and other material that does not fall within the scope of *Myths and Hero Tales*. (We use the term "writer," although both retellers and editors are represented. In a few instances, the writer is also the translator.)

The Index of Stories by Types classifies individual stories by subject matter and function (e.g., creation of the world, heavenly phenomena, warriors). A Table of Contents shows the overall order of types; this is followed by the titles of stories arranged by type. A reader, for example, seeking an account of the origin of the seasons or a tale of romance and chivalry, can glance through the table of contents and locate the type by number. In general, myths and hero tales are treated separately. Some figures, however, are not easily categorized (e.g., Loki, Anansi). Scholars do not agree on whether such characters are heroes or gods, and indeed, some figures participate in both categories. Rather than make distinctions that may not hold up under scrutiny, we have combined god and hero tricksters, goddesses and important female figures, and searches and quests as types that contain both hero tales and myths.

With respect to the Index of Cultures, some writers are explicit in listing where the stories originate. Others are more general (West Africa, Northern Europe). Although we have indicated broad cultural groups or geographical areas in the Index of Writers, Book Titles, and Stories, in the Index of Cultures we have used the most specific designation given in the books themselves, sometimes nationality, sometimes tribe, sometimes language group, sometimes geographical area.

One of the difficulties of dealing with retellings from oral tradition is that the names of figures often appear with variant spellings. In the Index of Characters, Places, and Other Significant Items we have combined items where the figures are clearly the same, although the spellings vary (Athena-Athene,

Bedevere-Bedivere). Some figures are related, but not identical (Odysseus-Ulysses), or the spellings are so different that a reader is not likely to find them in the index for the same character (Manabozo-Nanabozhoo-Winabijou). In such cases we have directed the reader with a "*See also*." Where we are not sure that the same figure is meant, we have provided separate index items.

The Index of Book Titles by Grade Levels poses some special problems. In general, we have followed publishers' age designations, except in cases where our experience leads us to a different conclusion. Particularly with retellings from oral tradition, suggested levels should not be followed slavishly. Since myths and hero tales were intended for all ages, the retellings can usually be treated with flexibility and, depending upon the proposed use, may have no age limits. Children differ greatly, and their receptivity to books often depends on the skill and enthusiasm of the adults working with them. While many highly illustrated, single-story books were issued for preschoolers and early elementary children, they are serious in tone and stylistically attractive and are just as appropriate for students in middle school and high school. They are, in reality, all-ages books. Similarly, even when a book is aimed at older children, it may be accessible to younger ones if introduced by a dedicated and sensitive adult, or books intended for middle graders may be of interest to teenagers for comparison or supplementary information. With this in mind, users of *Myths and Hero Tales* should take grade levels only as a general guide.

We ourselves have read and considered all the books included here, and the literary judgments are our own. For valuable assistance, we express our appreciation to the Eastern Michigan University Library and the Ann Arbor, Michigan, District Library. Specifically, we thank Brian Steimel and Thomas Staicar of the Interlibrary Loan Department of Eastern Michigan University for their help in obtaining books not available locally.

The assistance of the Ann Arbor District Library staff has been of immense value to us. We thank the reference librarians and the clerical and library staff, especially the following: Sherry Roberts, Paula Schaffner, Cynthia Chelius, Betsy Baier, and Yvette Shane (Director), all of the Main Library, and Ieva Bates of the Loving Branch. Our appreciation also goes to Kathy Wasil of the Ypsilanti, Michigan, District Library for helping in a variety of ways and especially for her interest in and ongoing support for all our projects.

The following abbreviations are used in the entries:

ad.	adapter	ret.	retelling; reteller
coll.	collection; collector	sel.	selector
comp.	compiler	trans.	translator
ed.	editor	unp.	unpaginated
illus.	illustrator		

Index of Writers, Book Titles, and Stories

(Numerals at the left refer to the book entries in the Guide; numerals after the story titles refer to page numbers within the books.)

1 Alderson, Brian, ret., *The Arabian Nights Or Tales Told by Sheherezade During a Thousand and One Nights* (collection, Arabia)

> "The Two Kings, Shah Shahryar and Shah Zaman, and the Wazir's Daughter Sheherezade," 9

2 Alexander, Ellen, ret., *Llama and the Great Flood: A Folktale from Peru* (single story, Native American, Quechua)

3 Allen, Paula Gunn, ed., *Spider Woman's Granddaughters: Traditional Tales and Contemporary Writing by Native American Women* (collection, Native American)

> "The Warrior Maiden," Oneida, 53
>
> "The Woman Who Fell from the Sky," Mohawk, 56
>
> "The Beginning and the End of the World," Okanagon, 106
>
> "Coyote Kills Owl-Woman," Okanagan, 112
>
> "Evil Kachina Steals Yellow Woman," Cochiti, 182
>
> "Sun Steals Yellow Woman," Cochiti, 186
>
> "Whirlwind Man Steals Yellow Woman," Laguna, 187

4 Al-Saleh, Khairat, ret., *Fabled Cities, Princes & Jinn from Arab Myths and Legends* (collection, Arabia)

> "Myths and Legends of the Extinct Arabs," 32
>
> "The Woman with the Wonderful Sight," 36
>
> "The Vengeance of God," 37
>
> "Iran of the Tall Columns," 44
>
> "Queen Balqis and King Sulayman," 50
>
> "The Queen Priestess and the Dyke of Ma'rib," 57

"The Story of Queen Zabba and King Jadhima," 60

"The Order of Creation," 88

"The Arabian Nights," 103

"The City of Brass," 108

5   Anderson, David A., ret., *The Origin of Life on Earth: An African Creation Myth* (single story, Sub-Saharan Africa)

6   Anderson, William, coll. and ret., *Green Man: The Archetype of Our Oneness with the Earth* (anthology)

"Cybele and Attis," Anatolia, Phrygia, 38

7   Armstrong, Carole, ret., *Lives and Legends of the Saints* (anthology)

"George," British Isles, 23

"Francis of Assisi," Italy, 24

"Joan of Arc," France, 41

8   Ashby, Gene, comp. and ed., *Never and Always: Micronesian Legends, Fables, and Folklore* (collection, Micronesia)

"The Demiurge Builders of Nan Madol," 31

"The Rock of Khlop on Satawal," 48

"The First Sakau on Pohnpei," 106

9   Bach, Alice, and J. Cheryl Exum, rets., *Moses' Ark: Stories from the Bible* (collection, ancient Israel)

"The Garden of Eden," 9

"The Flood," 19

"The Tower," 29

"Moses' Ark," 35

"The Exodus," 47

"The Promised Land," 65

"Deborah, Judge over Israel," 77

"The Adventures of Samson," 95

"The Wisdom of Solomon," 145

"Elijah, the Prophet of God," 159

10 Bascom, William, coll. and ed., *African Folktales in the New World* (anthology, Sub-Saharan Africa, African American, Native American; three main stories with more than 100 variants)

"Oba's Ear: A Yoruba Myth in Cuba and Brazil," Yoruba, Cuba, Brazil, 1 (several brief variants)

"Trickster Seeks Endowments; Measuring the Snake; Challenging Birds (Insects) to Fill a Container; Milking a Cow (Deer) Stuck in a Tree," Ashanti (Ghana) and others, 40

Stories 1, 2, Mandinka (Gambia), 44
Story 3, Temne (Sierra Leone), 44
Stories 4, 5, Temne (Sierra Leone), 45
Story 6, Liberia, 45
Story 7, Liberia, 46
Story 8, De (Liberia), 46
Story 9, Wobe (Ivory Coast), 46
Story 10, Fulani (Mali), 46
Story 11, Malinke (Mali), 47
Story 12, Mosi (Upper Volta), 47
Story 13, Mosi (Upper Volta), 48
Story 14, Ghana, 48
Stories 15, 16, 17, Ghana, 49
Stories 18, 19, 20, 21, Ashanti (Ghana), 50
Story 22, Ashanti (Ghana), 51
Story 23, Ewe (Ghana), 51
Story 24, Hausa (Nigeria), 51
Stories 25, 26, Hausa (Nigeria), 52
Story 27, Bura (Nigeria), 52
Story 28, Igbo (Nigeria), 53
Story 29, Mbala (Zaire), 53
Story 30, Native American, Hitchiti (Oklahoma), 53
Story 31, Native American, Natchez (Oklahoma), 54
Story 32, Native American, Chitimacha (Louisiana), 54
Story 33, African American (Mississippi), 54
Story 34, African American (Alabama), 54
Story 35, African American (Alabama), 55
Story 36, African American (Virginia), 55
Story 37, African American (South Carolina), 55
Stories 38, 39, 40, 41, 42, African American (South Carolina), 56
Stories 43, 44, 45, African American (South Carolina), 57
Stories 46, 47, 48, African American (South Carolina), 58
Stories 49, 50, 51, 52, African American (Georgia), 59
Stories 53, 54, 55, 56, African American (Georgia), 60
Stories 57, 58, Native American, Creek (Georgia), 61
Story 59, Native American, Seminole (Florida), 61
Story 60, Mexico (unspecified; probably Native American), 61
Story 61, Native American, Chuh (Guatemala), 62
Story 62, African (Bahamas), 62
Story 63, African (Dominican Republic), 63
Stories 64, 65, 66, African (Guadaloupe), 63
Story 67, African (Guadaloupe), 64
Story 68, African (Marie Galante), 64
Story 69, African (Les Saintes), 64
Story 70, African (Les Saintes), 65

Stories 71, 72, African (Dominica), 65
Story 73, African (Martinique), 65
Story 74, African (Saint Lucia), 65
Story 75, African (Grenada), 66
Story 76, African (Trinidad), 66
Story 77, Native American, Warao (Venezuela), 66
Story 78, Colombia, 67

"Moon Splits Hare's Lip (Nose)," Sub-Saharan Africa, 145
Story 1, African American (Georgia), 146
Story 2, Native American, Chitimacha (Louisiana), 147
Story 3, Hausa (Nigeria), 147
Stories 4, 5, Bushman (Botswana), 147
Stories 6, 7, 8, 9, 10, Bushman (Botswana), 148
Stories 11, 12, 13, 14, 15, 16, Bushman (South Africa), 149
Story 17, Bushman (Namibia), 149
Stories 18, 19, 20, Hottentot (South Africa), 150
Stories 21, 22, 23, 24, Hottentot (South Africa), 151
Stories 25, 26, 27, Hottentot (South Africa), 152
Stories 28, 29, 30, Hottentot (South Africa), 153
Stories 31, 32, Hottentot (Namibia), 153

11   Battle, Kemp P., comp., *Great American Folklore: Legends, Tales, Ballads and Superstitions from All Across America* (collection, United States)
"How Johnny Appleseed Brought Apple Blossoms to the West," 12

"Daniel Boone's Tale of the Three Notches," 51

"How Mike Fink Beat Davy Crockett in a Shooting Match," 99

"Mike Fink and the Deacon's Bull," 101

"John Henry, the Steel Driving Man," 134

"Mose Humphries, the Fighting Fireman," 141

"The Death of Crockett," 151

"Davy Crockett Meets His Match," 180

"Crockett Pops the Question," 224

"How Daniel Boone Found His Wife," 225

"The Queen of the Bull-Whackers," 239

"Coyote Turns into a Buffalo," (Native American, Pawnee), 343

"The Wonderful Tar-Baby Story," 346

"How Mr. Rabbit Was Too Sharp for Mr. Fox," 348

"Crockett Gets the Votes," 394

"Calamity's Bet," 478

"Annie Oakley Makes Her Name," 479

"The Saga of Pecos Bill," 517

"Sam Patch, the Jumping Man," 577

"Febold Feboldson, the Most Inventingest Man," 585

"Gib Morgan and the Whickles," 588

"Gib's Biggest Rig," 593

"How Gib Invented Rubber Boots," 595

"How Gib Saved His Tool Dresser," 596

"Paul Bunyan's Birth," 603

"Babe, Paul Bunyan's Blue Ox," 604

"Why the Great Lakes Have No Whales," 611

"The Round Drive," 620

"How Paul Bunyan Cleared North Dakota," 623

"Tony Beaver Meets Paul Bunyan," 626

12 Beck, Brenda E. F., Peter J. Claus, Praphulladatta Goswami, and Jawaharlal Handoo, eds., *Folktales of India* (collection, India)

"The Goddess of Mahi River," Gujarat, 5

"The Rain Prince's Bride," Gujarat, 9

"The Birth and Marriage of Siva," West Bengal, 71

"The Youngest Daughter-in-Law," West Bengal, 75

"Lord Siva and the Satwaras," Gujarat, 85

"Lord Krishna's Wives," Karnataka, 155

"Siva and Parvati," Karnataka, 171

"Vayanatu Kulavan," Kerala, 175

"The Origin of Man," Manipur, 269

"How Lijaba Created the World," Nagaland, 273

"Bhimnath Mahadev," Gujarat, 279

13 Belting, Natalia M., ret., *Moon Was Tired of Walking on Air* (collection, Native American)

"Moon Was Tired of Walking on Air," Chorote, 7

"The Traveling Sky Baskets," Apanyekra, 10

"What Happened When Fox Opened the Bottle Tree," Chorote, 12

"Daughter of Rain," Cayapo, 15

"Why Rainbow Is Bent," Selkam, 21

"Why Sun Has a Headdress and Moon Has None," Ramkokamekra, 22

"When Orekeke Wrestled Tornado," Teheulces, 25

"Ghosts and Souls," Tapirape, 29

"Fox and the Parakeet Women," Chorote, 30

"How Averiri Made the Night and the Seasons," Campas, 36

"What Happened When Armadillo Dug a Hole in the Sky," Cayapo, 38

"The Ancestors Are All around Us," Selkam, 42

"How the Birds Got New Beaks and Men Got Teeth," Bororo, 44

14   Bennett, Martin, ret., *West African Trickster Tales* (collection, Sub-Saharan Africa)

"Head Over Heart," 3

"The Glue of Greed," 11

"A Debt Made Profit, Or, Why Monkeys Live in Trees," 23

"Ananse Meets His Measure," 61

"The Opposite Party," 71

"Ananse's Harvest," 89

"The Monster at the Stream," 103

15   Bernhard, Emery, ret., *The Tree That Rains: The Flood Myth of the Huichol Indians of Mexico* (single story, Native American)

16   Berry, Jack, ret., *West African Folktales* (collection, Sub-Saharan Africa)

"The Scarecrow," Ga (Ghana), 11

"Why We Tell Stories About Spider," Ga (Ghana), 14

"Aja and the Enchanted Beast," Krobo (Ghana), 21

"Adene and the Pineapple Child," Ga (Ghana), 26

"Spider Finds a Fool," Ga (Ghana), 32

"Spider's Bargain with God," Sefwi (Ghana), 38

"The Yam Farm and the Problem Tongue," Ga (Ghana), 56

"Tortoise Buys a House," Yoruba (Nigeria), 63

"Why Bush Pig Has a Red Face," Ga (Ghana), 64

"Spider and the Nightjar," Sefwi (Ghana), 66

"Spider Learns to Listen," Sefwi (Ghana), 67

"Tortoise and the Singing Crab," Vane Avatime (Ghana), 69

"How Tortoise Got Water," Yoruba (Nigeria), 74

"The Cloud Mother," Krio (Sierra Leone), 75

"Spider the Artist," Ga (Ghana), 77

"Ata and the Messenger Bird," Krobo (Ghana), 78

"The Most Powerful Name," Avatime (Ghana), 89

"The Return of Ananse," Sefwi (Ghana), 90

"Ananse Is Put in His Place," Sefwi (Ghana), 101

"How Crab Got His Shell," Northern Ghana, 106

"Why Fowls Scratch," Twi (Ghana), 118

"The Bag of Salt," Ga (Ghana), 120

"The Stone with Whiskers," Krio (Sierra Leone), 122

"Why Lizard Bobs His Head," Ga (Ghana), 127

"Spider the Swindler," Sefwi (Ghana), 128

"Tortoise Sheds a Tear," Yoruba (Nigeria), 131

"Tortoise Disobeys," Yoruba (Nigeria), 135

"Dog Is Betrayed," Yoruba (Nigeria), 136

"The Wisdom of Aja," Krobo (Ghana), 140

"Why the Mason Wasp Has a Narrow Waist," Krobo (Ghana), 147

"The Fairies and the Flute," Adengme (Ghana), 148

"Why Hippo Wears No Coat," Krobo (Ghana), 158

"Why Spider Is Bald," Ga (Ghana), 163

"Spider and the Calabash of Knowledge," Twi (Ghana), 165

"Tortoise and the Stew Bowl," Ga (Ghana), 170

"Crab and Guinea Fowl Part Ways," Yoruba (Ghana), 170

"The Vultures and the Liver Cave," Krio (Sierra Leone), 175

"The Nefarious Fly," Sefwi (Ghana), 176

"The Gluttonous Monkey," Avatime (Ghana), 178

"The Price of Eggs," Sefwi (Ghana), 181

"The Coffin of God's Daughter," Twi (Ghana), 182

"The Quarrel Between Heaven and Earth," Yoruba (Nigeria), 183

"Ananse and God's Business," Larteh (Ghana), Twi (Ghana), 189

"Why the Sky Is High," Ga (Ghana), 190

17 Bierhorst, John, ed., *The Monkey's Haircut and Other Stories Told by the Maya* (collection, Native American)

"Chac," 66

"Rabbit and Coyote," 72

"Rabbit and Puma," 77

"Rabbit Gets Married," 81

"The Lord Sun's Bride," 84

"Blue Sun," 107

18 Bierhorst, John, sel., *The Mythology of Mexico and Central America* (collection, Native American)

"The Emergence of Ancestors," Aztec, 67

"The Man of Crops," Jicaque, 68

"Why the Earth Eats the Dead," Bribri, 74

"Opossum Steals Fire," Mazatec, 77

"The Loss of the Ancients," Tarahumara, 79

"The Flood Myth," Mixe, 80

"The Seeds of Humanity," Guaymi, 84

"The Tree and the Flood," Cabecar, 84

"The Sun and Fire," Huichol, 100

"The Childhood of Sun and Moon," Chatino, 102

"The Sun and His Brothers," Tzotzil, 110

"The Dead Wife," Miskito, 117

19 Bierhorst, John, sel. and ret., *The Mythology of North America* (collection, Native American)

"The Raven Cycle," Tsimshian, 28

"Mink," Kwakiutl, 36

"The House of Myths," Kwakiutl, 39

"Creation Tales," Nunivak, 60

"Creation Tales," Eskimo, 61

"The Mother of Animals," Eskimo, 62

"In the Beginning," Apache, 84

"In the Beginning," Zuni, 84

"The Bird Nester," Apache, 86

"Toads and Frogs," Gabrielino/Luiseno, 100

"Elder Brother," Pima, 103

"Coyote Releases Salmon," Salish, 142

"Coyote as Orpheus," Chinook, 144

"Star Boy," Crow, Arapaho, Blackfeet, Kiowa, 158

"The Woman Who Fell from the Sky," Iroquois, 196

"The Red Swan," Winnebago, 218

"The *Walam Olum*," Delaware, 222

"The Mind of *Wakonda*," Winnebago, 230

20 Bierhorst, John, sel., *The Mythology of South America* (collection, Native American)

"The Tree and the Flood," (prototype story), 12

"The Twin Myth," (prototype story), 12

"The Plant from the Grave," Yuracare (Bolivia), 31

"Moon and His Sister," Barasana (Brazil), 32

"The Origin of Night," Bororo (Brazil), 33

"The Origin of Male Domination," Mundurucu (Brazil), 44

"Alone in the Darkness," Tariana (Brazil), 55

"Creation by Thought," Witoto (Colombia), 57

"Creation of the Self," Mbya Guarani (Paraguay), 58

"The Twin Myth," Waiwai (Guiana), 86

"The Star Woman," Ge (Brazil), 96

"The Bird Nester and the Jaguar," Ge (Brazil), 101

"Tokwah, Lord of the Dead," Mataco (Argentina), 124

"Fire," Mataco (Argentina), 139

"Cold," Toba (Argentina), 143

"Darkness," Toba (Argentina), 144

"The Yoaloh Brothers," Yamana (Chile), 155

"Myths of the Kogi," Kogi (Colombia), 178

"Wirakocha," Inca (Peru), 200

21 Bierhorst, John, ed., *The White Deer and Other Stories Told by the Lenape* (collection, Native American)

"How the First Stories Came Out of the Earth," 17

"Snow Boy," 18

"The Giant Squirrel," 20

"The Big Fish and the Sun," 47

"Ball Player," 56

"The White Deer," 67

"Jack Babysits," 79

"Crazy Jack Puts His Nose to the Ground," 81

"Wehixamukes Story," 82

"More Wehixamukes," 85

"Six Stories About Wehixamukes," 89

"Why the World Doesn't End," 106

22 Bierhorst, John, ret., *The Woman Who Fell from the Sky: The Iroquois Story of Creation* (single story, Native American, Iroquois)

23 Bright, William, sel. and ed., *A Coyote Reader* (collection, Native American)

"Telling about Coyote," Pueblo, 30

"How Her Teeth Were Pulled," Northern Paiute, 37

"Coyote Gives Birth," Southern Paiute, 44

"Coyote Places the Stars," Hopi, 49

"Coyote Turns into Driftwood," Karuk, 65

"Coyote Steals Fire," Karuk, 84

"Coyote and the Prairie Dogs," Navajo, 92

"Sex, Fingers, and Death," Yana, 105

"First Woman Invents Compassion," Blackfeet, 117

"Coyote Continues Upriver," Karuk, 122

"Coyote and Badger," Kathlamet Chinook, 124

"Coyote Tricks Grey Fox," Apache, 131

"Two Coyotes," Nez Perce, 135

"Coyote Marries His Own Daughter," Karuk, 146

"Coyote on the Beach," Karuk, 152

24   Bruchac, Joseph, ret., *Between Earth & Sky: Legends of Native American Sacred Places* (collection, Native American)

"Mau-shop (Gay Head)," Wampanoag, 5

"Ne-ah-ga (Niagara)," Seneca, 7

"El Capitan," Navaho, 9

"Great Smokies," Cherokee, 11

"The Race," Cheyenne, 17

"Grand Canyon," Hopi, 19

"Lake Champlain," Abenaki, 23

25   Bruchac, Joseph, ret., *Iroquois Stories Heroes and Heroines Monsters and Magic* (collection, Native American)

"The Coming of Legends," 12

"The Creation," 15

"The Two Brothers," 19

"How Bear Lost His Tail," 32

"Chipmunk and Bear," 37

"The Gifts of the Little People," 41

"Turtle's Race with Beaver," 47

"Turtle's Race with Bear," 51

"Turtle Makes War on Men," 55

"How Buzzard Got His Feathers," 61

"Rabbit and the Willow Tree," 65

"Raccoon and the Crayfish," 69

"Rabbit and Fox," 74

"The Hungry Fox and the Boastful Suitor," 80

"The Dogs Who Saved Their Master," 85

"The Two-headed Snake," 97

"The Story of Okteondon or the Workers of Evil," 104

"The Two Daughters," 116

"The Girl Who Was Not Satisfied with Simple Things," 123

"The Stone Coat Woman," 135

"The Wife of the Thunderer," 146

"Skunny-Wundy and the Stone Giant," 161

"Hodadenon: The Last One Left and the Chestnut Tree," 169

"The Brave Woman and the Flying Head," 184

"The Hunting of the Great Bear," 189

Bruchac, Joseph, ret. *See* Caduto, no. 27.

26   Burn, Lucilla, ret., *Greek Myths* (collection, Greece)

   "Introduction," (Demeter and Persephone), 7

   "Introduction," (Ares, Aphrodite, Hephaistos), 14

   "The Labours of Herakles," 16

   "Theseus of Athens," 25

   "The Trojan War," 31

   "The Story of Odysseus," 43

   "Jason, Medea and the Golden Fleece," 59

   "Perseus and Medusa," 63

   "Oedipus and the Theban Cycle," 66

27   Caduto, Michael J., and Joseph Bruchac, rets., *Keepers of the Earth: Native American Stories and Environmental Activities for Children* (collection, Native American)

   "Of Science and Indian Myths," Seneca, 3

   "The Coming of Gluscabi," Abenaki, 21

   "The Earth on Turtle's Back," Onondaga, 25

   "Four Worlds: The Dine Story of Creation," Dine (Navajo), 31

   "Loo-Wit, The Fire-Keeper," Nisqually, 41

   "Old Man Coyote and the Rock," Pawnee, 57

   "Tunka-shila, Grandfather Rock," Lakota, 57

   "Gluscabi and the Wind Eagle," Abenaki, 67

   "The Hero Twins and the Swallower of Clouds," Zuni, 79

   "Koluscap and the Water Monster," Micmac, Maliseet, 81

   "How Thunder and Earthquake Made Ocean," Yurok, 93

   "Sedna, the Woman Under the Sea," Inuit, 95

   "How Raven Made the Tides," Tsimshian, 103

   "How Fisher Went to the Skyland: The Origin of the Big Dipper," Anishinabe, 117

   "Spring Defeats Winter," Seneca, 129

   "The Coming of Corn," Cherokee, 137

   "Manabozho and the Maple Trees," Anishinabe, 145

   "Kokopilau, the Hump-Backed Flute Player," Hopi, 151

   "How Turtle Flew South for the Winter," Dakota (Sioux), 157

   "Gluscabi and the Game Animals," Abenaki, 165

   "The Origin of Death," Siksika (Blackfeet), 181

   "The White Buffalo Calf Woman and the Sacred Pipe," Lakota (Sioux), 187

28   Chaikin, Miriam, ad., *Exodus* (single story, ancient Israel)

29   Chatterjee, Debjani, ret., *The Elephant-Headed God and Other Hindu Tales* (collection, India)

> "The Monkey Bridge to Lanka," 1
>
> "The Elephant-Headed God," 9
>
> "Shiva and the Mountain," 24
>
> "Ashes to Ashes," 28
>
> "The Dwarf's Three Steps," 36
>
> "Krishna—Man and God," 43
>
> "Bhima and the Monkey's Tail," 55
>
> "Yudhishtira's Journey," 60
>
> "Kunti's Secret Son," 65
>
> "For Love of Urvashi," 81

Claus, Peter J., ed. *See* Beck, no. 12.

30   Climo, Shirley, ret., *Atalanta's Race* (single story, Greece)

31   Climo, Shirley, ret., *Someone Saw a Spider: Spider Facts and Folktales* (anthology)

> "Arachne's Gift," Greece, 5
>
> "The Spider Brothers Make the Rainbow," Native American, Achomawi, 29

32   Climo, Shirley, ret., *Stolen Thunder: A Norse Myth* (single story, Norse)

33   Cohen, Caron Lee, ret., *The Mud Pony* (single story, Native American, Pawnee)

34   Connolly, James E., ret., *Why the Possum's Tail Is Bare and Other North American Indian Nature Tales* (collection, Native American)

> "How the Rabbit Lost Its Tail," Sioux, 43
>
> "Old Man and the Bobcat," Blackfeet, 50
>
> "Coyote in the Cedar Tree," Chinook, 61

Costas, ret. *See* Switzer, no. 155.

35   Craft, M. Charlotte, ret., *Cupid and Psyche* (single story, Graeco-Roman)

36   Crespo, George, ret., *How Iwariwa the Cayman Learned to Share* (single story, Native American, Yanomami)

37   Crespo, George, ret., *How the Sea Began: A Taino Myth* (single story, Native American)

Crossley-Holland, Kevin, ret. *See* Thomas, no. 163.

38   Curry, Jane Louise, ret., *Robin Hood and His Merry Men* (collection, British Isles)

39   Curry, Jane Louise, ret., *Robin Hood in the Greenwood* (collection, British Isles)

40   Dalley, Stephanie, trans., *Myths from Mesopotamia* (collection, Mesopotamia)

> "Atrahasis," 1
>
> "The Epic of Gilgamesh," 39
>
> "The Descent of Ishtar to the Underworld," 154
>
> "Nergal and Ereshkigal," 163
>
> "Adapa," 182
>
> "Etana," 189
>
> "Anzu," 203
>
> "The Epic of Creation," 228
>
> "Theogony of Dunnu," 278
>
> "Erra and Ishum," 282

41   DeSpain, Pleasant, coll. and ret., *Thirty-Three Multicultural Tales to Tell*
(anthology)

> "Grandfather Spider's Feast," Sub-Saharan Africa, 35
>
> "Coyote Steals Spring," Native American, Pacific Northwest, 63
>
> "Hungry Spider," Sub-Saharan Africa, Ashanti, 107

42   Ecun, Oba (Cecilio Perez), coll. and ret., *Ita: Mythology of the Yoruba
Religion* (collection, Santeria stories from Sub-Saharan Africa later told
in Brazil, Cuba, and Haiti)

> "Formation of the Earth," 38
>
> "Oddua and Yembo's Love," 41
>
> "Second Child—Oggun (Metals), 42
>
> "Sixth Child—Osain," 45
>
> "Seventh Child and First Female—Dada (Brain)," 47
>
> "Ninth Child—Oba Nani (Wisdom and Teacher of the World)," 48
>
> "Tenth Child—Oya (The Air We Breathe)," 49
>
> "Birth of Orula," 63
>
> "First Encounter Between Oggun and Shango," 78
>
> "Jeggua's Punishment," 98

43   Elder, John, and Hertha D. Wong, eds., *Family of Earth and Sky: Indigenous Tales of Nature from Around the World* (anthology)

> "The Emergence," Native American, Navajo, 17
>
> "The Creation," Native American, Mohawk, 32
>
> "Tangaroa, Maker of All Things," Tahiti, 40
>
> "In the Beginning . . . ," Australian Aboriginal, 42
>
> "*Kalevala*: The Mother of Water," Finland, 44
>
> "The Origin of Different Water Animals," Nagaland (India), 50

"Juruna Kills the Sun," Native American, Juruna (Brazil), 52

"How Moon Fathered the World," Sub-Saharan Africa, Wakaranga (Zimbabwe), 56

"Sun and Moon," Native American, Nivakle (Paraguay), 58

"The Origin of Fishes," Sub-Saharan Africa, Fon (Benin), 65

"How Gluskabe Brought the Summer," Native American, Abenaki, 66

"Halibu the Hunter," Mongolia, 75

"The Toad," Sub-Saharan Africa, Ibo (Nigeria), 79

"The Chameleon and the Lizard," Sub-Saharan Africa, Margi, 80

"The Origin of Death," Sub-Saharan Africa, Hottentot, 81

"The Song of the Birds," Native American, Mohawk, 109

"The Blossom Tree," Tibet, 112

"*Kalevala*: Song of the Bear," Finland, 123

"Anansi Owns All Tales That Are Told," Sub-Saharan Africa, Ashanti (Ghana), 195

"Anansi's Rescue from the River," Sub-Saharan Africa, Ashanti (Ghana), 198

"Anansi Plays Dead," Sub-Saharan Africa, Ashanti (Ghana), 200

"The Jackal and the Hen," Kabyle (Algeria), 203

"The Jackal and the Lion," Kabyle (Algeria), 205

"How Ijapa, Who Was Short, Became Long," Sub-Saharan Africa, Yoruba (Nigeria), 207

"Ijapa Cries for His Horse," Sub-Saharan Africa, Yoruba (Nigeria), 209

"T'appin (Terrapin)," African American, 212

"Sheer Tops," African American, 215

"The Monkey-Son," Tamiladu (India), 220

"The Raven and the Whale," Inuit (Eskimo), 223

"The Raven and the Hunter," Inuit (Eskimo), 225

"The Lustful Raven," Inuit (Eskimo), 226

"The Winnebago Trickster Cycle," Native American, Winnebago, 228

"The Stealing of the Sun," Native American, Kato, 233

"Sun's Arrival in the Sky," Native American, Miwok, 235

"Coyote Juggles His Eyes," Native American, Sioux, 237

44   Erdoes, Richard, coll., ed., and ret., *Tales from the American Frontier* (collection, United States)

"Tarzan Boone," 37

"Swallowing a Scalping Knife," 42

"A Damn Good Jump," 45

"The Warrior Woman," 49

"The Irrepressible Backwoodsman and Original Humorist," 57

"Grinning the Bark off a Tree," 60

"Davy Crockett on the Stump," 61

"The Drinks Are on Me, Gentlemen," 61

"Jim Bowie and His Big Knife," 63

"A Shooting Match," 75

"Did Such a Helliferocious Man Ever Live?," 77

"Like Father, Like Daughter," 80

"She Fought Her Weight in She-B'ars," 81

"Little Big Man," 95

"Kit Carson and the Grizzlies," 100

"Old Solitaire," 109

"Pegleg Smith and Headless Harry," 121

"Lover Boy of the Prairies," 128

"Paul Bunyan and His Little Blue Ox," 153

"Paul Bunyan Helps to Build the Railroad," 157

"Kidnapped by a Flea," 162

"Thunder Bay," 167

"The Saga of Pecos Bill," 197

"The Taming of Pecos Bill's Gal Sue," 203

"Coyote Makes a Texas Cowboy," Native American, 209

"No-Head Joaquin and Three-Fingered Jack," 225

"El Keed," 235

"El Chivato," 241

"He Rose from the Grave," 244

"The King of the Pistoleers," 255

"Jim Bowie Takes a Hand," 282

"Born Before Her Time," 299

"How Old Calam Got Her Name," 301

"Calamity Jane Meets a Long-Lost Lover," 305

"Deadwood Dick and the Grizzly," 312

"Deadwood Dick to the Rescue," 315

"The Law West of the Pecos," 323

"Ah Ling's Hommyside," 325

"Fining the Deceased," 328

"The Hanging of Carlos Robles," 330

"Roy Bean's Pet Bear," 332

Evernden, Margery, ret. *See* Hodges, no. 79.

Exum, J. Cheryl, ret. *See* Bach, no. 9.

45   Fairman, Tony, ret., *Bury My Bones But Keep My Words* (collection, Sub-Saharan Africa)

> "Hare and the White Man," Tswana, 106
>
> "Hare and His Friends," Luo, 116

46   Faulkner, William J., coll. and ret., *Brer Tiger and the Big Wind* (single story, African American)

47   Fisher, Leonard Everett, ret., *Jason and the Golden Fleece* (single story, Greece)

48   Fisher, Leonard Everett, ret., *William Tell* (single story, Switzerland)

49   Frost, Abigail, ret., *Myths and Legends of The Age of Chivalry* (anthology)

> "Arthur," British Isles, 4, 6, 8
>
> "The Round Table," British Isles, 8
>
> "Sir Lancelot of the Lake," British Isles, 10
>
> "Queen Guinevere," British Isles, 12
>
> "Percival of Wales," British Isles, 15
>
> "The Holy Grail," British Isles, 16
>
> "The Stormy Fountain," British Isles, 18
>
> "The Knight of Lion," British Isles, 21
>
> "The Deeds of Tristan," British Isles, 22
>
> "Tristan and Iseult," British Isles, 24
>
> "Merlin and Viviane," British Isles, 27
>
> "Charlemagne," France, 28
>
> "Ogier the Dane," France, 30
>
> "Oliver," France, 31
>
> "Young Roland," France, 32
>
> "Mission Impossible," France, 34
>
> "Hasty Huon," France, 37
>
> "Renaud the Rebel," France, 38
>
> "Magician and Rogue," France, 40
>
> "William Short-Nose," France, 42

50   Gakuo, Kariuki, ret., *Nyumba ya Mumbi: The Gikuyu Creation Myth* (single story, Sub-Saharan Africa)

51   Ganeri, Anita, ret., *Out of the Ark: Stories from the World's Religions* (anthology)

> "Baiame, the Great Spirit," Australian Aboriginal, 8
>
> "The Churning of the Sea of Milk," 11

"How Shiva Got His Blue Throat," Hindu, 14

"Izanagi and Izanami," Shinto, 16

"In the Beginning," ancient Israel, 18

"Old Spider and the Giant Clamshell," Polynesia, 21

"Men, Monkeys, and Mukulu," Sub-Saharan Africa, 22

"The Earth Diver," Native American, Cheyenne, 23

"Yin, Yang, and the Cosmic Egg," China, 24

"Inca Ancestors," Native American, Inca, 25

"Ea, Ziusdra, and the Great Flood," Mesopotamia, 26

"How the Fish Saved Manu," Hindu, 29

"The Lie and Evil Enter the Ark," Jewish, 32

"Fire, Ice, and Flood," Native American, Hopi, 35

"Fire, Ice, and Flood," Native American, Aztec, 35

"The Great Bronze Buddha and the Whale," Buddhist, 36

"The Valley of the Ants," Islam, 40

"Hanuman and the Search for Sita," India, 43

"The Hare and the Earthquake," Buddhist, 46

"The Story of Maryam's Son," Islam, 48

"The First Christmas," Christian (New Testament), 50

"How Dayamanti Chose Her Husband," Hindu, 52

"The Blue God's Birth," Hindu, 54

"How Ganesh Got His Elephant Head," Hindu, 57

"The Prince and the Guru's Cloak," Sikh, 63

"How Rama Defeated Ravana," India, 66

"The Battles of Badr and Uhud," Islam, 70

"The Ten Plagues of Egypt," ancient Israel, 71

"The Life of the Buddha," Buddhist, 74

"Muhammed Escapes from Mecca," Islam, 77

"Abraham and the Idols," Jewish, 80

"The Life of Guru Nanak," Sikh, 82

"The Merchant and the Five Hundred Gold Coins," Sikh, 86

"Jesus' Last Days," Christian (New Testament), 90

52   Gates, Frieda, ret., *Owl Eyes* (single story, Native American, Mohawk)

53   Geras, Adele, ret., *My Grandmother's Stories: A Collection of Jewish Folk Tales* (collection, Russian Jewish)

"Bavasi's Feast," 6

"The Golden Shoes," 21

54   Gerstein, Mordicai, ret., *The Shadow of a Flying Bird: A Legend from the Kurdistani Jews* (single story, Kurdistan)

55   Goble, Paul, ret., *The Lost Children* (single story, Native American, Blackfeet)

56   Gonzalez-Wippler, Migene, ret., *Legends of Santeria* (collection, Cuba)

"Creation of the World," 19

"Creation of the Ground," 22

"Creation of Humankind," 24

"Olokun," 25

"The Orishas in the World," 29

"Oddudua and Oloddumare," 172

Goswami, Praphulladatta, ed. *See* Beck, no. 12.

57   Greaves, Nick, ret., *When Hippo Was Hairy and Other Tales from Africa* (collection, Sub-Saharan Africa)

"In the Beginning," Bushman, 14

"In the Beginning," Swazi, 14

"How Cheetah Got His Speed," Bushman, 28

"How Jackal Got His Markings," Hottentot, 47

"The Elephant and the Rain," Bushman, 53

"No Fish for Hippo," Bushman, 67

"The Giraffe in the Sky," Bushman, 89

"The First Zebra," Angoni, 97

"How Tsessebe Got His Peculiar Horns," Bushman, 104

"The Foolishness of the Ostrich," Bushman, 127

"The Living Stones," Swazi, 134

58   Greaves, Nick, ret., *When Lion Could Fly and Other Tales from Africa* (collection, Sub-Saharan Africa)

"In the Beginning . . . ," Fon (Dahomey), 14

"In the Beginning . . . ," Pygmy, 15

"Why Pangolin Has Scales," Angoni, 46

"Why Guinea Fowl Calls at Dawn (and Why Flies Buzz)," Ekoi (Nigeria), 99

"The Birds' Great Race," Bushman, 107

"Why Python Can Shed His Skin," Mende, 121

"Chameleon and First Man," Ndebele, 125

"Chameleon and the Greedy Spider," Bushman, 126

"Dung Beetle's Burden," Ghana, 134

59   Greene, Ellin, ret., *The Legend of the Cranberry: A Paleo-Indian Tale* (single story, Native American, Delaware)

60 Greene, Jacqueline Dembar, ret., *Manabozho's Gifts: Three Chippewa Tales* (collection, Native American)

"How Manabozho Stole Fire," 1

"How Manabozho Found Rice," 15

"How Manabozho Saved the Rose," 29

61 Greger, C. Shana, ad., *Cry of the Benu Bird: An Egyptian Creation Story* (single story, Egypt)

62 Greger, C. Shana, ret., *The Fifth and Final Sun: An Ancient Aztec Myth of the Sun's Origin* (single story, Native American)

63 Gregg, Andy, ret., *Great Rabbit and the Long-Tailed Wildcat* (single story, Native American, Passamaquoddy)

64 Hague, Michael, sel., *The Book of Dragons* (anthology)

"Perseus and Andromeda," Greece, 16

"Sigurd and Fafnir," Norse, 72

"St. George and the Dragon," British Isles, 89

65 Hamilton, Virginia, ret., *The Dark Way: Stories from the Spirit World* (anthology)

"Rolling Rio, the Gray Man, and Death," African American, 5

"Manabozo," Native American, 27

"Medusa," Greece, 43

"Childe Rowland and Burd Ellen," British Isles, 65

"Everlasting Life," China, 75

"Fenris, the Wolf," Norse, 82

"The Free Spirits, Bouki and Malice," Haiti, 102

"Yama, the God of Death," India, 137

66 Hamilton, Virginia, sel. and ret., *Her Stories: African American Folktales, Fairy Tales, and True Tales* (collection, African American)

"Little Girl and Buh Rabby," 3

"Miz Hattie Gets Some Company," 15

"Woman and Man Started Even," 69

"Annie Christmas," 84

67 Hamilton, Virginia, ret., *In the Beginning: Creation Stories from Around the World* (anthology)

"The Pea-Pod Man," Inuit (Eskimo), 3

"Finding Night," Melanesia, 9

"An Endless Sea of Mud," Sub-Saharan Africa, Kono (Guinea), 15

"Bursting from the Hen's Egg," China, 21

"Traveling to Form the World," Native American, Blackfeet, 25

"First Man Becomes the Devil," Russian Altaic, 29

"Turtle Dives to the Bottom of the Sea," Native American, Maidu, 35

"Moon and Sun," Sub-Saharan Africa, Fon (Dahomey), 43

"Bandicoots Come from His Body," Australian Aboriginal, 47

"Spider Ananse Finds *Something*," Sub-Saharan Africa, Krachi (Togo), 53

"The Woman Who Fell from the Sky," Native American, Huron, 59

"Man Copies God," Sub-Saharan Africa, Lozi (Zambia), 65

"The Frost Giant," Norse, 69

"Owner of the Sky," Sub-Saharan Africa, Yoruba (Nigeria), 73

"Marduk, God of Gods," Mesopotamia, 79

"Four Creations to Make a Man," Native American, Maya, 87

"The Angry Gods," Tahiti, 101

"Sun, Life, Wind, and Death," Micronesia, 105

"The Sun-God and the Dragon," Egypt, 111

"Separation of Earth and Sky," Minyong (India), 117

"First Man, First Woman," ancient Israel, 123

"The Coming of All Things," Greece, 127

"The God Brings Fire to Man," Greece, 134

"Pandora," Greece, 139

"In the Beginning," ancient Israel, 149

Handoo, Jawaharlal, ed. *See* Beck, no. 12.

68   Harper, Piers, ret., *How the World Was Saved & Other Native American Tales* (collection)

"The Girl Who Married a Ghost," Nisqualli, 8

"Michabo and the Flood," Algonquin, 12

"Tirawa Creates the People," Pawnee, 18

"How the World Was Saved," Navajo, 20

69   Harrison, Michael, ret., *The Curse of the Ring* (collection, Norse)
70   Harrison, Michael, ret., *The Doom of the Gods* (collection, Norse)

"The Wall of Asgard," 6

"Utgard," 18

"Sif's Hair," 34

"Geirrod," 46

"The Apples of Iduna," 52

"Baldur," 61

"Ragnarok," 75

71   Hart, George, ed., *Egyptian Myths* (collection, Egypt)

"The Sun God of Heliopolis," 11

"Ptah of Memphis," 18

"The Ogdoad of Hermopolis," 19

"Khnum and the Theban Theogony," 25

"The Myth of Kingship," 29

"Plutarch's Version," 40

72 Hastings, Selina, ret., *Sir Gawain and the Loathly Lady* (single story, British Isles)

73 Haugaard, Erik, and Masako Haugaard, rets., *The Story of Yuriwaka* (collection, Japan)

74 Hausman, Gerald, ret., *Coyote Walks on Two Legs: A Book of Navajo Myths and Legends* (collection, Native American)

"The Great Flood," 4

"First Angry," 10

"The Day Magpie Tricked Coyote," 14

"Coyote's New Coat," 21

"The Guardian of the Corn," 25

75 Hayes, Sarah, ret., *Robin Hood* (collection, British Isles)

76 Helbig, Alethea K., ed., *Nanabozhoo, Giver of Life* (collection, Native American, Ojibwa)

"Manabozho," 8

"Nenebuc, the Transformer," 28

"The Birth of Nenebojo," 41

"Nanabush Kitche Manitou's Emissary," 45

"Heavenly Fire Gained and Lost," 57

"Legend About Tobacco," 62

"The Legend of the Three Sisters," 65

"The Gift of Corn; or, Mondamin, the Red Plume," 69

"The Midewewin," 74

"Paradise," 78

"The Story of Nana-Bo-Zhoo and His Brother," 83

"Nenebojo and His Brother," 91

"Indian Legend of the Deluge," 94

"Winabijou Looks for the Wolf," 98

"The 'Origin Legend' (King Version)," 104

"The 'Origin Legend' (Judge Version)," 107

"Nanabush and the Ducks," 113

"The Duck Dinner," 116

"Nenebojo and the Deer," 119

"How Nanbush Fixed the Eye of the Owl," 122

"Why the Squirel Coughs," 124

"Why the Geese Fly in a Line," 129

"Bagging Geese," 131

"How the Turtle Got Its Shell," 137

"Nenebojo Makes Ice Music," 139

"Nanabush and the Ducks," 141

"Nenebojo Visits Black Duck," 145

"Nanibozho Visits the Woodpecker," 147

"Nanabush and Manitou," 149

"Nenebojo Goes Hunting," 151

"Why the Porcupine Has Quills," 154

"Nanbush and the Mud Turtle," 156

"Why the Cat Falls on Her Feet," 158

"Why the Buffalo Has a Hump," 164

"Nenebojo Dives for Berries and Peaches," 168

"Ne-naw-bo-zhoo Spoils the Sugar Trees," 170

"Why the Birch Bark Is Spotted," 172

"Why Roses Have Thorns," 174

"Legend of the Creation of the Islands," 178

"Legend of the Great Lakes," 181

"Wife Is Turned to Stone," 186

"Menaboju's Marriage," 188

"The Seasons," 201

"How Manabozho Disguised Himself as a Woman," 207

"The First Robin," 210

"The Woodpecker," 212

"Manabozho Visits the Man Whom the People Are Afraid Of," 217

"Nanabush and the Four Men," 221

"Sugarloaf Rock," 224

"Nanabush and the Young Man and Wife," 228

77   Heyer, Carol, ret., *Excalibur* (single story, British Isles)

78   Hodges, Margaret, ret., *The Kitchen Knight: A Tale of King Arthur* (single story, British Isles)

79   Hodges, Margaret, and Margery Evernden, rets., *Of Swords and Sorcerers: The Adventures of King Arthur and His Knights* (collection, British Isles)

"Of Castles and Dragons," 1

"Of Swords and Sorcerers," 13

"Of Guinevere and the Round Table," 21

"Of True Love," 31

"Of the Sword Bridge," 43

"Of the Boy Who Would Be a Knight," 51

"Of the Coming of Sir Galahad," 65

"Of the Quest for the Holy Grail," 75

"Of the Last Battle," 85

80 Holt, David, and Bill Mooney, sels. and rets., *Ready-to-Tell Tales* (anthology)

"Rabbit and Possum Hunt for a Wife," Native American, Cherokee, 90

"The Twelve Labors of Hercules," Graeco-Roman, 138

"How the Turtle Cracked His Shell," Native American, Cherokee, 142

81 Horowitz, Anthony, ret., *Myths and Legends* (anthology)

"The Dragon and Saint George," British Isles, 153

"The Grendel," British Isles, 159

"The Ugly Wife," British Isles, 165

"Nidud the Cruel," Norse, 174

"The Death of Nornagest," Norse, 181

"The Wishes of Savitri," India, 195

"The Monkey Who Would Be King," China, 207

"The First Eclipse," Japan, 211

"Geriguiaguiatugo," Native American, Bororo, 221

"The Ten Fingers of Sedna," Eskimo, 227

"Catching the Sun," Polynesia, 236

82 Hull, Robert, ret., *Native North American Stories* (collection, Native American)

"The Beginning of Earth," Inuit, 6

"The Creation of People," Crow, 9

"Thunderbird," Blackfeet, Kwakiutl, Pawnee, Tlingit, 15

"Why Wolves Chase Deer," Tsimshian, 23

"Winter and Spring," Iroquois, 26

"Bluebird and Coyote," Pima, 32

"The First Love Music," Lakota Sioux, 35

"The Last Journey," Skidi Pawnee, 43

83 Hulpach, Vladimir, ret., *Ahaiyute and Cloud Eater* (single story, Native American, Zuni)

84 Hunt, Jonathan, ret., *Leif's Saga: A Viking Tale* (single story, Norse)

85 Hutton, Warwick, ret., *Perseus* (single story, Greece)

86   Jackson, Danny P., trans., *The Epic of Gilgamesh* (collection, Mesopotamia)

87   Jackson, Ellen, ret., *The Precious Gift: A Navaho Creation Myth* (single story, Native American)

88   Jaffe, Nina, and Steve Zeitlin, rets., *While Standing on One Foot: Puzzle Stories and Wisdom Tales from the Jewish Tradition* (collection, Jewish)

"The Case of the Boiled Egg," 18

89   Jaffrey, Madhur, ret., *Seasons of Splendour: Tales, Myths and Legends of India* (collection, India)

"The Birth of Krishna, the Blue God," 22

"Krishna and the Demon Nurse," 26

"The Serpent King," 30

"How Krishna Killed the Wicked King Kans," 32

"How Ram Defeated the Demon King Ravan," 48

"The Moon and the Heavenly Nectar," 71

"The Girl Who Had Seven Brothers," 75

"Lakshmi and the Clever Washerwoman," 81

"The King Without an Heir," 110

"The Girl in the Forest," 115

"How Ganesh Got His Elephant Head," 121

90   Johnson, James Weldon, ret., *The Creation* (single story, ancient Israel)

91   Johnston, Basil, coll., ed., and ret., *The Manitous: The Spiritual World of the Ojibway* (collection, Native American)

"Introduction," xv

"Muzzu-Kimmik-Quae: Mother Earth," 9

"Maudjee-kawiss: The First Son," 17

"Pukawiss: The Disowned," 27

"Cheeby-aub-oozoo: The Ghost of Rabbit," 37

"Nana'b'oozoo," 51

"The Manitous of the Forests and Meadows," 97

"The Spirit of Maundau-meen (Maize)," 103

92   Kellogg, Steven, ret., *Sally Ann Thunder Ann Whirlwind Crockett* (single story, United States)

93   Kimmel, Eric A., ret., *The Adventures of Hershel of Ostropol* (collection, Jewish)

"What Hershel's Father Did," 9

"The Goose's Foot," 13

"The Bandit," 16

"Money from a Table," 19

"Potatoes!," 28

"The Miracle," 32

"An Incredible Story," 37

"The Cow," 44

"The Candlesticks," 52

"Hershel Goes to Heaven," 61

94   Kimmel, Eric A., ad., *Rimonah of the Flashing Sword: A North African Tale* (single story, Egypt)

95   Koslow, Philip, ret., *El Cid* (collection, Spain)

96   Lankford, George E., coll. and ed., *Native American Legends: Southeastern Legends: Tales from the Natchez, Caddo, Biloxi, Chickasaw, and Other Nations* (collection, Native American; one legend from Sub-Saharan Africa)

"Mother Sun," Yuchi, 58

"The Daughter of the Sun," Cherokee, 61

"The Theft of Fire," Hitchiti, 68

"Bears and Fire," Alabama, 69

"Lightning and the People," Caddo, 81

"The Flood," Caddo, 97

"Earth-Diver," Yuchi, 107

"The Flood," Alabama, 110

"Emergence," Choctaw, 111

"The Origin of Animals (Clans)," Creek, 118

"Owner of the Animals," Caddo, 126

"Creation of the Whites," Yuchi, 136

"Origin of Races," Seminole, 140

"The Origin of Tobacco," Yuchi, 143

"Kanati and Selu," Cherokee, 148

"The Origin of Maize," Creek, 155

"The Origin of Maize," Abnaki, 156

"Journey to the Sky," Alabama, 211

"Orpheus," Yuchi, 213

"The Tasks of the Trickster," Ashanti (Gold Coast), 229

"A Tug of War," Creek, 234

97   Larry, Charles, ret., *Peboan and Seegwun* (single story, Native American, Ojibwa)

98   Larungu, Rute, ret., *Myths and Legends from Ghana for African-American Cultures* (collection, Sub-Saharan Africa)

"The Horse with the Golden Horn," Hausa (Ghana), 12

"The Spider and the Terrible Great Ones," Hausa (Ghana), 36

"The Coming of the Golden Stool," Ashanti (Ghana), 51

"How Wisdom Came to the Tribe," Ashanti (Ghana), 69

"The Nkorowa Dance," Ashanti (Ghana), 71

99   Lattimore, Deborah Nourse, ret., *Why There Is No Arguing in Heaven: A Mayan Myth* (single story, Native American)

100   Lawlor, Robert, ret., *Voices of the First Day: Awakening in the Aboriginal Dreamtime* (collection, Australian Aboriginal)

"How the Sun Was Made," 44

101   Leeson, Robert, ret., *The Story of Robin Hood* (collection, British Isles)

102   Lewis, Richard, ret., *All of You Was Singing* (single story, Native American, Aztec)

103   Lister, Robin, ret., *The Legends of King Arthur* (collection, British Isles)

104   London, Jonathan, with Larry Pinola, rets., *Fire Race: A Karuk Coyote Tale* (single story, Native American)

105   Manitonquat (Medicine Story), ret., *The Children of the Morning Light: Wampanoag Tales* (collection, Native American)

"The Song of Creation," 13

"Sky Woman and the Twins," 17

"Maushop Builds Turtle Island," 20

"Firstman," 25

"Story of the Sweat Lodge," 30

"How Death Came into the World," 35

"The Great Migration and Old Man Winter," 40

"Maushop and Grandfather Sun," 49

"Maushop and the Porpoises," 56

"Cheepii Keeps Himself Safe," 62

"Muckachuck," 67

Markman, Peter T., ed. *See* Markman, Roberta H., no. 106.

106   Markman, Roberta H., and Peter T. Markman, eds., *The Flayed God: The Mesoamerican Mythological Tradition* (collection, Native American)

"The Birth of All of Heaven and Earth," Maya, 104

"The Creation of the Sun and the Moon," Aztec, 120

"The Creation of the World," Aztec, 126

"Myths of the Suns and the Toltec-Chichimec Origins of the Mexica People," Toltec, 131

"The Mixtec Creation Myth," Mixtec, 149

"The Myth of Tlaltecuhtli," Aztec, 212

"The Myth of Mayahuel," Aztec, 212

"The Hero Journey of the Hero Twins," Maya, 316

"Quetzalcoatl's Hero Journey," Aztec, 352

"The Birth of Huitzilopochtli," Aztec, 380

"The Finding and Founding of Tenochtitlan," Aztec, 394

107 McCaughrean, Geraldine, sel. and ret., *The Golden Hoard: Myths and Legends of the World* (anthology)

"The Golden Wish," Greece, 1

"Shooting the Sun," China, 7

"George and the Dragon," Persia, 12

"Skinning Out," Ethiopia, 17

"Robin Hood and the Golden Arrow," British Isles, 20

"Brave Quest," Native American, Blackfeet, 29

"Saving Time," Polynesia, 35

"Admirable Hare," Ceylon, 49

"Rainbow Snake," Australian Aboriginal, 60

"Juno's Roman Geese," Rome, 66

"John Barleycorn," United States, 74

"The Singer Above the River," Germany, 77

"How Music Was Fetched out of Heaven," Native American, Aztec, 84

"Whose Footprints?," Sub-Saharan Africa, Fon (Benin), 89

"The Death of El Cid," Spain, 94

"The Man Who Almost Lived Forever," Mesopotamia, 100

"Stealing Heaven's Thunder," Norse, 103

"Anansi and the Mind of God," West Indies, 110

"How Men and Women Finally Agreed," Sub-Saharan Africa, Kikuyu (Kenya), 114

"First Snow," Native American, 120

108 McCaughrean, Geraldine, ret., *Greek Myths* (collection, Greece)

"In the Beginning Pandora's Box," 9

"Persephone and the Pomegranate Seeds," 15

"Echo and Narcissus," 21

"Arachne the Spinner," 32

"King Midas," 36

"Perseus," 41

"The Twelve Labors of Heracles," 51

"Apollo and Daphne," 60

"Theseus and the Minotaur," 62

"Jason and the Golden Fleece," 66

"Orpheus and Eurydice," 71

"Atalanta's Race," 75

"The Wooden Horse," 78

"Odysseus," 84

109 McCaughrean, Geraldine, ret., *Saint George and the Dragon* (single story, British Isles)

110 McDermott, Gerald, ret., *Raven: A Trickster Tale from the Pacific Northwest* (single story, Native American)

111 McGill-Callahan, Sheila, ret., *The Children of Lir* (single story, British Isles)

Medicine Story, ret. *See* Manitonquat, no. 105.

112 Mitchell, Robert Allen, ret., *The Buddha: His Life Retold* (collection, India)

113 Monroe, Jean Guard, and Roy A. Williamson, rets., *They Dance in the Sky: Native American Star Myths* (collection, Native American)

"Bright Shining Old Man," Onondaga, 4

"Raccoon's Children and Baby Coyote," Shasta, 7

"Wild Onion Women," Monache, 9

"Baakil and His Five Wives," Tachi Yokuts, 12

"The Celestial Bear," Micmac, 16

"Grizzly Bear Brother-in-Law," Coeur d'Alene, 21

"How Coyote Arranged the Night Sky," Wasco, 22

"The Elk Hunters," Snohomish, 25

"Black God and His Stars," Navajo, 29

"The Little Girl Who Scatters the Stars," Cochiti Pueblo, 37

"Coyote Scatters the Stars," Cochiti Pueblo, 40

"The Dove Maidens," Picuris Pueblo, 41

"Stone God," Skidi Pawnee, 49

"The Seventh Star," Skidi Pawnee, 56

"Basket Woman, Mother of the Stars," Skidi Pawnee, 58

"White Elk, the Bear Man," Pitahawirata Pawnee, 60

"The Fixed Star," Blackfeet, 65

"The Sacred Pole," Pawnee, 69

"The Sun Dance Wheel," Arapaho, 73

"The Seven Stars," Assiniboin, 76

"The Land of the Dead," Gabrielino, 80

"How Rattlesnake Had His Revenge," Luiseno, 83

"The Seven Boys-Turned-Geese," Chumash, 85

"Eight Wise Men," Chumash, 89

"The Seven Sisters," Luiseno, 91

"The Wolf and the Crane," Tachi Yokuts, 92

"The Elkskin," Quileute, 97

"Coyote Loves a Star," Klamath, 100

"Chinook Wind Wrestles Cold Wind," Wasco, 102

"The Celestial Canoe," Alabama, 111

"Anitsutsa—The Boys," Cherokee, 116

"Where the Dog Ran," Cherokee, 117

Mooney, Bill, sel. and ret. *See* Holt, no. 80.

114 Morris, Christopher, ed., *The Illustrated Children's Old Testament* (collection, ancient Israel)

"The Creation," 1

"The Garden of Eden," 6

"The Forbidden Fruit," 8

"Cain and Abel," 11

"The Lord Speaks to Noah," 13

"Noah and the Ark," 14

"Noah Hears God's Promise," 18

"The Tower of Babel," 19

"Abraham," 20

"Sodom and Gomorrah," 23

"Isaac and Rebekah," 26

"Jacob and Esau," 28

"Jacob's Ladder," 30

"Rachel and Leah," 32

"The Coat of Many Colors," 36

"Pharaoh's Dreams," 40

"The Birth of Moses," 46

"The Lord's Message to Moses," 50

"The Ten Commandments," 62

"The Death of Moses," 73

"The Walls of Jericho," 74

"Gideon's Trumpet," 76

"Samson," 79

"Samson and Delilah," 80

"Ruth and Naomi," 84

"David and Goliath," 94

"Solomon's Dream," 111

"King Solomon's Wisdom," 112

"The Queen of Sheba," 116

"The Prophet Elijah," 120

"Esther Becomes Queen," 124

"Mordecai and Haman," 126

"Handwriting on the Wall," 141

"Jonah and the Whale," 146

115 The National Association for the Preservation and Perpetuation of Storytelling, coll., *Best-Loved Stories Told at the National Storytelling Festival* (anthology)

"How Caedmon Got His Hymn," British Isles, 75

"Possum, Turtle, and the Wolves," Native American, Cherokee, 135

"The Girl and the Ghost," Native American, Nisqually, 210

116 The National Association for the Preservation and Perpetuation of Storytelling, coll., *More Best-Loved Stories Told at the National Story-telling Festival* (anthology)

"The Legend of Obi Obi Gui," Sub-Saharan Africa, Yoruba (Nigeria), 40

"Daughter of the Sun," Native American, Cherokee, 74

"Medusa," Greece, 104

"Gluscabi and the Wind Eagle," Native American, Abenaki, 125

"The Brave Little Parrot," Buddhist, 194

"Br'er Rabbit Builds a Home," African American, 197

117 Nye, Naomi Shihab, sel., *The Tree Is Older Than You Are: A Bilingual Gathering of Poems & Stories from Mexico with Paintings by Mexican Artists* (collection, Native American)

"The Three Suns," Zinacantec, 66

"Fire and the Opossum," Mazateco, 75

"The Rabbit's Ears," Maya, 82

118 Oliviero, Jamie, ret., *The Fish Skin* (single story, Native American, Cree)

119 Oodgeroo (Kath Walker), ret., *Dreamtime: Aboriginal Stories* (collection, Australian Aboriginal)

"The Beginning of Life," 61

"Biami and Bunyip," 64

"Mirrabooka," 67

"Curlew," 79

120 Oppenheim, Shulamith Levey, ret., *And the Earth Trembled: The Creation of Adam and Eve* (single story, Islam)

121 Oppenheim, Shulamith Levey, ret., *Iblis* (single story, Islam)

122 Osborne, Mary Pope, ret., *American Tall Tales* (collection, United States)

"Davy Crockett," 3

"Sally Ann Thunder Ann Whirlwind," 15

"Johnny Appleseed," 25

"Stormalong," 37

"Mose," 51

"Febold Feboldson," 63

"Pecos Bill," 73

"John Henry," 87

"Paul Bunyan," 97

123 Osborne, Mary Pope, ret., *Favorite Greek Myths* (collection, Graeco-Roman)

"Chariot of the Sun God: The Story of Phaeton and Helios," 1

"The Golden Touch: The Story of Bacchus and King Midas," 9

"Lost at Sea: The Story of Ceyx and Alcyone," 13

"The Weaving Contest: The Story of Arachne and Minerva," 19

"Apollo's Tree: The Story of Daphne and Apollo," 23

"The Face in the Pool: The Story of Echo and Narcissus," 29

"The Kidnapping: The Story of Ceres and Proserpina," 35

"The Great Bear: The Story of Callisto and Arcus," 41

"Journey to the Underworld: The Story of Orpheus and Eurydice," 45

"The Golden Apples: The Story of Atalanta and Hippomenes," 51

"The Four Tasks: The Story of Cupid and Psyche," 57

"The Mysterious Visitors: The Story of Baucis and Philemon," 67

124 Osborne, Mary Pope, ret., *Favorite Norse Myths* (collection, Norse)

"Creation: The Nine Worlds," 1

"Odin's Three Quests," 9

"The Magic Stallion," 14

"How Thor Got His Hammer," 20

"Loki's Children," 27

"The Giant's Bride," 33

"The Golden Apples," 36

"The Fairest Feet," 43

"Spell of the Giant King," 47

"Marriage of the Ice Maiden," 53

"The Giant's Cauldron," 58

"Thor and the Clay Giant," 65

"The Death of Balder," 70

"Twilight of the Gods," 77

125 O'Shea, Pat, ret., *Finn Mac Cool and the Small Men of Deeds* (single story, British Isles)

126 Oughton, Jerrie, ret., *How the Stars Fell into the Sky: A Navajo Legend* (single story, Native American)

127 Oughton, Jerrie, ret., *The Magic Weaver of Rugs: A Tale of the Navajo* (single story, Native American)

128 Page, R. I., ret. and ed., *Norse Myths* (collection, Norse)

"Where to Find Norse Myths," 10

"Aesir, Vanir and a Few Kings," 27

"Odin and Thor," 35

"Baldr and Loki," 47

"Beginnings, Middles and Ends," 56

"Gods and Heroes," 67

129 Pan, Cai-Ying, ad., *Monkey Creates Havoc in Heaven* (collection, China)

Perez, Cecilio, coll. and ret. *See* Ecun, no. 42.

130 Philip, Neil, ret., *The Illustrated Book of Myths* (anthology)

"First Things," Egypt, 16

"The Sweat of His Brow," Serbia, 17

"Out of the Ice," Norse, 18

"The Cosmic Egg," China, 22

"The Floating World," Japan, 24

"Izanami and Izanagi," Japan, 26

"The Dreamtime," Australian Aboriginal, 28

"An Earthly Paradise," Iran, 30

"The Old Man of the Ancients," Native American, Modoc, 32

"Made from Mud," Siberia, 34

"Children of the Sun God," Native American, Navajo, 36

"The Food of Life," Mesopotamia, 38

"The Sky World," Indonesia, 42

"Gilgamesh," Mesopotamia, 44

"The Great Flood," Serbia, 49

"The Origin of the Ox," China, 52

"First Creator and Lone Man," Native American, Mandan, 53

"Vainamoinen," Finland, 54

"The Gift of Fire," Greece, 58

"The Tree of Life," Norse, 62

"Loki the Trickster," Norse, 64

"Maui-of-a-Thousand Tricks," Polynesia, 68

"Hunting the Sun," Australian Aboriginal, 69

"The Sky God's Stories," Sub-Saharan Africa, Ashanti, 70

"The Apples of Youth," Norse, 72

"Earth-maker and Coyote," Native American, Maidu, 74

"Make Me a Man!," Sub-Saharan Africa, Baganda, 76

"Why Do We Die?," Sub-Saharan Africa, Ibo, 77

"Isis and Osiris," Egypt, 80

"Persephone," Greece, 82

"World Without Sun," Japan, 84

"The Sword in the Stone," British Isles, 86

"The Holy Grail," British Isles, 89

"Glooskap and the Wasis," Native American, Algonquin, 92

"Telepinu," Hittite, 94

"Cadmus and the Sown Men," Greece, 96

"Mother of Life and Death," India, 98

"The Golden Touch," Greece, 102

"King Midas's Ears," Greece, 104

"Beowulf," British Isles, 106

"Theseus and the Minotaur," Greece, 108

"The Fall of Icarus," Greece, 112

"Taliesin," British Isles, 114

"Going to the Palace," Haiti, 117

"Thor in the Land of the Giants," Norse, 118

"Cuchulain," British Isles, 125

"The Labors of Heracles," Greece, 130

"Romulus and Remus," Rome, 138

"The Plumed Serpent," Native American, Aztec, 140

"The Elephant God," India, 144

"The Cat Goddess," Egypt, 146

"King of the Birds," India, 147

"The Winged Horse," Greece, 148

"The Phoenix," China, 151

"The Phoenix," Egypt, 151

"Aeneas in the Underworld," Rome, 154

"The Death of King Arthur," British Isles, 156

"The Voyage of Bran," British Isles, 159

"The Death of Balder," Norse, 162

"Orpheus and Eurydice," Greece, 166

"Sedna," Inuit (Eskimo), 168

"Atlantis," Greece, 170

"The Rainbow Serpent," Sub-Saharan Africa, Fon, 173

"Ragnarok," Norse, 174

"The Purifying Stream," Iran, 176

131   Philip, Neil, ret., *The Tale of Sir Gawain* (collection, British Isles)

132   Pijoan, Teresa, coll. and ret., *White Wolf Woman and Other Native American Transformation Myths* (collection, Native American)

"Snakes," Arawak (Guiana), 21

"Wolves," Pueblo, 51

"Wolves," Inuit (Eskimo), 51

"Wolf Star," Pawnee, 65

"Bearskin-Woman," Blackfeet, 96

"Other Animals," Cherokee, 109

"Seneca Medicine," Seneca, 117

"First People," Inuit (Eskimo), 121

"Buffalo-Maiden," Arikara, 128

"Magic Beasts," Comanche, 145

133   Pilling, Ann, ret., *Realms of Gold: Myths & Legends from Around the World* (anthology)

"Iyadola's Babies," Sub-Saharan Africa, 10

"Naming the Winds," Native American, Iroquois, 15

"How Maui Stole Fire from the Gods," Pacific Islands, 18

"Water, Moon, and Sun," Sub-Saharan Africa, Nigeria, 25

"The Death of Baldur," Norse, 28

"Persephone," Greece, 37

"King Midas," Greece, 62

"The Giants Who Couldn't Swim," British Isles, 77

"How Perseus Killed the Gorgon," Greece, 85

Pinola, Larry, ret. *See* London, no. 104.

134   Riordan, James, coll. and trans., *The Sun Maiden and the Crescent Moon: Siberian Folk Tales* (collection, Siberia)

> "Akanidi the Bright Sunbeam," Saami, 30
>
> "How Happiness Came," Saami, 41
>
> "The Raven and the Owl," Eskimo, 48
>
> "How the Chukchi People Became Friends," Chukchi, 50
>
> "The Sun Maiden and the Crescent Moon," Ket, 55
>
> "Kotura, Lord of the Winds," Nenets, 59
>
> "Aioga," Nanai, 68
>
> "Brave Azmun," Nivkh, 71
>
> "Why Hares Have Long Ears," Mansi, 82
>
> "The Cuckoo," Nenets, 86
>
> "How Anga Fetched a Serpent's Skin and a Bear's Fur," Nanai, 88
>
> "The Silver Maid," Saami, 92
>
> "The Girl and the Moon Man," Chukchi, 94
>
> "Coot and the Fox," Itelmen, 102
>
> "Father of Sickness," Nganasan, 107
>
> "The Little Whale," Chukchi, 118
>
> "Bold Yatto and His Sister Tayune," Nenets, 120
>
> "Ankakumikaityn the Nomad Wolf," Kerek, 132
>
> "Net-Pos-Hu the Archer," Khanty, 134
>
> "Little Oonyani," Evenk, 141
>
> "Why the Sun Forsook the Tundra," Koryak, 150
>
> "How the Sun Was Rescued," Eskimo, 161
>
> "Mistress of Fire," Selkup, 176
>
> "The Two Suns," Udegei, 179
>
> "Daughter of the Moon, Son of the Sun," Saami, 197

135   Rodanas, Kristina, ad., *Dance of the Sacred Circle: A Native American Tale* (single story, Native American, Blackfeet)

136   Rohmer, Harriet, and Dorminster Wilson, rets., *Mother Scorpion Country/La Tierra de la Madre Escorpion* (single story, Native American, Miskito)

137   Rosen, Michael, ed., *South and North, East and West: The Oxfam Book of Children's Stories* (anthology)

> "The Beginning of History," Native American, Ticuna (Brazil), 42

138   Rosenberg, Donna, ret., *World Mythology: An Anthology of the World's Great Myths and Epics* (anthology)

> "The Creation of the Titans and the Gods," Greece, 3
>
> "The Creation of Human Beings: The Ages of Man," Greece, 12

"Demeter and Persephone," Greece, 15

"The Flood Cycle," Greece, 21

"The Labors and Death of Heracles," Greece, 28

"The *Iliad* of Homer," Greece, 33

"The *Odyssey* of Homer," Greece, 75

"Romulus and Remus," Rome, 113

"The *Aeneid* of Virgil," Rome, 116

"The Creation of the Universe, Gods, and Human Beings," Mesopotamia, 157

"Osiris, Isis, and Horus," Egypt, 166

"Telepinu," Hittite, 177

"*Gilgamesh*," Mesopotamia, 181

"The Creation, Death, and Rebirth of the Universe, Gods, and Human Beings," Norse, 219

"The Theft of Idun's Apples," Norse, 228

"The Death of Baldur," Norse, 232

"The Theft of Thor's Hammer," Norse, 239

"The *Saga of Sigurd the Volsung*," Norse, 244

"The Creation of Ireland: The Ages of the World," British Isles, 277

"Dagda the Good," British Isles, 285

"*Beowulf*," British Isles, 289

"*King Arthur*," British Isles, 314

"The Creation, Death, and Rebirth of the Universe," India, 353

"Indra and the Dragon," India, 358

"The *Ramayana*," India, 365

"The Creation of the Universe and Human Beings," China, 390

"Yi the Archer and the Ten Suns," China, 393

"The Quest for the Sun," China, 395

"The Creation of the Universe, Gods, and Japan," Japan, 401

"Ama-terasu," Japan, 406

"*Kotan Utunnai: The Ainu Epic Hero*," Japan, 411

"The Creation of the Universe, Ife, and Human Beings," Sub-Saharan Africa, Yoruba (Nigeria), 426

"The Quarrel between Sagbata and Sogbo," Sub-Saharan Africa, Fon (Dahomey), 432

"*Gassire's Lute*," Sub-Saharan Africa, Soninke (Faraka), 435

"*Mwindo*," Sub-Saharan Africa, Nyanga (Zaire), 441

"The Creation of the Universe and Human Beings," Native American, Tiahuanaco (pre-Inca Peru), 459

"The House of Origin," Native American, Inca (Peru), 462

"The Children of the Sun," Native American, Inca (Peru), 464

"Paraparawa and Waraku," Native American, Trio (Brazil), 467

"The Creation of the Universe and Human Beings," Native American, Maya (Guatemala), 470

"The Creation of the Universe," Native American, Toltec/Aztec (Mexico), 476

"Quetzalcoatl," Native American, Toltec/Aztec (Mexico), 484

"The Creation of the Navajo People: The Five Worlds," Native American, Navajo, 489

"Ahaiyuta and the Cloud-Eater," Native American, Zuni, 495

"Lodge-Boy and Thrown-Away," Native American, Crow, 497

"Raven and the Sources of Light," Native American, Haida/Tlingit (Canada), 500

139 Ross, Anne, ret., *Druids, Gods & Heroes from Celtic Mythology* (collection, British Isles)

"The Arrival of the Gods," 14

"The Second Battle of Moytura," 21

"The Sorrows of Storytelling," 25

"The Children of Lir," 29

"The Story of CuChulainn," 32

"The Story of Fionn," 53

"The Four Branches of The Mabinogion," 65

"Branwen, Daughter of Llyr," 69

"Manawydan, Son of Llyr," 72

"Math, Son of Mathonwy," 77

"The Legend of King Arthur," 82

"Magic Birds and Enchanted Animals," 105

"The Land of Promise," 109

"The Story of Saint Brendan," 112

"The Naming of Places," 123

"The Golden Idol," 124

"The Isle of Man," 126

"The Wonderful Head," 128

140 Ross, Gayle, ret., *How Rabbit Tricked Otter and Other Cherokee Trickster Stories* (collection, Native American)

"Flint Visits Rabbit," 6

"How Rabbit Tricked Otter," 13

"Why Possum's Tail Is Bare," 19

"How Deer Won His Antlers," 29

"Why Deer's Teeth Are Blunt," 33

"Rabbit Goes Duck Hunting," 43

141   Ross, Gayle, ret., *How Turtle's Back Was Cracked: A Traditional Cherokee Tale* (single story, Native American)

142   Roth, Susan L., ret., *Buddha* (single story, Buddhist)

143   Sabuda, Robert, ret., *Arthur and the Sword* (single story, British Isles)

144   Sanfield, Steve, coll. and ret., *The Feather Merchants & Other Tales of the Fools of Chelm* (collection, Jewish)

"A Beginning," 3

145   San Souci, Robert D., ret., *Cut From the Same Cloth: American Women of Myth, Legend, and Tall Tale* (collection, United States)

"The Star Maiden," Native American, Chippewa, 5

"Annie Christmas," African American, 35

"Sal Fink," United States, 51

"Pale-Faced Lightning," Native American, Pueblo, 77

"Pohaha," Native American, Tewa Pueblo, 87

"Hekeke," Native American, Miwok, 103

"Otoonah," Eskimo, 111

"Hiiaka," Hawaii, 121

146   San Souci, Robert D., ret., *Larger Than Life: The Adventures of American Legendary Heroes* (collection, United States)

"John Henry: The Steel-Driving Man," 1

"Old Stormalong: The Deep-Water Sailor," 13

"Slue-Foot Sue and Pecos Bill," 23

"Strap Buckner: The Texas Fighter," 35

"Paul Bunyan and Babe the Blue Ox," 47

147   Saxby, Maurice, ret., *The Great Deeds of Heroic Women* (anthology)

"Athena: Warrior Goddess of Wisdom," Greece, 14

"Aphrodite: Goddess of Love," Greece, 19

"Demeter: Goddess of the Grain," Greece, 25

"Atalanta: The Fleet-footed Huntress," Greece, 30

"Circe: The Enchantress," Greece, 36

"Medea: A Cruel and Savage Witch," Greece, 42

"Guanyin: The Goddess of Mercy," China, 50

"Rehab and the Fall of Jericho," ancient Israel, 62

"Esther: The Champion of Her People," ancient Israel, 68

"Judith and Holofernes," ancient Israel, 74

"Bilqis: The Queen of Sheba," Arabia, 82

"Scheherazade," Arabia, 91

"Boadicea: Queen of the Iceni," British Isles, 97

"Joan of Arc," France, 105

"The Hunter Maiden of the Zuni People," Native American, Zuni, 115

"Pocahontas," Native American, Algonkion, 131

"Mary Bryant," Australia, 141

148   Saxby, Maurice, ret., *The Great Deeds of Superheroes* (anthology)

"Perseus the Fearless," Greece, 17

"Heracles the Strong One," Greece, 25

"Theseus the Daring and the Bold," Greece, 38

"Jason the Voyager," Greece, 46

"Odysseus: Agile of Body and Mind," Greece, 50

"Gilgamesh: The Epic Hero of the Sumerians," Mesopotamia, 63

"Sigurd of the Volsungs," Norse, 76

"Vainamoinen: Hero, Singer and Enchanter," Finland, 91

"Moses the Lawgiver," ancient Israel, 104

"Samson the Nazirite," ancient Israel, 113

"Beowulf the Dragon Slayer," British Isles, 120

"King Arthur: The Stuff of Heroes," British Isles, 130

"Cuchulain the Champion," British Isles, 142

"Roland, Hero of France," France, 160

"El Cid Campeador of Spain," Spain, 171

149   Seymour, Tryntje Van Ness, ret., *The Gift of Changing Woman* (single story, Native American, Apache)

"Changing Woman," Native American, Apache, 7

"The Story of the Mountain Spirits," Native American, Apache, 16

150   Shepherd, Sandy, ret., *Myths and Legends from Around the World* (anthology)

"The Birth of Japan," Japan, 10

"Ta'aroa," Tahiti, 12

"Creating the World: Egypt," Egypt, 16

"Creating the World: Scandinavia," Norse, 16

"Creating the World: Guatemala," Native American, Maya, 17

"Creating the World: North America," Native American, Onondaga (Iroquois), 17

"Rangi and Papa," New Zealand, Maori, 18

"Indra and the Peacock," India, 20

"Plants and Animals: Canada," Inuit, 22

"Plants and Animals: Sierra Leone," Sub-Saharan Africa, 22

"Plants and Animals: Greece," Greece, 23

"Plants and Animals: Russia," Russia, 23

"The Divine Archer," China, 28

"The Sun, the Moon, and the Stars: Mexico," Native American, Aztec, 32

"The Sun, the Moon, and the Stars: Japan," Japan, 33

"The Sun, the Moon, and the Stars: North America," Native American, Micmac, 33

"Matsya," Hindu, 34

"The Forces of Nature: Scandinavia," Norse, 38

"The Forces of Nature: Central America," Native American, Maya, 39

"The Forces of Nature: Greece," Greece, 39

"The Forces of Nature: Indonesia," Sulawesi, 39

"Typhon and Zeus," Greece, 40

"Romulus and Remus," Rome, 46

"Discoveries: Madagascar," Madagascar, 50

"Discoveries: North America," Native American, Chippewa, 51

"Discoveries: South America," Native American, Amazon Kayapo, 51

"Shen Nung," China, 52

"Quetzalcoatl," Native American, Aztec, 56

"Gilgamesh," Mesopotamia, 58

"Great Warriors: Greece," Greece, 62

"Great Warriors: Russia," Tartar, 62

"Great Warriors: China," China, 63

"Great Warriors: Ireland," British Isles, 63

"Great Warriors: North America," Native American, Navajo, 63

"The Trojan War," Greece, 64

"Frigg and Odin," Norse, 70

"Osiris and Isis," Egypt, 72

"Great Deities: Phoenecia," Phoenecia, 76

"Great Deities: Burundi," Sub-Saharan Africa, 77

"Sedna," Inuit, 78

"Cagn," San (Bushman), 80

"Animal Gods: Australia," Binbinga Aboriginal, 83

"Animal Gods: North America," Native American, Haida, Tlingit, Tsimshian, 83

"Pandora's Jar," Greece, 88

"Battles: Mesopotamia," Mesopotamia, 92

"Battles: Scandinavia," Norse, 92

"Battles: India," India, 93

"Battles: North America," Native American, Mandan, 93

151   Shetterly, Susan Hand, ret., *Muwin and the Magic Hare* (single story, Native American, Passamaquoddy)

152   Shute, Linda, ret., *Rabbit Wishes* (single story, Cuba)

153   Sutcliff, Rosemary, ret., *Black Ships Before Troy: The Story of THE ILIAD* (single story, Greece)

154   Sutcliff, Rosemary, ret., *The Wanderings of Odysseus: The Story of THE ODYSSEY* (collection, Greece)

"The Cyclops," 11

"The Lord of the Winds," 18

"The Enchantress," 24

"The Land of the Dead," 32

"Sea Perils," 38

"Telemachus Seeks His Father," 46

"Farewell to Calypso," 54

"The King's Daughter," 63

"The Beggar in the Corner," 86

"The Slaying of the Suitors," 102

155   Switzer, Ellen, and Costas, rets., *Greek Myths: Gods, Heroes and Monsters* (collection, Greece)

"How the World Began: The Greek Version," 10

"Hades," 39

"Prometheus: The First of the Great Heroes," 65

"Pandora: The First Woman?," 68

"Persephone in Hades," 74

"Perseus and the Medusa: Everybody's Fairy Tale," 81

"Hercules: The Strongest Man on Earth," 91

"Theseus: The Favorite Hero of Athens," 100

"The Golden Fleece, Jason, and Medea," 114

"Oedipus: The Tragic Hero Who Might Have Asked 'Why Me?'," 126

"Antigone: A Hero Can Also Be a Woman," 133

"Orpheus and Eurydice," 139

"Midas," 141

"Narcissus and Echo," 146

"Hyacinth," 147

"Adonis," 148

"The Trojan War," 165

"The House of Atreus: Murder, Vengeance, and Forgiveness," 185

"The Adventures of Odysseus," 191

156 Talbott, Hudson, ret., *King Arthur and the Round Table* (single story, British Isles)

157 Talbott, Hudson, ret., *King Arthur: The Sword in the Stone* (single story, British Isles)

158 Taylor, C. J., ret., *Bones in the Basket: Native Stories of the Origin of People* (collection, Native American)

"Before All Things Began," Native American, Zuni, 6

"From Darkness to Light," Native American, Mandan, 8

"The Raft," Native American, Cree, 10

"Big Raven Creates the World," Russia, Siberia, Chuckchee, 13

"A Place to Have Children," Native American, Osage, 17

"Creation," Native American, Mohawk, 20

"Bones in the Basket," Native American, Modoc, 29

159 Taylor, C. J., ret., *How We Saw the World: Nine Native Stories of the Way Things Began* (collection, Native American)

"The Birth of Niagara Falls," Algonquin, 6

"Why Butterflies Cannot Sing," Tohono O'Odhan (Papago), 8

"How Eagle Man Created the Islands of the Pacific Coast," Bella Coola, 10

"How Snowmaker Was Taught a Lesson," Micmac, 13

"How Horses Came into the World," Blackfeet, 16

"Why the Dog Is Our Best Friend," Oneida, 21

"The First Tornado," Kiowa, 24

"Why Rabbits and Owls Look the Way They Do," Mohawk, 27

"How the World Will End," Cheyenne, 30

160 Tedlock, Dennis, ret., *Breath on the Mirror: Mythic Voices & Visions of the Living Maya* (collection, Native American)

"Breath on the Mirror," 1

"The Great Eastern City," 12

"The Death of Death," 31

"White Sparkstriker," 37

161 Tedlock, Dennis, trans., *Popol Vuh: The Definitive Edition of the Mayan*

Book of the Dawn of Life and the Glories of Gods and Kings (collection, Native American)

"Part One (creation of the world)," 73

"Part One (origin of animals)," 76

"Part One (creation of humans)," 79

"Part One (floods and destruction)," 84

"Part Two (adventures of gods)," 87

"Part Two (constellations)," 97

"Part Three (adventures of gods)," 105

"Origin of the Calabash Tree," 113

'The Tails of Animals," 128

"Part Four (creation of humans)," 163

"Part Four (fire)," 172

"Part Four (origin of the sun)," 181

"Part Four (the first prostitutes)," 189

162 Te Kanawa, Kiri, ret., *Land of the Long White Cloud: Maori Myths, Tales and Legends* (collection, New Zealand, Maori)

"The Birth of Maui," 11

"Maui and the Great Fish," 17

"Maui Tames the Sun," 23

"Kupe's Discovery of Aotearoa," 27

"Mataora and Niwareka in the Underworld," 67

"Lake Te Anau," 85

"Putawai," 91

"Rona and the Legend of the Moon," 101

"Hutu and Pare," 105

"Maui and the Birds," 117

163 Thomas, Gwyn, and Kevin Crossley-Holland, rets., *Tales from the Mabinogion* (collection, British Isles)

"Pwyll, Prince of Dyfed," 10

"Branwen, Daughter of Llyr," 30

"Manawydan, Son of Llyr," 46

"Math, Son of Mathonwy," 64

164 Thornhill, Jan, ret., *Crow & Fox and Other Animal Legends* (anthology)

"Tortoise and Crane," China, 10

"Crane and Crow," Australia, 14

"Fox and Bear," Northern Europe, 18

"Bear and Coyote," Western Canada, 20

"Mouse and Tapir," South America, 28

165   Time-Life Books Inc., *The Book of Beginnings* (anthology)

"The Water-Mother," Finland, 9

"A Terrestrial Paradise," China, 17

"First Fruits," Burma, 24

"Fall of the Sky Maiden," Native American, Iroquois, 26

"The Trembling Earth," Sub-Saharan Africa, 35

"A Hog's Itch," Celebes (South Seas), 36

"A Restless Frog," Mongolia, 37

"Fiery Lairs of Gods and Monsters," Graeco-Roman, 38

"Phaethon's Folly," Greece, 41

"The Twin Luminants," Korea, 56

"Lunar Denizens," Buddhist, 70

"Lindu's Astral Veil," Estonia, 72

"Hieroglyphics of the Heavens," Greece, 74

"Dark Dramas of the Firmament," Native American, Naskapi, 82

"Dark Dramas of the Firmament," Siberia, 86

"Dark Dramas of the Firmament," Burma, 90

"Dark Dramas of the Firmament," Sub-Saharan Africa, 94

"The Primal Potter," India, 99

"The Braggart's Bungle," Mongolia, 100

"How the Elephant Lost Its Wings," India, 105

"A Feathered Heraldry," Latvia, 110

"A Feathered Heraldry," India, 111

"A Muddy Metamorphosis," Greece, 114

"The Garden of the Gods," Greece, 118

"Bequest of a Golden Stranger," Native American, Iroquois, 124

"Noah's Miraculous Voyage," Jewish, 130

166   Time-Life Books Inc., *Fabled Lands* (anthology)

"A Man among Gods," Norse, 14

"Journeys into Wonder," British Isles, 20

"Journeys into Wonder," British Isles, 28

"Realms of Eternal Night," Norse, 49

"Realms of Eternal Night," Mesopotamia, 61

"Realms of Eternal Night," Norse, 65

"Daring the Dark," Rome, 77

"A Parting of Worlds," British Isles, 105

"The Countess of the Fountain," British Isles, 121

167   Troughton, Joanna, ret., *How Stories Came into the World* (collection, Sub-Saharan Africa)

"How Stories Came into the World," Ekoi (Nigeria), 1

"Why the Sun and Moon Live in the Sky," Efik Ibibio, 4

"How All Animals Came on Earth," Ekoi (Nigeria), 10

"Rubber Girl," Yoruba, 14

"Why Hippo Lives in Water," Efik Ibibio, 20

"The Story of Lightning and Thunder," Efik Ibibio, 26

168   Troughton, Joanna, ret., *How the Seasons Came: A North American Indian Folk Tale* (single story, Native American, Algonquin)

169   Tyler, Royall, ed. and trans., *Japanese Tales* (collection, Japan)

"Gyogi and Baramon," 33

"The Old Mackerel Peddler," 34

"Kobo Daishi," 35

"Come to My Kasaga Mountain," 42

"Princess Glory," 46

"The Wizard of the Mountains," 127

"Very High in the Mountains," 141

"The God of Fire and Thunder," 144

170   Ude, Wayne, ret., *Maybe I Will Do Something* (collection, Native American)

"Coyote's Cave," 1

"Coyote and Sun," 11

"Coyote Learns a Lesson," 21

"Coyote's Carving," 29

"Coyote and the Crow Buffalo-Ranchers," 35

"Coyote's Eyes," 41

"Coyote's Revenge," 53

171   Van Laan, Nancy, sel. and ret., *In a Circle Long Ago: A Treasury of Native Lore from North America* (collection, Native American)

"The Long Winter," Slavey, 24

"Raven, the River Maker," Tlingit, 40

"How Beaver Stole Fire," Nez Perce, 50

"How Spider Caught Flies," Wishosk, 60

"Coyote and the Blackbirds," Tewa, 68

"Mother Sun," Creek, 80

"A Tug of War," Creek, 82

"How Possum Got His Skinny Tail," Cherokee, 88

"The Earth on Turtle's Back," Lenape, 95

"Rabbit and the Willow," Seneca, 98

172   Van Laan, Nancy, ret., *Rainbow Crow: A Lenape Tale* (single story, Native American)

173   Volkmer, Jane Anne, ret., *Song of the Chirimia: A Guatemalan Folktale* (single story, Native American, Maya)

174   Vuong, Lynette Dyer, ret., *Sky Legends of Vietnam* (collection, Vietnam)

"Why the Rooster Crows at Sunrise," 1

"How the Moon Became Ivory," 9

"The Moon Fairy," 13

"The Miraculous Banyan Tree," 38

"The Weaver Fairy and the Buffalo Boy," 54

"The Seven Weavers," 81

Walker, Kath, ret. *See* Oodgeroo, no. 119.

175   Walker, Paul Robert, ret., *Big Men, Big Country: A Collection of American Tall Tales* (collection, United States)

"Davy Crockett Teaches the Steamboat a Leetle Patriotism," 15

"Old Stormalong Finds a Man-Sized Ship," 22

"Big Mose and the Lady Washington," 29

"John Darling and the Skeeter Chariot," 37

"Ol' Gabe in the Valley of the Yellowstone," 42

"Paul Bunyan and the Winter of the Blue Snow," 49

"John Henry Races the Steam Drill," 55

"Gib Morgan Brings in the Well," 62

"Pecos Bill Finds a Ranch but Loses a Wife," 69

176   Walker, Paul Robert, ret., *Giants! Stories from Around the World* (anthology)

"Kana the Stretching Wonder," Hawaii, 17

"The Cyclops," Greece, 35

"Coyote and the Giant Sisters," Native American, Pacific Northwest, 55

"David and Goliath," ancient Israel, 63

177   Warner, Elizabeth, ret., *Heroes, Monsters and Other Worlds from Russian Mythology* (collection, Russia)

"Mikula Selyaninovich the Peasant's Son and Vol'ga," 21

"Dunai and Nastas'ya," 37

"Sukhman," 41

"Sadko of Novgorod," 44

"How Sadko Angered the Sea Tsar," 45

"Dobrynya and the Dragon," 69

"Alesha the Priest's Son and Tugarin," 72

"Il'ya of Murom and Nightingale, the Brigand," 76

178 West, John O., comp. and ed., *Mexican-American Folklore: Legends, Songs, Festivals, Proverbs, Crafts, Tales of Saints, of Revolutionaries, and More* (collection, Mexican American)

"'Mana Sorra (Sister Fox) and 'Mano Coyote (Brother, or Br'er, Coyote)," 89

"Senor Coyote Acts as Judge," 91

179 Williams, Sheron, ret., *And in the Beginning . . .* (single story, Sub-Saharan Africa)
Williamson, Roy A., ret. *See* Monroe, no. 113.
Wilson, Dorminster, ret. *See* Rohmer, no. 136.

180 Wisniewski, David, ret., *Sundiata: Lion King of Mali* (single story, Sub-Saharan Africa)

181 Wolkstein, Diane, ret., *Esther's Story* (single story, ancient Israel)
Wong, Hertha D., ed. *See* Elder, no. 43.

182 Wood, Audrey, ret., *The Rainbow Bridge* (single story, Native American, Chumash)

183 Yolen, Jane, ret., *Wings* (single story, Greece)

184 Young, Ed, ad., *Moon Mother: A Native American Creation Tale* (single story, Native American)
Young, Judy Dockrey, coll. and ed. *See* Young, Richard Alan, nos. 185, 186, 187, and 188.

185 Young, Richard Alan, and Judy Dockrey Young, colls., eds., and rets., *African-American Folktales for Young Readers* (collection, African American)

"Brother Lion and Brother Man," 59

"How Br'er Rabbit Outsmarted the Frogs," 66

"Anansi Tries to Steal All the Wisdom in the World," 76

"Why Anansi Has a Narrow Waist," 78

"Anansi and Turtle," 81

"Fling-A-Mile," 87

"Anansi and Candlefly," 93

"Why Brother Alligator Has a Rough Back," 103

"John Henry," 124

"Annie Christmas," 130

"Casey Jones and His Friends," 133

"The Cabbage Inspector," 163

"Brother Possum and Brother Snake," 170

186   Young, Richard Alan, and Judy Dockrey Young, colls. and eds., *Outlaw Tales: Legends, Myths, and Folklore from America's Middle Border* (collection, United States)

"Belle and the Stuff of Legends," 21

"Wild Bill: The 'Prince of Pistoleers'," 45

"Belle at Devil's Den," 83

"Jesse and Frank," 133

"Belle at Marble Cave," 148

"Angel of Mercy—II," 164

"Angel of Mercy—III," 190

"Calamity Jane Explains Her Name," 202

187   Young, Richard, and Judy Dockrey Young, colls. and eds., *Race with Buffalo and Other Native American Stories for Young Readers* (collection, Native American)

"The Twin Brothers," Caddo, 23

"Grandmother Spider Steals the Fire," Choctaw, 37

"Old Man at the Beginning," Crow, 43

"Race with Buffalo," Cheyenne, 47

"Blue Corn Maiden and the Coming of Winter," Northern Pueblo, 51

"Bear's Lodge," Kiowa, 54

"The Evening Star," Caddo, 59

"Skunnee Wundee and the Stone Giant," Seneca, 70

"Long Hair and Flint Bird," Acoma Pueblo, 79

"The Bloodsucker," Northern Pueblo, 85

"Bear's Race with Turtle," Seneca, 91

"The Ballgame Between the Animals and the Birds," Cherokee, 105

"Where the Dog Ran Across the Sky," Cherokee, 108

"How Bear Lost His Tail," Seneca, 111

"Coyote's Sad Song to the Moon," Northern Pueblo, 114

"Kanati the Hunter and the Cave of Animals," Cherokee, 117

"How Buzzard Got His Clothing," Iroquois, 121

"The Seven Star Brothers," Seneca, 125

"How the Animals Came to Be of Many Colors," Kathlamet, 128

"Kuloskap and the Three Wishes," Micmac, 135

"Raccoon and the Crabs," Iroquois, 138

"Possum's Beautiful Tail," Cherokee, 143

"The Girl Who Married a Ghost," Chinook, 155

188 Young, Richard Alan, and Judy Dockrey Young, colls. and rets., *Stories from the Days of Christopher Columbus: A Multicultural Collection for Young Readers* (anthology)

  "In the Taino Village," Native American, Taino, 33

  "In the Aztec Palace: The Smoking Mountain," Native American, Aztec, 55

  "The Chests of Sand," Spain, 79

  "El Cid and the Lion," Spain, 88

  "The Tree of Life," Native American, Carib, 93

Zeitlin, Steve, ret. *See* Jaffe, no. 88.

189 Zeman, Ludmila, ret., *Gilgamesh the King* (single story, Mesopotamia)

The Guide: Annotated Bibliographical Entries

(Books are arranged in alphabetical order by the writers' names. Numerals within the entries refer to pages within the books.)

1   Alderson, Brian, ret., *The Arabian Nights Or Tales Told by Sheherezade During a Thousand and One Nights*, illus. Michael Foreman, Morrow, 1995 (hardcover), ISBN 0–688–14219–2, $20.00, 192 pp. Ages 5 up, grades K up.

This beautifully designed and elegantly written adaptation of the most familiar stories from "The Arabian Nights" collection follows the material as it appears in "the nineteenth-century translation of John Payne, as refurbished and augmented by Sir Richard Burton in the sixteen volumes of his 'Nights' and 'Supplemental Nights' (1885–1888)," according to the "Editor's Remarks" about sources and stories that appears at the end of the book. The writer employs "thees" and "thous" and similar archaic terms to excellent effect, keeps the action moving, and retains a good sense of the culture and ethic of the period. The stunning watercolors glow and shimmer like Persian miniatures on occasion; the smudginess of others projects a pleasing fairy-tale effect. Heading and closing the other eighteen folktales and fables of different lengths (including the hallmark ones of Sindbad, Aladdin, and Ali Baba) is the hero story of the clever Sheherezade, the daughter of the Shah's Wazir and betrothed of the Shah, who, to keep from getting her head chopped off, weaves for the king spellbinding tales night after night. After one thousand and one nights he is so much in love with her that he relents and absolves her of the judgment of death. This remarkably beautiful book will bring lasting enjoyment.

2   Alexander, Ellen, ret., *Llama and the Great Flood: A Folktale from Peru*, illus. Ellen Alexander, Crowell, 1989 (hardcover), ISBN 0–690–04727–4, $14.89, 39 pp. Ages 4 up, grades PS up.

This unusual, little-known myth from the Native American Quechua of Peru about how a llama saves human and animal life from extinction during a world-destroying flood is simply told in mostly summarized narrative but gives a strong sense of the enormity of the flood and the significance of the lowly animal's contribution. Single-page and double-spread watercolors dominate the book, extending the story with details of mountains and landscape, both close up and aerial, that convey the closeness of the culture to earth and sky and give some idea of how these ancient Americans might have lived. Although the tersely told text occupies only one or two lines on each page and the pictures often have a light touch, this book about a serious event has impact for all ages. An introduction and afterword tell about the Indian culture and the myth.

3   Allen, Paula Gunn, ed., *Spider Woman's Granddaughters: Traditional Tales and Contemporary Writing by Native American Women*, Beacon, 1989 (hardcover), ISBN 0–8070–8100–0, 19.95, 242 pp.; Fawcett, 1990 (paper), ISBN 0–449–90508–X, $12.00, 256 pp. Ages 12 up, grades 7 up.

Among these twenty-four short stories by and about Native American Indian women and their concerns are seven from the oral tradition. The remainder are short fiction and biographical accounts by Native American authors of the nineteenth and twentieth centuries. Two of the traditional stories are creation myths: the Mohawk (Iroquois) "The Woman Who Fell from the Sky" (56) and the Okanagan "The Beginning and the End of the World" (106). Another Okanagan tale, "Coyote Kills Owl-Woman" (112), tells how the wily trickster uses his cleverness to outwit a terrible old woman who abducts children and saves a brave young woman she has kidnapped. In "The Warrior Maiden" (53), an Oneida story, a courageous heroine gives her life to save her people from their traditional enemies. In the remaining three stories, all seasonal and fertility myths, two from the Cochiti Pueblo (182, 186) and the third from the Laguna Pueblo (187), Yellow Woman, who represents corn, is stolen by evil beings. In the Cochiti myths, Spider Woman helps to save her from her abductors and restore the natural order. Adventure, conflict, and regional color pervade these old narratives, which offer valuable contrasts to one another and underscore the importance of women in Native American culture. This version of the Mohawk creation presents an interesting contrast to the Iroquoian account given in the *The Book of Beginnings* (no. 165).

4   Al-Saleh, Khairat, ret., *Fabled Cities, Princes & Jinn from Arab Myths and Legends*, illus. Rashad N. Salim, Peter Bedrick Books, 1995 (hardcover), ISBN 0–87226–924–8, $22.50, 132 pp. Ages 10 up, grades 5 up.

This extensive book, first published in England, is a mix of myths, legends, discussions of Arabic history and belief, and folktales, sometimes difficult to separate. Among them are myths of the creation of the world (88), floods and destruction stories (32, 37, and 57), the tale of the fabulous Camel of God (32), the hero tale of the mighty king Shaddad (44), a quest story, "The City of Brass" (108), and four stories of heroic women: Zarqu Al-Yamama (36), whose prophecy was ignored; Queen Balqis of Saba (50); Queen Zabba of Malik (60); and Shahrazad (103). While the style is not difficult, the retellings are often confusing because of the many unfamiliar names and variations of familiar names (i.e., Saba for Sheba) and because many of the stories do not have ready parallels in European myths and hero tales. It is, nevertheless, a valuable source for stories not frequently retold in English. Illustrations are striking; some of them are pen drawings of symbols and characters in panels that ac-company the stories (and are explained in notes at the end), and others are full-page or double-page paintings, many of them with the intricate design in detail and borders associated with Islamic art. A note on pronunciation and a long list of sources follow.

5   Anderson, David A., ret., *The Origin of Life on Earth: An African Creation Myth*, illus. Kathleen Atkins Wilson, Sights Productions, 1991 (hardcover), ISBN 0–9629978–5–4, $18.95, unp.; Sights Productions, 1996 (paper), ISBN 1–886366–09–8, $9.95. Ages 8 up, grades 3 up.

In the sky the orishas, powerful spirits or assistants to the great god Olorun, live contentedly except for Obatala, who longs for a mission to put his powers to use. Olorun sends him to the watery waste below to begin his work. On the ad-vice of Orunmila, the diviner, Obatala gets all the other orishas to contribute their gold jewelry and clothing to make a great chain, on which he climbs down from the heavens. He takes with him a snail shell full of sand, palm nuts, maize, and other seeds in his shoulder bag, as well as what is known as the egg, which contains the personalities of all the other orishas. When he sprinkles the sand on the swirling waters, it spreads and becomes firm. When he drops from the end of the chain, the egg is shattered and out springs Sankofa, the bird, clutching all the personalities. It scratches sand in all directions, spreading personality into the soil, so that when Obatala walks over the land, sprinkling the seeds, they spring to life. At the edge of a pool, he scoops up mud to form figures in his shape as he sees it reflected in the water. When Chameleon, sent by Olorun to see what progress Obatala has made, reports that the figures are good but have no life, the great god blows his breath upon the place called Ife, and the figures wake and start doing "the things people do." This Yoruba myth is told in straightforward but not overly simple language and is illustrated by striking paintings with a great deal of gold color and the characters, all very black, shown either in silhouette or in featureless full face. The book is as much for older children and adults as for the early grades.

6 Anderson, William, coll. and ret., *Green Man: The Archetype of Our Oneness with the Earth*, illus. with photographs by Clive Hicks, HarperCollins, 1990 (paper), ISBN 0–06–250075–9, $17.00, 276 pp. Ages 14 up, grades 9 up.

Seasonal stories are often "Green Man" accounts, or, put the other way around, myths explaining the seasons or regeneration of life often embody the universal Green Man myth, for example, Venus and Adonis, Isis and Osiris, Demeter and Persephone, Saint George, and Robin Hood, to name but a few. Anderson's examination of the universal archetypal vegetation or life spirit is compelling in its scholarly treatment of a vast amount of detailed and disparate material, which the collector sifts through for commonalities as well as distinguishing unusual elements. Almost all figures appear elsewhere in far better story versions than are given here, since Anderson is less concerned with the stories as narratives as with what the stories mean, that is, scholarly analysis and speculation about the narratives' essence. The book is almost all commentary, but the lesser-known seasonal myth of the goddess Cybele and her lover Attis (38) from Phrygia (Anatolia) and adopted by the Romans is related in some detail, with telling descriptions of the attendant rites. Notes, bibliography, index, and numerous photographs perfectly complementing the text are included.

7 Armstrong, Carole, ret., *Lives and Legends of the Saints*, illus. with museum works, Simon & Schuster, 1995 (hardcover), ISBN 0–689–80277–3, $17.00, 43 pp. Ages 5 up, grades K up.

This unusual book tells about twenty saints in single-page biographies, each accompanied by a beautifully reproduced painting from an art museum, most from Europe, one from the National Gallery in Washington, D.C. The art works range in period from Giotto's *Saint Francis Preaching to the Birds*, probably dating from the early fourteenth century, to Ingres's *Joan of Arc* from the nineteenth century. Although all the text pieces contain some material obviously from legend, only the stories of Saint George (23), who wounds and then beheads a dragon in the fashion of monster slayers of the oral tradition; Francis of Asissi (24), beloved of animals; and Joan of Arc (41), whose story outstripped historical fact even in her lifetime, are heroic beyond their stature as martyrs and religious figures. Each piece also lists the symbols (the red cross of Saint George and the fleur-de-lis of Joan, for instance) associated with the figure and identifiable in the painting. The endpapers give a calendar of saints' days.

8 Ashby, Gene, comp. and ed., *Never and Always: Micronesian Legends, Fables and Folklore*, illus. Thomas Joel, Rainy Day Press, 1989 (paper), ISBN 0–931742–11–0, $8.95, 128 pp. Ages 10 up, grades 4 up.

In this large collection of mostly folk and legendary tales explaining physical features and customs, three stories deal with supernaturals of a higher order. "The Demiurge Builders of Nan Madol" (31) involves two heroic brothers who have magical powers that enable them to construct settlements and unite clan chiefs on Pohnpei. "The Rock of Khlop on Satawal" (48) tells of the rivalry between two brothers over a girl and gives a brief view of the afterlife. "The First Sakau on Pohnpei" (106) describes an unusually compassionate relationship between the god Luk and an old man and ends by giving the origin of the plant called kava, from which a beverage is made. The stories, told by students of the Community College of Micronesia, overflow with details of local customs and origins. They show how homogeneous in literature this vast and widespread territory is. The illustrations, by a Micronesian artist, contribute a strong sense of place. A commentary introduces the stories, and a list of further readings concludes the book.

9 Bach, Alice, and J. Cheryl Exum, rets., *Moses' Ark: Stories from the Bible*, illus. Leo and Diane Dillon, Delacorte, 1989 (hardcover), ISBN 0–385–29778–5, $14.95, 164 pp. Ages 7–13, grades 2–8.

Unlike *The Illustrated Children's Old Testament* (no. 114), which adheres to the King James translation and for the sake of clarity changes such outdated language as "thees" and "thous" and pares away extraneous or unnecessary details, this book retells the Biblical tales in the generally accepted sense of a retelling. Thus, details of character, action, and setting are added, and dialogue is created, all in contemporary, less formal diction. Each method has merits, but in this case the King James book is more impressive because of the beauty of the diction, while the Bach and Exum book is probably more accessible to young readers to read for themselves. Bach and Exum employ such narrative devices as flashbacks and foreshadowing, to flesh out the stories, and some extra-canonical material is included. Sometimes the stories seem fulsome, like that of Samson, and even melodramatic, but the narratives always hold the attention, and the romantic, gray-toned illustrations are a handsome complement. The introduction and notes that follow every story add such valuable information as the specific chapters and verses retold and cultural and linguistic aids, and the bibliography at the end points the reader toward significant resources. The book starts appropriately with "The Garden of Eden" (9), which tells of the creation of the world and humans and the origin of certain human woes (but not, in this retelling, of death). "The Flood" (19) is about the hero Noah, the ark, and the origin of the rainbow, while the explanatory "The Tower" (29), a tale better known by the name of Babel, concerns the origin of different tribes and languages. The rest of the stories are hero tales: "Moses' Ark" (35), "The Exodus" (47), and "The Promised Land" (65) take Moses from infancy through the exodus from Egypt and the Ten Commandments to the hero's death, does not neglect the contribution of women to the story, and introduces the warrior hero Joshua and Rahab, the woman hero who aids him and the Hebrews; "Deborah, Judge over Israel" (77) tells of the Hebrews' defeat of the Canaanite general, Sisera, under her leadership and the action of the bold Jael; "The Adventures of Samson" (95) is about the unfortunate life of the ancient strong man; "The Wisdom of Solomon" (145) emphasizes the intellectual aspect of the king's character and describes the visit of the Queen of Sheba; and "Elijah, the Prophet of God" (159) deals mainly with the prophet's tribulations with Ahab and Jezebel.

10   Bascom, William, coll. and ed., *African Folktales in the New World*, Indiana University Press, 1992 (hardcover), ISBN 0–253–31128–4, $39.95, 282 pp.; (paper), ISBN 0–253–20736–3, $16.95, 243 pp. Ages 15 up, grades 10 up.

This very large compendium of stories that Bascom assembled from various African groups and that are also told by African Americans and Native American Indians in the Western Hemisphere offers a treasury of valuable reading and will especially appeal to those interested in comparative folklore. Most of the stories reproduced and discussed in these "technical essays" (which first appeared in *Research in African Literature*, 1976–1982) are folktales, which this eminent authority on African art and folklore collected, edited, and annotated during his lifetime. Typically, each chapter is devoted to a single story, which is introduced by a discussion of sources, summarized to the narrative basics, and then presented in different versions. The variants have been reproduced from work done by such eminent collectors and scholars as Franz Boas, John R. Swanton, Elsie Clews Parsons, Joel Chandler Harris, George Dorsey, Leo Frobenius, and dozens of other linguists and folklorists. Of the fourteen analyzed in this fashion, one can clearly be classed as myth and two as hero tales, and of these some one hundred variants appear, most of them short and lively. "Oba's Ear: A Yoruba Myth in Cuba and Brazil" (1) focuses on an important, originally Yoruban (Nigerian) river goddess, the account of whose unfortunate adventures in love was later transported to the New World and retold in several versions by African Americans in Cuba and Brazil. "Trickster Seeks Endowments; Measuring the Snake; Challenging Birds (Insects) to Fill a Container; Milking a Cow (Deer) Stuck in a Tree" (40) receives much more extensive treatment, with altogether seventy-eight versions, each of which can stand alone, from such African groups as appear in Gambia, Sierra Leone, Liberia, Ivory Coast, Mali, Fulani, Upper Volta, Ghana, and Nigeria, to make up about one-third of the variants. The remaining versions are about equally divided between Africans in the New World from the United States through the Caribbean to Colombia and from the Native American groups Hitchiti, Natchez, Chitimacha, Creek, Seminole, Chuh (Guatemala), and Warao (Venezuela). Briefly summarized, the trickster, called variously Rabbit, Hare, Spider, or Anansi, seeks wisdom, cleverness, or power and to get it must perform some task or tasks enjoined upon him by a superior being. Most of these narratives are versions of the story of how Anansi the spider secured stories from the Sky God. In most, Rabbit is the trickster and receives long ears for an act of misbehavior. "Moon Splits Hare's Lip (Nose) (145) concerns the origin of death, a story sometimes known as "The Message That Failed" or "The Perverted Message." God, or some superior being, sends a message to inform people that they will return to this life after dying, but the messenger changes the intent and as a result people die to this life forever. The messenger, usually a rabbit, is punished for his duplicity with a characteristic physical feature. Of the thirty-two versions included, one is Native American Indian (Chitimacha), one is African American, and the remainder come from Sub-Saharan groups in Nigeria, Botswana, South Africa, and Namibia. Although this is a very scholarly book, the versions are consistently interesting, move quickly, and are told with obvious affection and relish. Attentive readers should gain a healthy respect not only for the stories but also for the science of folklore and the importance of honoring sources. A foreword by Alan Dundes, notes and bibliographies for each story, and an index are also included.

11 Battle, Kemp P., comp., *Great American Folklore: Legends, Tales, Ballads and Superstitions from All Across America*, illus. John M. Battle, Doubleday, 1986 (hardcover), ISBN 0–385–18555–3, $16.95, 646 pp. Ages 12 up, grades 7 up.

This hefty, highly entertaining compendium contains some three hundred stories, jokes, and ballads gleaned mostly from the published works of such eminent collectors of American oral traditions as Richard Dorson, Carl Carmer, Walter Burns, Frank Dobie, and several dozen others of importance on the American folklore scene. Most of the stories are short, a few pages long, and are classified into thirteen sections, among them tales of travelers, pioneers, fighters, hunters and fishermen, preachers, animals, the Wild West, cowboys, and lying and boasting. One section is devoted entirely to Paul Bunyan. Appearing are stories about Johnny Appleseed (12); Daniel Boone (51, 225), in which the Indians are presented in what many today would consider an objectionable light; Mike Fink (99, 101); John Henry (134), in which his wife is given as Polly Ann; Mose Humphries, the fighting fireman (141); Davy Crockett (99, 151, 180, 224, 225, 394); Mother Jurgenson, the bull-whacker (239); Coyote, (343, Pawnee); Br'er Rabbit (346, 348); Calamity Jane (478); Annie Oakley (479); Pecos Bill (517); Sam Patch, the jumper (577); Febold Feboldson, the farmer and inventor (585); Gib Morgan, the oil man (588, 593, 595, 596); and Paul Bunyan (603, 604, 611, 620, 623, 626). Included also are stories of Jesse James, Wyatt Earp, Billy the Kid, Roy Bean, Sam Bass (ballad), Casey Jones (ballad), and Butch Cassidy, among other similar figures. Since the book is thick and the print fairly small, the appeal would be to older, more accomplished, or more highly motivated readers. An informative introduction opens the book, and introductions precede each section and some stories. There are also a helpful list of acknowledgments, a bibliography, and indexes. This book is chockful of entertaining, valuable material on American, mostly tall-tale, heroic figures.

12   Beck, Brenda E. F., Peter J. Claus, Praphulladatta Goswami, and Jawaharlal Handoo, eds., *Folktales of India*, University of Chicago Press, 1987 (hardcover), ISBN 0–226–04080–1, $19.95, 357 pp. Ages 14 up, grades 9 up.

   This excellent collection of ninety-nine stories, mostly folktales, is both scholarly and interestingly written. The stories have been recorded from oral sources, are indentified by subcultural group, and are classified into eight categories: Suitors and Maidens, New Brides and Grooms, Parents and Children, Sisters and Brothers, Domestic Strife, Moral Virtue or its Lack, Knowledge and the Fool, and Origin Tales. The collectors indicate which narratives can be regarded as myths. Most of these significantly involve goddesses or important female figures, even though a god may be the leading character: "The Goddess of Mahi River" (Gujarat, 5); "The Rain Prince's Bride" (Gujarat, 9), which is also a seasonal and fertility story; "The Birth and Marriage of Siva" (West Bengal, 71), which also tells of the creation of the world; "The Youngest Daughter-in-law" (West Bengal, 75), which also explains the origin of the worship of the goddess Manasa; "Lord Krishna's Wives" (Karnataka, 155); and "Siva and Parvati" (Karnataka, 171), which shows Parvati's trickster side well. "Lord Siva and the Satwaras" (Gujarat, 85) explains the origin of a particular caste community; "Vayanatu Kulavan" (Kerala, 175) relates the adventures of Siva; "The Origin of Man" (Manipur, 269) explains how the first god, man, and tiger came to be; and the thrust of "How Lijaba Created the World" (Nagaland, 273) is explained by the title. "Bhimnath Mahadev" (Gujarat, 279) concerns the adventure of the Pandevs from the *Mahabharata*. Pushker Chandervaker, Asutosh Bhattacharyya, Amrit Someshwar, Raghavan Payyanad, Irom Babu Singh, Dulal Chaudhuri, and J.T.P. Ao collected these stories from the informants. The introduction capably describes the similarities of these stories to others in India and in the world in fascinating detail, and salient and helpful commentaries precede each section and story. The whole presents not only a collection of lively and action-filled stories but also enlightening glimpses into Asian-Indian customs and beliefs. A map, a foreword of the history of collecting in India contributed by A. K. Ramanujan, notes to the tales, a fine bibliography, brief sketches of the contributors, an index of tale types and motifs by story, an index of tale types, an index of motifs, and a general index all increase the book's value.

13 Belting, Natalia M., ret., *Moon Was Tired of Walking on Air*, illus. Will Hillenbrand, Houghton Mifflin, 1992 (hardcover), ISBN 0–395–53806–8, $15.95, 48 pp. Ages 9 up, grades 4 up.

Fourteen myths of South American Indian groups are retold in this handsome book, all briefly but in dignified language, varied enough from story to story to give a sense of diversity among the people. The title story is of the creation of the world (7). Two myths deal with the arrival of people (30, 38); two concern the afterlife, both seeing the spirits of the dead inhabiting living animals (29, 42). "When Orekeke Wrestled Tornado" (25) is about the absence of the great storms of the past. The rest are explanations and origin stories of natural features: night and the seasons (36); rivers (12); agriculture (15); the appearance and paths of the sun and the moon (10, 22); the shape of the rainbow (21); and the beaks of birds and teeth of men (44). The illustrations, powerful full-page or larger paintings, are semirealistic, giving a sense of the area from which the myths come.

14 Bennett, Martin, ret., *West African Trickster Tales*, Oxford, 1994 (paper), ISBN 0–19–274172–1, $12.95, 130 pp. Ages 9 up, grades 4 up.

The distinguishing feature of these ten tales is the storytelling style, in a modern idiom, with references to refrigerators, telex, ballpoint pens, and other twentieth-century elements, not as part of the original story but as things the audience is familiar with, as introductory material or comparisons the listener can understand. A brief preface and an afterstory set the retelling outdoors on a moonlit night before a mixed-age group. The stories are mostly trickster-buffoon tales, featuring Ananse the spider (11, 71, 89), Tortoise (23, 103), or Monkey (3). Two are of animal appearance, telling why the spider has a narrow waist (61, 71), and one is of animal behavior, telling why monkeys live in trees (23). Within some of the tales are others, as in "The Opposite Party," where Farmer tells Ananse how Snake stole the fresh skins sent by the Sky God and doomed man to old age and presumably death. The book makes no pretense of a scholarly approach, giving no indication of where in West Africa the individual tales originated and adding no notes or bibliography. The story-telling is in some places self-consciously informal, but on the whole the tales are lively and easily approachable.

15 Bernhard, Emery, ret., *The Tree That Rains: The Flood Myth of the Huichol Indians of Mexico*, illus. Durga Bernhard, Holiday House, 1994 (hardcover), ISBN 0–8234–1108–7, $15.95, unp. Ages 4 up, grades PS up.

Bright, detailed, primitive gouaches adorn and extend the story of this myth from the Huichol Native American Indians of Mexico about a world-destroying flood, the survival of a peasant and his dog in a boat with the help of Great-Grandmother Earth, and the recreation of life after the waters recede. The tree of the title is a great fig that releases gentle rains upon the new fields and is purported to stand yet today near Lake Chapala in central Mexico. The book, whose text is simply and directly related with a minimum of dialogue, can be readily comprehended by young listeners but holds undertones of meaning that only older readers will appreciate. Both text and illustrations reflect the particular characteristics of the landscape where the story developed and where it is still in oral tradition. A note at the end of the book gives helpful information.

16 Berry, Jack, ret., *West African Folktales*, Northwestern University Press, 1991 (hardbound), ISBN 0–8101–0979–4, $26.95; (paper), ISBN 0–879094–304, $6.95, 229 pp. Ages 12 up, grades 7 up.

These 123 tales were collected from African storytellers by Berry and his associates and are identified by the country and by the language in which they are told, in Ghana (Ga, Sefwi, Krobo, Avatime, Vane Avatime, Twi, Larteh, and Adengme), in Nigeria (Yoruba), and in Sierra Leone (Krio). A few lack a language designation and are listed only by the area ("How Crab Got His Shell," 106, Northern Ghana). Although many are fables or folktales of other kinds, a large number are explanatory stories: of animal appearance (26, 63, 64, 78, 106, 120, 135, 147, 163, 170, 175, 178, 181, 183); of animal behavior (11, 21, 56, 66, 77, 89, 90, 101, 118, 148, 158, 170, 176); of flower or plant origins (67, 140), and of geographical features, as in "Why the Sky Is High" (190). The origin of thunder and lightning is the subject of "The Coffin of God's Daughter" (182) and of knowledge in "Spider and the Calabash of Knowledge" (165). Tricksters figure in many of these stories, but the purpose seems to be the explanation. In others, the focus is clearly on the trickster, most often the spider-man, called usually Ananse or Anaanu, as in "Spider Finds a Fool" (32), "Spider's Bargain with God" (38), "The Yam Farm and the Problem Tongue" (56), "The Return of Ananse" (90), "The Stone with Whiskers" (122), "Spider the Swindler" (128), and "Ananse and God's Business" (189). Other trickster figures include Tortoise, in "Tortoise and the Singing Crab" (69), "How Tortoise Got Water" (74), "Tortoise Sheds a Tear" (131), and "Dog Is Betrayed" (136), and Rabbit in "The Cloud Mother" (75). This is a scholarly collection, with an attempt to retell the tales just as they were heard by the field-workers. The predominant motivation is hunger or thirst. A great many of the stories open by saying that it was a time of famine or of drought; in others, the character is simply a glutton. Cannibalism is frequent. Most are short, a page or less. Many are earthy, with emphasis on farting and excrement, but very few have any sexual elements. The stories are preceded by Berry's preface about spoken art in West Africa and an introduction by Richard Spears, who edited the collection after Berry's death and added the titles, and are followed by notes on each story and a guide to pronunciation.

17   Bierhorst, John, ed., *The Monkey's Haircut and Other Stories Told by the Maya*, illus. Robert Andrew Parker, Morrow, 1986 (hardcover), ISBN 0–688–04269–4, $13.00, 152 pp. Ages 8–12, grades 3–7.

While some of these Native American Indian stories can be found in the *Popol Vuh*, the ancient sacred book of the Quiche Maya, most are folktales. Of the myths, "Chac" (66) relates how the rain god, Chac, has troubles with his servant in a "foolish apprentice" type of story. In "The Lord Sun's Bride" (84), the Sun steals a wife, whose father calls upon the rain god for help. The story concludes by explaining the origin of snakes and such flying creatures as wasps and flies. The bride eventually becomes the moon. "Blue Sun" (107) tells how a boy gets rid of his cruel brother, brings about the origin of animals, and becomes the sun. His grandmother becomes the moon and holds a rabbit in her arms. In three trickster tales, Rabbit gets the better of Coyote and Puma: "Rabbit and Coyote" (72), "Rabbit and Puma" (77), and "Rabbit Gets Married" (81). Notes, a fine introduction about Maya belief and story, and a bibliography add to the value of these skillful retellings.

18   Bierhorst, John, sel., *The Mythology of Mexico and Central America*, Morrow, 1990 (hardcover), ISBN 0–688–06721–2, $17.00, 239 pp.; Quill, 1992 (paper), ISBN 0–688–11280–3, $10.00, 256 pp. Ages 14 up, grades 9 up.

This third in Bierhorst's series on the mythologies of the Native American Indians of the Western Hemisphere "is different from its companions [on North American and South American myths] in that it surveys the stories of just one, more or less unified area. . . ." It "treats its material in great detail; and . . . incorporates an anthology of basic myths. . . ." (Preface, v) Preceding the collection of stories is an introduction about the peoples of the area, primarily Aztec and Maya, and their most important stories, and concluding the book are comments on still more myths and their function in the lives of the people today. A glossary and an extensive list of references also appear. Of the myths, "The Emergence of Ancestors" (Aztec, 67) and "The Seeds of Humanity" (Guaymi, 84) tell of the origin of people, the latter also of the origin of monkeys; "The Man of Crops" (Jicaque, 68) deals with the beginnings of various crops; "Why the Earth Eats the Dead" (Bribri, 74) speaks of how death originates; and fire comes to the earth in "Opossum Steals Fire" (Mazatec, 77). "The Loss of the Ancients" (Tarahumara, 79), "The Flood Myth" (Mixe, 80), and "The Tree and the Flood" (Cabecar, 84) offer contrasting views of destruction by floods, and the last also explains the sea. The sun and moon originate in "The Sun and Fire" (Huichol, 100), "The Childhood of Sun and Moon" (Chatino, 102), and "The Sun and His Brothers" (Tzotzil, 110), the last of which also tells how pigs came into being. A view of the afterlife appears in "The Dead Wife" (Miskito, 117), in which a husband accompanies his deceased wife to the world of the dead. The stories are edited for readability and are pleasing in style, and the background information is fascinating.

19   Bierhorst, John, sel. and ret., *The Mythology of North America*, Morrow, 1985 (hardcover), ISBN 0–688–04145–0, $16.00, 258 pp. Ages 14 up, grades 9 up.

As with its companion volumes on South and Central American mythologies, most of the Native American Indian stories in this scholarly yet very readable collection present only the most important plot details and compare the stories with those from neighboring or culturally similar groups. The myths are divided by geographical areas: Northwest Coast, Far North, Southwest, West Central, Coast Plateau, Plains, East, and Midwest. Within each area, the tales are grouped by type of story. Included also are a number of Inuit (Eskimo) narratives. A fine introduction on North American myth begins the collection, and background material appears throughout, most of the time along with the myths, a practice that often makes it hard to separate story from commentary. Maps show the groups and the main kinds of stories from each group, and detailed notes on sources and an index end the book. Included are myths of the creation of the world from the Apache (84), Zuni (84), Iroquois (196), and Winnebago (230); the creation of the world and humans from the Kwakiutl (39), Nunivak (Eskimo, 60), Inuit (Eskimo, 61), Gabrielino and Luiseno (100), Pima (103), and Delaware (Lena Lenape, 222); floods from the Kwakiutl (36), Pima (103), and Delaware (Lena Lenape, 222); goddesses and women heroes from the Inuit (Eskimo, Sklumyoa, 60; Sedna, 62); the origin of animals from the Inuit (Eskimo, 62); the origin of such necessities and realities as daylight from the Tsimshian (28), the moon from the Gabrielino and Luiseno (100), salmon from the Salish (142), and work from the Winnebago (218); the origin of death from the Tsimshian (28), Gabrielino and Luiseno (100), and Chinook (144); views of the world of the dead and the afterlife from the Chinook (144); and hero stories from the Tsimshian (Raven, 28), Kwakiutl (Mink, 36), Apache (Coyote, 86), Salish (Coyote, 142), Chinook (Coyote, 144), and Crow, Arapaho, Blackfeet, and Kiowa (Star Boy, 158). Although most stories are brief, sticking to just the main details, this book contains so much valuable information that it must be deemed an authoritative source for the stories of the Native American Indians of the North American continent.

20 Bierhorst, John, sel., *The Mythology of South America*, Morrow, 1988 (hardcover), ISBN 0–688–06722–0, $16.00, 269 pp.; Quill, 1991 (paper), ISBN 0–688–10739–7, $9.00, 272 pp. Ages 14 up, grades 9 up.

After dividing the continent into several regions, Bierhorst recounts the principal myths of each area and points out the likenesses and differences among them. The retellings vary in their literary value. In many instances, the tales are hard to separate from the accompanying commentary. In spite of this shortcoming, or perhaps because of it, the accounts carry a conviction that many versions of myths produced by a less knowledgeable writer do not. The sense of the geographic area and the values the stories are intended to transmit are clearly evident, as well as occasional intrusions from Christianity. Bierhorst says that two myths stand out across the continent: "The Twin Myth," which normally tells of the adventures of two brothers, and "The Tree and the Flood," which is a flood story. He summarizes these two story types in the introduction (12) and then illustrates them in versions from several regions. Among the Waiwai of Guiana, "The Twin Myth" (86) becomes "a modest-sized epic of creation" that explains such matters as humans, hearth fires, manioc, and different tribes. A variant from the Yuracare of Bolivia, "The Plant from the Grave" (31), tells of the origin of death. Other versions include "Moon and His Sister" (32), a myth from the Barasana of Brazil that cautions against incest and also explains the moon's spots, and "The Origin of

Night" (33) from the Bororo of Brazil. Among the Mataco of northern Argentina, Tokwah the trickster is the leading character in a tree and the flood (124) story, and "Fire" (139) from the same group tells how the world is destroyed by fire. "Cold" (143) from the Toba of Argentina has the means of destruction being ice, sleet, and frost, and in "Darkness" (144), also Toba, a long period of night wipes out life. The Mundurucu of Brazil tell "The Origin of Male Domination" (44), a story whose content is obvious, while a woman creates the world and people in a Tariana (northwestern Amazon, Brazil) story, "Alone in the Darkness" (55). The Creator thinks the universe into existence in "Creation by Thought" (57), a Witoto (northwestern Amazon, Colombia) myth, and in a Mbya Guarani story from eastern Paraguay, "Creation of the Self" (58), the Creator first creates himself, then paradise, earth, and the cosmos. Among the Ge of the Brazilian highlands, various foods originate in "The Star Woman" (96), and fire comes in "The Bird Nester and the Jaguar" (101), also a variant of the twin myth. Among the Yamana of Tierra del Fuego (Chile), in a story similar to the twins-in-opposition-to-each-other type of North America, one of "The Yoaloh Brothers" (155) discovers fire by accident, and both brothers are responsible for other such realities as death and sexual intercourse. Their older sister, a mythological figure even cleverer than they, makes arrowheads and harpoons. The Kogi of northern Colombia have a female Creator and an elaborate creation story involving nine "preliminary worlds" described in "Myths of the Kogi" (178). In a long, complex myth set after the flood, "Wirakocha" (200), the Inca god-culture hero of that name, molds people from clay and creates nations, seeds, and the heavenly bodies, among other aspects of life. This volume also includes an excellent introduction, notes on pronunciation and sources, a list of references, and an index.

21   Bierhorst, John, ed., *The White Deer and Other Stories Told by the Lenape*, Morrow, 1995 (hardcover), ISBN 0–688–12900–5, $15.00, 160 pp. Ages 9 up, grades 4 up.

Half of the twenty-five mostly short stories included in this collection from the Native American Lenape are folktales, stories that reflect actual happenings, and prediction or prophecy stories. Of the remaining myths and hero tales, "How the First Stories Came Out of the Earth" (17) explains the origin of Lenape oral literature. "Snow Boy" (18) is a seasonal myth, "The Giant Squirrel" (20) and "The White Deer" (67) tell how animals came to be, and "The Big Fish and the Sun" (47) concerns the origin of fire. Along with "Ball Player" (56), it is also a hero tale of the monster-slayer variety. "Why the World Doesn't End" (106) is eschatological, and similar Lenape stories are briefly described in a prefatory note. The rest of the narratives feature two tricksters whose predominant mode is that of fool: "Jack Babysits" (79) and "Crazy Jack Puts His Nose to the Ground" (81), in which Jack's literalness gets him into trouble, and several stories about the popular Wehixamukes, who is mostly fool and occasionally trickster, "Wehixamukes Story" (82), "More Wehixamukes" (85), and "Six Stories About Wehixamukes" (89). The narrative style varies from teller to teller, whose names are given for each story. Some stories have been translated, some recorded directly from the tellers in English, and some were written down as they were remembered and then edited. Thus some are more literary than others, but all move well and hold the attention with plenty of action and dialogue. They have a pleasing storytelling attitude. An introduction tells about the Lenape (Delaware), who once occupied the Hudson and Delaware valleys and later were located in Ontario, Indiana, Kansas, and Oklahoma, where some still live. Bierhorst also compares the stories to those of other related groups and appends helpful notes, a glossary, and a bibliography of references. Photographs of storytellers add to the book's sense of authenticity.

22 Bierhorst, John, ret., *The Woman Who Fell from the Sky: The Iroquois Story of Creation*, illus. Robert Andrew Parker, Morrow, 1993 (hardcover), ISBN 0–688–10680–3, $15.00, unp. Ages 5 up, grades K up.

Presented as a picture book, this Native American Iroquois origin myth is simply told but with a seriousness and dignity that make it suitable for all ages. The woman, who falls through a hole in the sky, lands on the back of a turtle. The muskrat dives and returns with a bit of mud in its claws. From this the woman creates the world. Two sons born to her represent the opposite qualities of the world: Sapling, the life-giving, nourishing, helpful aspects; his brother Flint, the hard, difficult, and painful aspects. Sapling creates humans and teaches them to make houses and fire. The illustrations in gouache and pen and ink are impressionistic, with a dreamy quality appropriate to the story. A note at the end discusses sources.

23 Bright, William, sel. and ed., *A Coyote Reader*, University of California Press, 1993 (hardcover), ISBN 0–520–08061–0, $30.00, 202 pp.; (paper), ISBN 0–520–08062–9, $13.00. Ages 15 up, grades 10 up.

This scholarly study of the Native American trickster figure Coyote draws from the oral traditions of western groups, predominately from the Karuk people of Northern California (65, 84, 122, 146, and 152). Other Native American groups represented are the Pueblo (30), the Northern Paiute (37), the Southern Paiute (44), the Hopi (49), the Navajo (92), the Yana (105), the Blackfeet (117), the Kathlamet Chinook (124), the Apache (131), and the Nez Perce (135). Although Coyote is throughout a trickster figure, some stories treat this aspect primarily, as in "How Her Teeth Were Pulled" (37), "Coyote Turns into Driftwood" (65), "Coyote Steals Fire" (84), "Coyote and the Prairie Dogs" (92), "Coyote Tricks Grey Fox" (131), "Two Coyotes" (135), and "Coyote Marries His Own Daughter" (146). Other sorts of myths included are explanations of animal appearance—"Telling about Coyote" (30), "Coyote Continues Upriver" (122), and "Coyote on the Beach" (152)—and of animal behavior— "Coyote and Badger" (124). Among the origin stories are those of death ("Sex, Fingers, and Death," 105, and "First Woman Invents Compassion," 117), of seasons ("Telling about Coyote," 30), of star patterns ("Coyote Places the Stars," 49), of fire ("Coyote Steals Fire," 84), and of human troubles ("Coyote Gives Birth," 44). Many of the stories are bawdy. Some are cast into an ethnopoetic form, in an attempt to recreate in English a feel for the cadence and rhythm of the oral telling. Besides the traditional legends there are literary pieces about the coyote figure, both in prose and poetry, by Gary Snyder, Jarold Ramsey, Peter Blue Cloud and others, even Mark Twain, and brief discussions of the biological coyote and speculations about why this particular mythic figure is so widespread. This interesting book is valuable for mature readers.

24 Bruchac, Joseph, ret., *Between Earth & Sky: Legends of Native American Sacred Places*, illus. Thomas Locker, Harcourt, 1996 (hardcover), ISBN 0-15-200042-9, $16.00, unp. Ages 8 up, grades 3 up.

Within a frame story of a young Indian boy learning from his uncle about the sacred places in all seven directions—East, West, North, South, Above, Below, and Within—the book describes ten such sites in addition to the Hudson River land where their Delaware ancestors lived. Myths are not related about all the sites; little is known about the beliefs of the people who built the incredible serpent mound in southern Ohio or the dwellers of the Mesa Verde pueblo in Colorado, for instance. Most of the others are explanations of geographical features: the islands in Lake Champlain (23); the Great Smoky Mountains (11); the whale-shaped headland off Martha's Vineyard known as Mau-shop or Gay Head in Massachusetts (5); the huge stone called El Capitan in the Navaho lands of Arizona (9). The Grand Canyon is explained as a reminder to people of the destructive flood that drove them from the land below to our world (19). The story of the race from the Black Hills to the Rocky Mountains between Buffalo and Man to see who will be dominant is not connected to any specific place but to mountains in general and explains why dog lives with humans (17). The story told about Ne-ah-ga or Niagara Falls concerns the meaning of thunder (7). While the frame story is unnecessarily didactic, the place stories are simply and sometimes poetically told. The book's strength, however, lies in its gorgeous illustrations, full-page oil landscape paintings wider than they are high, evocative of the part of the country depicted and the mood of the tale. A brief list of further readings is given at the book's opening, and a map, showing the location of the sites pictured and of the Native American groups as well as a pronouncing glossary, is added at the end.

25 Bruchac, Joseph, ret., *Iroquois Stories Heroes and Heroines Monsters and Magic*, illus. Daniel Burgevin, Crossing Press, 1985 (hardcover), ISBN 0–89594–234–8, $12.95; (paper), ISBN 0–89594–167–8, $8.95, 198 pp. Ages 8–12, grades 3–7.

The more than thirty stories presented are all generally from Native American Iroquois peoples; a few are identified from more specific groups. Many of them are origin or explanatory tales. One is about creation of the world (15); one is about the creation of animals (19). Others concern the origin of stories (12), of troubles (19), of knowledge (41), of thunder and lightning (146), of seasons (189), and of agriculture (19). Some explain animal appearance: bear's tail (32), chipmunk's stripes (37), rattlesnake's flat head and turtle's cracked shell (55), the varied colors of birds (61), and the cleft nose of the rabbit (65); some concern animal behavior: raccoon's habit of washing food (69) and buzzard's appetite for rotting meat (61). Others explain the constellations (189) and the geographical features of Niagara Falls (146). Heroes come in both genders. Heroic women are brave and clever when confronted by evil forces: the Flying Head (184), the Stone Coat Woman (135), a husband who is really a serpent (123), and an old man masquerading as a handsome prospective husband (116). Men sometimes slay monsters: the two-headed snake (97) and the Workers of Evil (104). One is on a quest (169). In one story the heroes are dogs who die saving their master from an unnamed horror (85). Tricksters of various types appear: fox (32 and 80), turtle (47 and 51), and Skunny-Wundy (161). The style is storytelling, though not entirely consistent, and the stories tend to seem similar when one reads straight through the book. They are followed by a glossary of Iroquois terms. No published sources are given.

Bruchac, Joseph, ret. *See* Caduto, no. 27.

26 Burn, Lucilla, ret., *Greek Myths*, British Museum and University of Texas Press, 1990 (paper), ISBN 0–292–72748–8, $9.95, 80 pp. Ages 15 up, grades 10 up.

In spite of its title, this scholarly but never stuffy collection, also published in Great Britain by the British Museum where the writer is a curator, consists almost entirely of tales about the major Greek heroes. A lucid and salient introduction lists and briefly describes the major gods and discusses how the myths and hero tales functioned in fifth century B.C.E. Greece. The stories of Demeter and Persephone (7; seasons and fertility) and Ares, Aphrodite, and Hephaistos (14; adventures of gods) are summarized to illustrate the points made. The rest of the book considers the heroes one by one, telling of the exploits of each in unadorned narrative without dialogue, judiciously inter-jecting explanatory or elucidating comments as the stories proceed, specifying major sources, and occasionally quoting from the sources: Herakles (16), The-seus (25), Achilles and the Trojan War (31), Odysseus (43), Jason (59), Perseus (63), and Oedipus (66), in whose story Cadmus also appears. Although inci-dents are not expanded into full-fledged episodes and few characters except the heroes themselves are given much space, a few female figures receive attention: Calypso, Circe, and Penelope in the story of Odysseus; Medea in the story of Jason; and Antigone in the story of her father, Oedipus. The myth of Dionysus and the Maenads appears as a sidebar in the story of Oedipus (66). The last chapter of the book briefly discusses the "imaginative legacy" of the Greek myths in the music, art, and literature of the Western world. The book concludes with suggestions for further reading. Numerous black-and-white photographs of vases and other artifacts bearing scenes from the myths and drawings taken from artifacts accompany the stories and add a good deal of information about them and the gods. Although style for the most part is pedestrian, this book gives the gist of the tales in more detail and more interestingly than the handbooks, and the explanatory material is fascinating and valuable.

27   Caduto, Michael J., and Joseph Bruchac, rets., *Keepers of the Earth: Native American Stories and Environmental Activities for Children*, illus. John Kahionhes Fadden and Carol Wood, Fulcrum, 1988 (hardcover), ISBN 1–55591–027–0, $19.95, 209 pp. Ages 5–12, grades K–7.

   This book is made up largely of apparatus for teachers, activities very loosely related to the retold legends and couched in educational jargon with sugges-tions for questions and discussion groups. It also contains many stories told in a pedestrian fashion simple enough to be read to preschoolers or by chil-dren at about fourth-grade level. The stories come from a variety of Native American groups, including Seneca (3 and 129), Abenaki (21, 67, and 165), Onondaga (25), Dine [Navajo] (31), Nisqually (41), Lakota (57 and 187), Paw-nee (57), Zuni (79), Micmac (81), Maliseet (81), Yurok (93), Inuit (95), Tsim-shian (103), Anishinabe (117 and 145), Cherokee (137), Hopi (151), Dakota (157), and Siksika [Blackfeet] (181). Creation stories are "The Earth on Turtle's Back" (25), "Tunka-shila, Grandfather Rock" (57), and "Four Worlds: The Dine Story of Creation" (31). Explanations of animal appearance occur in

"How Turtle Flew South for Winter" (157), of geographical features in "How Thunder and Earthquake Made Ocean" (93), of constellations in "How Fisher Went to the Skyland: The Origin of the Big Dipper" (117). The origins of various animals are told in "Sedna, the Woman Under the Sea" (95) and "Koluscap and the Water Monster" (81), of fire in "Loo-Wit, The Fire-Keeper" (41), of wind in "Gluscabi and the Wind Eagle" (67), of corn in "The Coming of Corn" (137), of maple syrup in "Manabozho and the Maple Trees" (145), of stories in "Of Science and Indian Myths" (3), of seasons in "How Fisher Went to the Skyland" (117) and "Spring Defeats Winter" (129), of tides in "How Raven Made the Tides" (103), and of death in "The Origin of Death" (181). Trickster figures appear in "Gluscabi and the Game Animals" (165), "Kokopilau, the Hump-Backed Flute Player" (151), and "Old Man Coyote and the Rock" (57); monster slayers in "The Hero Twins and the Swallower of Clouds" (79); and heroic women in "The White Buffalo Calf Woman and the Sacred Pipe" (187) and "Sedna, the Woman Under the Sea" (95). Most of these stories can be found in livelier and more authentic versions elsewhere without the questionable attempt to tie them in with almost unrelated activities. A companion volume, also illustrated with photographs, black-and-white drawings, and a map of Native North America, is *Keeper of the Animals* (Fulcrum, 1991).

28 Chaikin, Miriam, ad., *Exodus*, illus. Charles Mikolaycak, Holiday House, 1987 (hardcover), ISBN 0–8234–0607–5, $15.95, unp. Ages 4 up, grades PS up.

According to the introductory note, Chaikin consulted various translations of the Bible, including the King James Version, in preparing this retelling, which tells of the ancient Israelites' dramatic departure from slavery in Egypt and their problem-filled journey to the Promised Land of Canaan. Chaikin pares away extraneous details well, but on the whole the retelling, though consistently interesting, lacks the flavor and euphony of accounts that stay closer to the King James. She starts her narrative with the birth of Moses, continues through his encounter with God in the burning bush, his appearances before the pharaoh, whose stubborn refusal to let the people go culminates with the ten plagues, the Red Sea crossing, the receipt of the Ten Commandments, and the making of the golden calf and the building of the Tabernacle. She concludes her account with the people continuing on their way toward Canaan, rather than with the death of Moses, which seems a peculiar way to end since she began with the birth of Moses. Mikolaycak's magnificent paintings, grandiose and extremely striking in their stylized, close-up views, bolster the text and give a keen sense of the significance of events and journey. They make this very handsome book one all ages can appreciate.

29   Chatterjee, Debjani, ret., *The Elephant-Headed God and Other Hindu Tales*, illus. Margaret Jones, Oxford, 1992 (hardcover), ISBN 0–19–508112–9, $13.00, 88 pp. Ages 9 up, grades 4 up.

Most of the twelve Hindu tales in this attractively written collection have no exact counterparts in other mythologies, being complicated because many of the human figures are the incarnations of gods. They also differ in tone, in which humility and compassion are the ideals rather than glory or power. Still, there are a variety of recognizable heroes: kings and rulers (Krishna, 43; Rama, 1), warriors (Arjuna, 43), voyagers (Yudhishtira, 60), and strong men (Bhima, 55). The title story tells of the origin of wisdom (9). Embedded in the story of Rama and the monkey bridge to Lanka is an explanatory story of the squirrel's appearance (1). Godlike tricksters are the main characters in "Ashes to Ashes" (28) and "The Dwarf's Three Steps" (36). Stories of goddesses and heroic women are "Kunti's Secret Son" (65) and "For Love of Urvashi" (81). The god of the mountains, Himalaya, goes adventuring in "Shiva and the Mountain" (24), planning to shower his daughter with gifts and shame his son-in-law, Shiva, only to end by humbly thanking him and building a temple in his honor. Some of the possible confusion for Western readers is eliminated by a list of main characters, which precedes the stories and points out the double nature of some figures as both man and god. The illustrations are ink drawings, usually a full page for each story, suggesting the intricate detail found in Hindu sculpture. Although the author says that the stories are from ancient India, among the oldest in the world, no specific sources are given.

Claus, Peter J., ed. *See* Beck, no. 12.

30   Climo, Shirley, ret., *Atalanta's Race*, illus. Alexander Koshkin, Clarion, 1995 (hardcover), ISBN 0–395–67322–4, $15.95, 32 pp. Ages 5 up, grades K up.

Strongly executed, full-color paintings that recall ancient murals establish the setting, picture the characters, and depict episodes from the hero story of a stalwart and determined woman. Cast out as an infant, reared by a bear and a woodsman, and later restored to her rightful position as the daughter of a king in ancient Greece, Atalanta distinguishes herself as a warrior, huntress, and athlete, especially talented at running. When Atalanta declares that she will wed only the youth who can best her in a footrace, the goddess Aphrodite assists a handsome young warrior, Melanion, to defeat her by providing him with golden apples that he uses to distract the princess while they compete.

Later, offended by the young couple's lack of attention to her, Aphrodite successfully appeals to the mother goddess Rhea to change them into lions, which race and hunt forevermore throughout the countryside. Climo, who sorted through the vast amount of disparate material about Atalanta and Melanion, has produced a readable and exciting account, which is ably complemented by the expressive illustrations and thus can appeal to a wide age range. Although the author's note at the end does not specify sources, it gives some idea of the importance of the story and relates it to the Olympic Games.

31 Climo, Shirley, ret., *Someone Saw a Spider: Spider Facts and Folktales*, illus. Dirk Zimmer, Crowell, 1985 (hardcover), ISBN 0–690–04436–4, $13.95, 128 pp. Ages 9–12, grades 4–7.

Of the nine stories in this book, only two are myths: the Greek story of Arachne (5), the expert weaver who challenged Minerva and was punished for her hubris by being shriveled into the form of a spider but allowed to go on spinning and weaving elaborate webs forever, and the Native American Achomawi myth, "The Spider Brothers Make the Rainbow" (29). In this story, the spider brothers are heroes who persuade Old-Man-Above to stop the rain that has been nearly drowning everything and causing both Indians and animals to starve. Both stories are retold with much dialogue. In one of the extensive notes at the end of the book, Climo explains that she uses Roman names in the Arachne retelling because she has followed the version of the Roman writer Ovid. The rest of the book is composed of folktales, rhymes, remedies, superstitions, and factual comments about spiders. A good-sized bibliography is divided into three sections: Spider Facts, Spider Fiction, and Spider Folk Beliefs.

32 Climo, Shirley, ret., *Stolen Thunder: A Norse Myth*, illus. Alexander Koshkin, Clarion, 1994 (hardcover), ISBN 0–395–64368–6, $15.95, 32 pp. Ages 4–11, grades PS–6.

This is a vigorously told version of the rollicking Norse myth of how Thor, the thunder god, dresses as a bride in order to recover his hammer from the giant king, Thrym, who has stolen it. Accompanying the story are robust, deep-color, expressive paintings that catch the story's conflict, suspense, and humor. Here and there they incorporate symbols and scenes from iconography found on runic stones and scenes from other artwork that has come from the time when the stories were told. No source is given for the version, nor is the source of the pictures' inspiration indicated.

33 Cohen, Caron Lee, ret., *The Mud Pony*, illus. Shonto Begay, Scholastic, 1988 (hardcover), ISBN 0–590–41525–5, $12.95, unp.; 1989 (paper), ISBN 0–590–41526–3, $3.95. Ages 5–11, grades K–6.

This hero story of the Skidi Pawnee tells of a poor boy who yearns for a pony of his own and fashions one with a white face from clay. After Mother Earth brings the pony to life, the boy, mounted on the white-faced mare, leads his people to victory in battle and then to great success on a buffalo hunt. Many years later, when the boy is grown and has become a noted chief, the horse returns to Mother Earth from whom she had come and who assures the man that she (Mother Earth) will remain with him always. The spare, powerful text is extended well by the soft-toned, full-color, impressionistic pictures. The sense of the culture comes across in such small details as leggings, travois, and knife cases. Although the pictures are somewhat idealized, the people seem real and not cliché Plains Indians. In an introductory note, Begay, who is Navajo, acknowledges the assistance he received from such authorities as the Museum of the American Indian in New York City, among others, and Cohen cites as her source the turn-of-the-century collection of Pawnee stories of George Dorsey.

34 Connolly, James E., ret., *Why the Possum's Tail Is Bare and Other North American Indian Nature Tales*, illus. Andrea Adams, Stemmer House, 1985 (hardcover), ISBN 0–88045–069–X, $15.95, 64 pp.; (paper), ISBN 0–88045–107–6, $7.95, 64 pp. Ages 8 up, grades 3 up.

The thirteen animal stories retold in this book come from eight Native American Indian groups of the Eastern Woodlands, Western Plains, and West Coast. They tell how animals originated or came to look or behave as they do. Action filled and humorous, they employ dialogue for interest, exhibit such familiar motifs as repeatedly forgetting instructions and not keeping one's mind on one's business, and convey cautionary advice. A brief essay about the Native American groups involved opens the book, and italicized introductions before each story give factual information but also add an unfortunate didactic note. The tales are taken from reputable sources, which are named, but Connolly's retellings occasionally seem somewhat condescending in diction and tone. Three stories involve the divine, or semidivine, order. In "How the Rabbit Lost Its Tail" (43, Sioux), the supreme being, Wakan-Tanka, helps a foolish rabbit out of several predicaments. Old Man, the Blackfeet creator-god, exhibits his trickster-buffoon side in "Old Man and the Bobcat" (50); he is tricked by a bobcat and retaliates by docking the bobcat's tail. "Coyote in the Cedar Tree" (61, Chinook) shows Coyote tricking his enemy, Cougar, in an unusual version of the "eye-thrower" motif type of story.

Costas, ret. *See* Switzer, no. 155.

35 Craft, M. Charlotte, ret., *Cupid and Psyche*, illus. Kinuko Y. Craft, Morrow, 1996 (hardcover), ISBN 0–688–13163–9, $16.00, unp. Ages 8 up, grades 3 up.

Cupid, the god of love, falls in love with a beautiful mortal girl, Psyche, who disobeys him. To regain his love, she must complete impossible tasks enjoined upon her by his mother, the goddess Venus. In a style recalling the romanticism of Botticelli, extravagant, colorful landscapes, portraits, and close-ups with borders of tiny flowers, hearts, Greek keys, leaves, and similar designs dominate the text. Craft gives no source for this familiar tale, which is known only from the writings of the Roman author Apuleius of the second century C.E. Although the Greek counterpart of Cupid was Eros, Craft appropriately uses the Roman name for him and the other characters. Unfortunately, the descriptors that appear on the reverse of the title page are confused; Cupid is rightly identified as a Roman deity, but Psyche is here incorrectly called a Greek goddess, and the mythology is incorrectly identified as Greek.

36 Crespo, George, ret., *How Iwariwa the Cayman Learned to Share*, illus. George Crespo, Clarion, 1995 (hardcover), ISBN 0–395–67162–0, $14.95, unp. Ages 5 up, grades K up.

This myth of the Native American Yanomami people of the Amazon rain-forest in Venezuela and northern Brazil is retold in picture-book format with brilliant, rather cartoonlike illustrations in oil. The cayman or crocodile has obtained fire from a lightning-struck tree, but he has kept it a secret, hiding it in a basket in his mouth. The other animals, wanting to share in the delicious-smelling hot food, trick him into laughing and exposing the basket, which first the bird, then the tortoise, then the armadillo make off with in a wild chase, until Iwariwa follows the armadillo down a tunnel and gets stuck. He then bargains with the other animals to share with them if they dig him out. Although published for young children, the myth is interesting for all ages as a comparison to other origin-of-fire myths.

37 Crespo, George, ret., *How the Sea Began: A Taino Myth*, illus. George Crespo, Clarion, 1993 (hardcover), ISBN 0–395–63033–9, $14.95, unp. Ages 6–11, grades 1–6.

This Native American Taino myth tells of the origin of Puerto Rico. When Guabancex, the dreaded goddess of hurricanes, sends a storm that kills Yayael, the most skillful hunter in the village, his parents place his magic bow and arrows in a gourd, which some recalcitrant boys accidentally break. The water that gushes forth creates a salt ocean filled with sea life and isolates the mountains that become the Caribbean islands, including Boriquen, or Puerto Rico. The retelling, based on a story collected in Christopher Columbus's time, has a strong storytelling flavor. The colorful oil paintings have amusing touches but remain respectful to the story and culture and extend the narrative with details of culture, setting, and action. The endnote about sources and the prounciation guide are helpful.

Crossley-Holland, Kevin, ret. *See* Thomas, no. 163.

38 Curry, Jane Louise, ret., *Robin Hood and His Merry Men*, illus. John Lytle, McElderry, 1994 (hardcover), ISBN 0–689–50609–0, $13.95, 42 pp. Ages 7–11, grades 2–6.

This brief retelling of seven stories about Robin Hood is aimed at young readers able to handle chapter books but not ready for complicated language or plotlines. Since all Robin Hood stories are based on a series of ballads which are sometimes fragmentary and even contradictory, there is no definitive source, and retellers often invent episodes and even characters. This collection follows well-known patterns of how Robin (here called Robin of Barnesdale) becomes an outlaw, how he meets and fights Little John at the bridge, how Little John becomes a servant of the Sheriff of Nottingham and steals his silver, and how the Sheriff comes to Sherwood and is dined against his will. The other three chapters deal with Sir Richard of Lee, who, unable to repay a debt, is losing his land to the abbot of Saint Mary's Abbey. Robin lends him the necessary money and robs the abbot's cellarer to replenish his funds. The style is pleasant and not in oversimplified diction, but it lacks the vigor of such earlier versions as the retellings by Howard Pyle. For children who know Robin Hood only through the television series, this is an adequate introduction.

39 Curry, Jane Louise, ret., *Robin Hood in the Greenwood*, illus. Julie Downing, McElderry, 1995 (hardcover), ISBN 0–689–80147–5, $15.00, 53 pp. Ages 7–11, grades 2–6.

A companion to Curry's *Robin Hood and His Merry Men* (no. 38), this book contains the stories of Friar Tuck, of Maid Marian coming to Sherwood Forest disguised as a page, of the archery contest in Nottingham designed to trap Robin and his men, of their escape to the castle of Sir Richard of Lee, of the capture of Sir Richard by the Sheriff of Nottingham, and of his subsequent rescue by Robin. The other two chapters deal with the coming of the king to Sherwood and of Robin's going into the king's service and eventually returning to the forest. Strangely, the king is not identified as Richard, nor is there any mention that John has been the wicked regent in his absence. As in the earlier book, the style is pleasant and not difficult, but the stories are bland compared with more vigorous retellings.

40   Dalley, Stephanie, trans., *Myths from Mesopotamia*, Oxford, 1991 (paper), ISBN 0–19–281789–2, $7.95, 337 pp. Ages 15 up, grades 10 up.

Dalley translates several ancient Mesopotamian (Sumerian, Babylonian) poems transmitted in the Akkadian language, adhering strictly to the texts, providing generously detailed introductions to each poem, and following each with copious notes. "Atrahasis" (1), the Utnapishtim of the Gilgamesh story, tells how the goddess Mami creates the first man. After humans multiply and the gods decide to send a flood to reduce the population, a friendly god, Enki, warns Atrahasis, who survives in a boat. "The Epic of Gilgamesh" (39), the longest extant composition in cuneiform Akkadian, relates that ancient king-hero's exploits in both standard and Old Babylonian versions. Several short stories combine into the long, widely known, and influential epic, including those of Enkidu, Humbaba, and the Utnaphistim flood story. A seasonal fertility story, "The Descent of Ishtar to the Underworld" (154) concerns the search of the goddess Ishtar for her lover, Dummuz, in the world of the dead, which is ruled by the goddess Ereshkigal. Another seasonal fertility story is "Nergal and Ereshkigal" (163). In "Adapa" (182), the antedeluvian sage of that name is sent by the wise god Ea to bring humans the arts of civilization and in the adventure loses the opportunity for immortality, both for himself and all humankind. "Etana" (189) relates the ascent of an ancient quasi-historical hero-king to heaven on an eagle, and "Anzu" (203) describes the epic deeds of Ninurta, the warrior god, in recovering the Tablet of Destinies, which the lion-headed eagle, Anzu, has stolen from the gods, thus usurping their power. "The Epic of Creation" (228) is the story of how, after the gods come into being, one of them, Marduk, slays the water-monster, Tiamat, and creates heaven and earth, thus bringing order from chaos. An alternate account of creation appears in "Theogony of Dunnu [an ancient town]" (278), in which Plough and Earth are the originators of creation and the parents of land and sea. In an adventure story, "Erra and Ishum" (282), the herald god, Ishum, placates the angry Erra, god of war and plague, and prevents him from going on a rampage and destroying everything. A fine introduction discusses sources and versions with fascinating, detailed information and relates the stories to other Mediterranean and Middle-Eastern writings. A map, chronological chart, extensive glossary, and bibliography complete the book. An excellent discussion of these texts, making use of Dalley's translations, appears in *Mesopotamian Myths* by Henrietta McCall, University of Texas Press, 1993.

41   DeSpain, Pleasant, coll. and ret., *Thirty-Three Multicultural Tales to Tell*, illus. Joe Shlichta, August House, 1993 (hardcover), ISBN 0–87483–265–9, $25.00; (paper), ISBN 0–87483–266–7, $15.00, 126 pp. Ages 4–10, grades PS–5.

DeSpain, a storyteller, has assembled these thirty-three stories, almost all of them folktales, from twenty-one countries. Chosen for their "tellability, universality, and cultural integrity" and tested in storytelling situations, they are intended "for both beginning and professional educators, parents (bedtime story experts!)[*sic*], and storytellers." The versions are short, told in simple, uncomplicated language with lots of dialogue, and encompass a range of characters from spirits to kings with assorted animals and humans in between. A short introduction and brief endnotes with the main story motifs identified by number enhance the book's value. "Hungry Spider" (107) is an amusing trickster tale from the African Ashanti. "Grandfather Spider's Feast" (35) is also a trickster tale, but unfortunately it is identified only as coming from Sub-Saharan Africa. It explains why the spider has a very small waist. In like fashion, no specific group is given for "Coyote Steals Spring" (63), a seasonal tale about how the ubiquitous trickster wrests spring from Old Woman with the help of various animals. The tale is described only as "A Native American Tale, From the Pacific Northwest." The exact sources of the stories are not given, but variants are occasionally indicated.

42   Ecun, Oba (Cecilio Perez), coll. and ret., *Ita: Mythology of the Yoruba Religion*, Obaecun Books, 1989 (paper), ISBN 0–926603–00–0, $29.95, 141 pp. Ages 15 up, grades 10 up.

The Yoruba beliefs and practices known as *Santeria* originated in Nigeria and came with the slaves to the Western Hemisphere, in particular to Cuba, Brazil, and Haiti. Immigrants to the United States from these areas brought their beliefs with them. A very large pantheon exists, among whom is Oloddumare, the Supreme Being. How this very abstract and elevated god brings the world and the first human into being and begins the process of creating the gods is told in "Formation of the Earth" (38). The origin of the sun occurs in "Oddua and Yembo's Love" (41); of troubles in "Second Child—Oggun (Metals)" (42) and in "Tenth Child—Oya (The Air We Breathe)" (49); of animals and plants in "Sixth Child—Osain" (45); of wisdom and knowledge in "Seventh Child and First Female—Dada (Brain)" (47) and "Ninth Child—

Oba Nani (Wisdom and Teacher of the World)" (48); of death and burial in "Birth of Orula" (63) and "Jeggua's Punishment" (98); and of war and earthquake in "First Encounter Between Oggun and Shango" (78). This slim volume is slow going, since it combines story, religion, and philosophy. The style is dense and often shows a lack of careful editing. The writer's own knowledge of the religion provides the source of the stories. Included are an introduction about the Yoruba, a glossary, a bibliography, and photographs of Yoruba artifacts.

43 Elder, John, and Hertha D. Wong, eds., *Family of Earth and Sky: Indigenous Tales of Nature from Around the World*, Beacon, 1994 (hardcover), ISBN 0–8070–8528–6, $30.00, 323 pp.; 1996 (paper), ISBN 0–8070–8529–4, $15.00, 336 pp. Ages 12 up, grades 7 up.

This anthology of forty multicultural stories mostly about creation and tricksters presents a "global array of vivid responses to nature from indigenous oral traditions" (flap) by such eminent collectors as Elias Lonnrot, Ulli Beier, and Harold Courlander, and a few personal responses from such contemporary writers as Leslie Marmon Silko and N. Scott Momaday. The tales have been reproduced from a wide variety of sources, some of them important but no longer readily accessible. While some of the stories are familiar, like that of the Navajo creation, many, especially those in the trickster section, are relatively unknown. The editors' purposes "have been to illustrate some of the many possibilities for a response to nature that is grounded in the experience of a specific homeland, and at the same time to highlight continuities among the imaginations of people living in very different bio-regions" (4). They understand the term "indigenous" as defined by the organization Cultural Survival: "culturally distinct groups that have occupied a region longer than other immigrant groups or colonist groups" (6). Since this is an anthology, the stories, which have not been retold, offer varied voices and views, one of the book's delights. Brief but helpful introductions precede each of the four sections: Origins, Animal Tales and Transformations, Tricksters, and Tales to Live By; an introduction about the characteristics of the stories and about nature literature opens the book; and a list of sources and an index close it. "In the Beginning . . ." (Australian Aboriginal, 42) and "*Kalevala*: The Mother of Water" (Finland, 44) describe the creation of the world. "The Emergence" (Native American, Navajo, 17), "The Creation" (Native American, Mohawk, 32), "Tangaroa, Maker of All Things" (Tahiti, 40), and "How Moon Fathered the World" (Africa, Wakaranga, 56) tell of both the creation of the world and humans. "The Creation" (32) also explains the origin of evil and of the earthquake. The Mohawk story of "The Creation" (32) and "*Kalevala*: The Mother of Water" (44) both involve important female figures, Sky Woman and Mother of Water, respectively. The title explains the content of "The Origin of Different Water Animals" (Nagaland, India, 50), as does the African Fon "The Origin of Fishes" (65), while "Juruna Kills the Sun" (Brazil, Juruna, 52) presents both the origin of the sun and of such creatures as snakes, spiders, and centipedes. "How Moon Fathered the World" (56) describes the gaining of fire. The Paraguayan Nivakle "Sun and Moon" (58) tells of the origin of those heavenly bodies, while "Anansi's Rescue from the River" (Africa, Ashanti, 198) explains the moon. "How Gluskabe Brought the Summer" (Native American, Abenaki, 66) is a seasonal story. The Mongolian "Halibu the Hunter" (75) tells of a world-destroying flood. The African Ibo "The Toad" (79), the African Margi "The Chameleon and the Lizard" (80), and the African Hottentot "The Origin of Death" (81) are explanations of how death came to be. The Mohawk "The Song of the Birds" (109) tells how certain birds got their songs. Heroes include the Abenaki Gluskabe (66), the Buddha (Tibet, 112), the Finnish Vainamoinen from the *Kalevala* (123); the Ashanti Anansi (195, 198, 200), the Algerian Kabyle jackal (203, 205), the African Yoruba Ijapa the tortoise (207, 209), the African American T'appin (Terrapin) (212) and Br'er Rabbit (215), the Asian Indian Tamiladu "The Monkey-Son" (220), the Inuit (Eskimo) Raven (223, 225, 226), the Native American Winnebago Trickster (228), and Coyote from the California Native American Kato (233) and Miwok (235), which also explain the heavenly bodies, and from the Native American Sioux (237). The tale of T'appin (Terrapin) also gives an interesting view of the afterlife. This anthology is a treasure trove of entertaining and mind-expanding reading.

44   Erdoes, Richard, coll., ed., and ret., *Tales from the American Frontier*, illus. Richard Erdoes, Pantheon, 1991 (hardcover), ISBN 0–394–51682–6, $25.00, 443 pp. Ages 12 up, grades 7 up.

This hefty volume of 132 highly entertaining narratives is rightly advertised on the jacket flap as "a wonderfully boisterous treasury of tall tales and fanciful yarns . . . [about] pioneers, trappers, and Indian fighters, the settlers, keelboatmen, and cowboys, the gunfighters, outlaws, and shootists, the gamblers, prospectors, and railroaders" who actually and figuratively peopled the American West in reality and in story. The tales are related in appropriately mouthfilling, grandiloquent language that captures the essence of the figures, along with plenty of stylistic winks, grins, and guffaws. Some stories are reproduced from other printed sources, but most are retold by Erdoes himself and range from a half page to a half-dozen pages in length. The tales are classified both by region (e.g., Ohio River) and by type of figure (e.g., Long Hunters). Real historical figures include Daniel Boone (37, 42); Sam Brady of the famous leap (45); Mad Ann Bailey, the notorious warrior woman (49); Davy Crockett (57, 60, 61, 75); Jim Bowie, (63; 282); Mike Fink (75, 77); Sal Fink, Mike's daughter and a hell-raiser in her own right (80, 81); Kit Carson (95, 100); Bill Williams the trapper, called Old Solitaire (109); trapper, fighter, and brawler Pegleg

(Tom) Smith and his companion and partner in escapades, Headless Harry (121); Jim Beckwourth, mountain man and infamous lover and breaker of women's hearts (128); Pine Leaf, a Crow Indian amazon, who becomes Beckwourth's wife (128); Billy the Kid (235, 241, 244); Wild Bill Hickok (255); Calamity Jane (255, 299, 301, 305); and Judge Roy Bean (323, 325, 328, 330, 332). Fictitious figures are represented by lumberman Paul Bunyan, he of the famous Babe the Blue Ox (153, 157, 162, 167); Pecos Bill, the archetypal cowboy (197, 203); Slue-foot Sue, Pecos Bill's sometime sweetheart (197, 203); Coyote, the Native American trickster, here not identified by tribal group, who creates the first human, a Texas cowboy (209); No-Head Joaquin and Three-Fingered Jack Garcia, a pair of notoriously bad hombres (225); and Deadwood Dick, hearty rescuer of many in distress (312, 315). Numerous other lesser known figures also appear, as well as stories of witches and ghosts and sundry lyin' tales, yarns, and jests. A short biography with background information introduces almost every hero, whose story is then fleshed out by representative narratives. Readers will find plenty of hilarity here, and will also gain insights into what has come to be known as typical American humor. A fine introduction, endnotes, and a bibliography are included.

Evernden, Margery, ret. *See* Hodges, no. 79.

Exum, J. Cheryl, ret. *See* Bach, no. 9.

45 Fairman, Tony, ret., *Bury My Bones But Keep My Words*, illus. Meshack Asare, Holt, 1991 (hardcover), ISBN 0–8050–2333–X, $15.95, 192 pp. Ages 8–13, grades 3–8.

Two of the thirteen stories in this collection of African tales are hero stories; the rest are folktales. All are related in an intimate, conversational tone with the writer introducing the situations under which elders will tell the traditional tales to a child audience. The children often interrupt the narratives with comments or questions, thus contributing to the taletelling. The stories move fast with lots of action and dialogue. "Hare and the White Man" (106), from the Tswana, is a classic underdog tale, with a clever trickster rabbit cheating a white man by pretending he has a pot that can cook food without fire. In the Luo "Hare and His Friends" (116), Sungura the trickster hare displays his buffoon side by trying unsuccessfully to emulate the hospitality of several friends for an amusing "bungling host" story. The writer, who has been a teacher of English to non-English speaking people, heard some of these stories while working in Africa and adapted others from written sources. The book has a helpful map near the beginning and a list of sources at the end.

46 Faulkner, William J., coll. and ret., *Brer Tiger and the Big Wind*, illus. Roberta Wilson, Morrow, 1995 (hardcover), ISBN 0–688–12985–4, $15.00, unp. Ages 4 up, grades PS up.

Hints of African American speech rhythms and bits of dialect enliven and distinguish this humorous trickster tale, in which Brer Rabbit and his friends teach selfish Brer Tiger a lesson about sharing. Framed, realistic, full-color, textured, quarter-page, full-page, and double-spread paintings retell the story, depict the animals in various situations, and enhance the action. Their use of emotion and their comic touches reveal a good deal about human nature that older readers and viewers will especially appreciate. A note about the writer indicates that the late Faulkner, a reputed African American folklorist, story-teller, pastor, and teacher, heard this story as a child from Simon Brown, a former slave who worked on the Faulkner farm.

47 Fisher, Leonard Everett, ret., *Jason and the Golden Fleece*, illus. Leonard Everett Fisher, Holiday House, 1990 (hardcover), ISBN 0–8234–0794–2, $14.95, unp. Ages 5 up, grades K up.

This dramatically told and powerfully illustrated portrayal of an important ancient Greek hero recounts the main episodes in the lengthy story of Jason's quest for the golden fleece and concludes with his nonheroic abandoning of his benefactress and wife, Medea, in favor of a young princess. The illustrations are especially impressive; powerful, dramatic, up-close, deep-toned oils offer striking, memorable views, for example, the *Argo* departing on its journey under so blazing a sun that the entire sky glows red and the shoreline and water have purply tones; the horrible harpies with ragdoll reddish hair, glowing red eyes, extended yellowish talons, scaly green bodies; the clashing rocks of the Symplegades that loom dark and menacing over the tiny ship below; the powerfully muscular, fire-breathing bulls; Jason holding the fleece high over his head in triumph; and at the end, the hero no longer so heroic, wandering the country as a homeless mendicant in punishment for his misdeeds and ingratitude toward Medea. Sources, a map, and a very brief introduction are included. Other retellings of Greek myths by Fisher include books about Theseus, the Cyclops, and the Olympians, the last a book of short essays about the gods; on the Biblical Moses and David's battle with Goliath; and the Swiss hero William Tell (no. 48). All are most notable for their powerfully executed paintings.

48   Fisher, Leonard Everett, ret., *William Tell*, illus. Leonard Everett Fisher, Farrar, 1996 (hardcover), ISBN 0–374–38436–3, $16.00, unp. Ages 5 up, grades K up.

Politics and fatherly and filial love combine in a legend that Fisher calls "a metaphor for freedom" (flap). Although Fisher does not specify his sources, the details of Fisher's version of the historical Swiss early fourteenth-century freedom fighter and marksman follow the well-known pattern: Gessler, the tyrant governor of the Swiss canton of Uri, orders everyone to bow down to his hat, which is displayed on a pole in the town square, as a sign of fealty to the Austrian overlords. Tell refuses and is ordered to shoot an apple off the head of his son with a bow and arrow. Tell does so but is found to have another arrow intended for Gessler. He is imprisoned as punishment, escapes, kills Gessler, and helps his countrymen gain their independence. The illustrations are typical of Fisher's work: deep palette, strongly executed, expressive oils, which wrap around and flow over the text and very often overwhelm it. Both text and illustrations are occasionally melodramatic, especially in the portrayal of Gessler, but the confrontation involving marksmanship is tense with drama, an unforgettable scene, a point of high emotion that even the too cleanly divided apple does not diminish. This is a stunningly handsome book about a remarkable hero.

49   Frost, Abigail, ret., *Myths and Legends of The Age of Chivalry*, illus. Francis Phillips, Marshall Cavendish, 1990 (hardcover), ISBN 1–85435–235–0, $9.95, 48 pp. Ages 9–13, grades 4–8.

These twenty-one tales retold are slightly more than half from the Arthurian tradition; the remainder are legends of Charlemagne. The style is bald, with little development, and many stories reduced to bare-bones incidents. Where there is a choice of fanciful or realistic versions, these are the less believable. For instance, Merlin's parentage is ascribed to the Devil (4), and Arthur's earliest campaign as king is against the giant Ryon (8). Other knights of Britain include Lancelot (10), Percival (15), Yvain (18, 21), and Tristan (22). There are also the stories of the doomed romances of Guinevere (12) and Iseult (24), Merlin's entrapment by Viviane (27), and the quest for the Holy Grail (16), although Galahad is not mentioned. The legends of Charlemagne include stories of the king himself (28), Ogier the Dane (30), Oliver (31), Roland (32), Huon (37), Renaud the Rebel (38), Maugis the Magician (40), and William Short-Nose (42). Since the Arthurian stories are more attractively told in a number of other sources, the main value of the book is in the French stories from the *Chansons de Geste*, which are not as well known or commonly retold. Illustrations are attractive, with some good monsters and action scenes, though the faces of heroes are similar and idealized. An afterword titled "Chivalry, True and False" discusses the differences between the factual and fictional Middle Ages, mentions sources for the retellings, and gives useful maps for both the world of Arthur and that of Charlemagne.

50 Gakuo, Kariuki, ret., *Nyumba ya Mumbi: The Gikuyu Creation Myth*, illus. Mwaura Ndekere, Jacaranda, 1992 (paperback), ISBN 9966–884– 72–6, $8.95, 36 pp. Ages 6 up, grades 1 up.

Although published in picture-book form, this strikingly illustrated retelling of an ancient Gikuyu (Kikuyu) myth, one in the publisher's African Art and Literature Series, has great dignity and conveys a sense of the importance of first things appropriate to creation myths. In poetic, sensory language, it tells how this Kenya tribe originated through the grace and action of the creator god Mugai, who gave the land surrounding the sacred mountain to the hero Gikuyu, his wife, Mumbi, and their nine daughters, from whom descended the nine major clans of the group. The paintings, which show panoramic views of the landscape, catch the nature of characters, and reveal them in action, are strongly executed. Included also are brief explanatory notes, information about the writer and illustrator, and a short bibliography of sources. This picture book will appeal to a wide age range. An expanded, less formal, modernized version appears in McCaughrean's *The Golden Hoard* (no. 107).

51 Ganeri, Anita, ret., *Out of the Ark: Stories from the World's Religions*, illus. Jackie Morris, Harcourt, 1996 (hardcover), ISBN 0–15–200943–4, $18.00, 96 pp. Ages 8–15, grades 3–10.

First published in Great Britain in 1994, this is a large and attractive collection of stories from major religions from around the globe, classified by subject, for example, stories of creation, animals, floods, marriages, and so on, almost all from "living" religions. Some stories, like those from the Bible of the birth of Jesus and of the ten plagues of Moses, are familiar, but most are not well known. Some, such as the life of the Buddha, are told in summarized narrative, almost like that found in an encyclopedia, but others are related in greater detail with dialogue, drama, and suspense. All are told with respect for the culture, story, and audience and are judiciously placed for good effect. While on the whole this is a fine and consistently interesting collection, some drawbacks include the lack of page numbers and identification of cultures for individual tales in the table of contents and the lack of specific sources for the stories. A few errors appear. For example, the story "In the Beginning" is identified as "in the Christian religion," when in fact it comes from Genesis in the Old Testament of the Bible, and in the otherwise very helpful "Who's

Who?" glossary of names that concludes the book, Krishna is identified as "the god Vishnu in disguise" and a similar attribution is given to Rama, when, in fact, they are both avatars (incarnations) of Vishnu, which is quite a different matter from a disguise. The book's strengths lie in its broad coverage; its inclusion of many seldom retold tales; its respectful and dignified narratives; the glossary and section entitled "Religions—Fact Files"; and the numerous colorful, detailed watercolors, which, although often tinged with the comic, do not seem inappropriate and make the book attractive. Creation of the world stories include "Baiame, the Great Spirit" (8, Australia); "The Churning of the Sea of Milk" (11, India, Hindu); "How Shiva Got His Blue Throat" (14, India, Hindu); "Izanagi and Izanami" (16, Japan, Shinto), which also tells how the Japanese islands originated, gives a view of the world of the dead, and focuses on a goddess; "Old Spider and the Giant Clamshell" (21, Polynesia), which also features a figure with the stature of a goddess; "The Earth Diver" (23, Native American, Cheyenne); and "Yin, Yang, and the Cosmic Egg" (24, China). "In the Beginning" (18, Judaeo-Christian) tells of the origin of the world and humans, as does "Inca Ancestors" (25, Native American, Inca), which also tells how the Incas and their city of Cuzco came to be. "Men, Monkeys, and Mukulu" (22, Africa) explains the origin of humans and of monkeys. Flood stories include "Ea, Ziusdra, and the Great Flood" (26, Mesopotamia/Babylon); "How the Fish Saved Manu" (29, India, Hindu); "The Lie and Evil Enter the Ark" (32, Judaism), which also explains the existence of evil in the world; and "Fire, Ice, and Flood" (35, Native American, Aztec and Hopi). A large number of stories revolve around heroic figures: "The Great Bronze Buddha and the Whale" (36), "The Hare and the Earthquake" (46), and "The Life of the Buddha" (74), all about the Buddha from southeastern Asia. From Islam come "The Valley of the Ants" (40) about Sulaiman (Solomon); "The Story of Maryam's Son" (48) about the Messiah (Jesus). Also from Islam are "The Battles of Badr and Uhud" (70) and "Muhammed Escapes from Mecca" (77), both about Muhammed. "The First Christmas" (50) and "Jesus' Last Days" (90) are Christian stories from the Bible. "Hanuman and the Search for Sita" (43) and "How Rama Defeated Ravana" (66) concern Rama of India. "The Prince and the Guru's Cloak" (63), "The Life of Guru Nanak" (82), and "The Merchant and the Five Hundred Gold Coins" (86) are Sikh stories from India and Pakistan. "The Ten Plagues of Egypt" (71) concerns the Judaeo-Christian Moses, and "Abraham and the Idols" (80) is a Jewish story. Adventures of gods appear in "How Dayamanti Chose Her Husband" (52), "The Blue God's Birth" (54), and "How Ganesh Got His Elephant Head" (57), all Hindu stories from India that concern an enterprising woman and clever goddesses.

52   Gates, Frieda, ret., *Owl Eyes*, illus. Yoshi Miyake, Lothrop, 1994 (hardcover), ISBN 0–688–12472–0, $15.00, unp. Ages 4 up, grades PS up.

When he meddles with the work of the Native American Mohawk Everything-Maker Raweno in creating the world and giving animals their appearances and attributes, a troublesome owl receives eyes that see best in the dark, a short neck that restricts his ability to view what is going on, and a dull, muddy-colored coat in punishment for interfering. Richly colored, strongly conceived, representational paintings extend across the pages, enclose the text, and portray the gradually evolving landscape and animals as Raweno develops them. Raweno is shown as a gentle, strong-muscled young Indian father figure. The simple dignity of the narrative, the humorous commentary on human nature, and the powerful illustrations result in a book that spans the viewing and reading generations.

53   Geras, Adele, ret., *My Grandmother's Stories: A Collection of Jewish Folk Tales*, illus. Jael Jordan, Knopf, 1990 (hardcover), ISBN 0–679–80910–4, $17.95, 96 pp. Ages 8–13, grades 3–8.

Among these ten folk stories from the Russian Jewish tradition are two hero tales. In "Bavasi's Feast" (6), King Solomon teaches a rich merchant what it feels like to be hungry. "The Golden Shoes" (21) concerns the Chief Sage of Chelm, the village in which everyone is a fool. The Sage can be identified as the wisest man in town because he wears his golden shoes on his hands to keep them from getting muddy. The vigorously told, witty, amusing stories are presented as though they were being told by a grandmother to her visiting granddaughter.

54   Gerstein, Mordicai, ret., *The Shadow of a Flying Bird: A Legend from the Kurdistani Jews*, illus. Mordicai Gerstein, Hyperion, 1994 (hardcover), ISBN 0–7868–2012–8, $15.95, unp. Ages 5 up, grades K up.

This legend, taken from a Kurdistani version of the Biblical story, tells of the very last days on earth of the ancient, highly revered Hebrew leader Moses. Although in essence a very serious story, it has amusing moments. When Moses reaches 120 years of age and God decides that his soul should return to God, Moses unsuccessfully prays to be allowed to continue to live, then appeals to the forces of nature to help him escape his fate, all to no avail. God then asks angels to bring Moses's soul to him, and when each in turn refuses, Gabriel, Michael, Zagzagle, and even the evil Sammael, God himself takes Moses's soul with a kiss. This gentle story of loving compassion and ironic character revelation is accompanied by slightly comic, full-color expressive paintings that capture the story's emotional turbulence and make the book appropriate for those well beyond picture-book age. A note at the beginning gives the source of the story.

55   Goble, Paul, ret., *The Lost Children*, illus. Paul Goble, Bradbury, 1993 (hardcover), ISBN 0–02–736555–7, $14.95, unp. Ages 5–8, grades K–3.

Six brothers, orphans, are neglected and tormented in the village, their only friends the camp dogs. Unable to bear the abuse, they decide to become something other than humans and settle on stars. One of them blows a feather upward, and they are lifted to the sky. Although warned not to look back, one does and becomes Smoking Star, a comet. The others explain their plight to Sun Man and his wife, Moon Woman. Angered at their treatment, Sun Man shines down fiercely on the earth, causing a terrible drought. The camp dogs howl and pray for rain, and Sun Man relents. Now the boys can be seen in the constellation called Pleiades, a bunched group surrounded by many tiny stars, explained as the camp dogs. This Blackfeet version of a legend told by many Native American peoples is accompanied by a long list of references, an author's note, and a description of the tipi designs. It is decorated with Goble's hallmark brilliant colors and slightly stylized illustrations drawn with pen and India ink, then filled in with thickly applied watercolors. Another myth explaining a constellation appears in Goble's earlier book, *Her Seven Brothers* (Bradbury, 1988), which tells the Cheyenne story of the origin of the Big Dipper.

56   Gonzalez-Wippler, Migene, ret., *Legends of Santeria*, Llewellyn Publications, 1994 (paper), ISBN 1–56718–328–X, $9.95, 274 pp. Ages 13 up, grades 8 up.

This substantial volume, which is a greatly expanded revision of the *Tales of the Orishas*, gives a sampling of the many stories or patakis in the Cuban version of the religion known as Santeria, a complex mix of Yoruban and Christian tradition practiced variously also in Brazil, Trinidad, Haiti, some other parts of the New World, and Nigeria and neighboring countries. The patakis include the creation of the world (19 and 22) and of humans (24 and 172), flood stories (25), and the origin of enmities and tribal rivalries (29), but most of the stories concern the adventures of the orishas or gods, mostly sexual relationships and conflicts resulting from rapes or seductions. Since each of the orishas personifies some elemental power, these can be taken metaphorically to describe the forces of the natural world. They also make robust and entertaining tales more comparable to those of the Greek gods than to the Catholic saints with which they are said to be associated. The favorite orisha is Chango, god of fire and volcanoes, who represents passion and irresistible desire. Among the female orishas the most prominent is Oshun, goddess of love and dance. Others include Obatala, symbol of peace and purity, father of many of the other orishas; Oggun, god of war and metals; Yemaya, representation of sea waters and protector of women; and Eleggua, messenger and trickster, who knows all and punishes evil. Since many patakis were lost when Yorubans were brought to the Western Hemisphere in the slave trade, some disappeared from Yoruba when whole villages were transported or destroyed, and others arose in South America, Mexico, and the Caribbean islands, there are no definitive versions. Even in the sampling retold in this book, those in Part II differ considerably from those in Part I, mainly in the inclusion of a devil figure, Olosi, who influences happenings among the orishas and humans. Little is included about the rituals that are part of Santeria, but the appendices include a set of invocations, an essay on the divination system which is said to be the origin of the patakis, and a set of proverbs, as well as a glossary and bibliography. The whole suffers from stylistic and grammatical errors, especially lie-lay confusion, which a good editing should have eliminated.

Goswami, Praphulladatta, ed. *See* Beck, no. 12.

57   Greaves, Nick, ret., *When Hippo Was Hairy and Other Tales from Africa*, illus. Rod Clement, Barron, 1988 (hardcover), ISBN 0–8120–4131–3, $12.95; 1991 (paper), ISBN 0–8120–4548–3, $8.95, 144 pp. Ages 7–14, grades 2–9.

Ten of these thirty-six short and lively, if plainly told, stories concern Creator and Rain Spirit, obviously mythological figures, who interact with mostly large African animals in an unfinished world of an early, far-off age. An animal's appearance or behavior is usually altered or fixed because of some shortcoming of action or attitude. Droughts, dust, waterholes, exotic trees, savannah grasses, and rocky passes awaken the sense of the varied African terrain, and gentle, often ironic humor relieves the morals. Although the stories come from several groups, each of whom undoubtedly has its own name for him, the high god is referred to in all the stories as Creator. The accounts are largely narrative, with only occasional dialogue. Dramatic, realistic, highly tactile paintings and sketches, many of them striking portraits, bring the animals into the viewers' dimension with startling clarity. Intended as a text, the book includes maps, information about the animals, a glossary of terms, and a bibliography. Seven Bushman stories appear. "In the Beginning" (14) is a brief creation of the world and coming of humans story that concludes with a one-paragraph summary of the corresponding Swazi story. The content of "How Cheetah Got His Speed" (28) and "How Tsessebe Got His Peculiar Horns" (104) is evident from their titles, while "No Fish for Hippo" (67) explains why hippopotami prefer to spend time in the water; "The Elephant and the Rain" (53) shows Rain Spirit teaching Elephant who's boss; and "The Foolishness of the Ostrich" (127) tells how a Bushman steals from Ostrich the fire that Mantis, Creator's assistant, had instructed Ostrich to guard. "The Giraffe in the Sky" (89), also Bushman, describes the origin of the Southern Cross constellation; "How Jackal Got His Markings" (47) is Hottentot; "The First Zebra" (97), an Angoni story, tells how the zebra's coat gained stripes; and the Swazi "The Living Stones" (134) explains why tortoises do not take care of their eggs.

58 Greaves, Nick, ret., *When Lion Could Fly and Other Tales from Africa*, illus. Rod Clement, Barron, 1993 (hardcover), ISBN 0–8120–6344–9, $13.95; (paper), ISBN 0–8120–1625–4, $8.95, 144 pp. Ages 7–14, grades 2–9.

This sequel complements the same writer and artist's collection *When Hippo Was Hairy and Other Tales from Africa* (no. 57) with thirty more animal stories, most of them folktales, from the early, unfinished times of myth. In appearance, design, and content it parallels its predecessor. Several tales involve the Creator, and one story revolves around the antics of the trickster Anansi and another around an otherwise anonymous Spider, who functions as the counterpart of Anansi. "In the Beginning" (14), from the Fon, tells how Creator commands Ancient Snake to create and sustain the earth. The story also explains the earthquake and foretells the end of the world. A Pygmy tale (15) tells of the creation of the earth, a great flood, and the first pygmies. The Angoni story "Why Pangolin Has Scales" (46) not only explains the anteater's scales but also the honey badger's taste for honey. The content of the Ekoi "Why Guinea Fowl Calls at Dawn (and Why Flies Buzz)" (99) is evident from the title. "The Birds' Great Race" (107), from the Bushmen, explains the guiding propensity of the honeyguide bird. The Mende story, "Why Python Can Shed His Skin" (121), not only explains that feature of the python but also why it is a solitary being, why the jackal is so cunning, and why humans die. Also about the coming of death is the Ndebele "Chameleon and First Man" (125), which also tells how chameleons acquired the ability to change color. The Ghana story "Dung Beetle's Burden" (134) concerns the trickster spider, Anansi, and explains why spiders hide and trap their food. "Chameleon and the Greedy Spider" (126) is a Bushman tale about a figure called Spider whose trickery goes awry, resulting in the small waists that all spiders have today. The story also explains why spiders eat very little at one time and why they wrap their prey in webs.

59 Greene, Ellin, ret., *The Legend of the Cranberry: A Paleo-Indian Tale*, illus. Brad Sneed, Simon & Schuster, 1993 (hardcover), ISBN 0-671-75975-2, $15.00, unp. Ages 6-11, grades 1-6.

This old Native American Indian Delaware (Lenape) myth tells how the Great Spirit becomes angry when Yah-qua-whee (mammoths and mastodons) go on rampages and attack people and small animals. The Great Spirit instructs the people and animals to band together in defense against the common enemy. After many Yah-qua-whee are trapped in pits and killed, the rest attack, and in a tremendous battle, the Great Spirit unleashes his thunderbolts to ensure victory against the aggressors. As a sign of peace and his "abiding love," he creates the cranberry. The smooth, flowing quality of the text and the conflict of the story are well supported by the full-page, often dramatic, watercolors. Some are panoramic views; some are close-ups of people and animals. Especially effective are the head-on perspective of a huge, charging Yah-qua-whee and a long-range shot of the combatants from the elevated perspective of the Great Spirit. An endnote provides information about sources.

60 Greene, Jacqueline Dembar, ret., *Manabozho's Gifts: Three Chippewa Tales*, illus. Jennifer Hewitson, Houghton, 1994 (hardcover), ISBN 0-395-69251-2, $14.95, 42 pp. Ages 7-11, grades 2-6.

These three freely retold tales of the many hundreds surrounding Manabozho, the culture hero-trickster-buffoon of the Native American Chippewa, or Ojibwa, Indians, show the figure as a benefactor. In "How Manabozho Stole Fire" (1), Manabozho suffers considerable discomfort in order to make life easier on earth; in "How Manabozho Found Rice" (15), he receives an answer from the Great Spirit to his supplications for food in an unexpected and amusing way; and in "How Manabozho Saved the Rose" (29), it is explained why rabbits have long ears and cleft upper lips. The stories are dramatically retold, with good pacing, well-built suspense, and lively dialogue. A foreword gives important introductory information, and notes at the end specify sources. The first story is retold from retellings done for children in the 1960s, instead of from primary sources. The other two narratives rely on primary material, although, in the second one, Greene alters the action by combining the tale with buffoon material. The last story relies mainly on the account of the eminent Canadian Ojibwa authority, Basil Johnston. The black-and-white, smoothly stylized illustrations appear to be woodcuts. Skillfully executed, not only are they decorative but they also catch the spirit and important action of the episodes. Unfortunately, they are not always synchronized with the texts they portray. This beautiful and entertaining set of tales for younger or reluctant readers can serve as an introduction to this important heroic figure. An erratic bibliography concludes the book.

61   Greger, C. Shana, ad., *Cry of the Benu Bird: An Egyptian Creation Story*, illus. C. Shana Greger, Houghton, 1996 (hardcover), ISBN 0–395–73573–4, $14.95, unp. Ages 5 up, grades K up.

Combining traditions from the religious center of Heliopolis, Greger retells an ancient Egyptian myth about the creation of the gods, world, and humans. The portion about the Benu Bird, an ancient symbol of eternity and a protector against darkness, comes from a story told by the Greek historian Herodotus; the other sources named are ancient Egyptian. Accompanying the somewhat pedestrian retelling and lending it great dignity and sophistication are stylized, fluid, occasionally ethereal full-color paintings. The text, divided into brief chapters to mark the stages of creation, is framed by borders bearing ancient motifs. The whole projects a distinctively Egyptian flavor and, although a picture book, will appeal to all ages, being a handsome coffee-table production.

62   Greger, C. Shana, ret., *The Fifth and Final Sun: An Ancient Aztec Myth of the Sun's Origin*, illus. C. Shana Greger, Houghton Mifflin, 1994 (hardcover), ISBN 0–395–67438–7, $14.95, unp. Ages 4–11, grades PS–6.

In picture-book form, this tells of the five attempts of the Aztec gods to create the sun. First Tezcatlipoca, the God of the Night, then Quetzalcoatl, the jealous God of the Wind, then again Tezcatlipoca become the sun, each trying to destroy the other. The other gods, tired of the fighting, chose Tlalloc, God of the Rain, to be the sun, angering the God of the Wind, who, in his wrath, covers the entire world with lava. Then, ashamed of the destruction he has caused, he chooses Tlalloc's wife, Chalchihuitlicue, to become the fourth sun. The God of the Night insults this Goddess of Waters until her tears cover the land and turn all the creatures into fish. After some time of darkness, the gods convene and realize that a permanent sun can be achieved only through sacrifice. Two gods offer themselves: Tecciztecal, the God of the Snails, and Nanautzin, scorned as the Scabby-Pimply One. The God of the Snails is unable to jump into the fire, but Nanautzin rushes into the center of the blaze, and becomes the fifth and final sun. Written in simple but dignified language, the book will probably appeal to older readers, although the illustrations in predominately golds and oranges may attract some younger children. Borders are based on Aztec patterns and initial letters on hieroglyphics on a pre-

Hispanic Calendar Stone. An author's note says that the story is taken mostly from a sixteenth-century manuscript and the Calendar Stone.

63 Gregg, Andy, ret., *Great Rabbit and the Long-Tailed Wildcat*, illus. Cat Bowman Smith, Albert Whitman, 1993 (hardcover), ISBN 0–8075–3047–6, $13.95, 32 pp. Ages 6–10, grades 1–5.

A Native American Passamoquoddy version of a tale first recorded in a nineteenth-century Algonquin collection, this story tells how the wildcat, through greed and overconfidence, loses his beautiful long tail. Full-page pictures, predominantly blue and brown, alternate with pages of text framed with Indian motifs. The story is retold in an informal humorous tone, and the illustrations are slightly cartoonish, suitable for the type of tale but probably appealing most to an audience of the very young.

64 Hague, Michael, sel., *The Book of Dragons*, illus. Michael Hague, Morrow, 1995 (hardcover), ISBN 0–688–10879–2, $18.00, 146 pp. Ages 8 up, grades 3 up.

Three tales of oral tradition dragon-slaying heroes appear in this collection of stories about dragons: "Perseus and Andromeda" (16), reprinted from the now-classic set of retellings from Greek mythology by Padriac Colum, *The Golden Fleece*; "Sigurd and Fafnir" (72), taken from the Norse and retold by Andrew Lang in euphonious, romantically formal tones; and an irreverent, grandiloquent, tongue-in-cheek, always lively and interesting version by William H. G. Kingston of "St. George and the Dragon" (89) from English tradition. Deep-toned, romantic, full-page paintings—some humorous, others starkly dramatic—and black-and-white sketches portray dragons and humans in appropriate poses and make this a collector's book.

65 Hamilton, Virginia, ret., *The Dark Way: Stories from the Spirit World*, illus. Lambert Davis, Harcourt, 1990 (hardcover), ISBN 0–15–222340–1, $19.95, 154 pp. Ages 9 up, grades 4 up.

Eight pleasing, freely retold myths and hero tales from as many cultures appear in this well-designed and attractively illustrated anthology of mostly lesser known folktales. The tone is intimate and conversational, and the stories are well supported by the expressive, full-color paintings. In a few instances, the specific cultural group is not indicated, and, although an extensive bibliography is appended, the stories are not linked to specific sources. Information about each story appears at the end of the tale. An introduction at the beginning of the book provides insights into the intent and meaning of the tales. Hero tales appear from the African Americans with a rollicking tall tale involving a John Henry–type named Rolling Rio (5); adventurous ones about the Native American Manabozo (27), the Greek Perseus who slays Medusa (43), and the English (Celtic) Merlin (65), who advises Childe Rowland on how to recover his lost sister; and a humorous story from Haiti involving the trickster rabbit Malice (102). The Chinese myth "Everlasting Life" features the goddess Ho Hsien ku (75), while a tale involving the Norse wolf named Fenris (82) and one revolving around the Indian god of death, Yama (137), are incidents or adventures featuring gods. This last story also gives a view of the world of the dead.

66 Hamilton, Virginia, sel. and ret., *Her Stories: African American Folktales, Fairy Tales, and True Tales*, illus. Leo and Diane Dillon, Blue Sky, 1995 (hardcover), ISBN 0–590–47370–0, $19.95, 114 pp. All ages, grades 1 up.

These nineteen mostly fictitious or old stories, a few from personal experience, collected and retold by a prolific narrator of tales from world folklore and mythology, "focus on the magical lore and wondrous imaginings of African American women" (book jacket). While some tales are more fluently told than others, all retain the important oral quality, many employ dialect but never ponderously, and all suggest African American speech cadences. Some stories are serious, some humorous, some downright funny—tone and atmosphere vary, but all claim the attention well. Like Hamilton's other folklore anthologies, this has a helpful introduction that gives background to the stories as well as section introductions, a valuable "Comment" that closes each story, and a list entitled "Useful Sources" that appears at the end of the book. The book's attractively framed, strongly conceived full-color paintings—dramatic, suspenseful, or funny as appropriate—and framed, cream-toned text pages result in a remarkably handsome volume. "Little Girl and Buh Rabby" (3) is a trickster tale about the figure better known as Brer Rabbit. In "Miz Hattie Gets Some Company" (15), the Lord God creates the cat out of his glove to give the old woman relief from the hordes of mice that are bothering her. "Woman and Man Started Even" (69) tells how, at the very beginning of the world, the devil helps the woman get power from the Lord God to counterbalance man's greater physical strength. "Annie Christmas" (84) is a tall tale about a legendary, very powerful and enterprising African American woman keelboat operator on the Mississippi River.

67 Hamilton, Virginia, ret., *In the Beginning: Creation Stories from Around the World*, illus. Barry Moser, Harcourt, 1988 (hardcover), ISBN 0–15–238740–4, $22.95; 1991 (paper), ISBN 0–15–238742–0, $14.95, 163 pp. Ages 9 up, grades 4 up.

This strikingly designed and very readable anthology contains twenty-five retellings of myths from around the globe that explain how the world and humans originated. They range from myths where the gods themselves come into being, through those in which the gods bring matter into being, to cosmic-egg, monster-slaying, and primal-water versions. Some stories were set down in writing in very early times, among them the Mesopotamian tale of Marduk, while others were more recently put into written form, among them those of the Native American Raven and Old Man and the African stories. Some myths are frequently found in collections, including those about Prometheus and Pandora of the ancient Greeks, while others, for example, the Tahitian story of Ta-aroa, are known mostly from scholarly volumes. Although all hold the attention and move well, some retellings seem to capture the essence of the cultures and the intrinsic importance of the genre more aptly than others. The retelling of Pandora's story, for example, inaccurately portrays her as a petulant, disobedient teenager, an attitude unfortunately reinforced by the accompanying illustration. At their best, Moser's strong paintings convey the grandeur of the genre, in the brooding, primal scenes and especially in the stunning, powerful portraits. Following each retelling is an italicized "Comment" about the story, and an introduction and afterword give added information. An extensive list of "Useful Sources" completes the book. The specific source for each story is not given. Appearing are stories of the creation of the world from the Fon (Africa, 43), Krachi (Africa, 53), Native American Huron (59), Minyong (India, 117), and Greece (127); the origin of humans from Greece (139); the world and humans from the Inuit (Eskimo, 3), Melanesia (9), Kono (Guinea, 15), China (21), Native American Blackfeet (25), Russian Altaic (29), Native American Maidu (35), Australian Aboriginals (47), Lozi (Africa, 65), Norse (69), Yoruba (Africa, 73), Mesopotamia (Sumer/Babylon, 79), Native American Maya (87), Polynesia (Tahiti, 101), Micronesia (Marshall Islands, 105), Egypt (111), and ancient Israel (Biblical, 123, 149); the origin of death from Melanesia (9), Kono (Africa, 15), Native American Blackfeet (25) and Huron (59), Polynesia (Tahiti, 101), and Micronesia (Marshall Islands, 105); views of the world of the dead from Micronesia (Marshall Islands, 105); the origin of such necessities and realities as night from Melanesia (9), pain and suffering from China (21), the devil or evil from Russian Altaic (29), and arts, crafts, wisdom, knowledge, fire, troubles, diseases, and hope from Greece (134, 139); floods from the Native American Maya (87); goddesses and women heroes from the Fon (Africa, 43), Native American Huron (59), and Polynesia (Tahiti, 101); the origin of tattooing from Micronesia (Marshall Islands, 105);

and a variety of heroes from the Inuit (Eskimo, Raven, 3), Native American Blackfeet (Old Man Napi, 25) and Maidu (Coyote, 35), and Krachi (Africa, Ananse, 53). This is a substantial and well-retold anthology of myths.

Handoo, Jawaharlal, ed. *See* Beck, no. 12.

68 Harper, Piers, ret., *How the World Was Saved & Other Native American Tales*, illus. Piers Harper, Western, 1994 (hardcover), ISBN 0–307–17507–3, $14.95, 23 pp. Ages 5–12, grades K–7.

Bold, bright, dramatic illustrations whose motifs and settings are drawn from the culture depicted in the tale decorate and extend the simple, directly told versions of Native American myths. A Nisqualli myth takes a young woman to the world of the dead, of which the reader receives a vivid picture, in "The Girl Who Married a Ghost" (8); in "Michabo and the Flood" (12), from the Algonquin, the great and powerful spirit known as Michabo recreates the world after a mighty flood destroys it; Tirawa, the greatest god of the Pawnee, oversees the work of lesser gods in creating such physical features as trees and other plants to accommodate humans, who are then also brought into being (18); and in "How the World Was Saved" (20), twin Navajo heroes, Monster-Slayer and Child-of-the-Water, render the world habitable by ridding it of many of the monsters that plague it. A note about the purpose and function of myths introduces this slim, attractive book but unfortunately fails to specify sources.

69 Harrison, Michael, ret., *The Curse of the Ring*, illus. Tudor Humphries, Oxford, 1987 (hardcover), ISBN 0–19–274131–4, $13.95, 80 pp. Ages 8 up, grades 3 up.

Following the basic story of Sigurd and the cursed ring in the *Volsunga Saga*, this retelling expands the dialogue and description but remains true in spirit to the ancient tale. Some changes have been made for brevity and ease of comprehension: the episode of Andvari and the gods has been moved to the opening (6), the legends of Sigmund much abbreviated (21), and those of his sister Signy eliminated. There follow the stories of the marriage of Queen Hiordis to Ilf and the birth of Sigurd, her son by Sigmund (26), and of Sigurd's childhood and the reforging of his father's broken sword, Cleave (28). Urged on by the blacksmith, Regin, Sigurd slays the dragon Fafnir and, when Regin attacks him for the gold, turns the knife to wound the blacksmith mortally (34). Alerted by birds, whose language he now understands, Sigurd rides through a ring of fire to the great hall where Brynhild, the Valkyrie, sleeps (45), makes love to her, and gives her the ring from the dragon's hoard. Setting off again to avenge his father's death, he comes to the country of King Gunnar, where Gunnar's mother practices witchcraft and gives Sigurd a potion that makes him forget Brynhild and fall in love with Gunnar's sister, Gudrun (50). Gunnar, who has heard stories of Brynhild, gets Sigurd, disguised to resemble him, to ride once more over the flames, claim Brynhild, and retrieve the ring from her (53). Later, having forgotten to pass the ring on to Gunnar, Sigurd gives it to Gudrun (58), and the curse continues through the slaying of Sigurd by Gunnar's brothers, Gudrun's unhappy marriage to King Atli who covets the dragon's gold (68), the slaying of the brothers at Atli's command (76), and Gudrun's eventual suicide in the sea (79), while wearing the doomed ring. The book is printed in oversize format with large, dramatic illustrations on almost every page, many in color, but the text is much more extensive and demanding than that in most picture books. This is an exciting and readable version of the most popular of all Norse hero tales.

70 Harrison, Michael, ret., *The Doom of the Gods*, illus. Tudor Humphries, Oxford, 1985 (hardcover), ISBN 0–19–274128–4, $13.95, 80 pp. Ages 8 up, grades 3 up.

First published in Great Britain and one in the Oxford Myths and Legends series, this readable, lively collection of some of the main Norse myths has at its center Loki, the half-giant half-god trickster of many adventures. Although Harrison changes some motivations, introduces authorial speculation, takes some liberties with the standard versions, and, by sometimes overwriting, deviates from the spare, dramatic spirit and tragic grandeur of the originals, his novelistic narratives use dialogue with good effect, move well, and claim the attention throughout. Adventure abounds in "The Wall of Asgard" (6), "Utgard" (18), and "Geirrod" (46), in all of which Loki becomes involved with giants. "The Apples of Iduna" (52) and "Baldur" (61) are seasonal stories, and Loki's trickery drives the action in "Sif's Hair" (34), "The Apples of Iduna" (52), and "Baldur" (61). "Baldur" also contains a view of the world of the dead, and "Ragnorak" (75) is clearly eschatological. A brief account of the creation of the world appears on page 37 of "Sif's Hair." "Sif's Hair," "The Apples of Iduna," and "Baldur" all involve searches or quests. Colorful representational paintings bring out the human side of the gods.

71 Hart, George, ed., *Egyptian Myths*, British Museum Publications and University of Texas Press, 1990 (paper), ISBN 0–292–72076–9, $9.95, 80 pp. Ages 14 up, grades 9 up.

The several myths in this scholarly volume are described rather than narrated, with explanatory comments inserted as the action occurs. All are set in historical, archaeological, and geographical contexts and are accompanied by a map to show where particular stories were commonly told in ancient Egypt, by photographs of artifacts to illustrate characters and concepts, and by charts of the gods. Most of the book is about religious beliefs concerning the gods rather than a recreation of the actual stories. Myths included are creation of the world (and the gods) accounts popular at Heliopolis, "The Sun God of Heliopolis" (11), Memphis, "Ptah of Memphis" (18), and Hermopolis, "The Ogdoad of Hermopolis" (19), and a story from Upper Egypt of how the god Khnum created humans, "Khnum and the Theban Theogony" (25). "The Myth of Kingship" (29) tells of the adventures of the gods Isis and Osiris, a more detailed story than the other myths given, here related as a tale of dynastic rivalry and succession or a ritual drama of kingship. "Plutarch's Version" (40) of the same story relies on the seasonal, fertility, and arts of civilization aspects of the myth. An index of names and suggestions for further reading conclude the book.

72 Hastings, Selina, ret., *Sir Gawain and the Loathly Lady*, illus. Juan Wijngaard, Lothrop, 1985 (hardcover), ISBN 0–688–05823–X, $13.00, 29 pp. Ages 5 up, grades K up.

Intricately beautiful, this retelling of one Arthurian legend is presented in dignified, modern language that captures the intensity of the story of chivalry and honor. Challenged by the Black Knight to answer the question, "What do women most desire?," or die, Arthur takes the word of a misshapen hag that it is to have their own way. He escapes death but in return must promise that one of his knights will marry the ugly woman. Young Sir Gawain volunteers and bravely goes through the wedding ceremony, only to find in the bridal chamber that the loathsome creature has become a lovely young woman. When he learns that she is doomed by a spell to be her beautiful self only at night or only in the daytime, Gawain cannot decide which he prefers and allows his bride to choose. This giving of the woman her own way breaks the spell, and the whole court rejoices in their love and happiness. This book deservedly won the British Greenaway Award for its illustrations, which are elaborate and detailed, bordered with chivalric designs. Page numbers are set on shields, the lady is realistically hideous, action scenes are dramatic, and court scenes are sumptuously rich.

73 Haugaard, Erik, and Masako Haugaard, rets., *The Story of Yuriwaka*, illus. Birgitta Saflund, Roberts Rinehart, 1991 (hardcover), ISBN 1–879373–02–5, $12.95, 42 pp. Ages 9–12, grades 4–7.

The Emperor, petitioned by the people of Kyushu who are beset by sea raiders, orders Yuriwaka, the strongest man in the kingdom, to take three ships and deal with the pirates. Although happy with his wife, Lady Kasuga, and his work as governor in the district of Bungo, Yuriwaka sets off, fights for three years, and sails for home, after losing two of his ships but defeating the raiders. Two jealous officers, the brothers Taro and Jiro Beppu, steal his iron bow while he sleeps, maroon him on a small, rocky island, and report that he is dead. Lady Kasuga, who refuses to marry Taro, is arrested. Her only word from Yuriwaka is a message written in blood, bound to the leg of his hawk, Midorimaru, and delivered through the window of her tower prison. When Yuriwaka is rescued by fishermen, he has no way to prove who he is, and he works in the stables until, in an archery contest, he is the only one able to wield the iron bow and thereby kills the usurpers and claims his rightful place. Although described as a Japanese *Odyssey* and thought to be an outgrowth of the stories of Odysseus brought to Japan in the sixteenth century, it has long been in the oral tradition and has lost most of the elements of the Greek tale except for the shipwrecked hero, the faithful wife, and the exceptional bow. It is, however, a stirring hero tale retold skillfully and illustrated handsomely with three double-page paintings, four full-page black-and-white pictures, and numerous smaller scenes and decorations, all using Japanese costume and design.

74   Hausman, Gerald, ret., *Coyote Walks on Two Legs: A Book of Navajo Myths and Legends*, illus. Floyd Cooper, Philomel, 1994 (hardcover), ISBN 0–399–22018–6, $15.95, unp. Ages 5 up, grades K up.

In large, highly illustrated format, five stories of the trickster-buffoon-culture hero figure Coyote are retold from the Navajo oral tradition. The first is the myth of the great flood caused by Coyote (4), from which the animal people escape to a new world, presumably ours, in the sky. The others are more typical trickster-buffoon tales, telling how Coyote got his name, First Angry (10); how he lost his eyes by trying to copy Magpie's trick of throwing them away and recalling them (14); how he tried to steal corn from its guardian, Horned Toad (25); and how he tried to get a spotted coat, like the fawn, by letting sparks burn holes in his hair (21). All the illustrations are realistic full-page paintings bleeding to the edges in southwestern colors of orange, gold, and tan, with the text in the form of free-verse poems superimposed on the picture. Despite its picture-book format, older children could benefit from this striking collection.

75   Hayes, Sarah, ret., *Robin Hood*, illus. Patrick Benson, Holt, 1989 (hardcover), ISBN 0–8050–1206–0, $12.95, 76 pp. Ages 9–11, grades 4–6.

A brief but lively retelling of the Robin Hood stories in thirteen chapters, this book captures the zest and humor that are the distinguishing features of the hero tale. In this version, Robin is Robert Locksley, son of a farmer, not a noble, and he is deliberately entrapped by Sir Guy of Gisborne and arrested for killing a deer he did not shoot. He is saved by a band of outlaws led by Will Scarlet and joins the group of which Much the Miller and Jack Smithy are already members. Now known as Robin Hood, he soon becomes the leader and sets the pattern of stealing from the rich to give to the poor. The episodes of fighting Little John on the bridge, of carrying and being carried across the stream by Friar Tuck, of meeting Maid Marian disguised as a page, of saving Fair Ellen from a forced marriage and wedding her to Alan a Dale, of Little John's entering the service of the Sheriff of Nottingham and stealing his silver, and of the archery contest in Nottingham designed to trap the outlaws all appear, as does one less familiar about saving three condemned children from the gallows. Guy of Gisborne, a prominent figure in this retelling, eventually is slain in hand-to-hand combat by Robin. King Richard arrives in Sherwood Forest dressed as a pilgrim and enlists Robin and many of his followers into his service to instruct his men in the use of the longbow, but within months they are back in the forest. The final chapter deals with Robin's death, after he is betrayed by the Prioress who is pretending to heal him. Although not more difficult to read than the books by Curry (no. 38 and no. 39), this retelling is more spirited.

76 Helbig, Alethea K., ed., *Nanabozhoo, Giver of Life*, Green Oak, 1987 (hardcover), ISBN 0–931600–06–5, $15.95, 269 pp. Ages 11 up, grades 6 up.

In this thorough and entertaining study of the Native American Woodlands Indian god-hero-trickster are more than sixty out-of-print or unpublished tales from Southeastern Ojibwa sources. The various aspects of this complex figure are well represented. After a great flood (8, 28, 83, 91, 94, 98, 104), which in most versions he causes, he recreates the world (8, 28, 83, 91, 94, 98, 104). He is also a benevolent character in many other stories, slaying monsters (8, 41, 45, 217), undertaking quests (8, 45), giving the people such important agricultural crops as corn, squash, and tobacco (62, 65, 69, 201), even creating Paradise, at the direction of the Great Spirit (78). As a magician in his old age, he grants the requests of young men brave enough to seek him out (221, 224). He is responsible for many changes in animal appearance (8, 28, 83, 91, 98, 122, 137, 151, 154, 156, 164) and in animal behavior (62, 124, 129, 149, 158, 164), as well as various geographical features (178, 181, 186, 224) and other things in nature: the red willow (113, 116), the markings on birch bark (172), red granite (113), thorns on roses (174), the woodpecker (212), and the first robin (210). Also through him humans receive some great benefits: heavenly fire for sacred ceremonies (57) and the knowledge of healing through medicine rites (74, 107). Many of the stories concentrate on his aspect as a rascal or trickster (8, 113, 116, 119, 124, 131, 170, 188, 207). Frequently his tricks backfire and he becomes the butt of his own joke, or he simply acts in a foolish way, to be pictured as a buffoon (8, 28, 113, 116, 119, 139, 141, 145, 147, 168). Several stories have views of the world of the dead—two briefly as a place in the west ruled over by his brother, the wolf (104, 107), and one in much more detail in a story in which Nanabozhoo helps a young man retrieve his wife from death (228). Each of the eight sections, which follow the pattern of his life, starts with a general introduction describing the group of tales and their meaning, and each story is preceded by a discussion of where and by whom it was told or written and its special significance, often with mention of other versions and important stylistic elements. Some of the retellings are literary in nature, including those by Henry Rowe Schoolcraft in the nine-teenth century; others, often directly from storytellers, are informal in the style of the oral tradition. Many are humorous, even scatological. Extensive notes and an index support this scholarly but lively work. Several variations of his name are used, including Manabozo, Nanabush, Nenebuc, and others.

77   Heyer, Carol, ret., *Excalibur*, illus. Carol Heyer, Ideals Children's Books, 1991 (hardcover), ISBN 0–8249–8487–0, $14.95, unp. Ages 8 up, grades 3 up.

In picture-book format, this volume tells of King Arthur's acquiring of the wondrous sword with its magical scabbard from the Lady of the Lake, after having the sword he pulled from the stone broken in a conflict with the Black Knight. Despite simple language, the book deals with complex ideas of the nature of true honor, with Merlin the wizard as the young king's guide. The illustrations, in pencil and acrylic on canvas, are full-page paintings in rich colors, many of them in purples and blues, frequently seen from unusual angles, as in the pictures of the Black Knight framed by Arthur's sword and the edge of his shield and of Excalibur rising from the lake with only the water, the hand that wields the sword, a bit of white samite, and the jeweled hilt showing. Arthur is depicted as a serious youth with dark hair flowing below his shoulders. This is an interesting addition to fuller treatments of the Arthur stories.

78   Hodges, Margaret, ret., *The Kitchen Knight: A Tale of King Arthur*, illus. Trina Schart Hyman, Holiday House, 1990 (hardcover), ISBN 0–8234–0787–X, $14.95; 1993 (paper), ISBN 0–8234–1063–3, $5.95, unp. Ages 4 up, grades PS up.

With her characteristic verbal dexterity, fidelity to the speech rhythms usu-ally associated with the medieval period, and obvious love for Arthurian lit-erature, Hodges retells the story of King Arthur's determined nephew, Sir

Gareth, as he wins his knighthood, kills the dreaded Sir Ironside, the Red Knight of the Red Plain, and wins the fair Linesse. Hodges's sources are Sir Thomas Malory's *Le Morte D'Arthur* and the Winchester text, according to an afternote. Hyman's colorful paintings are typically and appropriately dramatic, romantic, and filled with action and pagentry, portraying stalwart, armored knights on their ponderous, muscled mounts, ladies with flowing tresses (including Hyman's trademark big-eyed brunette), hilltop castles, streaming flags and flowing pennants, moody night scenes, landscapes of old England, and resplendent castle interiors, all enclosed in her usual framed pictures that give the sense of windows on a long-ago and far-gone era. Numerous symbols appear for the discerning viewer, like the two treetop crows that peer at Gareth while he is riding with the surly, scornful Linette. Anyone familiar with Hodges's work will appreciate this product of her skillful hand and ear, and those acquainted with Hyman's pictures will applaud this evidence of her ability to capture the essence of the Arthurian hero tale.

79 Hodges, Margaret, and Margery Evernden, rets., *Of Swords and Sorcerers: The Adventures of King Arthur and His Knights*, illus. David Frampton, Scribner's, 1993 (hardcover), ISBN 0–684–19437–6, $14.95, 96 pp. Ages 9–14, grades 4–9.

In dignified, slightly formal but not archaic diction, this book tells the story of King Arthur, Guinevere, and the main knights in nine chapters that begin with Arthur's birth and identification as king through the coming of the knights and the search for the Holy Grail to Arthur's death in battle at the hand of one of the knights, Sir Mordred. The contributions of the evil enchantress Morgan le Fay and of the wise Lady of the Lake are not neglected, and Sir Lancelot appears with imperfections as well as virtues—in short, in spite of the magic and enchantment that pervade the tales, the king, knights, and ladies are presented as human beings with aspirations and failings. Frampton's woodcuts add to the glory and to the reality of Camelot and the knights. "Of Castles and Dragons" (1) tells about Arthur's coming to kingship, and "Of Swords and Sorcerers" (13) describes how Arthur secures, loses, and regains Excalibur, the sword, and its scabbard. Arthur's marriage is related in "Of Guinevere and the Round Table" (21). "Of True Love" (31) concerns Sir Lancelot and his love for Guinevere and the love of two maidens named Elaine for him, while "Of the Sword Bridge" (43) describes how Lancelot battles a wicked knight on behalf of Guinevere. "Of the Boy Who Would Be a Knight" (51) revolves around Sir Percival, and "Of the Coming of Sir Galahad" (65) and "Of the Quest for the Holy Grail" (75) around Sir Galahad. "Of the Last Battle" (85) treats Arthur's problems with Lancelot and Arthur's death. The strong narrative pull and fluidity of these retellings probably derives from the writers' years of experience in telling stories to children and young people.

The foreword cites as sources Sir Thomas Malory's *Le Morte d' Arthur* (*sic*), the *Mabinogion*, and the work of Howard Pyle.

80 Holt, David, and Bill Mooney, sels. and rets., *Ready-to-Tell Tales*, August House, 1994 (hardcover), ISBN 0–87483–380–9, $24.95, 224 pp.; (paper), ISBN 0–87483–381–7, $16.95, 224 pp. Ages 5–13, grades K–8.

This multicultural collection by thirty-nine storytellers includes forty-one stories, all but three of which are folktales. "The Twelve Labors of Hercules" (138) is an unusual adaptation of the hero tale of the ancient Graeco-Roman strongman. Two Cherokee (Native American Indian) tales, which straddle the line between myth and folktale, explain animal behavior and appearance. "Rabbit and Possum Hunt for a Wife" (90), an action-filled account, concludes with Possum's protecting himself by pretending to play dead, thus initiating that species' peculiar defense mechanism. "How the Turtle Cracked His Shell" (142) explains the characteristic markings on the turtle's back in a spirited version that recalls Brer Rabbit in the briar patch. The adaptations, which project a strong narrative flavor, have been tested in storytelling situations. No sources are given.

81 Horowitz, Anthony, ret., *Myths and Legends*, illus. Francis Mosley, Kingfisher, 1994 (paper), ISBN 1–85697–975–X, $6.95, 254 pp. Ages 9–14, grades 4–9.

More than half of the thirty-five stories in this collection are Greek, Roman, and Norse myths frequently and better retold elsewhere. A few are legends without mythological elements. Of the rest, however, most are less well known or appear in unfamiliar versions. Saint George, for instance, does not slay a dragon but, in what is now Lebanon, rebukes it and leads the repentant beast by a ribbon around its neck back to the town it has been harassing (153). The Beowulf story (159) consists of only the episode of Grendel, omitting that of Grendel's mother and the dragon slaying in the hero's old age, as well as all the tales within the tale that make up much of the original. Two of the Norse stories are not frequently retold: "Nidud the Cruel" (174), about Volsung the Smith, and "The Death of Nornagest" (181), about the death of the poet as a result of the fanatical Christianity of King Olaf. The King Arthur stories are represented by "The Ugly Wife" (165), about Sir Gawain's marriage to a hideous woman. Two contrasting women are Savitri (195) of India and Sedna (227) from the Eskimo. Other myths and hero tales are Japanese, "The First Eclipse" (211); Chinese, "The Monkey Who Would Be King" (207); Polynesian, "Catching the Sun" (236); and Bororo Indian of South America, "Geriguiaguiatugo" (221). The weakness of the collection is in its breezy tone and a style not suited to the seriousness of myths and epic hero tales, especially in the dialogue, of which there is a great deal. Characters say, "You dirty rat!" and "What the . . . what the blazes!," and even the Buddha speaks informally: "Not bad," he tells monkey. Its value is in the variety of stories, not all of which are easily obtainable, and as a contrast to other retellings. This has also been published in hardcover, titled *Myths and Mythology*.

82 Hull, Robert, ret., *Native North American Stories*, illus. Richard Hook and Claire Robinson, Thomson Learning, 1993 (hardcover), ISBN 1–56847–005–3, $15.95, 48 pp. Ages 10–14, grades 5–9.

A handsome, originally British retelling of eight Native American Indian stories, at least seven of them myths, this collection has well-developed selections, an introduction about the native peoples of North America, a map showing their cultural areas, notes including the pronunciation of various group names, and a bibliography titled "Further Reading." The style is simple but serious and respectful. Illustrations are of two types: lavish, realistic, full-color paintings, some of them double-page, and stylized strips, mostly in black and white, bordering the text and employing motifs appropriate to the story, for example, totem pole figures beside a Tlingit tale and snowflake designs beside one of the origin of seasons. Included are myths of the creation of the world from the Inuit (6); the creation of people from the Crow (9); thunder from the Pawnee, Blackfoot, Tlingit, and Kwakiutl (15); the origin of the hunting pattern of wolves from the Tsimshian (23); the origin of seasons from the Iroquois (26); how the bluebird got its color from the Pima (32); and the origin of music from the Lakota Sioux (35). An unusual view of the world of the dead is presented in "The Last Journey" (43) from the Skidi Pawnee.

83 Hulpach, Vladimir, ret., *Ahaiyute and Cloud Eater*, illus. Marek Zawadzki, Harcourt, 1995 (hardcover), ISBN 0–15–201237–0, $16.00, unp. Ages 5 up, grades K up.

Sophisticated, full-color paintings illustrate episodes and characterize the principals in this seasonal, fertility Native American Zuni hero tale retold from the authoritative collection of Ruth Benedict of 1935. The youth Ahaiyute, helped by Grandmother and a mole, journeys far to the east searching for the giant monster called in the text Cloud Eater and shown in the pictures as a huge, writhing, bluish sky snake. Cloud Eater is responsible for a terrible, long-lasting drought that has afflicted the entire region. Ahaiyute kills the monster with a well-placed arrow and thus proves himself a man of the tribe. Striking visual effects capture the eye and play up the poetic prose. For example, the pictures' subdued, misty tones both emphasize the dryness of the desert and foreshadow the coming rain. This unusual book offers new avenues of appreciation every time it is read and viewed.

84   Hunt, Jonathan, ret., *Leif's Saga: A Viking Tale*, illus. Jonathan Hunt, Simon & Schuster, 1996 (hardcover), ISBN 0–689–80492–X, $16.00, unp. Ages 5–11, grades K–6.

Years afterward, a Norse boatbuilder tells his young red-haired daughter the story of Leif Ericson's journey to the western lands sighted by a sea trader named Bjarne Herfjolfsson. When he is nineteen, Leif takes the place of his father, Eiric, who is disabled with a broken arm, at the head of a ship's crew and sails from Greenland to the places he names Helluland, Markland, and Vinland, today's Baffin Island, Labrador, and Newfoundland. After spending the winter in dwellings they construct on Newfoundland, still to be seen in ruins there, they return to Greenland with a shipload of dried fish, skins, other foods, and sturdy oak logs from that plentiful land. Although there is little attempt to build suspense or create excitement, the narrative works satisfactorily to convey the main aspects of the voyage to a broad age range. More impressive are the large, framed, full-color paintings that accompany the action and extend the story. The double-page close-ups and long-range views of land and sea and small inset pictures offer an abundance of details and, in particular, extend the setting. Also included are a lengthy author's note, a small map, explanations of the runes that appear here and there and in the frames, and a short bibliography.

85   Hutton, Warwick, ret., *Perseus*, illus. Warwick Hutton, McElderry, 1993 (hardcover), ISBN 0–689–50565–5, $14.95, unp. Ages 5 up, grades K up.

Hutton humanizes Perseus, one of the best-known heroes of ancient Greece, presenting him as brave and worthy but also somewhat naive and worried about the safety of his mother and stepfather, Danae and Dictys, in view of the deviousness of the local king; mindful of his humble origins; gentle toward Andromeda, the maiden he rescues by bravely slaying a sea monster; quick to dispatch his foe, the snaky-haired Medusa; cognizant that he has received necessary help from the gods Hermes and Athena; and moral about returning the magical gifts they have loaned him. The loose and sketchy watercolors sometimes glow and at other times appear muted, and unusual perspectives add interest. For example, as the book opens, the fisherman Dictys discovers the wooden chest with Danae and her baby Perseus inside; both text and pictures reflect his point of view. When Perseus prepares to kill the sea monster, the viewpoint is that of the monster, threatening indeed as his huge body arches toward the slim, young hero. Hutton does not indicate his sources. Although better told versions exist, this one has appeal, covers the most important ground, and holds the attention. Hutton has also published books about Theseus, the Trojan War, and Persephone, also of Greek story, and Adam and Eve and Moses of ancient Hebrew tradition.

86 Jackson, Danny P., trans., *The Epic of Gilgamesh*, illus. Thom Kapheim, Bolchazy-Carducci, 1992 (hardcover), ISBN 0–86516–251–4, $35.00, 140 pp.; 1992 (paper), ISBN 0–86516–352–9, $4.95, 96 pp. Ages 14 up, grades 9 up.

This is a graceful, free-verse translation of the twelve ancient Mesopotamian tablets that make up the epic of Gilgamesh, one of the world's most magnificent poems, among the oldest of writings, and the prototype literary creation that informed Biblical and ancient Greek literatures, among others. The story tells of a feared and powerful legendary king in Uruk in about 2700 B.C.E. After he and his dearest friend, Enkidu, slay a monster-man, Humbaba, Gilgamesh is griefstricken when Enkidu dies, having angered especially Ishtar, the goddess of love. Obsessed with the prospect of his own ultimate death, Gilgamesh travels far and wide in search of the secret of immortality, arriving eventually in the paradise called Dilmun, where he confers with Utnapishtim, the hero who had survived the world-destroying flood. The epic is notable for several features, among them the incorporation of a flood story that long antedates in writing its Biblical Noachic counterpart; the stirring, poignant lament of Gilgamesh over the body of Enkidu, which predates and prefigures that of David over Saul and Jonathan; its quest for the secret of life eternal, which recalls other later quest stories, in particular those of Odysseus for advice from Achilles and of Aeneas for the Golden Bough; and such themes as the exploration of the meaning and value of human existence. Included also are excellent introductory material, photographs of ancient artifacts pertaining to the story, original drawings of significant scenes, list of important characters, a map, and glossary.

87 Jackson, Ellen, ret., *The Precious Gift: A Navaho Creation Myth*, illus. Woodleigh Marx Hubbard, Simon & Schuster, 1996 (hardcover), ISBN 0–689–80480–6, $16.00, unp. Ages 4–11, grades PS–6.

Amusing, detailed, full-color primitives follow the characters' actions and add imaginative facets to one of the last sections of the very long Navajo creation story of how humans began in the underworld and started their lives here. Upon evolving through a thin reed into the fifth, or current, world, people are tired and thirsty but can find no water in the parched, arid desert of the Southwest. First Man sends Beaver, Otter, Frog, and Turtle in pairs down into the underworld to bring back water. After they fail, the little Snail, tenacious and persevering, succeeds and is rewarded for his efforts when First Man attaches the flask to his back to be his home henceforth. All rivers, streams, and lakes evolve from the water Snail brings to the upper world. The story also explains why beavers and otters live in swampy areas, how turtles acquired shells, and why frogs are hunched up. Vivid poetic touches appear in story and pictures. For example, First Man uses a piece of coral as a stopper for the flask, which he then attaches to Otter's neck with a cord of rainbow. An author's note indicates that the story comes from Franc Newcomb's collection of Navajo tales and that the story intends to remind hearers of the importance of water and its conservation. Although horses, which came with the Spaniards, anachronistically appear in the illustrations, this is otherwise a pleasingly rendered account.

88   Jaffe, Nina, and Steve Zeitlin, rets., *While Standing on One Foot: Puzzle Stories and Wisdom Tales from the Jewish Tradition*, illus. John Segal, Holt, 1993 (hardcover), ISBN 0–8050–2594–4, $14.95, 120 pp. Ages 8–15, grades 3–10.

Among these eighteen conversationally told folk stories taken from throughout Jewish history and all parts of the world is "The Case of the Boiled Egg" (18). Even as a child, King Solomon shows "unusual powers of perception and insight" in helping one of his father's weavers. The man is in debt to a greedy innkeeper, who demands a sum of money equal to the worth of all the chickens that might have descended from the single boiled egg the weaver ate at the innkeeper's table. Notes on the stories give sources, and a bibliography is included.

89   Jaffrey, Madhur, ret., *Seasons of Splendour: Tales, Myths and Legends of India*, illus. Michael Foreman, Puffin, 1987 (paper), ISBN 0–317–62172–6, $7.95, 128 pp. Ages 9 up, grades 4 up.

These eighteen stories, about half of which are myths and hero tales, are set in the context of the writer's childhood memories. Jaffrey grew up as the daughter of a large, extended, affluent Indian family, in which the old tales were regularly told by female elders to the assorted second- and third-generation cousins. Preceding each major section is a personal reminiscence of the occasions on which the tales were told that leads into the events of the story. The narratives are related with affection and verve, and even when events are serious, there are touches of humor. Dialogue is extensive, and action abounds. Accompanying major events are colorful paintings in jewel-like tones. They recall ancient Indian art and are impressionistic and occasionally comic. Included are four hero stories about the monster-slayer Krishna, who is the embodiment of the god Vishnu: "The Birth of Krishna, the Blue God" (22), "Krishna and the Demon Nurse" (26), "The Serpent King" (30), and "How Krishna Killed the Wicked King Kans" (32). The epic *Ramayana* is summarized in five chapters as "How Ram Defeated the Demon King Ravan" (48). "The Moon and the Heavenly Nectar" (71) tells of both the creation of the world and the origin of the eclipse of the moon. "The Girl Who Had Seven Brothers" (75), "Lakshmi and the Clever Washerwoman" (81), and "The King Without an Heir" (110) are fertility myths. "How Ganesh Got his Elephant Head" (121) tells how the son of the god Shiva and the goddess Parvati acquires the head of an animal. This story and "The King Without an Heir" and "The Girl in the Forest" (115), a Rumpelstiltskin type, feature the goddess Parvati. The book concludes with an excellent glossary of names and a pronunciation guide.

90 Johnson, James Weldon, ret., *The Creation*, illus. James E. Ransome, Holiday House, 1994 (hardcover), ISBN 0–8234–1069–2, $15.95, unp. Ages 4 up, grades PS up.

The short free-verse narrative poem retells with deep reverence, true elegance, and hints of humor the story of the creation of the world and the first man from Genesis 1 and 2 in the Bible. Phrases and rhythms aptly catch the flavor of southern African American storytelling and preaching. One of the poetic sermons from Johnson's *God's Trombones: Seven Negro Sermons in Verse* (1919, 1927), it is accompanied by highly expressive, full-color, deep palette paintings. This is a stunning book that appeals to the emotions and intellect of all ages.

91 Johnston, Basil, coll., ed., and ret., *The Manitous: The Spiritual World of the Ojibway*, illus. David Johnson, HarperCollins, 1995 (hardcover), ISBN 0–06–017199–5, $24.00, 247 pp.; (paperback), ISBN 0–06–092735–6, $12.00, 272 pp. Ages 14 up, grades 9 up.

This collection, one of several by this writer, focuses on manitous, supernatural beings of various degrees of importance and power of the Anishinaubae (the northeastern woodlands) people, more specifically, the Native American Indian Ojibway. An Ojibway from the Cape Croker Indian reserve in Ontario, Canada, Johnston gathered and retold these myths, legends, tales, and spiritual teachings from his own recollections and from interviews with tribal elders. The book projects an authoritative appeal similar to that of his best-known book, *Ojibway Heritage* (Columbia University, 1976), but it is more tightly organized and displays a firmer sense of substance. The stories also have a stronger affinity to the storytelling situation, even though philosophical comments and explanatory information occasionally impede the flow of events. The "Introduction" (xv) tells of the creation of the world and humans, a flood, and Sky Woman, an important mythological figure. "Muzzu-Kimmik-Quae: Mother Earth" (9) provides background on Mother Earth or Earth Woman and also tells of the action of the prototypical hero, Nana'b'oozoo, in recreating the earth after a world-destroying flood. Also about Nana'b'oozoo and his three heroic brothers are "Maudjee-kawiss: The First Son" (17), which, in addition to being a first-rate adventure story, tells of the origin of recording events on sashes, scrolls, and the like, and of stories; "Pukawiss: The Disowned" (27), about the trickster who is the first dancer, actor, and entertainer; "Cheeby-aub-oozoo: The Ghost of Rabbit" (37), concerning the first holy man or spiritual leader who originates vision quests and becomes the ruler of the underworld or afterlife; and of "Nana'b'oozoo" (51), a long, detailed version of the life and adventures of the mightiest trickster and warrior of them all. "The Manitous of the Forests and Meadows" (97) explains how fire, tobacco, and evergreen and birch trees came to be, and is a seasonal story involving a search and the goddess Mother Earth. "The Spirit of Maundau-meen (Maize)" (103) explains how the Ojibway received the gift of corn. A preface and an introduction open the book, and an extensive glossary of names and terms concludes it.

92   Kellogg, Steven, ret., *Sally Ann Thunder Ann Whirlwind Crockett*, illus. Steven Kellogg, Morrow, 1995 (hardcover), ISBN 0–688–14042–4, $15.00, unp. Ages 4 up, grades PS up.

Drawing his material from the Davy Crockett almanacs, according to a prefatory note, and employing his typical snappy, detailed, comic, sometimes purposely anachronistic watercolors, Kellogg has produced another frisky retelling in his series of American folk heroes, which includes Mike Fink, Paul Bunyan, Pecos Bill, and Johnny Appleseed. Born two hundred years ago, the only daughter and youngest child in a family of nine boys, Sally Ann Thunder Ann Whirlwind announces at birth that she can "out-talk, out-grin, out-scream, out-swim, and out-run any baby in Kentucky" and she proceeds to do all. Later she uses these talents to establish herself as one of the most famous American frontier heroines. After she rescues Davy Crockett, in an episode that results in her creating the American bald eagle, and then marries him and he leaves for Congress, she defeats a huge herd of attacking hooligan alligators and bests with wit and physical strength champion wrestler and riverboatman Mike Fink, among other outrageous exploits that should delight young feminists and all lovers of tall tales.

93   Kimmel, Eric A., ret., *The Adventures of Hershel of Ostropol*, illus. Trina Schart Hyman, Holiday House, 1995 (hardcover), ISBN 0–8234–1210–5, $15.95, 64 pp. Ages 5 up, grades K up.

These peppy retellings of the escapades of the scapegrace whose antics and mischief became legendary in eastern Europe exude comic humor for younger readers and offer insightful views of human nature for older readers. A real person who lived in the Ukraine in the late eighteenth and early nineteenth centuries, Hershel, a ritual slaughterer, became the center of a cycle of stories told in Yiddish, the language of eastern European Jews. The stories reveal him as a lazy and improvident trickster, who cleverly outwits the wealthy men in the community to support himself and his family, at the same time exposing their greed and arrogance and making them look foolish. These ten stories (9, 13, 16, 19, 28, 32, 37, 44, 52, 61) are typical of the many told about Hershel and range from the truly funny to tall-tale outrageous. An introduction gives historical background, and a selection of witty sayings attributed to Hershel appears in an afterword.

94   Kimmel, Eric A., ad., *Rimonah of the Flashing Sword: A North African Tale*, illus. Omar Rayyan, Holiday House, 1995 (hardcover), ISBN 0–8234–1093–5, $15.95, unp. Ages 5 up, grades K up.

This dramatic retelling of an Egyptian story combines motifs from Snow White and the Arabian Nights. At its center is an intrepid heroine who in childhood suffers through the schemes of a wicked stepmother queen. She is rescued by forty Ali Baba–like thieves, who shelter her in their sumptuous cavern castle and train her to ride and fight. She becomes known far and wide as the boldest in their desert bedouin band. Poisoned by the wicked queen, she is awakened by a good and handsome prince, and together she, the prince, and the thieves slay the queen and restore her father the king to his rightful position. Rimonah, staunch, fearless, and skilled with horse and sword, is a heroine who accomplishes her own delivery. A forenote indicates the source of the story. Rayyan's opulent, full-color, action-filled paintings reveal character and dramatize moments in hues, costumes, and motifs drawn from old Egypt and other parts of North Africa and the Middle East. Although presented in picture-book format, the story and illustrations are sufficiently sophisticated to appeal to a broad age range.

95   Koslow, Philip, ret., *El Cid*, Chelsea House, 1993 (hardcover), ISBN 0–7910–1266–2, $18.95, 92 pp. Ages 11 up, grades 6 up.

More biography than hero tale, this version of the life of Rodrigo Diaz, the Spanish military leader who became known as El Cid, concentrates on the historical records of the early eleventh century and what facts are known about the real life of the hero. Only in the final chapter does it treat the legend that grew up around this figure, and even there it comments on what parts of the story seem to depart from fact and indulge in the romantic exaggeration typical of oral tradition. It is followed by a chronology starting with Rodrigo's birth in 1040 in Vivar, Spain, and ending with the death of his wife, Dona Jimena, who outlived him by seventeen years, in 1116, and by a bibliography for further reading. One of a series called Hispanics of Achievement, it is illustrated with some photographs of historically important sites and many reproductions of medieval and later artworks connected to the story of El Cid. Although not in itself a retelling of the legend, the book should be a valuable addition to a study of the famous Spanish hero.

96 Lankford, George E., coll. and ed., *Native American Legends: Southeastern Legends: Tales from the Natchez, Caddo, Biloxi, Chickasaw, and Other Nations*, August House, 1987 (hardcover), ISBN 0–87483–040–0, $25.95, 265 pp.; (paper), ISBN 0–87483–041–9, $9.95. Ages 14 up, grades 9 up.

Scholarly but interesting introductions precede the more than 130 stories, many of them variants of one another, drawn mostly from printed collections from Native American groups of the American Southeast. The stories are divided into sections by setting (e.g., The Above World), kind of character (e.g., The Twins), and miscellaneous adventures (e.g., Other Adventures). The notes that follow the stories give the sources and significant motifs, sometimes by number, and often compare the stories with others of their type. Most tales are short, ranging from a quarter of a page to two pages in length. The Yuchi "Mother Sun" (58) gives an unusual account of the origin of human beings, while "Emergence" (111) from the Choctaw tells how the Muscogees, Cherokees, Chickasaws, and Choctaws came to be. The origin of white people appears in the Yuchi "Creation of the Whites" (136) and of whites, blacks, and Native Americans in "Origin of Races" (140) from the Seminole. "Earth-Diver" (107) tells the Yuchi version of the creation of the world. How death became a reality is described in "The Daughter of the Sun" (61), a Cherokee quest tale that also gives the origin of the cardinal bird and a view of the world of the dead. Another look at the world of the dead appears in "Orpheus" (213), a Yuchi quest story in which four men travel to the world of the dead to recover their wives. Fire becomes a reality for humans when the trickster hero Rabbit steals it from its owners in the Hitchiti "The Theft of Fire" (68), while in the Alabama "Bears and Fire" (69) humans discover fire after its owners, the bears, have abandoned it. Another reality of life is explained in "Lightning and the People" (81) from the Caddo. Devastating floods appear in two stories, both entitled "The Flood," from the Caddo and the Alabama (97 and 110, respectively). How various common animals originate appears in the Creek "The Origin of Animals (Clans)" (118), which also explains Creek clans. Coyote the trickster stars in his beneficent mode in "Owner of the Animals" (126, Caddo) by releasing buffalo that the Buzzards have kept for themselves. The origin of commonly hunted animals appears in "Kanati and Selu" (148, Cherokee), along with the explanation of why they are hunted. "The Origin of Tobacco" (Yuchi, 143) tells how that important plant originated, and three tales explain how corn came: "Kanati and Selu" (Cherokee, 148) and two tales entitled "The Origin of Maize" from the Creek and the Abnaki (155 and 156, respectively). Various foods originate in "Journey to the Sky" (211, Alabama), which also gives an interesting view of the sky world. The trickster Rabbit puts one over on a tie-snake in "A Tug of War" (234) from the Creek. A good version of how the African Ashanti trickster Ananse (Kwaku Ananse) acquires stories from the sky god is given in "The Tasks of the Trickster" (229). Although the language of these stories is not difficult, well within the capacity of most fifth graders and the plots are uncomplicated, the book's format may intimidate readers below high school level. Extensive notes and the fine bibliography at the end of the book increase its usefulness and value.

97 Larry, Charles, ret., *Peboan and Seegwun*, illus. Charles Larry, Farrar, Straus and Giroux, 1993 (hardcover), ISBN 0–374–35773–0, $16.00, unp. Ages 5 up, grades K up.

Into the lodge of the old man at the end of winter comes a young man, bright eyed and smiling. As they smoke a pipe together, they converse about their contrasting skills: the old man, Peboan, has only to blow upon the land and all the streams turn to stone; the young man, Seegwun, breathes and flowers spring up. As day comes to the lodge, the old man begins to stream away and wither to nothing. The spring beauty, the earliest of the northern flowers, blooms. In fewer than three hundred words, Larry retells the myth of the changing of the seasons originally recorded by Henry Schoolcraft from the Ojibwa oral tradition in the 1830s. Although the language is spare, it is descriptive and the syntax is not overly simple, so that what may at first seem a story for the very young is really suitable for all ages. Gorgeous, full-page paintings illustrate the tale, showing the geographical area and the lifestyle of the Ojibwa people before the coming of the whites.

98 Larungu, Rute, ret., *Myths and Legends from Ghana for African-American Cultures*, illus. Lou Turechek, Telecraft, 1992 (hardcover), ISBN 1–878893–21–1, $14.95; (paper), ISBN 1–878893–20–3, $8.95, 94 pp. Ages 8 up, grades 3 up.

Two of these eight Hausa and Ashanti are myths and three are hero tales featuring the spider trickster. Now a "grandmother person," the reteller heard the stories when she was young and lived in the Gold Coast, as Ghana was then known. The retellings have a strong oral quality and are intended, Larungu says, as "lovegifts" to present-day hearers and readers. Three "letters" appear among the stories, in which she explains cultural features and gives information about the tales. Proverbs appear here and there, enhancing the cultural atmosphere, as do the frequent black-and-white sketches of characters and incidents. There is also a helpful pronunciation guide. Explaining how the Hausa nation came to be is "The Horse with the Golden Horn" (12), and the origin of the Ashanti kingdom appears in "The Coming of the Golden Stool" (51). In the remaining three stories, Spider, as the Hausa know him, outwits animal friends in "The Spider and the Terrible Great Ones" (36) and behaves in a similar fashion as does Ananse in the Ashanti "The Nkorowa Dance" (71). On the other hand, Ananse reveals a more beneficial side in the Ashanti "How Wisdom Came to the Tribe" (69). This is a pleasing collection, humorous, exciting, and revealing of the cultural values.

99   Lattimore, Deborah Nourse, ret., *Why There Is No Arguing in Heaven: A Mayan Myth*, illus. Deborah Nourse Lattimore, HarperCollins, 1989 (hardcover), ISBN 0–06023–717–1, $13.95, unp. Ages 5–12, grades K–7.

This adaptation of a Native American Indian myth describes the creation of the earth and humans. In order to stop the fussing among the lesser gods as to who is the most important among them, the first Creator God, Hunab Ku, having created the earth, challenges his subordinates to create "a being worthy of worshipping him" to prove their superiority. After humans of mud and of wood prove unsuitable and are destroyed, the Maize God uses corn seeds and produces a satisfactory race. Although the narrative does not always move logically, as it should in a retelling, the humor and drama that arise from the bickering among the anthropomorphic gods and their unsuccessful attempts build suspense well. The distinctive illustrations capture the flavor of the myth and the sense of the culture. Blue-green, sometimes full-color framed paintings wrap around the text and show the gods in deliberation or at work, the unworthy humans and their destruction, and finally the beautiful creatures that develop from the corn. All the paintings draw their inspiration from painted art and stonework reliefs and sculptures, in particular, those presented in the green tones. The endpapers are fascinating reproductions of glyphs from codices with the English translations. A reteller's note about the people and their literature appears at the end of this unusual book.

100 Lawlor, Robert, ret., *Voices of the First Day: Awakening in the Aboriginal Dreamtime*, Inner Traditions, 1991 (paper), ISBN 0–89281–355–5, $24.95, 412 pp. Ages 6 up, grades 1 up.

Only one story appears in this very scholarly and exhaustive anthropological examination of Australian Aboriginal indigenous rituals and beliefs. Other tales can be found here and there in bits and pieces interspersed among commentary but are hard to appreciate as narratives. "How the Sun Was Made" (44) is an entertaining account of how the sun got into the sky and light came into the world and why the Goo-goor-gaga bird, better known as the kookaburra, greets the dawn with loud cackling. He was chosen to prepare people for the light that will soon appear in the sky, a task he undertakes each morning to this day.

101 Leeson, Robert, ret., *The Story of Robin Hood*, illus. Barbara Lofthouse, Kingfisher, 1994 (hardcover), ISBN 1–85697–988–1, $16.95, 96 pp.; (paper), ISBN 0–7534–5021–6, $6.95, 160 pp. Ages 9 up, grades 4 up.

Longer and more detailed than most of the recent retellings of the Robin Hood stories, this version strives for the lively and humorous style vital to the tone of the hero tale but often falls short, perhaps because of the mix of slightly archaic language and extensive dialogue. An author's note at the end points out that the version follows the earliest tellings and ballads, which do not specify which king comes in disguise to the Greenwood, but has added Maid Marian (48) from fifteenth- and sixteenth-century plays. The most familiar stories appear: Little John on the bridge (6); the wedding of Allan-a-Dale (11), Little John as the servant of the Sheriff of Nottingham (27), Friar Tuck and his dunking Robin Hood in the stream (40), the duel with Sir Guy of Gisbourne (61), the contest for the golden arrow (72), and the king's appearance in Sherwood Forest (83). Several stories involve Sir Richard of Lee, to whom Robin lends money owed the rich abbot of Saint Mary's and who later gives shelter to Robin's band as they flee from the Sheriff's men (16, 22, 75, 78). Robin's death (92) is attributed, as usual, to the Prioress of Kirklees, but also involves the less familiar figure of Sir Roger the Red, an evil parish priest. Illustrations in bright colors, predominantly and appropriately green, picture Robin and his men as rather too young and clean-cut, but have some attractive features, like the illuminated ovals that enclose initial letters for each chapter.

102 Lewis, Richard, ret., *All of You Was Singing*, illus. Ed Young, Atheneum, 1991 (hardcover), ISBN 0–689–31596–1, $13.95; Aladdin, 1994 (paper), ISBN 0–689–71853–5, $4.95, unp. Ages 5 up, grades K up.

In dignified, poetic prose, Lewis retells the two Native American Aztec (Nahuatl) myths of the creation of the world and the securing of music. After earth and sky come into being from the pieces of a slain water monster, the wind god goes to the house of the sun from which he brings back heavenly musicians to relieve the silence of the earth. This version deviates from the usual story in not naming the gods and in having the earth and not the trickster god Tezcatlipoca suggest that Quetzalcoatl (the wind god) get music. The expressive, sophisticated paintings support significant moments. Notes give sources and background information. The title seems grammatically incorrect but in context is part of a concluding statement sky makes to earth.

103 Lister, Robin, ret., *The Legends of King Arthur*, illus. Alan Baker, Doubleday, 1988 (hardcover), ISBN 0–385–26369–4, $15.95, 96 pp. Ages 9–14, grades 4–9.

The Arthurian stories are retold from the point of view of Merlin, the enchanter, framed by passages spoken from his long imprisonment in a limestone cave. It opens with a substantial chapter about his childhood in South Wales, where he is seized by Vortigern's men who need to sacrifice a fatherless boy to keep the walls of their fortress from crumbling. By prophesying defeat for Vortigern and the coming of a dragon named Arthur, the boy, a bastard who is thought to be a child of a devil and has inherited second sight from his human grandfather, brings confusion to the troops and escapes. The story goes on to the building of Stonehenge (16), the trickery for Uther Pendragon which results in the birth of Arthur (22), Arthur's coming to power (28), his gift of the sword Excalibur from the Lady of the Lake (44), the establishment of the Round Table (48), and then the familiar stories of Lancelot, Elayne, and Guinevere. The quest for the Holy Grail and maimed King Pelleam (78) dominate the Round Table stories, and are followed by the love of Lancelot and Guinevere exposed by Mordred and Agravaine (79), the planned execution of Guinevere at the stake (81), her rescue by Lancelot (83), and the ensuing battles which lead to the death of Arthur (90). Although clear and without undue simplification, the style is not compelling, and the dialogue is too modern to give a sense of the ancient romance. The device of using Merlin's point of view gets lost about half way through and is not as successful as that of using Gawain's voice in Neil Philip's *The Tale of Sir Gawain* (no. 131). Illustrations are dramatic, with some especially effective borders of silhouettes. There is no bibliography or discussion of sources.

104   London, Jonathan, with Larry Pinola, rets., *Fire Race: A Karuk Coyote Tale*, illus. Sylvia Long, Chronicle, 1993 (hardcover), ISBN 0–8118–0241–8, $13.95, unp. Ages 5–12, grades K–7.

This legend of the Native American Karuk peoples of the Klamath River region in northwest California tells how Coyote, in his role as culture hero, steals fire from the Yellow Jackets and, with the help of the other animals, makes it available to people. Having decorated the Yellow Jackets, who alone have fire, with black charcoal stripes, Coyote persuades them that he can make them even more beautiful if they will close their eyes, whereupon he grabs a burning brand in his teeth and races away. As he trips and rolls downhill in the snow, Eagle snatches the glowing coal and flies off, and so it passes to Mountain Lion, Fox, Bear, Measuring Worm, Turtle, and Frog, with the furious Yellow Jackets swarming after each in turn. Frog leaps into the river and hides the fire in his mouth until the Yellow Jackets give up the pursuit. Then he bursts from the water and spits the hot coal into the roots of the willow tree, which swallows it. The baffled animals again turn to Coyote, who shows them how to coax fire from the willow again by rubbing two sticks together over dry moss. The rich, detailed illustrations cover the large pages, with text imprinted in boxes or on wide margins. Except for Coyote, who wears a leather robe and a skull cap, and for necklaces on Eagle, Mountain Lion, and Bear, the animals are depicted realistically in settings of wintry mountainous scenery. At the end are a brief essay on the Karuk people and a bibliography.

105   Manitonquat (Medicine Story), ret., *The Children of the Morning Light: Wampanoag Tales*, illus. Mary F. Arquette, Macmillan, 1994 (hardcover), ISBN 0–02–765905–4, $16.95, 72 pp. Ages 8 up, grades 3 up.

Manitonquat heard these eleven often dramatic, occasionally humorous, action-filled stories in his youth. From the Wampanoag, or Pokonoket, Indians of what is now the northeastern United States, they are retold with flair, respect, and obvious enjoyment and affection. Although some stories are patently didactic, the reteller skillfully keeps the instruction from getting in the way of the entertainment and adheres to a storytelling mode. The stories are presented within the framework of an old tale-teller's passing them on, a device that seems condescending and unnecessary since the stories are strong enough to carry in their own right. Included are narratives about the creation of the world and humans, "The Song of Creation" (13), "Sky Woman and the Twins" (17), "Maushop Builds Turtle Island" (20), and "Firstman" (25); a goddess figure, "Sky Woman and the Twins" (17); the origin of such realities as troubles and evil, "Sky Woman and the Twins" (17) and "Story of the Sweat

Lodge" (30); the origin of wisdom, knowledge, arts, and crafts, "Maushop Builds Turtle Island" (20), "Firstman" (25), "The Great Migration and Old Man Winter" (40), "Maushop and Grandfather Sun" (49), and "Cheepii Keeps Himself Safe" (62); the gaining of the healing arts, "Story of the Sweat Lodge" (30); acquiring fire, sun, and daylight, "Story of the Sweat Lodge" (30); and "Maushop and Grandfather Sun" (49); the origin of foods, "The Great Migration and Old Man Winter" (40); learning sun rituals, "Maushop and Grandfather Sun" (49); the origin of animals, "Maushop Builds Turtle Island" (20) and "Maushop and the Porpoises" (56); the origin of death and views of the world of the dead, "How Death Came into the World" (35); the beginning of seasons, "The Great Migration and Old Man Winter (40); floods, "The Great Migration and Old Man Winter" (40); searches and quests, "The Great Migration and Old Man Winter (40); and trickster tales, "Maushop and Grandfather Sun" (49) and "Muckachuck" (67). The reteller is a Wampanoag elder, and the creator of the accompanying powerful, realistic paintings is Mohawk. This is a substantial, consistently interesting, attractive collection, one that reveals the cultural values well.

Markman, Peter T., ed. *See* Markman, Roberta H., no. 106.

106 Markman, Roberta H., and Peter T. Markman, eds., *The Flayed God: The Mesoamerican Mythological Tradition*, Harper, 1992 (hardcover), ISBN 0–06–250528–9, $30.00, 456 pp. Ages 15 up, grades 10 up.

This examination of pre-Columbian mythology (Native American Aztec, Maya, Mixtec, Toltec, and Chichimec) written by two eminent literary scholars follows the work of Joseph Campbell in that area. The book contains a selection of texts from antiquity, among them myths, hymns, and fables, but is mostly commentary, fascinating in the insights presented but very challenging for all but the most accomplished or determined readers. The writers include detailed discussions of the iconography of the numerous photographs of mythological statues and the like that illustrate the stories. The main myths are reproduced as translated by other scholars. To facilitate appreciation, each is preceded by an introduction that explains important aspects of the myth and sometimes relates it to similar American or other myths. The creation of the world appears in "The Myth of Tlaltecuhtli" (Aztec, 212), and of the world and humans in "The Birth of All of Heaven and Earth" (Maya, 104), "The Creation of the World" (Aztec, 126), "Myths of the Suns and the Toltec-Chichimec Origins of the Mexica People" (131), and "The Mixtec Creation Myth" (149). Accounts of the origin of the sun and moon appear in "The Birth of All of Heaven and Earth" (Maya, 104); in "Myths of the Suns and the Toltec-Chichimec Origins of the Mexica People" (131); in "The Creation of the Sun and the Moon" (Aztec, 120), and in "The Hero Journey of the Hero Twins" (Maya, 316); "The Mixtec Creation Myth" (Mixtec, 149) is limited to the origin of the sun. World-destroying floods, sometimes sets of them, appear in "The Birth of All of Heaven and Earth" (Maya, 104); "The Creation of the World" (Aztec, 126); "Myths of the Suns and the Toltec-Chichimec Origins of the Mexica People" (131); and "The Mixtec Creation Myth" (149). The origin of corn is given in "The Birth of All of Heaven and Earth" (Maya, 104); in "Myths of the Suns and the Toltec-Chichimec Origins of the Mexica People" (131); and in "The Creation of the World" (Aztec, 126); of fire in "The Creation of the World" (Aztec, 126); of divine pulque (a drink important in ritual) in "The Myth of Mayahuel" (Aztec, 212); and of the settlement called Mexico City today in the "The Finding and Founding of Tenochtitlan" (Aztec, 394). Views of the afterlife (underworld) appear in "Myths of the Suns and the Toltec-Chichimec Origins of the Mexica People" (131) and in "The Hero Journey of the Hero Twins" (Maya, 316). "The Myth of Tlaltecuhtli" (Aztec, 212) and "The Myth of Mayahuel" (Aztec, 212) revolve around goddesses and are fertility stories, as is "The Birth of Huitzilopochtli" (Aztec, 380), which features the mother-goddess Coatlicue. "The Hero Journeys of the Hero Twins" (Maya, 316) and two versions of the story of the Aztec hero-god Quetzalcoatl, both entitled "Quetzalcoatl's Hero Journey" (Aztec, 352) are dramatic hero tales. The book includes an extensive introduction, pronunciation guide, map, time charts, color and black-and-white plates, endnotes, references, and index.

107 McCaughrean, Geraldine, sel. and ret., *The Golden Hoard: Myths and Legends of the World*, illus. Bee Willey, McElderry, 1996 (hardcover), ISBN 0–689–80741–4, $19.95, 130 pp. Ages 8–14, grades 3–9.

The strengths of this anthology of twenty-two stories, first published in Great Britain, lie in the vigorous storytelling, the variety of tones and cultures, the attractive overall design of the book, and the colorful paintings that skillfully blend drama and humor and extend and enhance the narratives. The retellings are free; added details of plot and character and extensive dialogue expand and enliven the stories and heighten suspense and action, strengthen the climax, and expand the conclusion. Detracting elements are the lack of information about sources, the superficial endnotes, and such mistakes as attributing the story "Brave Quest" about Scarface to the Sioux instead of the Blackfeet Indians; saying that Theseus instead of Perseus slew a dragon in the manner of the hero in "George and the Dragon"; making Freya instead of Frigga the wife of Odin; and having a centaur instead of a satyr contribute to Midas's unfortunate experience, to name some. In spite of the need for more careful attention to source material, the book offers good entertainment and ready access to stories not usually included in such anthologies. Among the hero tales are those of King Midas from Greece, "The Golden Wish" (1); "George and the Dragon" (12) from Persia, a version of the story of Saint George of England; the Blackfeet Scarface's search for the sun in "Brave Quest" (29); the Buddha in "Admirable Hare" (49), from Ceylon; Camillus, the legendary Roman fighter, in "Juno's Roman Geese" (66); and the remarkable last days of the Spanish warrior El Cid in "The Death of El Cid" (Spain, 94). Trickster tales include the rousingly retold "Robin Hood and the Golden Arrow" (20; England); the Polynesian account of how the strong man Maui snared the sun and made it rise and set in a regular fashion, "Saving Time" (35); and "Anansi and the Mind of God" (110), an amusing West Indies story in which Anansi tricks God by ostensibly reading his mind. Stories of the origin of necessities and realities include the Chinese "Shooting the Sun" (7), about how the present sun came to be, which is also an excellent adventure story; and a story from the Native Americans west of the Mississippi (no group given), "First Snow" (120), in which Coyote, intent on the first snow, almost forgets to present people with squash, corn, and beans. "Skinning Out" (17) is the Ethiopian account of why people die and also tells why snakes shed their skins, while "The Man Who Almost Lived Forever" (100), the Mesopotamian story of Adapa, also explains human mortality. Explantory tales concern why there appears to be a rabbit dancing in the moon, "Admirable Hare" (49), from Ceylon; the origin of indigenous animals and various phenomena on the Australian landscape in "Rainbow Snake" (60), an Aboriginal myth; seasonal and agricultural aspects in the American "John Barleycorn" (74); the origin of music for the Aztecs in "How Music Was Fetched out of Heaven" (84); why God lives in heaven in the Fon "Whose Footprints?" (89); and the origin of the Kikuyu (Kenya) and of women as head of their clans among the Kikuyu in "How Men and Women Finally Agreed" (114). "The Singer Above the River" (77) is the German story of the maiden who lures sailors to their deaths in the Rhine. "Stealing Heaven's Thunder" (103), a rousing and humorous adventure story, comes from the Norse.

108 McCaughrean, Geraldine, ret., *Greek Myths*, illus. Emma Chichester Clark, McElderry, 1993 (hardcover), ISBN 0–689–50583–3, $18.95, 96 pp. Ages 8–13, grades 3–8.

Originally published in Great Britain, this collection contains retellings of the most familiar Greek myths and hero tales, with the exception of the stories of the creation of the world and the great flood. "In the Beginning Pandora's Box" (9) tells of the creation of humans and animals and of the coming of troubles, death, hope, and fire. "Persephone and the Pomegranate Seeds" (15) explains the seasons and gives a view of the world of the dead. "Echo and Narcissus" (21) tells of the origin of the narcissus flower and of the echo phenomenon, "Apollo and Daphne" (60) of the laurel tree, and "Arachne the

Spinner" (32) of the spider. The remaining stories concern the exploits of King Midas (36), Perseus (41), Heracles (51), Theseus (62), Jason (66), Orpheus (71), Atalanta (75), and Odysseus (78, 84). The versions are lively with much dialogue and interesting details of character and action, but the Roman names are used instead of the Greek for some figures, and some errors affect the meaning of the stories significantly. For example, McCaughrean has Heracles kill his family while drunk instead of in the fit of madness visited upon him by Hera, and she presents Ariadne and Persephone as children. No sources are indicated, but tone, attitude, and details suggest that McCaughrean has drawn her material from less desirable Roman sources rather than the better Greek ones. The many colorful comic illustrations also lessen the dignity of the accounts. The book has the advantage of making available a large number of basic Greek stories in readable form and projects a late twentieth-century look and feel, but the effect is more that of Saturday morning cartoons than a respectful introduction to an important mythology. Better versions appear in the now-classic D'Aulaires' *Book of Greek Myths* (Doubleday, 1962) by Ingri and Edgar D'Aulaire and *Greek Myths* (Macmillan, 1962) by Padriac Colum for the same age range, and in the also classic, highly recommended *Mythology* (Little, Brown, 1942) by Edith Hamilton for junior high up.

109 McCaughrean, Geraldine, ret., *Saint George and the Dragon*, illus. Nicki Palin, Doubleday, 1989 (hardcover), ISBN 0–385–26529–8, $13.95, unp. Ages 4–10, grades PS–5.

This version of the story of how the legendary hero who became England's patron saint slays a marauding dragon and saves a princess lacks the drama and color of the more familiar, longer retelling by Margaret Hodges, illustrated by Trina Schart Hyman, also called *Saint George and the Dragon* (Little, Brown, 1984). McCaughrean's version emphasizes the dragon's ravages and the triumph of good over evil and also tells something of the hero's post-dragon-slaying feats. The pictures reveal George as a homely, hard-muscled man, but the princess sometimes seems just adolescent and at other times more mature. Since the illustrations are suffused with gold tones, George's charger, described as white in the text, appears as a light bay. Scenes in the village call attention to the communal beneficence of George's deed. Background information is included, but no specific source for this version is given.

110 McDermott, Gerald, ret., *Raven: A Trickster Tale from the Pacific Northwest*, illus. Gerald McDermott, Harcourt, 1993 (hardcover), ISBN 0–15–265661–8, $14.95, unp. Ages 4–10, grades PS–5.

Although no specific native group is given and the narrative is identified only as coming from the Pacific Northwest, the details of story and pictures seem characteristic in a general way of the native peoples of that wide area. In very early, far-off times, Raven displays his trickster mode as he puts the sun in the sky. Born the grandson of the Sky Chief, Raven fusses until the old man gives him the shining ball of the sun to hold. Raven then changes into his bird form, flies off, and flings the sun high into the sky, thus bringing light into a hitherto dark and cold world. Typical of McDermott's art, the illustrations are sophisticated, dramatic, deeply toned, stylized abstracts, patterned after Northwest Indian visual art. In deep palette reds, blues, and greens, they retell the spare, poetic text, adding details of place, character, and action. Raven's appearance is based on coastal raven masks. The narrative, which consists almost entirely of simple declarative sentences, highly repetitive in diction, is interrupted occasionally by questions addressed to the reader, probably an attempt to recreate the storytelling situation that unfortunately comes off as condescending. Nevertheless, this is a stunning, eye-catching book, with powerfully executed interiors, exteriors, and close-ups appropriate for so momentous an event. Other recent, noteworthy versions of the same story are those by Ann Dixon, *How Raven Brought Light to People* (McElderry, 1992), and by Susan Hand Shetterly, *Raven's Light* (Atheneum, 1991). McDermott's hero stories also include *Zomo the Rabbit: A Trickster Tale from West Africa* (Harcourt, 1992), in which Zomo (specific group not identified) must accomplish three impossible tasks to win wisdom from the Sky God; and *Coyote: A Trickster Tale from the American Southwest* (Harcourt, 1994), a Zuni story about Coyote as a fool that explains why coyotes are the color of dust and have black-tipped tails. Both books have understated texts and humorous, stylized, highly dramatic illustrations. Earlier, McDermott published *Arrow to the Sun* (Viking, 1974), a retelling of a Pueblo myth that won the Caldecott Medal, *Anansi the Spider: A Tale from the Ashanti* (Holt, 1987), and *The Voyage of Osiris: A Myth of Ancient Egypt* (Windmill, 1977), to name some, all also picture-story books with appeal to a broad age range.

111 McGill-Callahan, Sheila, ret., *The Children of Lir*, illus. Gennady Spirin, Dial, 1993 (hardcover), ISBN 0–8037–1121–2, $14.99, 32 pp. Ages 5 up, grades K up.

The enchantment of the four children of the Irish King Lir is the subject of this beautiful picture book lavishly decorated with watercolors reproduced as partial, full-page, and double-page illustrations. The story, based on a myth of the Celtic sea god Lir or Llyr, is of the wicked stepmother, Aiofe, who turns Lir's four children into swans. In this version they are eventually saved and reunited with their father by the intervention of the whale, Jasconius, and wild swans, who contrive to break the spell. Although the story should be comprehensible to young children, the language is dignified and not simple, more appropriate for older readers.

Medicine Story, ret. *See* Manitonquat, no. 105.

112 Mitchell, Robert Allen, ret., *The Buddha: His Life Retold*, Paragon House, 1989 (hardcover), ISBN 1–55778–151–6, $19.95, 274 pp. Ages 12 up, grades 7 up.

This life of Siddhartha Gautama opens with brief stories of two previous incarnations of the Buddha as Sumedha (1) and as Visvantara (5). The remainder starts with the birth of Siddhartha in a well-to-do family of India and continues through his youth until, at the age of twenty-nine, shortly after the birth of his first child, he renounces the world, changes his costly raiment for a saffron-dyed monk's robe, and sets off to seek enlightenment. Eventually he reaches Nirvana, the Supreme Wisdom, and becomes a wandering teacher, bringing his spiritual knowledge to others, including, some time later, his wife and young son. His cousin Ananda joins him as a disciple, then his attendant, and is with him for many years until Siddhartha passes from this world. Although the numerous little stories of teachings and conversions are interesting individually, they have a sameness of tone that makes for slow reading, and they contain sermons and lists of many kinds—for instance, ten strange and wondrous things, eight strict rules for the ordination of women, the four Fine-Material Absorptions and the four Immaterial Absorptions—that interrupt the narrative and are unlikely to appeal to young people not avidly seeking spiritual enlightenment.

113 Monroe, Jean Guard, and Roy A. Williamson, rets., *They Dance in the Sky: Native American Star Myths*, illus. Edgar Stewart, Houghton, 1987 (hardcover), ISBN 0–395–39970–X, $12.95, 130 pp. Ages 10 up, grades 5 up.

This substantial collection contains Native American myths concerning stars seen in the Northern Hemisphere. Of these, twenty-five are direct explanations of constellations and other star patterns, from a wide variety of Indian groups. Some, although they have a connection to stars, primarily concern other matters: explanations of animal appearance (16), of animal behavior (40), of geographical features (100), of the origin of peace and friendship among the Pawnees (69), of the seasons (102), and of wisdom and knowledge, especially of the proper way in which to perform ceremonies (58, 60, 73). One has a detailed view of the world of the dead (80). The first section is devoted to legends of the Pleiades, the second to the Great Bear or Big Dipper. The next six sections tell myths of separate regions. Each story is preceded by a commentary discussing the background of the myth, the star patterns as they appear to the people of a particular area, and sometimes briefly the comparable myth in the European and Near Eastern traditions. A preface explains the importance of the stories to the Native American cultures. Included are an extensive glossary, a bibliography, and a list of suggested further readings. The stories, most of which have not appeared previously outside scholarly collections, are retold clearly, with occasional humor, and without pretentious language, and they are illustrated attractively with realistic drawings.

Mooney, Bill, sel. and ret. *See* Holt, no. 80.

114 Morris, Christopher, ed., *The Illustrated Children's Old Testament*, illus. Bill Farnsworth, Harcourt, 1993 (hardcover), ISBN 0–15–238220–8, $14.95, 192 pp. Ages 8–14, grades 3–9.

Approved by cross-sectarian consultants, this impressive volume presents all the major Old Testament stories in King James Version language minus such archaicisms as "thee" and "thou" and phrases peculiar to the ancient and Elizabethan periods but with enough of their formal flavor to retain the narratives' dignity and power. The chapters are short, so that, for example, the story of the patriarch Abraham is presented in five chapters, only the most important information about Abraham's charge and about Sarah and Lot being included. Magnificent paintings from portraits to sweeping landscapes, many based on Biblical masters, support and extend the stories and make this an exceptionally beautiful book. Maps; information about the Holy Land, plants, animals, and ancient Egypt; notes on the text; and a Bible dictionary are welcome helps intended for adults but not beyond the reach and appreciation of older young readers. Creation of the world and humans stories appropriately open the book, "The Creation" (1), "The Garden of Eden" (6), and "The Forbidden Fruit" (8), with their attendant explanations of death and troubles. "Cain and Abel" (11) gives the origin of the crime of murder, and the familiar story of Noah's flood appears in "The Lord Speaks to Noah" (13), "Noah and the Ark" (14), and "Noah Hears God's Promise" (18), which contains the beautiful account of the rainbow. The final explanatory story of the "first things" part of the Old Testament occurs in "The Tower of Babel" (19), which tells of the origin of nations and languages. Hero stories follow, mostly of the holy men, spiritual leader variety, starting with Abraham, in "Abraham" (20); "Sodom and Gomorrah" (23), which is also a flood story, and several other chapters about him; Isaac in "Isaac and Rebekah" (26) and others; Jacob in

"Jacob and Esau" (28), "Jacob's Ladder" (30), and "Rachel and Leah" (32); Joseph in "The Coat of Many Colors" (36) and "Pharaoh's Dreams" (40), among others; Moses in "The Birth of Moses" (46), "The Lord's Message to Moses" (50), "The Ten Commandments" (62), "The Death of Moses" (73), and others; Joshua the warrior in "The Walls of Jericho" (74); Gideon the fighter in "Gideon's Trumpet" (76); Samson the strong man in "Samson" (79) and "Samson and Delilah" (80); David the future king in "David and Goliath" (94), and some passages about King Saul; the youthful Solomon in "Solomon's Dream" (111), his famous judgment between the two women in "King Solomon's Wisdom" (112), and the well-known visit of the Queen of Sheba in a story by that name (116); and the leaders and prophets Elijah (120), Daniel (141), and Jonah (146). The contributions of such women as Rebekah, Rachel, Leah, and Rahab are not neglected in these hero stories, and the stalwart Ruth and Naomi (84) have a story of their own, as does the courageous Esther in "Esther Becomes Queen" (124) and "Mordecai and Haman" (126). *The Illustrated Children's Bible* (1993), a companion volume that begins with *The Illustrated Children's Old Testament* and includes only the stories of Jesus from the New Testament, seems less successful, neglecting as it does narratives about Paul and other important New Testament figures.

115 The National Association for the Preservation and Perpetuation of Storytelling, coll., *Best-Loved Stories Told at the National Storytelling Festival*, August House, 1991 (hardcover), ISBN 1–879991–01–2, $19.95; (paper), ISBN 1–879991–00–4, $14.95, 223 pp. Ages 7 up, grades 2 up.

The thirty-seven stories by as many tellers were selected from those performed at the National Storytelling Festival held annually at Jonesborough, Tennessee. Some selections have been retold from written sources, and some are stories the tellers heard related by friends or relatives. All have spirit and verve and reflect the tellers' enjoyment. While most of the tales in the collection are folk stories, three are relevant for this study: the Anglo-Saxon "How Caedmon Got His Hymn" (75), a poignant hero story retold from the Venerable Bede; a humorous Native American Cherokee trickster tale, "Possum, Turtle, and the Wolves" (135), which is reminiscent of Bre'r Rabbit's briar patch experience and explains the cracks in the turtle's shell; and an eerie, Native American Nisqually story of the afterlife, "The Girl and the Ghost" (210). An introduction by Jane Yolen on the nature and power of oral narrative opens the book, and alphabetical indexes of tellers and stories conclude the volume. Notes on sources and background accompany each tale. More stories appear in a sequel (*see* no. 116).

116 The National Association for the Preservation and Perpetuation of Storytelling, coll., *More Best-Loved Stories Told at the National Storytelling Festival*, August House, 1992 (hardcover), ISBN 1-879991-09-8, $24.95; (paper), 1-879991-08-X, $14.95, 223 pp. Ages 7 up, grades 2 up.

Here are thirty-nine more sprightly tales from the annual Jonesborough, Tennessee, National Storytelling Festival, a sequel to no. 115. Three are explanatory stories: "The Legend of Obi Obi Gui" (40), from the Yoruba in Nigeria, tells of the origin of the coconut; the Buddhist "The Brave Little Parrot" (194) explains why the parrot is multicolored; and "Daughter of the Sun" (74), from the Native American Cherokee, describes how the redbird came to be. The "Daughter of the Sun" also tells of the origin of death, gives a view of the afterlife, and revolves around the sun, who has the stature of a goddess. "Medusa" (104) is a lively, modernized, and irreverent retelling of the story of the ancient Greek female figure who affords the hero Perseus the opportunity to function as a monster slayer. "Gluscabi and the Wind Eagle" (125), from the Native American Abenaki, and the African American "Br'er Rabbit Builds a Home" (197) are amusing trickster tales.

117 Nye, Naomi Shihab, sel., *The Tree Is Older Than You Are: A Bilingual Gathering of Poems & Stories from Mexico with Paintings by Mexican Artists*, Simon & Schuster, 1995 (hardcover), ISBN 0-689-80297-8, $19.95, 111 pp. Ages 8 up, grades 3 up.

Within this large collection of mostly authored poems and stories from Mexico, each of which is presented in both the original Spanish and English translation, are three explanatory myths. The Zinacantec story "The Three Suns" (66) explains the origin of the pig and the peccary, and tells why the moon's glow is fainter than the sun's rays. In "Fire and the Opossum" (75), from the Mazateco Native American Indians, an opossum steals fire from the selfish old woman who had captured it from the stars and planets and in the process burns his tail bare. "The Rabbit's Ears" (82), from the Maya, tells how the God of the Animals enlarged the rabbit's tiny ears. The stories are told with dignity and verve, and strongly executed, full-palette paintings make this an especially attractive book. An introduction about the writings and illustrations opens the book, and notes on the writers and stories and lists of titles in Spanish and English, of writers and artists, and of illustrations appear at the end.

118   Oliviero, Jamie, ret., *The Fish Skin*, illus. Brent Morrisseau, Hyperion, 1993 (hardcover), ISBN 1–56282–402–5, $14.95, unp. Ages 5 up, grades K up.

To save his dying grandmother in a time of drought, a young Native American Cree boy goes to the dreaded heart of the forest seeking Wisahkecahk, the maker and shaper, to ask for rain. While he is sleeping, the Great Spirit, pleased with the boy's bravery, emerges from the dense forest and lays a little fish skin beside him. When he awakes, the boy tries to put it on and finds that it stretches to cover him. He becomes enormous, swallows a great quantity of water, and persuades Cloud to return to the area. Then he blows the water so high that it hits the cloud, drops back as rain, and saves his people. He is given a new name, Okwapayikew, which means "water hauler." The story is told simply, with little elaboration or description, but the illustrations, done in gouache, are startlingly vivid, with brilliant blue, purple, green, and cerise figures and settings. While published for an audience in the early grades, the book would interest older children and young adults.

119   Oodgeroo (Kath Walker), ret., *Dreamtime: Aboriginal Stories*, illus. Bronwyn Bancroft, Lothrop, 1993 (hardcover), ISBN 0–688–13296–0, $16.00, 96 pp. Ages 9 up, grades 4 up.

Oodgeroo, an Australian Aboriginal whose Anglo name is Kath Walker, tells twenty-seven stories of two main types. The first half of the book, "Stories from Stradbroke," describes remembered incidents from her childhood on Stradbroke Island in Queensland. The other half of the book, "Stories from the Old and New Dreamtime," contains her retellings of Aboriginal myths and tales that she heard as a child and also her own original stories patterned on the traditional tales. Unfortunately, there is no note to indicate which are genuine oral tradition and which are fiction. Of those that appear to be genuine myths, "The Beginning of Life" (61) tells of the origin of the world and humans and features the Rainbow Serpent, the Mother of Life. "Biami and Bunyip" (64) describes the coming of evil. "Mirrabooka" (67) relates how the constellation the whites call the Southern Cross originated. "Curlew" (79) tells of the beginning of death and gives a view of the spirit's journey to the world of the dead. It also explains the origin of the curlew species. The latter two stories are possibly fiction but carry the conviction of oral tradition. The remaining tales are largely explanatory stories of how various plants and trees came to be and appear to imitate the *pourquoi* type of folktale. All the stories are related in a poetic, affectionate style and are accompanied by full-color paintings. The artist, who is also Aboriginal, has painted them in an elaborate style and filled them with indigenous patterns and motifs with good effect.

120   Oppenheim, Shulamith Levey, ret., *And the Earth Trembled: The Creation of Adam and Eve*, illus. Neil Waldman, Harcourt, 1996 (hardcover), ISBN 0–15–200025–9, $16.00, unp. Ages 4 up, grades PS up.

God's angels and even the Earth, from whom God commands that clay be fetched, rise in protest when God decides to create a man. They fear that the magnificently beautiful world around them will be destroyed if the potential for evil they sense the creature will have is allowed to become reality. God continues with his work of creation anyway and fashions Adam, and later Eve, and places them in Eden. Iblis, one of the angels, becomes so angry and resentful that God banishes him from Paradise. Waldman's full-page impressionistic paintings are strikingly beautiful, ethereal, and dramatic, suffused with earth and sky colors for the most part. They complement the strongly written text. Especially effective is the picture in which Iblis is banished; the tones of red emphasize his anger and hatred and foreshadow the devil figure he becomes. This creation story, which elaborates upon the Biblical story of the creation of Adam and Eve, comes from the collected legends of the Islamic religious authority and historian, Abou-Djafar al Taban, of the ninth century, according to the reteller's introductory note. This is a sophisticated book, one with layers of meanings.

121   Oppenheim, Shulamith Levey, ret., *Iblis*, illus. Ed Young, Harcourt, 1994 (hardcover), ISBN 0–15–238016–7, $15.95, unp. Ages 5 up, grades K up.

According to the reteller, this Islamic tale explains the beginnings of humankind and troubles and dramatizes the dangers of disobeying God's orders as well. Iblis, the devil or Satan, banished from Paradise, flatters the serpent into helping him evade the guardian angel, Ridwan, and enters Paradise. There he deceitfully persuades Eve to eat the "fruit that alone gives eternal youth and health," the seeds of the wheat tree, which then Adam also eats. In anger, God pronounces curses, and all the participants in disobedience are expelled from Paradise, including Iblis, who falls into the "River Eila, which flows into Hell." The spare, poetic prose of this ancient legend, a close parallel to the Biblical account, is amplified by off-the-page, full-color, highly sophisticated impressionistic paintings that extend the appeal of the book well beyond the picture-book set. Background information on the story and sources are included.

122 Osborne, Mary Pope, ret., *American Tall Tales*, illus. Michael McCurdy, Knopf, 1991 (hardcover), ISBN 0–679–80089–1, $18.00, 115 pp. Ages 8–13, grades 3–9.

Nine delightfully entertaining American hero tales reflect the economic and geographic diversity of the United States. They range from the Plains farmer Febold Feboldson (63), the backwoods Tennessee Davy Crockett (3), and the spunky, monster-slaying woman he eventually marries, Sally Ann Thunder Ann Whirlwind (15), through the benevolent, ecologically oriented Johnny Appleseed (25), the tragic steel driver John Henry (87), the feisty New England sailor Stormalong (37), New York City firefighter Mose Humphries (51), and cowboy Pecos Bill (73) to the northwoods forest tamer Paul Bunyan (97). Except for Mose Humphries, whose exploits grew out of a Broadway play, and Sally Ann Thunder Ann Whirlwind, the figures and their deeds are familiar. The writer's style is appropriately zippy and overblown, and the storytelling is accomplished with relish to produce the outrageous, tongue-in-cheek, poker-faced humor that typifies the genre and these particular examples of what has come to be known as America's contribution to mythological and heroic lore. In addition to Sally Ann, America's heroic women are also represented by Slue-foot Sue, who becomes Mrs. Pecos Bill but is a strong figure in her own right, and by John Henry's wife, Lucy, who also drove spikes. A map and an introduction about the genre open the volume, notes on sources and the particular figure precede each story, and an extensive bibliography, divided by figure, completes the book.

123 Osborne, Mary Pope, ret., *Favorite Greek Myths*, illus. Troy Howell, Scholastic, 1989 (hardcover), ISBN 0–590–41338–4, $14.95, 81 pp. Ages 7–11, grades 2–6.

The twelve retellings that make up this collection reproduce important, well-known stories for the most part, many of which revolve around women, and present the main plot details in lively fashion. Several problems are evident, however. The title clearly specifies Greek myths, and the introduction invites the readers/listeners to imagine themselves back in ancient Greece. Osborne, however, relies on such Roman writers as Ovid, whose versions are late and deviate from the earlier, standard Greek sources, a method that alters both content and tone. The most obvious problem is that Osborne employs the Roman names for the mythological figures, yet calls the stories Greek. These retellings can serve as an introduction to Graeco-Roman mythology, but not Greek mythology. Explanatory stories include "Lost at Sea: The Story of Ceyx and Alcyone" (13), about the origin of certain sea birds and the weather phenomonen called halcyon days; "The Weaving Contest: The Story of

Arachne and Minerva" (19), about the origin of the spider; "Apollo's Tree: The Story of Daphne and Apollo" (23), about the origin of the laurel tree; "The Face in the Pool: The Story of Echo and Narcissus" (29), about the origin of the echo phenomonen and the flower; "The Kidnapping: The Story of Ceres and Proserpina" (35), about how the seasons began, an account that also includes a view of the afterlife and involves a search; and "The Great Bear: The Story of Callisto and Arcus" (41), about the constellations great and little bear. Hero tales are represented by "Chariot of the Sun God: The Story of Phaeton and Helios" (1), about Phaeton's wild ride; "The Golden Touch: The Story of Bacchus and King Midas" (9); "Journey to the Underworld: The Story of Orpheus and Eurydice" (45), which also includes a view of the afterlife and a search; and "The Golden Apples: The Story of Atalanta and Hippomenes" (51), about an able woman athlete. "The Four Tasks: The Story of Cupid and Psyche" (57) involves a long, difficult search; and "The Mysterious Visitors: The Story of Baucis and Philemon" (67) culminates with a great flood. Although this is a representative collection of consistently interesting accounts, preferable versions exist for this age range. See the comment on McCaughrean, *Greek Myths* (no. 108). The book includes full-page paintings, a short introduction, a glossary, a list of some modern terms of Greek mythological origin, a short bibliography, and an index.

124   Osborne, Mary Pope, ret., *Favorite Norse Myths*, illus. Troy Howell, Scholastic, 1996 (hardcover), ISBN 0–590–48046–4, $17.95, 88 pp. Ages 7 up, grades 2 up.

Although this book is intended for young readers, the retellings are done with such obvious liking for the tales, respect for the stories and culture, and careful diction and are illustrated so imaginatively and appropriately that readers of all ages can get caught up in the drama and the ultimate tragedy of these old northern European and Icelandic myths. The reteller has focused on the main events of the most familiar stories, those that are basic to a knowledge of the ancient literature and are most frequently alluded to, and she has drawn her material from reputable translations of the *Poetic Edda* and the *Prose Edda*, short selections from which head each chapter. Similarly, to introduce each chapter, the artist has redrawn portions of Viking art in brown line sketches, each of which also appears as faint scratching overlays of figures in the magnificent paintings, mostly double spreads, that appear throughout the book and reveal character, establish setting, and depict action. Of the book's fourteen chapters, the creation of the world and humans, as well as an introduction to the most important deities, appears in "Creation: The Nine Worlds" (1). Other chapters are devoted to the origin of such important necessities of Norse life as poetry, wisdom, and knowledge, which appears in

"Odin's Three Quests" (9), a story which also explains why Odin has only one eye and the origin of runes; and to seasonal and fertility stories: "The Magic Stallion" (14), about the building of the walls of Asgard; "The Giant's Bride" (33), in which Thor loses and regains his hammer; "The Golden Apples" (36), about the loss of Idun's apples, without which the gods will grow old; "The Fairest Feet" (43), in which the giantess Skadi inadvertently chooses the god Njord to be her husband instead of Balder; "Marriage of the Ice Maiden" (53), in which Frey gives up his sword to gain the woman he loves; and "The Death of Balder" (70), which also gives a view of the world of the dead and heralds the end of the Norse world, a cataclysmic event described in "The Twilight of the Gods" (77). Loki the trickster giant god figures significantly in several stories, and since most involve searches and quests and conflict with the giants, who are the gods' traditional enemies, they are high in adventure: "The Magic Stallion" (14); "How Thor Got His Hammer" (20); "Loki's Children" (27), in which Tyr loses a hand in binding Fenrir the wolf; "The Giant's Bride" (33); "The Golden Apples" (36); "Spell of the Giant King" (47), in which Thor visits a giant's realm; "The Giant's Cauldron" (58), in which Thor goes fishing and catches the Midgard Serpent; and "Thor and the Clay Giant" (65), a story of deceit and conflict in which Thor is rescued, amusingly, by his infant son, Magni. The action revolves around goddesses or giantesses in "The Golden Apples" (36), "The Fairest Feet (43)," and "Marriage of the Ice Maiden" (53), while the beautiful Freya is to be the price of the stolen hammer's return in "The Giant's Bride" (33). Although the primary purpose of "The Death of Balder" (70), is probably seasonal, it is a poignant family story, high in emotional intensity. An introduction gives a brief but helpful historical overlook to the stories, and an appendix offers much of value: information on primary sources; lists of gods and goddesses, other important figures, and significant places; a brief exposition of symbols and runes; a fine if short bibliography; and an index.

125 O'Shea, Pat, ret., *Finn Mac Cool and the Small Men of Deeds,* illus. Stephen Lavis, Holiday House, 1987 (hardcover), ISBN 0–8234–0651–2, $12.95, 88 pp. Ages 8–13, grades 3–8.

Only one of the many tales about the legendary Irish fighting chieftain of the Fianna (who is also claimed by Scotland), this retelling treats novelistically and lightheartedly with how Finn and eight little men, each of whom possesses a special talent, restore the giant king's kidnapped sons. Finn is appropriately slothful, irascible, generous, and brave; evil is overcome by luck and good magic; and witty dialogue and playful narrative give the version zest and good humor. Comic illustrations contribute to the fun. No sources or background information are given.

126   Oughton, Jerrie, ret., *How the Stars Fell into the Sky: A Navajo Legend*, illus. Lisa Desimini, Houghton, 1992 (hardcover), ISBN 0–395–58798–0, $14.95, unp.; Sandpiper (paper), ISBN 0–395–77938–3, $5.95. Ages 4–14, grades PS–9.

This adaptation of a creation myth told by Hosteen Klah, a renowned Navajo medicine man of the very early 1900s, tells how, at the beginning of things, First Woman informs First Man that people need a way of finding out about the laws. He suggests that she write them in the night sky with her jewels, the stars. Coyote asks to help but soon grows impatient at the slow progress and flings the remaining stars into the sky. Therefore, "confusion . . . would always dwell" among the people because of the constellations' helter-skelter arrangement. The understated narrative has a quiet, dignified, poetic movement that is pleasingly supported by the simple, dark-toned, sparsely detailed, dramatic paintings, although the Madonna-like presentation of First Woman is sometimes startling. A touch welcome for its accuracy is the early conical shape of the Navajo hogan.

127   Oughton, Jerrie, ret., *The Magic Weaver of Rugs: A Tale of the Navajo*, illus. Lisa Desimini, Houghton Mifflin, 1994 (hardcover), ISBN 0–315–66140–4, $14.95, 32 pp. Ages 8 up, grades 3 up.

In a time of hardship for the Navajo people, two women go far from camp to be alone and to pray for help. They are heard by Spider Woman, who has pity on them, and in her voice that can split rocks she shows them how to build a loom, to shear sheep and dye the wool, and to weave rugs. Although terrified and doubting that this knowledge will be of use, they do as she directs, then return to their people and teach them the skill. The Navajo weave for themselves and trade rugs for food and other necessities and through their weaving prosper and express their love for their land. The text is brief, but the women's fear and distrust of Spider Woman are well evoked. In the illustrations, dominated by browns and dark earth colors, the figures are stiff, and Spider Woman is a shapeless female with curious straight hair standing on end. Young children may be put off by the grimness of the pictures.

128   Page, R. I., ret. and ed., *Norse Myths*, illus. with photographs, British Museum and University of Texas Press, 1990 (paper), ISBN 0–292–75546–5, $8.95, 80 pp. Ages 15 up, grades 10 up.

Wittily retold, laced with scholarly comments succinctly and interestingly related, slim in size but chockful of information, this book presents in retellings of different lengths most of the Norse myths from the Eddic sources as well as the saga of the Volsung line, of which the best-known hero is Sigurd. Some retellings incorporate portions of the source poems or prose, which increases their tone of authenticity and makes them very convincing. After an outline map of the regions from which the stories come and an introduction about the gods, the myths are presented by broad type. Within the section entitled "Where to Find Norse Myths" (10), which is mainly about the *Poetic Edda* and the *Prose Edda* and such features of Norse literature as kennings and audience involvement, are found the story of the theft of Thor's hammer, an adventurous tale of a search that is also a seasonal and fertility myth; a fertility myth that revolves around the giantess Skadi; the adventurous tale about the building of the walls of Asgard that shows Loki as a trickster and is also a fertility story; the origin of poetry, a story that involves Odin; and the story of the loss and recovery of Idunn's apples of youth, another fertility story that revolves around a goddess. The chapter "Aesir, Vanir and a Few Kings" (27) tells about the war between the Vanir and the Aesir, the adventure in which the Aesir emerge triumphant, and about how Frey wins the giantess Gerd, a narrative that involves a quest and is a seasonal or fertility myth. "Odin and Thor" (35) deals with the adventures in which Thor defeats the giant Hrungnir and goes fishing for the Midgard Serpent. The events surrounding the death of Baldr appear in "Baldr and Loki" (47), an adventurous and suspenseful myth, which shows Loki in his evil trickster mode, involves a search that ironically fails in its objective of guaranteeing Baldr's safety and in bringing him back from the world of the dead, and gives a view of the world of the dead, Hel's realm. The same chapter also tells the story of how Loki cut off the hair of Sif, Thor's wife, and brought to the gods their greatest treasures as penance, and the strange but eventful journey of Thor and Loki to the realm of the giant Utgard-Loki. "Beginnings, Middles and Ends" (56) tells of the creation of the world and humans, incorporates a short flood story in the slaying of the giant Ymir, and gives views of the world of the dead in Valhalla, here called Volholl, and the goddess Hel. In this chapter appears the story of the end of the Norse world, Ragnarok, and the new beginnings for gods and humans. The last chapter, "Gods and Heroes" (67), summarizes the hero story of the Volsung family, whose main male figures are Volsung, Sigmund, and Sigurd and most significant female figures are Signy, Gudrun, and the Valkyrie Brynhild. The clear and detailed photographs of Norse artifacts add much information, and the book concludes with suggestions for further reading and an index. Although this is a demanding book, it is also exceedingly valuable for learning about the Norse myths.

129   Pan, Cai-Ying, ad., *Monkey Creates Havoc in Heaven*, illus. Xin Kuan Liang, Zhang Xui Shi, Fei Chang Fu, and Lin Zheng. Viking Kestrel, 1987 (hardcover), ISBN 0–670–81805–4, $9.95, unp. Ages 8 up, grades 3 up.

This story of the Chinese mythological Monkey King, an irrepressible trickster and buffoon figure, is based on the sixteenth-century novel *The Pilgrimage to the West* by Wu Cheng En. Seeking more power, the Monkey King gets the special as-you-wish magic staff that can be transformed into many shapes and sizes. When he learns of this, the Celestial Emperor decrees that Monkey become Master of the Imperial Stables, the lowest-ranking position in Heaven, where he can be kept under surveillance. At first flattered, Monkey discovers his lowly status, frees the imperial steeds, and assaults those sent to arrest him. He continues to create havoc, eating the divine peaches of eternal life, devouring the golden pills of immortality, fighting off an army of 10,000 troops, and, when he is finally captured, resisting death by swords, axes, and fire. Finally, Buddha Hu Lai agrees that, if he can somersault out of his hand, Monkey will become Celestial Emperor, but this he cannot do. He is imprisoned in the mountain of Wu Hong, where he remains for 500 years, when at last he is released to guard the monk Trilpitaka on his journey to the West. The illustrations are brilliantly colored and highly stylized. Some are full page; others are in small boxes, like comic strips, several on a page, with background sheets in a variety of colors. All are alive with action and detail. Although the text is brief, this beautiful and unusual book is clearly not just for the very young.

Perez, Cecilio, coll. and ret. *See* Ecun, no. 42.

130   Philip, Neil, ret., *The Illustrated Book of Myths*, illus. Nilesh Mistry, Dorling Kindersley, 1995 (hardcover), ISBN 0–7894–0202–5, $19.95, 192 pp. All ages, grades PS up.

This exceptionally handsome anthology contains sixty-five retellings of myths and hero tales from twenty-three cultures. Some stories are familiar from classical sources, but most come from such lesser known traditions both ancient and modern as Hittite, Sumerian, Iranian, Indonesian, and Serbian; six come from Native American Indian groups and four from African. The stories are divided by major myth types, and each section is preceded by a short introduction pointing out story features common to that type. The style is straightforward and unadorned, the tone is consistently respectful, and details contribute to a sense of culture. Some full-color paintings depict important scenes; especially compelling are the color photographs of artifacts. The illustrations are judiciously arranged to complement and extend the traditions without overwhelming the tales. Captions add valuable information. An essay about myths opens the book, which also includes annotated maps, a glossary, and a name and subject index. No list of sources appears, unfortunately, and there are a few errors. For example, a caption says that "the *Kalevala* was the basis for the poem *Hiawatha* by Longfellow," when in fact the Finnish epic inspired Longfellow's choice of meter. Nevertheless, this collection is unusually attractive and offers a wealth of reading and listening enjoyment for a wide age range. Included are myths of the creation of the world and humans from Egypt (16), Serbia (17), the Norse (18), China (22), Japan (24), the Australian Aboriginals (28), Iran (30), the Native American Modoc (32), Siberia (34), the Native American Navajo (36); the creation of humans from Indonesia (42), Greece (58), East African Baganda (76), and the Native American Aztecs (140); the creation of the world from the Native American Mandan (53) and Finland (54); the origin of animals from China (52) and the Native American Mandan (53); stories of the seasons, agriculture, and fertility from the Norse (72), Egypt (80), Greece (82), Japan (84), the Celts (89), the Hittites (94), India (98), the Native American Aztecs (140), and Egypt (146); views of the world of the dead from Japan (26), the Native American Modoc (32), Rome (154), Ireland (159), the Norse (162), Greece (166), and the Inuit (Eskimo, 168); floods from Mesopotamia (44), Serbia (49), the Native American Maidu (74), and Greece (170); goddesses and significant female figures from Japan (Izanami, 26; Amaterasu, 84), Egypt (Isis, 80; Bast, 146), Greece (Demeter and Persephone, 82), India (Devi, 98, 144), Inuit (Eskimo; Sedna, 168), and the Norse (Idun, 72); the origin of death from Mesopotamia (38, 44), the Native American Maidu (74), and the West African Ibo (77); views of the end of the world from Egypt (16), Greece (170), the West African Fon (173), the Norse (174), and Iran (176); the origin of such realities and necessities as troubles, wisdom, daylight, fire, important foods, literature, and arts and crafts from Iran (30), Mesopotamia (38), Serbia (49), the Native American Mandan (53), Finland (54), Greece (58, 104), the Norse (62), Polynesia (68), the Australian Aboriginals (69), the West African Ashanti (70), Japan (84), and the Native American Aztecs (140); gods' adventures from the Norse (72, 118); the activities of fabulous animals from India (peacock, 147), Greece (winged horse, 148), and China and Egypt (phoenix, 151); searches and quests from Mesopotamia (Gilgamesh, 44), the Norse (Idun's apples, 72), Egypt (Isis, 80), the Celts (the Holy Grail, 89), Greece (Demeter, 82; Theseus, 108; Heracles, 130; Perseus, 148); tricksters (god figures) from Serbia (49), the Norse (64, 72), Polynesia (68), the Native American Maidu (74), and Haiti (117); and a wide variety of heroes from Mesopotamia (Gilgamesh, 44), the Celts (Arthur, 86, 89, 156), the Native American Algonquin (Glooskap, 92), the Anglo-Saxons (Beowulf, 106), Greece (Cadmus, 96; Midas, 102, 104; Daedalus, 112; Theseus, 108; Heracles, 130; Perseus and Bellerophon, 148), Wales (Taliesin, 114), Ireland (Cuchulain, 125), Rome (Romulus and Remus, 138; Aeneas, 154), the Native American Aztecs (Quetzalcoatl, 140), the Native American Maidu (Coyote, 74), and Polynesia (68). The adventures of humans, gods, and heroes abound in these stories, which are fast moving and well told.

131 Philip, Neil, ret., *The Tale of Sir Gawain*, illus. Charles Keeping, Putnam, 1987 (hardcover), ISBN 0–399–21488–7, $13.95, 112 pp. Ages 10 up, grades 5 up.

In the voice of dying Sir Gawain, who, fevered by his wounds and sometimes rambling, speaks to his young squire, the major Arthurian stories are related. In general, they follow the version written in the fifteenth century by Sir Thomas Malory, including the birth of Arthur, the pulling of the sword from the stone, the start of the Round Table, and the romance of Lancelot and Guinevere, with its tragic consequences. Also included are the stories of the marriage of Sir Gawain, of Sir Gawain and the Green Knight, and of The Fair Unknown, all from early English poems; the adventures of Sir Owain from the Welsh *Mabinogion*; and the quest for the Holy Grail, drawn mainly from French sources. Telling the stories from the point of view of Sir Gawain, a practical, loyal, and valiant knight, close enough to the main events to be a plausible narrator, is an interesting and successful technique. The result is a highly readable and moving version, neither elaborate nor oversimplified. The dozen full-page, black-and-white drawings by Keeping are dramatic.

132 Pijoan, Teresa, coll. and ret., *White Wolf Woman and Other Native American Transformation Myths*, August House, 1992 (hardcover), ISBN 0–87483–201–2, $17.95, 167 pp.; (paper), ISBN 0–87483–200–4, $11.95. Ages 8 up, grades 3 up.

Pijoan, whose family ran the general store at San Juan Pueblo in New Mexico, an honored "storyholder" of the pueblo and a teacher at a school at Canyon de Chelly, Arizona, collected these three dozen stories, mostly folktales, from thirty Native American Indian groups, the Eskimo, and Guiana. The stories are divided into four sections—tales about snakes, wolves, bears, and other animals—and tell of the "wonder of transformation." They demonstrate that, in Native American thought, "[t]here is no division between animals and people." As is the case with most tales from oral tradition, the retellings are spare in details of character and setting and emphasize plot. On the whole, they are lively and consistently high in interest while uncomplicated in vocabulary and sentence and plot structure. An Arawak story from

Guiana, "Snakes" (21) tells of the origin of death. "Wolves" (51), a passage that encompasses several brief stories, tells how wolves came to be for the Pueblo and the Eskimo and how humans originated for the Pueblo. The world and humans originate in "Wolf Star" (65) for the Pawnee and in "Other Animals" (109) for the Cherokee. An Eskimo tale of how different races originate is told in "First People" (121), while the Arikara nation and buffalo come into existence in "Buffalo-Maiden" (128) and the horse for the Comanche in "Magic Beasts" (145). "Bearskin-Woman" (96) is an exciting Blackfeet version of the origin of the constellation Great Bear. Various animals originate in "Other Animals" (109), according to the Cherokee, and medicine and healing in "Seneca Medicine" (117) for the Seneca. The book opens with a helpful essay by Richard and Judy Dockrey Young, themselves accomplished collectors and retellers, about the nature of Native American oral tradition and a short preface by Pijoan and concludes with notes about the stories. This book, by an eminent southwestern storyteller, offers valuable storytelling material and important insights into the traditions.

133 Pilling, Ann, ret., *Realms of Gold: Myths & Legends from Around the World*, illus. Kady MacDonald Denton, Kingfisher, 1993 (hardcover), ISBN 1-85697-913-X, $16.95, 93 pp. Ages 9–12, grades 4–8.

Among fourteen well-developed stories arranged in three sections (Earth, Air, Fire, and Water; Love and Death; Fools and Heroes), five are folktales and nine are myths or hero tales. Three of these are familiar stories from Greece: "Persephone" (37), "King Midas" (62), and "How Perseus Killed the Gorgon" (85). The Norse myth "The Death of Balder" (28) is also frequently retold, but the other five are less widely known, including a West African creation myth, "Iyadola's Babies" (10); a Native American Iroquois myth of the origin of weather features, "Naming the Winds" (15); a story of a trickster culture hero from the Pacific Islands, "How Maui Stole Fire from the Gods" (18); a Nigerian flood myth, "Water, Moon, and Sun" (25); and a story of the Irish hero Finn MacCool in "The Giants Who Couldn't Swim" (77). In an introduction, Pilling says she chose her selections because they are good stories, but she gives no sources. She has retold them with considerable dialogue in a simple, straightforward style suitable in tone to the type of story. The illustrations on the whole or part of every page are lively and colorful with attractive designs around titles and in borders. Unfortunately, the cartoon-like figures are suitable for the folktales but not serious or splendid enough for the myths.

Pinola, Larry, ret. *See* London, no. 104.

134   Riordan, James, coll. and trans., *The Sun Maiden and the Crescent Moon: Siberian Folk Tales*, Interlink Books, 1991 (hardcover), ISBN 0–940793–66–0, $24.95, 224 pp. Ages 12 up, grades 7 up.

This large, scholarly collection contains forty-three stories from twenty-three diverse Siberian peoples, some from the icy tundra, some from the coniferous taiga forest, and others from the scrubland steppe, in an area stretching from the Ural Mountains to the Pacific Ocean and the Aleutian Islands, a third of the way around the world. Although their lifestyles may be very different, clues from language and from folktale motifs and characters indicate a common origin in the warm plains of central Asia. Some of the stories are simply folktales, but many are explanatory myths: of animal appearance (raven and owl, 48; swan, 68; hare, 82; red fox, 132); of animal behavior (swan, 68; cuckoo, 86); or of heavenly bodies (Milky Way, 92; moon cycles, 55; woman in the moon, 197; the sun, 179). Several deal with threats to the moon or the sun, all important in the cold land: "How the Sun Was Rescued" (Eskimo, 161), "The Girl and the Moon Man" (Chakchi, 94), and "Mistress of Fire" (Selkup, 176). Seasons are explained in "Why the Sun Forsook the Tundra" (Koryak, 150). Other sorts of origins include both bad (sickness, 107; wicked witches, 30; tribal enmities, 118) and good (friendship, 50; arts and crafts, 41). The fox, the chief trickster figure, uses his wiles to deceive Coot or Raven (102) and the she-dog, girlfriend of the nomad wolf (132). Heroes slay monsters in "Little Oonyani" (Evenk, 141) and "Net-Pos-Hu the Archer" (Khanty, 134). They go on quests in "Bold Yatto and His Sister Tayune" (Nenets, 120), "How Anga Fetched a Serpent's Skin and a Bear's Fur" (Nanai, 88), and "Brave Azmun" (Nivkh, 71). A heroic woman appears in "Kotura, Lord of the Winds" (Nenets, 59). The stories are preceded by an interesting twenty-eight-page introduction about the land, the peoples, the tales, and the storytellers, and they are followed by a glossary and a bibliography of major works of reference. The group from whom each tale was collected is identified. This is a comprehensive work in a readable, storytelling style.

135   Rodanas, Kristina, ad., *Dance of the Sacred Circle: A Native American Tale*, illus. Kristina Rodanas, Little Brown, 1994 (hardcover), ISBN 0–316–75358–0, $4.95, unp. Ages 8 up, grades 3 up.

This myth of the Blackfeet tells the origin of the horse, so vital to the Indians of the plains. When the buffalo disappear, the people suffer. An orphan boy sets out to seek the Great Chief in the Sky, hoping to persuade him to assist them. After his arduous journey, the Great Chief appears to him and shapes, from mud, a new animal. He then calls the trees and all the other animals to him and asks each to contribute something useful to the creature. The pine and fir trees give it a tail and mane; Hawk, speed; Turtle, hardness of foot; Elk, size; and Wolf, courage. Finally Fawn contributes gentleness, so that its rider can trust it. They all dance around the statue, until the Great Chief stops their motion and breathes life into the horse. While riding this new animal back to his people, the boy crosses a wide river and is amazed to see horses' heads popping up through the surface until a whole herd is following him back to the camp and the men are able to find and chase the buffalo. Although the text is fuller and more detailed than that in most picture books and the illustrations, done in colored pencil over watercolor wash, are rich and dignified, the boy is pictured as quite young, so that the intended audience, which could be of any age, seems to be children in the early grades.

136 Rohmer, Harriet, and Dorminster Wilson, rets., *Mother Scorpion Country/La Tierra de la Madre Escorpion*, illus. Virginia Stearns, Children's, 1987 (hardcover), ISBN 0–89239–032–8, $10.95, 32 pp. Ages 10–17, grades 5–12.

In this myth from the Miskito Indians of Nicaragua, a courageous young husband accompanies his beloved, beautiful, just-deceased wife to the land of the dead where Mother Scorpion rules. Although Mother Scorpion is kind and welcoming, he soon discovers he does not wish to remain there because everything appears to be vague, colorless, or skeleton-like if nonthreatening. He returns to his own people, who no longer fully accept him, and decides to rejoin his wife. This compelling version of what is known as an "Orpheus type" story is told in both English and Spanish on each page and decorated by rich, full-color, bold paintings, which support the story's warm and loving atmosphere. A note about how Rohmer discovered the tale is included. Although a 1990 reissue (Children's) of a book originally published in 1976 by the same retellers, *How We Came to the Fifth World/Como Vinimos al Quinto Mundo* is a pleasingly told adaptation of the Aztec "myth of the ages," in which each age, or world or sun (terms vary), was created and then destroyed until the current one, the fifth, came to be. Brilliant, decorative, abstract collages emphasize the story's dramatic mood. The text appears in both English and Spanish, and a note at the end reports that, according to the Aztecs, this world will also also eventually come to an end unless evil is eradicated from human hearts. This legend provides an excellent comparison to other eschatological accounts.

137 Rosen, Michael ed., *South and North, East and West: The Oxfam Book of Children's Stories*, intro. Whoopi Goldberg, illus. various artists, Candlewick, 1992 (hardcover), ISBN 1–56402–117–3, $19.95, 95 pp.; (paper), ISBN 1–56402–396–6, $12.99, 96 pp. Ages 5 up, grades K up.

An amusing tale from the Native American Ticuna of the Amazon Basin in Brazil, "The Beginning of History" (42) says that people originated because of a dispute between two primeval, humanoid beings, one male and one female. When they quarrel because of a misunderstanding, she angrily hurls wasps' nests at him. His knees swell from the stings until they split open, and the first human beings pop out. This story is illustrated by Cathie Felstead with sophisticated, decorative, deep-palette, abstract paintings. Twenty-four folktales complete this handsome, readable book, originally published in Great Britain to benefit self-help projects and disaster relief for the poor in Africa, Asia, Latin America, and the Caribbean. Included also are notes on the stories and illustrators.

138 Rosenberg, Donna, ret., *World Mythology: An Anthology of the World's Great Myths and Epics*, National Textbook, 1986 (paper), ISBN 0–8442–5565–3, $23.95, 545 pp. Ages 14 up, grades 9 up.

This anthology contains forty-six pleasingly retold, highly readable myths and hero tales from seventeen countries or cultures, divided by major geographic areas. They vary in length from a page or two to about forty pages each for the *Iliad* and the *Aeneid*. About one-third of the stories come from less well-known literatures, for example, the Native American Trio of Brazil, the Native American pre-Incan Tiahuanaco, and the African Soninke. Mature, lively, and individualized in tone, the retellings convey something of the spirit of the original as transmitted through the translations from which Rosenberg worked. The titles of the translations and the translators are not specified. In some instances, the original sources are not indicated either. An extensive bibliography of references, however, appears at the end of the book. The stories are divided into seven major geographic sections: Greece and Rome, the Middle East, the Norse, the British Isles, the Far East, Africa, and the Americas. An introduction opens each section, and each story is preceded by an introduction of its own. Some stories have lists of characters as an aid in keeping events straight. Although one might quarrel with such statements as "Myths were originally created as entertaining stories with a serious purpose" (xv), the historical sketches and analyses of myths and hero tales as literary forms are on the whole well organized, cogent, and pertinent. There is also an alternate table of contents in which the stories are arranged by three themes: creation myths, fertility myths, and hero myths. Maps, which are not provided, would be helpful. An extensive index and study questions end this large, well-chosen collection of stories. Included are myths of the creation of humans from Greece (12, 21); the creation of the world from Greece (3), India (353), and Japan (401); the creation of the world and humans from Mesopotamia (Babylonia, 157), the Norse (219), Ireland (277), China (390), the African Yoruba (426), the Native American Tiahuanaco (459), the Native American Maya (470), the Native American Aztec (476), and the Native American Navajo (489); floods and similar destructions from Greece (12, 21), Mesopotamia (Sumer/Babylonia, 181), Ireland (277), India (353), the African Yoruba (426), the Native American Tiahuanaco (459), the Native American Maya (470), the Native American Aztec (476), and the Native American Navajo (489); the end of the world from the Norse (219) and India (353); the origin of Cuzco, the Inca capital, and the Inca nation (462, 464) and of Japan (401); the origin of such necessities and realities as fire, music, the sun and moon, arts and crafts, and foods from Greece (21), the Native American Tiahuanaco (459), the Native American Inca (464), the Native American Trio of Brazil (467), the Native American Aztecs (476, 484), and the Native American Haida/Tlingit (500); the origin of death from Mesopotamia (Sumer/Babylonia, 181), Ireland (277), India (358), Japan (401), the African Yoruba (426), the Native American Tiahuanaco (459), the Native American Maya (470), the Native American Aztec (476), the Native American Navajo (489), and the Native American Haida/Tlingit (500); goddesses and women heroes from Greece (Demeter, 15), Rome (Juno, 116; Dido, 116), Egypt (Isis, 166), Mesopotamia (Sumer/Babylonia; Ishtar, 181), the Norse (Idun, 228; Brynhild, 244), India (Sita, 365), and Japan (Izanami, 401; Ama-terasu, 406); searches and quests from Greece (Demeter, 15; Odysseus, 75), Rome (Aeneas, 116), Egypt (Isis, 166), Hittite (Telepinu, 177), Mespotamia (Sumer/Babylonia; Gilgamesh, 181), India (Rama, 365), and China (Bao Chu, 395); views of the underworld and afterlife from Greece (15, 75), Rome (116), Mesopotamia (Sumer/Babylonia, 181), Egypt (166), the Norse (219, 232), Japan (401), and the African Nyanga (441); divine tricksters from the Norse (Loki, 228, 232, 239) and the Native American Aztecs (Tezcatlipoca, 484); seasons, agriculture, and fertility from Greece (15), Egypt (166), the Hittite (177), the Norse (228, 232), Ireland (285), India (358), China (393), Japan (406), the African Fon (432), the Native American Aztec (484), and the Native American Zuni (495); a god's adventures from the Norse (Thor, 239); and a wide variety of heroes from Greece (Heracles, 28; Achilles, 33; Odysseus, 75), Rome (Romulus and Remus, 113; Aeneas, 116), Mesopotamia (Sumer/Babylonia; Gilgamesh, 181), the Norse (Sigurd, 244), the British Isles (Beowulf, 289; King Arthur, 314), India (Rama, 365), China (Bao Chu, 395), Japan (unnamed narrator, 411), the African Soninke (Gassire, 435), the African Nyanga (Mwindo, 441), the Native American Aztec (Quetzalcoatl, 484), the Native American Zuni (Ahaiyuta, 495), the Native American Crow (Lodge-Boy, Thrown-Away, 497), and the Native American Haida/Tlingit (Raven, 500). This comprehensive and impressive book gives valuable views of this literature for both neophyte and initiated and does it in a respectful and at the same time entertaining fashion.

139   Ross, Anne, ret., *Druids, Gods & Heroes from Celtic Mythology*, illus. Roger Garland and John Sibbick, Peter Bedrick, 1986 (hardcover), ISBN 0–87226–918–3, $22.50; (paper), ISBN 0–87226–919–1, $14.95, 132 pp. Ages 10 up, grades 5 up.

This substantial and readable volume in the Peter Bedrick World Mythology series retells and comments on Celtic myths and legends from a wide span of periods, with their roots dating from as far back as 2500 B.C. to the Arthurian tales of the Middle Ages. Since most were not written down by the Celtic people themselves but by the Romans who conquered and displaced them or by later scholars who studied surviving Irish and Welsh tales, inscriptions, place names, and artifacts and pieced together the myths from this evidence, it is not always clear which stories are about gods and which are about human heroes. All, however, are richly imaginative and involve enchantments and easy passage from our world to the Otherworld, a place of beauty and happiness unlike the land of the dead in many mythologies. Stories of invasions of Ireland by four groups (14)—the Children of Nemed, who fought against the indigenous Formorians; the Fir Bolg, who established social and political order; the Tuatha De Danann or Children of Danu; and the Gaels, known as the Sons of Mil—record a mix of history and mythology and include a number of such myths, mostly of the Tuatha De Danann, as "The Second Battle of Moytura" (21), which tells how Lugh Long Arm helps them defeat the Formorians, and "The Sorrows of Storytelling" (25), about Lugh's father, Cian the Mighty. A more widely known legend, like these a story of shape changing and enchantment, is "The Children of Lir" (29), also set in the time of the Tuatha De Danann. Two major hero tales, that of CuChulainn (32), greatest of the Red Branch heroes of Ulster, and of Fionn (53), whose stories are full of folktale-like transformations and exaggerations, are retold at some length. The four branches of *The Mabinogion* (65, 69, 72, 77), ancient Celtic hero tales first written down in medieval Wales, are summarized briefly but clearly. The stories of King Arthur (82) suffer more from condensation, although they are handled competently. Other assorted early Celtic legends about kings include that of Etain and Eochaid Airem, high king of Ireland (105), and of King Cormac (109), whose visit to the Otherworld or the Land of Promise is caused by Manannan mac Lir, god of the sea. Stories of holy men include that of Saint Brendan (112), who traveled for seven years among magical islands of the west, and that of Saint Patrick (124), who destroyed the golden idol, Crom Dubh, and sent its demon to the Otherworld. Severed heads that retain the powers of the living, sometimes of speech or evil, occur in a number of stories, notably in the flood of Riach (128). Like the other books in the series, this is highly illustrated with large paintings, black-and-white drawings, and borders formed of a collage of motifs from the stories. There is also a bibliography and a pronunciation glossary.

140   Ross, Gayle, ret., *How Rabbit Tricked Otter and Other Cherokee Trickster Stories*, illus. Murv Jacob, HarperCollins, 1994 (hardcover), ISBN 0–06–021285–3, $17.00, 80 pp. Ages 6 up, grades 1 up.

This handsome book contains fifteen stories from the Native American Cherokee tradition, all featuring Rabbit, the trickster who usually fools the other animals in "the days when the people and the animals still spoke the same language," but sometimes is too clever for himself and becomes the butt of his own jokes. Some of the tales are also explanatory stories of animal appearance: the cleft in rabbit's nose, in "Flint Visits Rabbit" (6); rabbit's tail, in "How Rabbit Tricked Otter" (13); possum's tail in "Why Possum's Tail Is Bare" (19); deer's antlers in "How Deer Won His Antlers" (29); and deer's teeth in "Why Deer's Teeth Are Blunt" (33). Others explain animal behavior: otter's preference for water (13), possum's way of playing dead when frightened (19), rabbit's ability to gnaw at stems and twigs (29), and rabbit's peculiar habit of chewing on his own fur when starving (43). Rabbit's attack on sleeping Flint with a wooden wedge (6) also accounts for the widespread distribution of the highly useful stone. Introduced with phrases like "Long ago in the beginning days of the world" and "This is what the old people told me when I was a child," the tales have the relaxed simplicity of oral retellings but also the careful construction of a skilled stylist. The illustrations are full-page paintings in brilliant colors, each in a circle or square framed by a wide band patterned with Indian motifs. Each text page has a black-and-white border of similar designs. The total effect is understated but unusually attractive.

141   Ross, Gayle, ret., *How Turtle's Back Was Cracked: A Traditional Cherokee Tale*, illus. Murv Jacob, Dial, 1995 (hardcover), ISBN 0–8037–1728–8, $14.99, unp. Ages 4 up, grades PS up.

This old Cherokee story, retold by the professional storyteller descendant of John Ross, the Cherokee chief at the time of the Trail of Tears, comes from James Mooney's comprehensive collection of Cherokee stories and explains the characteristic pattern on the turtle's shell. Although Possum was really responsible, Turtle takes credit for killing a troublesome wolf and shows off. Captured by the vengeful pack which seeks to kill him, he tricks them into throwing him into a river, where he cracks his shell. Although occasional awkward phrases break the rhythm, a strong oral quality gives vibrancy and fluency to the narrative. The stylized, highly patterned, bright paintings, done by a part-Cherokee artist, incorporate Cherokee motifs, demand repeated viewings to appreciate the wealth of detail, enhance the story's drama and humor, and produce an exceedingly beautiful book.

142   Roth, Susan L., ret., *Buddha*, illus. Susan L. Roth, Doubleday, 1994 (hardcover), ISBN 0–385–31072–2, $15.95, unp. Ages 5 up, grades K up.

This dramatically illustrated picture-story book tells of the birth and early years of Siddhartha, the prince who becomes "the enlightened one" or Buddha. Represented in the Indian *Vedas* as the ninth incarnation of the god Vishnu, Buddha is regarded by his followers as a mortal prince, who renounced his royal estate and lived a life of asceticism. The colorful, delicate cut-paper collages capture the flavor of India and southeastern Asia. A short afterword gives information about the life of Buddha and about Buddhism.

143   Sabuda, Robert, ret., *Arthur and the Sword*, illus. Robert Sabuda, Atheneum, 1995 (hardcover), ISBN 0–689–31987–8, $16.00, unp. Ages 5 up, grades K up.

Brilliant stained-glass artwork, often suffused with shades of royal purple, decorates and extends the story of how the youth Arthur pulls the ancestral sword from the anvil on the stone and assumes the kingship of England to which he is entitled by birth. The text, which is appropriately formal, dignified, and suspenseful, relies on the *Le Morte D'arthur* of Sir Thomas Malory. A historical note concludes this stunningly handsome, all-ages book.

144   Sanfield, Steve, coll. and ret., *The Feather Merchants & Other Tales of the Fools of Chelm*, Orchard, 1991 (hardcover), ISBN 0–53–05958–8, $15.99, 112 pp.; Beech Tree, 1993 (paper), ISBN 0–688–12568–9, $4.95, 114 pp. Ages 8 up, grades 3 up.

The first story in this highly entertaining collection of tales from European Jewish tradition explains why so many fools and simpletons live in the village of Chelm. Right after creating the world, God puts the wise and foolish souls into two sacks respectively. When an angel, instructed to distribute them throughout the world, flies over the jagged peaks just north of Chelm, the sack containing the foolish ones tears on an outcropping. The foolish souls all pour into the valley of Chelm, where they have lived ever since. The book includes a foreword, an afterword, a glossary of names and terms, and a bibliography.

145 San Souci, Robert D., ret., *Cut From the Same Cloth: American Women of Myth, Legend, and Tall Tale*, illus. Brian Pinkney, Philomel, 1993 (hardcover), ISBN 0–399–21987–0, $16.95, 144 pp. Ages 10 up, grades 5 up.

In fifteen stories, about half of them folktales, a wide variety of feisty and powerful but not widely known women of American tale are celebrated. Several of the African Americans are clearly folktale figures, but Annie Christmas (35), a huge dockworker and keelboat owner, is in the tradition of the tall-tale work hero, like Paul Bunyan. Sal Fink (51), daughter of the legendary Mike Fink, is another such outsized heroine, like Annie Christmas probably originally a literary invention later absorbed into the oral tradition. Of those from Native American Indian groups, Star Maiden (5) is an explanatory myth from the Chippewa; Pohaha (77) is a hunter and warrior who leads her Tewa Pueblo people against raiding parties; Hekeke (103) is instrumental in killing a monster that preys on the Miwok people of central California; Pale-Faced Lightning (77) is a culture hero of mysterious origin who befriends an equally mysterious tribe of little people in a Pueblo story. The Eskimo heroine Otoonah (111) survives and triumphs although her family has deliberately abandoned her. Hiiaka (121), sister of the Hawaiian fire goddess, Pele, sets off on a quest and encounters numerous perils in the familiar hero tale pattern. Each story is preceded by a short discussion of its origins and the people who told it. A thorough list of sources appears at the end of the book. The style, which varies with the story, employs dialect where appropriate. Full-page black-and-white illustrations, which look like etchings, are bordered by suitable motifs for each story.

146 San Souci, Robert D., ret., *Larger Than Life: The Adventures of American Legendary Heroes*, illus. Andrew Glass, Doubleday, 1991 (hardcover), ISBN 0–385–24907–1, $16.00, 59 pp. Ages 8–12, grades 3–7.

As the title indicates, these five tall tales are about American work heroes of exaggerated size whose exploits were never meant to be taken seriously. All are bigger and stronger than rationally possible, although John Henry's feat of outworking the steam drill, at least in this version (1), has less hyperbole than the other four: Old Stormalong, the sailing vessel mariner from the American Revolutionary period (13); Pecos Bill, the cowboy, and his daring girlfriend, Slue-Foot Sue (23); Strap Buckner, the brawler from Texas (35); and Paul Bunyan, the logger (47). The style is colloquial, and the humor is broad. The book is in oversized format with frequent colorful and lively illustrations. No sources are given.

147 Saxby, Maurice, ret., *The Great Deeds of Heroic Women*, illus. Robert Ingpen, Peter Bedrick, 1990 (hardcover), ISBN 0–87226–348–7, $24.95, 151 pp. Ages 9 up, grades 4 up.

Originally published in Australia as a companion book to Saxby's *The Great Deeds of Superheroes* (no. 148), this anthology presents a wide variety of stories, some of them myths, some hero tales from oral tradition, some folktales, and some records of historical figures. From Greek mythology are Athena (14), Aphrodite (19), Demeter (25), Atalanta (30), Circe (36), and Medea (42). The story of Guanyin (50) comes from ancient China; Rehab (62), Esther (68), and Judith (74) are Old Testament figures; Bilqis (82) and Scheherazade (91) are from Arabia; and the maiden hunter of the Zuni (115) is a heroine of Native American legend. Historical women include Boadicea (97), Joan of Arc (105), Pocahontas (131), and Mary Bryant (141), whose story starts and ends in Cornwall, but who is remembered chiefly in Australia for her daring escape from the penal colony at Botany Bay and her amazing sea journey in an open boat. Saxby opens the book with an essay, "The Many Faces of the Heroic Woman," in which he says he could find no overall pattern in their stories as he did for the superheroes; instead, he was impressed by the great variety of lives in which women proved themselves heroic, often against heavy odds. The retellings of stories from myth and legend are standard versions augmented by dialogue and detail. Those of historical women are supported by dates, quotations from contemporary accounts, and factual details. The style is readable, neither difficult nor exciting. Illustrations consist of handsome, full-page portraits of each woman, imaginatively individualized. A brief bibliography divided by cultures follows the main text.

148 Saxby, Maurice, ret., *The Great Deeds of Superheroes*, illus. Robert Ingpen, Peter Bedrick (hardcover), ISBN 0–87226–342–8, $24.95, 184 pp. Ages 9 up, grades 4 up.

This large anthology contains the stories of fifteen heroes from six cultures, each preceded by a short essay discussing the mythology behind the hero tale, the area in which the tale originated, and something of the literary sources. In the largest group, the heroes are Greek: Perseus (17), Heracles (25), Theseus (38), Jason (46), and Odysseus (50). Gilgamesh (64) is the only hero from Mesopotamia; Sigurd (76) and Vainamoinen (91) represent Scandinavia; Moses (104) and Samson (113) are Hebrew heroes from the Old Testament of ancient Israel; Beowulf (120), Arthur (130), and Cuchulain (142) are listed as from Old England; Roland (160) and El Cid (171) are medieval heroes of France and Spain, respectively. A general introduction discusses the heroic pattern and includes a two-page table containing for each figure such elements as Circumstances of Birth, Tasks and Trials, Strengths, Weaknesses, and Death. The retellings are standard versions told with more dialogue and detail than the originals but without added incidents or motivations. More exciting than the style are the illustrations, full-page portraits of each hero, individualized and often strikingly different from the usual heroic depictions. Beowulf, for example, is painted as a dreamy-eyed youth dressed in furs, with skin darker than the Anglo-Saxons from whom his story comes; Vainamoinen is a hooded old man shielding his musical instrument from falling snow. A few additional illustrations show dramatic scenes. A brief bibliography for each culture suggests books for both children and adults.

149 Seymour, Tryntje Van Ness, ret., *The Gift of Changing Woman*, illus. various Apache artists, Henry Holt, 1993 (hardcover), ISBN 0–8050–2577–4, $16.95, 38 pp. Ages 10–14, grades 5–9.

Almost buried in a description of the Native American Apache ceremony of Changing Woman, which celebrates a girl's coming of age, are myths of the re-creation of humans after a great flood (7) and of the creation of the world and its stabilization on the figures of four Gaans (Mountain Spirits) that hold it steady (16). The rest of the book tells of the four-day ceremony and includes quotations from Apache leaders, artists, and women who have gone through the experience. Illustrations are of various types, mostly of the black-painted Gaan figures or of the dance itself. A long author's note at the end discusses the difficulty of a non–Native American's giving a picture of the Apache culture that is accurate, sensitive, and respectful. It also gives biographical information on the speakers quoted and the artists and adds a bibliography of books about the Apache and a brief glossary of Apache words used in the text.

150 Shepherd, Sandy, ret. *Myths and Legends from Around the World*, illus. Tudor Humphries, Macmillan, 1995 (hardcover), ISBN 0–02–762355–6, $17.95, 96 pp. Ages 8–12, grades 3–7.

This extensive and highly decorated anthology contains forty-eight retellings of myths and hero tales from many cultures. Of these, seventeen are developed in one to three full pages; the other thirty-one are brief, each taking up about a quarter of a page. Several other entries, among them the one on Ale, the Ibo earth goddess, describe the culture and the worship but include no stories that could be considered myths. The book is divided into six parts: The World We Live In, The Heavens and the Earth, Founders and Inventors, Heroes and Heroines, Gods and Spirits, and Good and Evil. Each section is preceded by an introductory discussion of the type, and the whole is introduced by a brief essay on mythology. These are written at an elementary level, and, unfortunately, many of the myths are introduced by such phrases as, "The Inuit tell a story . . ." or "The Hawaiians once believed . . .", a style that produces a tone condescending to both the material and the reader. The illustrations are lavish, often full-page paintings of scenes and characters, with many smaller pictures of artifacts, such natural products as corn and ginseng, weapons, sculptures, masks, and wall and vase paintings. A double-page map at the end locates the cultures geographically. No sources are given. The longer entries include myths of the creation of the world from Japan (10) and New Zealand Maori (18); the creation of the world and humans from Tahiti (12); the origin of the sun from China (28); floods from the Hindus (34); volcanoes from Greece (40); sea creatures from the Inuit (78); evil from Greece (88); the peacock's plumage from India (20); agriculture from China (52); wisdom and knowledge from the Norse (70) and Egypt (72); and hero tales from Rome (Romulus and Remus, 46), Greece (the Trojan War, 64), the Aztecs (Quetzacoatl, 56), Mesopotamia (Sumer, Gilgamesh, 58), and the San Bushmen (Cagn, 80). Among the briefer entries are origin stories of the world from Egypt (16), the Norse (16), the Mayan (17), Onondaga (Iroquois, 17), and Mesopotamia (Sumer, 92); of animal appearances from the Inuit (22), Sierra Leone (22), and Russia (23); of flowers from Greece (23); of the sun, moon, and stars from the Aztec (32), Japan (33), and the Micmac (33); of thunder and lightning from the Norse (38); of seasons from Greece (39); of fire from the Amazon Kayapo (51); of agricultural products from Madagascar (50) and the Chippewa (51); of floods from the Maya (39) and the Mandans (93); of earthquakes from the Sulawesi (39); of death from the Burundi (77); of the boomerang from the Binbinga Aboriginals (83); of the world of the dead from Phoenecia (76); of a warrior goddess from India (Durga, 93); of a trickster figure from the Pacific Northwest (Raven, 83); and hero tales from Greece (Heracles, 62), the Tartars (Guinara, 62), China (Guan Yu, 63), Ireland (Cuchulainn, 63), and the Navajo (Nayenezgani, 63).

151 Shetterly, Susan Hand, ret., *Muwin and the Magic Hare*, illus. Robert Shetterly, Atheneum, 1993 (hardcover), ISBN 0–689–31699–2, $14.95, unp. Ages 5–12, grades K–7.

When Muwin, the big black bear, decides to have rabbit for dinner before he retires to his den for the winter, he does not suspect that the Passamaquoddy Indian hunter, medicine woman, and chief whom he meets and who feed and entertain him are really the trickster and creator rabbit, the Great Hare, Mahtoqehs, his prey transformed. Impressive, full-color paintings juxtapose Muwin's physical power and also his slow wit against the cleverness and resourcefulness of the seemingly weaker rabbit. They support the story by slowing the rhythm so the viewer can take in landscapes, concentrate on close-ups of the characters, and savor the humor. Sometimes they speed up the action and add details to the narrative. The portrait pictures are particularly arresting, and the Indians are individualized and given personality. The book opens with a glossary of Passamaquoddy terms and a note about the efforts of the Waponahki Nation, to which the Passamaquoddy belong, to preserve and perpetuate their culture.

152   Shute, Linda, ret., *Rabbit Wishes*, illus. Linda Shute. Lothrop, 1995 (hardcover), ISBN 0–688–13180–8, $16.00, unp. Ages 4 up, grades PS up.

This African-Cuban myth tells how, shortly after Papa Dios (Father God) has finished creating the world, tio Conejo (Uncle Rabbit) complains that he is too small, completes several tasks as payment, he thinks, for being made larger, and discovers that Papa Dios has only given him longer ears. The story's comic aspects are deftly supported by the active, colorful, cartoonish illustrations that portray tio Conejo as a Bugs Bunny sort. Behind the tomfoolery lies a serious moral about the nature of personal satisfaction and the importance of appearance that extends the audience well beyond the usual picture-book range. Occasional Spanish words lend a Caribbean lilt to the text. They are translated in parentheses as they appear, and a collected glossary opens the book. Source materials and information about the tio Conejo figure are given at the end.

153   Sutcliff, Rosemary, ret., *Black Ships Before Troy: The Story of THE ILIAD*, illus. Alan Lee, Delacorte, 1993 (hardcover), ISBN 0–385–31069–2, $19.95, 128 pp. Ages 8 up, grades 3 up.

Sutcliff's retelling of *The Iliad*, published posthumously, is listed as for "all ages" and is in highly illustrated large format, but its length and elevated language are clearly not for the very young. She starts the story not with the wrath of Achilles, more than nine years into the war as does Homer, but with the marriage feast of the sea nymph Thetis, at which the goddess of discord tosses a golden apple, marked "To the fairest," onto the table, thus fueling the rivalry between the goddesses Hera, Athene, and Aphrodite. The story of how they choose Paris, the son of Priam, King of Troy, as their judge and how Aphrodite bribes him with the promise of the most beautiful woman in the world, Helen, for his wife, follows, so flashbacks leading up to the Trojan War and the first years of the conflict are not necessary. She also carries the story beyond the funeral of Hector to the trick of the wooden horse and the sack of Troy, as told in the *Aeneid*, although she does not include the escape of Aeneas with his father and little son from the burning city. Otherwise, she follows the original story line faithfully, perhaps slightly underplaying the role of the gods but emphasizing the very human aspects of the heroes and the other figures caught in the ten-year war. The lavish illustrations, watercolors predominantly in shades of grey-blue and gold, are formal and well suited to the seriousness of the narrative.

154 Sutcliff, Rosemary, ret., *The Wanderings of Odysseus: The Story of THE ODYSSEY*, illus. Alan Lee, Delacorte, 1996 (hardcover), ISBN 0–385–32205–4, $22.50, 120 pp. Ages 8 up, grades 3 up.

This companion book to Sutcliff's retelling of *The Iliad, Black Ships Before Troy* (no. 153), is equally impressive, a faithful following of the original with stirring language and stunning illustrations. It does not overburden the narrative with names and details, but it includes all the important figures and incidents, starting with the departure of Odysseus and his twelve ships from the main Greek fleet sailing home from Troy. Well-developed stories include those of Polyphemus, the Cyclops (11); the visit to the island of Aeolus, Lord of the Winds, and the calamitous curiosity of the crew (18); and the nearly disastrous stop at the island of Circe, the enchantress (24). After Odysseus's visit to the land of the dead (32), where he gets advice from Tiresias of Thebes about how to avoid the perils of the sirens and of Scylla and Charybdis (38), the narrative is interrupted by a shift to his son Telemachus, who sets off in search for news of his father (46). The remainder of the return trip centers on the departure of Odysseus from the island of the nymph Calypso (54) and his shipwreck and arrival at the land of the Phaeacians, where the Princess Nausicaa finds him, naked and battered, and falls in love with him (63). In face of his determination to return to rocky Ithaca and his aging wife, Penelope, Nausicaa forgoes her desire, and he is at last sent on to his homeland. There, with the aid of his faithful swineherd, Eumaeus, he makes contact with Telemachus, who has just returned from his search, and together they work out a trick whereby Odysseus will pose as a beggar (86) and come to his own hall where greedy suitors feast and riot, trying to force Penelope to marry one of them who will then become king in his stead. The plan culminates in a bloody slaughter of the suitors (102) and a touching reunion with Penelope. Although the wrath of Poseidon and the aid of the goddess Athene are factors in many of these adventures, the emphasis is placed upon the human characters, each well distinguished and memorable, including the four women who love the voyager.

155 Switzer, Ellen, and Costas, rets., *Greek Myths: Gods, Heroes and Monsters*, photographs by Costas, Atheneum, 1988 (hardcover), ISBN 0–689–31253–9, $18.00, 208 pp. Ages 12 up, grades 7 up.

This book of myths from ancient Greece covers a lot of ground, if unevenly and pedestrianly. The selection of stories is broad, although mostly they are familiar narratives, but most are merely summaries, like passages in hand-books, and not retellings in the usual sense, while others include a good deal more detail. Most simply cover the action, and the writers interject commentaries here and there, sometimes about how the myth functions in today's world. Others, like that of Prometheus, unfold against a theme, in this case presenting Prometheus as the prototype rebel who reacts against the unjust tyranny of Zeus. The introductions giving sources and background information are generally excellent, and the photographs of statues, temples, landscapes, and the like are superb. Thus the book provides a moderately good introduction to Greek mythology for those for whom better versions, like those of Edith Hamilton and Padriac Colum, are not available. The book begins with "How the World Began: The Greek Version" (10), which explores Greek variants of the beginning of things, and then moves into separate chapters describing each of the major gods. The chapter on "Hades" (39) provides a description of the underworld that shows the limitations of the Switzer-Costas approach, since, for the purpose apparently of economy of space, the names and functions of the rivers there are not specified. "Prometheus: The First of the Great Heroes" (65) discusses Prometheus's motives, as well as describing his deeds, and gives the origin of fire; "Pandora: The First Woman?" (68) speculates on whether indeed she was the first human female, and also gives the origin of troubles and hope. "Persephone in Hades" (74) is a classic seasonal story that also involves a search, but the intensely emotional aspect of Demeter's loss of her beloved daughter to Hades, the god of the underworld, is not exploited as in better retellings. Many of the narratives deal with the most important adventures of the famous Greek heroes: "Perseus and the Medusa: Everybody's Fairy Tale" (81); "Hercules: The Strongest Man on Earth" (91), which unfortunately uses the Roman name for the hero instead of Heracles, the proper Greek one; "Theseus: The Favorite Hero of Athens" (100); "The Golden Fleece, Jason, and Medea" (114); "Oedipus: The Tragic Hero Who Might Have Asked 'Why Me?'" (126); "Antigone: A Hero Can Also Be a Woman" (133); "Orpheus and Eurydice" (139); "Midas" (141); "The Trojan War" (165); "The House of Atreus: Murder, Vengeance, and Forgiveness" (185); and "The Adventures of Odysseus" (191). "Narcissus and Echo" (146) gives the origin of the narcissus and of the echo, "Hyacinth" (147) of the hyacinth, and "Adonis" (148) of the anemone, and the last story, "The Adventures of Odysseus" (191), gives a striking picture of the world of the dead as well. This is a useful but not outstanding collection of Greek stories.

156 Talbott, Hudson, ret., *King Arthur and the Round Table*, illus. Hudson Talbott, Morrow, 1995 (hardcover), ISBN 0–688–11340–0, $16.00, 48 pp. Ages 5 up, grades K up.

This book, which concentrates on the romance between young King Arthur and Lady Guinevere, is carried by its lavish illustrations rather than its pedestrian text. It tells of an invented or little known meeting of the two on a battlefield the day after one of Arthur's early victories when Guinevere is studying the healing arts with the nuns ministering to the wounded. Although neither knows the other's identity, they both lose their hearts. Later, after his army has broken the siege on the castle of his ally King Leodegrance of Cameliard, Arthur meets his fair daughter, Guinevere, they recognize each other, are married, and receive as a gift from her father the fabulous Round Table. Only Merlin has any foreboding about this happy union, and his warning is not emphasized. The illustrations, in dazzling color, are full-page or two-page spreads, alive with action and many figures, notably scenes of the storming of the castle at Cameliard and of the knights pledging loyalty around the huge circle of the Round Table. Arthur, in close-ups and in the gold-hued wedding scene, is shown as a blond, beardless youth with curly hair trimmed at his collar. The first book in the series is *King Arthur: The Sword in the Stone* (Morrow, 1991; no. 157). Third in this series and similarly illustrated is *Excalibur* (Morrow, 1996), which deals with Arthur's acquiring the marvelous sword from the Lady of the Lake after his earlier weapon is broken in a conflict with a dark knight, here identified as King Pellinore.

157   Talbott, Hudson, ret., *King Arthur: The Sword in the Stone*, illus. Hudson Talbott, Morrow, 1991 (hardcover), ISBN 0–688–09403–1, $14.95, unp. Ages 5 up, grades K up.

   Although intended as a simplified version for young listeners to follow easily, readers of all ages will find this a bare-bones but dignified text of how Arthur was catapulted to the kingship of Britain. After summarizing the events leading up to and following his birth when Merlin the wizard, as he is called here, took him from his father into fosterage, the retelling mentions the turmoil in the land after the death of his father, Uther Pendragon, then leaps ahead to the tournament in London at which the naive Welsh country youth proves his kingship, not once but several times, and concludes with his coronation after public acclaim. Merlin is presented as the wise force of destiny, the archbishop as doltish and slow, the foster father, Ector, and foster brother, Kay, as worthy knights, and Arthur as gaining greatly in maturity in the approximately one year of the story's main events. Magnificent paintings convey medieval pagentry, though sometimes the dwellings look Tudor or Victorian, and for the most part echo the story in tone and theme. Occasionally, as in the text, the comic touches seem incongruous, perhaps taking their cue from T. H. White's novelized version. The sword is truly a wondrous implement, Kay and Ector on their charges suitably imposing, Merlin mysterious and inscrutable, views of the throngs in London vibrant with humanity, the knights in melee breathtaking, and Arthur crowned, resplendent and hopeful in white under a flowering (probably) apple tree. An afterword by Peter Glassman presents information about the Arthurian cycle, of which this narrative is one part adequately but not remarkably retold. Other books Talbott has done on the Arthur cycle include *King Arthur and the Round Table* (1995, no. 156) and *Excalibur* (1996), both published by Morrow.

158 Taylor, C. J., ret., *Bones in the Basket: Native Stories of the Origin of People*, illus. C. J. Taylor, Tundra Books, 1994 (hardcover), ISBN 0–88776–327–8, $17.95, 32 pp. Ages 6 up, grades 1 up.

These seven origin stories come from a variety of Native American groups in the United States and Canada; one, "Big Raven Creates the World" (13), comes from the Chuckchee of Russian Siberia. This myth also includes the origin of humans and animals. Also concerned with the creation of both the world and the people in it are the Zuni story "Before All Things Began" (6), the Mohawk myth "Creation" (20), and the Osage "A Place to Have Children" (17). The Mandan story "From Darkness to Light" (8), concerns the discovery, not the creation, of the world. In the Cree flood story "The Raft" (10), animals, at least, are already in existence when the two creators, Giant Beaver and Wisagatcak, battle over whether the world should be covered by earth or water. The title story, from the Modoc of northern California and southern Oregon (29), is an especially appealing myth of how Creator and his daughter bring the spirits of people, in the form of dry bones, up from an underworld not unlike that from which people emerge in the Mandan story. It also accounts for the origin of animals and the distribution of people in different parts of the world. Although in a large format and highly illustrated (each story is accompanied by at least one full-page, rather expressionistic painting), the book clearly is not limited to the usual picture-book age. Style is clear, but not overly simplified. A page at the end describes the various groups from which the myths come.

159 Taylor, C. J., ret., *How We Saw the World: Nine Native Stories of the Way Things Began*, illus. C. J. Taylor, Tundra, 1993 (hardcover), ISBN 0–88776–302–2, $17.95, 32 pp. Ages 6–10, grades 1–5.

In simple, dignified language with a storytelling rhythm, nine stories, each from a different Native American Indian group, tell of a variety of origins: of such geographical features as Niagara Falls from the Algonquin (6) and the islands of the Pacific Coast from the Bella Coola (10); of such animal behavior and appearance as the dog's loyalty to man from the Oneida (21), the first horses from the Blackfeet (16), the colors and inability to sing of the butterfly from the Tohono O'Odhan (Papago, 8), and the physical characteristics of owls and rabbits from the Mohawk (27); of the seasons from the Micmac (13); of the first tornado from the Kiowa (24). How the world will end, when Great Beaver gnaws through the pole that supports it, according to the Cheyenne (30), is the subject of the last story. A brief description of each tribe, where they lived in earlier periods, and where they live today follows the main text. A list of sources appears opposite the title page. Illustrations are full-page paintings of the action in each story, often with more than one incident depicted and a perspective slightly off to give a surrealistic quality. Although designed for readers in the early grades, the book could easily appeal to older children. Taylor has also written and illustrated a number of single-story books, also concerning origins, including *How Two-Feather Was Saved from Loneliness: An Abenaki Legend* (Tundra, 1990), about the beginning of agriculture and the use of fire; *Little Water and the Gift of the Animals: A Seneca Legend* (Tundra, 1992), in which the animals teach people the songs and dances to cure illness; and *The Secret of the White Buffalo: An Oglala Legend* (Tundra, 1993), about the institution of the peace pipe among the Oglala Sioux.

160   Tedlock, Dennis, ret., *Breath on the Mirror: Mythic Voices & Visions of the Living Maya*, HarperSanFrancisco, 1993 (hardcover), ISBN 0–06–250900–4, $21.00, 256 pp. Ages 15 up, grades 10 up.

Embedded in a narrative that is partly travelogue, partly anthropological study, and partly a record of the present-day practice of rituals are creation and origin myths from the Quiche Maya people of Guatemala. The title chapter (1) tells of the creation of the androgynous first four vigesimal creatures, or those with twenty digits (i.e., humans), called motherfathers, who could see and understand all. To decrease their potential power, the gods decide to make them male and provide them wives, a process which clouds their vision and understanding like "breath on the mirror." In other chapters are the myths of the origin of fire (12) and of the sun (31 and 37). Most of the rest of the book is a narrative of the study made by Tedlock and his wife of the intensely complicated system of keeping track of time by the "daykeepers," who name and trace the days that are dangerous or propitious for a wide variety of activities. There are also descriptions of expeditions with informants to sacred or magical spots at which they enact ritualistic observances. A very interesting section is a wildly revisionist account of Biblical events and characters, but it is not clear whether this is the interpretation of a single speaker or whether it is a more widely accepted version. This is a difficult and unusual book.

161   Tedlock, Dennis, trans., *Popol Vuh: The Definitive Edition of the Mayan Book of the Dawn of Life and the Glories of Gods and Kings*, Simon and Schuster, 1985 (hardcover), ISBN 0–671–45241–X, $19.95, 380 pp. Ages 15 up, grades 10 up.

This scholarly work is a translation of a dual-language (Quiche and Spanish) copy of the "Council Book" of the Quiche Mayan people made by a friar just after 1700, itself a transcription of a translation into alphabetic Quiche of a much more ancient heiroglyphic book that secretly escaped the mass book burning conducted by missionaries. Since it is both a mythology and a folk history of the Quiche and was also used as a divination tool, much of the book is obscure and subject to interpretation, and Tedlock spent a long period studying among the present-day Quiche people, apprenticing himself to a "daykeeper," a diviner who was also a motherfather, or patrilineage head, and who interpreted passages and difficult ideas. After a long introduction that summarizes the narrative to follow, Part One tells how the gods create the world, although all is still darkness (73). They try three times to create man: the first turn into animals (76), the second, made of mud, dissolve, and the third, made of wood, seem promising but fail to worship or acknowledge their makers and are destroyed in a massive flood (79 and 84). In Parts Two and Three, the narrative turns back to an earlier time and relates the adventures of two sets of gods, some on earth and some in the Mayan underworld, Xibalba (87 and 105). Included are explanatory stories, among them of constellations (97), of the calabash tree (113), and of animal appearance (128). In Part Four, the gods finally create man out of ground corn (163)—four androgynous beings with perfect knowledge and understanding. Alarmed that they have fashioned rivals for themselves, the gods repair the damage by making wives for these four, effectively turning them into males and clouding their sight and understanding. After this, the gods give them ways to make fire (172) and at last comes the first dawning of the sun, moon, and stars (181). Also there are explanations of the Mayan practice of blood sacrifice and of the first prostitutes (189). Part Five is essentially a folk history of tribal migrations and genealogies. This is followed by nearly 100 pages of notes, a long glossary, and an extensive bibliography.

162   Te Kanawa, Kiri, ret., *Land of the Long White Cloud: Maori Myths, Tales and Legends*, illus. Michael Foreman, Arcade, 1994 (hardcover), ISBN 1–55970–046–7, $16.95, 119 pp. Ages 7 up, grades 2 up.

Internationally acclaimed opera singer Dame Kiri Te Kanawa, the daughter of an Irish mother and a Maori father, retells in plain yet evocative style nineteen Maori (indigenous New Zealand) stories she remembers from her childhood. Five concern the trickster hero-god Maui, who, after an eventful birth, fishes up the New Zealand islands, tames the sun, and gives certain native birds their distinctive appearance (11, 17, 23, 117). Three stories describe heroic trips to the underworld: "Mataora and Niwareka in the Underworld" (67), "Putawai" (91), and "Hutu and Pare" 105), the first of which also tells of the origin of tattooing and death (67). Other tales tell of an earth-destroying flood, "Lake Te Anau" (85); the woman in the moon, "Rona and the Legend of the Moon" (101); and the legendary voyage of the hero Kupe, during which New Zealand was discovered, "Kupe's Discovery of Aotearoa" (27). The stories not listed here are folktales. Full-color impressionistic paintings point up significant scenes, contribute atmosphere, and make this an unusually attractive book. A glossary is a welcome help.

163 Thomas, Gwyn, and Kevin Crossley-Holland, rets., *Tales from the Mabinogion*, illus. Margaret Jones, Overlook Press, 1985 (hardcover), ISBN 0–87951–978–8, $14.95, 88 pp. Ages 10 up, grades 5 up.

These retellings of the first four branches or sections of the *Mabinogion* are ancient Celtic myths set mostly in what is now Wales. They are stories full of enchantments and strange prohibitions and wonders, describing a world where magic and the Other World are always near at hand. In the first branch, "Pwyll, Prince of Dyfed," Pwyll trades places with Arawn, king of the Other World, for a year. In this Celtic view, the Other World, or the world of the dead (10), is a happy place, very like the world of the living. This branch also includes stories of various enchantments, including that of Rhiannon, Pwyll's wife from the land of fairy, who is accused of killing her own baby and is punished with humiliation and physical degradation, until a boy who has mysteriously appeared and been adopted by a nearby lord, Teyrnon, is returned to Pwyll's court. Seeing his resemblance to Pwyll and learning his story, the king and his court accept him as Pwyll's son and heir and rename him Pryderi. The second branch, "Branwen, Daughter of Llyr," concerns the marriage of the heroic woman Branwen (30) to Matholwch, the king of Ireland; the misunderstandings between Matholwch and Bendigeidfran (called Bran in other versions), the king of the Island of Britain, caused by his half brother Efnisien; and the resulting war. Despite Bendigeidfran's great size and courage (30), only seven men from Wales escape, carrying with them Bendigeidfran's severed head, which remains able to talk and advise them for many years. The third branch concerns Bendigeidfran's brother Manawydan, who marries the widowed Rhiannon and rules over Dyfed, a kingdom in southwest Wales, until a spell is cast over his land (46) by a magician, Llwyd, to avenge an ancient wrong. Manawydan, his wife, her son, Pryderi, and Pryderi's wife, Cigfa, wander over England engaging in various crafts, finally returning to Dyfed, where Manawydan captures Llwyd's wife, changed into the shape of a mouse, and is able to force the magician to lift the spell. The fourth branch, "Math, Son of Mathonwy," is another story full of enchantments (64). The best-known part of this section concerns Lleu Llaw Gyffes, son of Math's niece, Arianrhod, and how her brother, the magician Gwydion, creates a wife of flowers for Lleu and names her Blodeuwedd. This lovely woman, however, is unfaithful to her husband with Gronw Pebyr, and eventually she is changed into an owl by Gwydion. Although greatly simplified from a direct translation, these stories are long and full of complications, too difficult for the very young, although the format of the book, large size and highly illustrated, might be deceptive. A pronouncing glossary of names and places is provided.

164 Thornhill, Jan, ret., *Crow & Fox and Other Animal Legends*, illus. Jan Thornhill, Simon & Schuster, 1993 (hardcover), ISBN 0–671–87428–4, $10.95, 32 pp. Ages 8–12, grades 3–7.

These nine legends, of which five are explanatory stories, come from a wide variety of cultures. "Tortoise and Crane" (10), which tells how the tortoise got his patterned shell, is from China. "Crane and Crow" (14), from Australia, explains both the crow's dark color and the crane's hoarse voice. The version of how the bear got its short tail, "Fox and Bear" (18), comes from Northern Europe. From Western Canada comes "Bear and Coyote" (20), about how neither animal could prevail in an argument about whether day or night should last all the time, with the result that we have both. "Mouse and Tapir" (28), about the beginning of banana trees, corn, and other growing foods, is from South America. All the stories are simply told, and each is accompanied by a full-page color illustration bordered by motifs from the culture of the tale. A map at the end locates the sources geographically.

165 Time-Life Books Inc., *The Book of Beginnings*, illus. John Sibbick et al., Time-Life Books Inc., 1986 (hardcover), ISBN 0–8094–5270–7, $19.95, 144 pp. Ages 11 up, grades 6 up.

One in a set of myths and legends by the editors of Time-Life for which folklore authority Tristram Potter Coffin of the University of Pennsylvania served as consultant, this book is the counterpart of *Fabled Lands* (no. 166) and shares with it characteristics of presentation and content. The illustrations are dramatic and opulent, sometimes mystical, sometimes sturdily realistic, sometimes small, simple, and scattered, most often full page, spread across two pages, or double paged. Some are stunning portraits, while many are up-front, close to the viewer's plane. The stories are divided into three broad groups, each category of which is introduced by a brief passage about that particular kind of myth: creation of the world and humans and such phenomena as earthquakes and volcanoes; stories about the heavenly bodies; and tales about the origin of animals, trees, and flowers. Several legends come from such lesser known cultures as Burma, Latvia, the Celebes, and Mongolia. Creation of the world stories are represented by "The Water-Mother" (9) from Finland, in which, waterborne, a mother goddess fashions aspects of the world and gives birth, after a long gestation, to Vainamoinen, the first farmer, poet, and storyteller. In the Chinese "A Terrestrial Paradise" (17), the god Pan Ku creates the universe, while humans are fashioned by the goddess Nu Kua. The story also explains the origin of work (fishing), music, fire, the alphabet, and the art of writing. The myth concludes with a mighty world-destroying flood, after which the goddess puts things to rights. "First Fruits" (24), a Burmese story, tells of the origin of humans and animals, which emerge from giant gourds. The Iroquois "Fall of the Sky Maiden" (26) presents a fascinating view of the upper world before following the adventures of a sky maiden who falls from there onto the back of a turtle, after which the present earth and animals come into being. The same story tells of the coming of evil into the world. From India is "The Primal Potter" (99), which tells of the origin of the world, people, the horse, and the dog. Very brief stories from Africa ("The Trembling Earth," 35), Celebes ("A Hog's Itch," 36), and Mongolia ("A Restless Frog," 37) give imaginative reasons for earthquakes; "Fiery Lairs of Gods and Monsters" (38) from Rome and Greece explain volcanoes. The Greek "Phaethon's Folly" (41) describes the sun as a blazing chariot that traverses the sky and also explains the deserts and dark races of Africa. A Korean story, "The Twin Luminants" (56), gives the origin of the sun and moon as twin children who flee to the sky to escape a ravening tiger. The Buddhist "Lunar Denizens" (70) describes the shadows on the moon's surface as the figure of a hare, and "Lindu's Astral Veil" (72) is the Estonian explanation of the Milky Way. "Hieroglyphics of the Heavens" (74) gives the ancient Greek account of the origin of several constellations, including within the larger story the hero tale of Perseus, who slew the snaky-locked Medusa. "Dark Dramas of the Firmament" (82) deals with the origin of the rainbow and the hurricane, from Burma (90) and thunderstorms from Africa (group unspecified, 94), as well as discusses views of the world of the dead from the Native American Naskapi (82) and Siberia (86). About animals are "The Braggart's Bungle" (100), a very short, amusing Mongolian story of the origin of the horse and the camel; "How the Elephant Lost its Wings" (105) from India; and "A Feathered Heraldry" (110), which contains a Latvian story about why woodpeckers have red heads and an Indian myth about why the peacock has eyes in its tail (111). About the origin of frogs is the Greek "A Muddy Metamorphosis" (114), while "The Garden of the Gods" (118), also Greek, is a composite account of the origin of several trees and flowers and the horse. "Bequest of a Golden Stranger" (124), from the Iroquois, tells how corn (maize) came to be. Concluding the book is a long, detailed, and suspenseful account of the Devil's unsuccessful attempt to scuttle Noah's ark, "Noah's Miraculous Voyage" (130), a Jewish extra-canonical story from Europe, which also explains the origin of the cat and of such pests as the mosquito and midges. A fine, lengthy bibliography at the end of the book indicates story sources and alternate references. Although a few errors have crept in, for example, Perseus is said to ride Pegasus although that winged steed belonged to the hero Bellerophon, this is an attractive book, filled with entertaining and insightful, if inconsistently told stories.

166 Time-Life Books Inc., *Fabled Lands*, illus. Michael Hague et al., Time-Life Books Inc., 1986 (hardcover), ISBN 0–8094–5254–5, $18.95, 143 pp. Ages 11 up, grades 6 up.

The consultant for the narratives in this handsome volume, one of a set on myths, legends, and folktales, was a leading authority on folklore, Tristram Potter Coffin. Varying in length from one to a dozen pages, some presented as individual texts without any illustrations and others profusely and provocatively illustrated, the stories revolve around visits to other worlds of ancient lore, to lands where fairy folk have been thought to dwell and worlds of departed souls, and the regulations and claims these otherworlds place on humans who go there and on the people who live in them and become involved with mortals. The storytelling varies from the plain and unadorned whose chief emphasis is on plot to longer, more elaborate, detailed narratives with extensive dialogue. The many dramatic, often mystical, and even ethereal largely deep-toned paintings support the atmosphere of the stories and project an elegant tone that recalls a long ago and far-off age. Of the various traditional materials reproduced, seven are hero tales. Of these, the Norse culture is represented by Hadding, Prince of Denmark, "A Man among Gods" (14), who in time of need is taken by Odin to Asgard and healed of grievous wounds; and by Thorkil, "Realms of Eternal Night" (49), who voyages far to the north and the world of the dead, which is presided over by a dreaded giant. Irish lore appears in the stories of Nera, "Journeys into Wonder" (20), who also travels into the world of the dead, or perhaps it is the Otherworld, where he is given visions that enable him to affect future events in his own world; Diarmuid, "Journeys into Wonder" (28), who goes Under-Wave where he becomes embroiled in a series of mysterious battles; and Oisin, son of Finn, who in "A Parting of Worlds" (105) falls in love with an otherworld woman, the daughter of the god of the sea, from whom he must inevitably part. Other fabled heroes are Owein, a knight of English Arthurian story, who battles on behalf of and becomes the consort of the mysterious woman who is "The Countess of the Fountain" (121), and the valiant Aeneas, who eventually founds the settlement from which Rome springs. In "Daring the Dark" (77), Aeneas descends to the realm of Hades with the help of the Sibyl, in an especially well-told story accompanied by a series of highly atmospheric black-and-white illustrations that graphically picture the ancient world of the dead. From Babylon in old Mesopotamia comes the quest of the goddess Ishtar to the Land of No Return to gain release for her dead lover, Tammuz (61), while the story of Hermod's attempt to bring the slain god Balder back from the Norse world of the dead is told in "Realms of Eternal Night" (65), another vividly told tale. The stories of Ishtar and Balder are also seasonal myths. All the stories are presented without formal introduction, and the reader is plunged almost immediately into the world of fairy and mystery. The narrative about Owein abruptly concludes the story portion of the book and is immediately followed by an excellent bibliography in which those books relied on for source material are starred. Although on occasion one wishes that the stories were presented more systematically, the book offers imaginative and entertaining insights into ancient thought about what lies beyond and exists concurrently with the natural world.

167   Troughton, Joanna, ret., *How Stories Came into the World*, illus. Joanna Troughton, Peter Bedrick, 1990 (hardcover), ISBN 0–216–92605–X, $13.95, unp. Ages 8–12, grades 3–7.

Embedded in the title story (1) are five other explanatory or origin myths from West Africa: two about animal behavior, "Why Hippo Lives in Water" (20) and "Rubber Girl" (14), telling why hares live in the grasslands; one about the origin of animals on earth (10); one explaining why the sun and the moon are located in the sky (4); and one about why thunder and lightning were banished from the land to the heavens (26). This last story ties in directly with the reason stories are spread throughout the world. Originally they were kept by Mouse, who wove them and kept them safe in her home, but when lightning broke her door, they all ran out and are still traveling up and down all over the earth. The illustrations, which look like brilliantly colored chalk or crayon, are semiprimitive and dominate the book with bold borders of African motifs; the text is confined to white inserts.

168   Troughton, Joanna, ret., *How the Seasons Came: A North American Indian Folk Tale*, illus. Joanna Troughton, Peter Bedrick, 1992 (hardcover), ISBN 0–87226–464–5, $14.95, unp. Ages 5 up, grades K up.

Although the subtitle indicates a generic Indian origin, a note points out that the myth comes from the Algonquin group in the northeastern United States. In a world that is always winter, the wolf's son is ill. To save his friend's child, the fisher leaps high enough to break a hole through the sky into a warm, sunny land above. There caged birds are hanging in the doorways of three lodges. Each sings a song of its season—spring, summer, and autumn. The fisher and the wolf, who has followed him, free the birds and direct them to fly through the hole to the land below, but the Thunderers, who have caged the birds, attack to avenge the loss. The wolf escapes but the fisher is hit by an arrow, and his body stretches across the hole, preventing the Thunderers from coming to earth or the birds from returning to the land in the sky. The song of each bird is printed separately as a poem dependent on the rhythm of repetition rather than regular meter or rhyme. Although the myth is of interest to all ages and the illustrations of the three birds are brilliant, most of the figures have a slightly cartoonish appearance which may relegate the book to a young audience.

169 Tyler, Royall, ed. and trans., *Japanese Tales*, Pantheon, 1987 (hardcover), ISBN 0–394–52190–0, $19.95, 340 pp. Ages 12 up, grades 7 up.

These 220 stories come primarily from medieval collections put together between 1100 and 1350, relating incidents that supposedly occurred between 850 and 1050. These are not folktales but what is known as "tale literature"— Buddhist stories, legends, and court anecdotes, most of them originating with the more privileged classes. Some are bawdy, some intensely pious. Many feature ghosts, demons, tengu, wizards, trickster foxes, dragons, and other creatures with supernatural power. The hero tales concern Buddhist holy men, including the Indian monk Baramon (33 and 34), Kobo Daishi (35), the Venerable Myoe (42), En no Gyoja or En the Ascetic (127), the monk Giei (141), and the Venerable Nichizo (144). Nichizo is credited with dying and visiting the Afterworld, where he has a long conference with Daijo Tenjin, the Celestial God of Fire and Thunder, and learns the reason for this god's rage. Returned to life, he is able to mitigate the god's fury with purification rites. The only woman of comparable stature is Princess Glory (46), who turns out to be the Immortal Lady of Mount Fuji and whose lover, distraught after her disappearance, leaps from a precipice and dies. His burning love kindles the fire that creates the smoke from the mountain. Since Buddhism in Japan adopted many local gods, the stories incorporate immortals both benign and wicked with fantastic powers of many sorts. Although the tales vary widely in style, some being brief, bare-bone skeletons, others lovingly embellished, they have in common a gentle or downplayed ending.

170 Ude, Wayne, ret., *Maybe I Will Do Something*, illus. Abigail Rorer, Houghton Mifflin, 1993 (hardcover), ISBN 0–395–65233–2, $14.95, 75 pp. Ages 9 up, grades 4 up.

Seven Coyote stories are retold in an entertaining and attractive way, illustrated by black-and-white engravings that skillfully bridge the gap between the man and the animal. All are trickster tales, appropriate to the central figure who is sometimes a con artist, sometimes a buffoon, sometimes a culture hero; a few focus more on his role as creator or at least originator: the beginning of the world and the origin of animals in "Coyote's Cave" (1) and the creation of people in "Coyote's Carving" (29). One explains why coyote is mostly active at night, "Coyote and Sun" (11); and one tells why the crow is black, "Coyote and the Crow Buffalo-Ranchers" (35). In the others, Coyote is both a trickster and a fool (21, 41, 53). No specific sources are given, but an Afterword tells that Ude grew up next door to the Belknap Reservation in northern Montana and went to school with Native American Indian children. He developed an interest he later pursued in college anthropology courses and as director of community action programs on the reservation. The stories are retold with perhaps more coherence and explanation of the Coyote character than collections of tales transcribed directly from oral sources, but the literary elements are not intrusive, and the book could serve as a good introduction to this literature.

171   Van Laan, Nancy, sel. and ret., *In a Circle Long Ago: A Treasury of Native Lore from North America*, illus. Lisa Desimini, Knopf, 1995 (hardcover), ISBN 0–679–85807–5, $20.00, 128 pp. Ages 4–11, grades PS–6.

This collection of twenty-five folktales, myths, hero tales, and a few poems is intended for elementary-aged readers but, since the language and tone are dignified and respectful, can have appeal as high interest, low vocabulary reading for older, less able readers. The book is attractively designed with illustrations that range from bold, bright, and dramatic to subtle and muted tones and black-and-white line drawings. They vary from double spreads to spots and attempt to capture the sense of the region as well as the spirit of the story. While most are told in simple prose that projects a storytelling tone, a few appear in the form of poetry. A colorful, easy-to-read map and an introduction about how Van Laan came to do the book and about the nature of the stories open the book, and short introductions head each of the eight sections, which contain stories from a particular geographical region. Information about the Native American groups, notes about the individual stories and their sources, which are mostly long out of print, and a short bibliography with additional, also respected, mostly older sources appear at the end of the book. "The Long Winter" (24) is a Slavey seasonal story about how several animals end a long period of cold weather by securing heat and also tells of a vast flood. The Creek "Mother Sun" (80) is a gently told poem about how light and human beings originated, and "The Earth on Turtle's Back" (95) is the Lenape account of the creation of the earth. Trickster tales include "Raven, the River Maker" (40) from the Tlingit, in which Raven steals water from greedy Wolf and in the process his feathers turn black; the Nez Perce "How

Beaver Stole Fire" (50), in which pine trees have possessed and not shared fire; "Coyote and the Blackbirds" (68; Tewa), which explains the origin of war; "A Tug of War" (82; Creek), which shows Rabbit tricking some tie snakes; "How Possum Got His Skinny Tail" (88), a Cherokee story, in which Rabbit changes Possum's elegantly bushy tail to the skinny one Possum has today, a story that also explains why the Possum plays dead; and "Rabbit and the Willow" (98), from the Seneca, in which Rabbit gains the appearance he has today and willows produce their cottonlike balls in the spring. In a myth involving the Great Maker of the Wishosk, "How Spider Caught Flies" (60), the Spider receives the ability to spin webs. This is an attractive, useful book.

172 Van Laan, Nancy, ret., *Rainbow Crow: A Lenape Tale*, illus. Beatriz Vidal, Knopf, 1989 (hardcover), ISBN 0–394–89577–0, $12.95, unp.; 1991 (paper), ISBN 0–679–81942–8, $5.99, unp. Ages 4–11, grades PS–6.

In the "long, long ago" before the "Two-Legged[s] walked the earth," so much snow falls that it begins to bury all the animals. Crow, who at that time had rainbow-hued feathers and a sweet singing voice, volunteers to fly to the Great Sky Spirit for help. The Spirit gives him fire with which to melt the snow, but before Crow can fly back to earth, the soot turns his feathers black and the ashes make his throat hoarse. The Great Sky Spirit rewards Crow's bravery and unselfishness with the gift of freedom, and the fire Crow has brought back becomes the "grandfather of all fires." The text has greater strength than the stylized, calendar-art pictures, in which the animals tend to be cute and cuddly and the snowscapes antiseptic. The occasional little verses are closer to doggerel than poetry and interject incongruous cuteness into a tale of true grit. The pictures of rainbow-hued Crow going to and returning from the Sky Spirit are more strongly composed as is that of the blackened Crow, whose feathers are palpably textured and subtly tinted. An interesting feature is the depiction of the Great Sky Spirit. Although he is exceedingly powerful, he is unable to stop the snow from falling and the weather from being cold. A note about sources opens the book.

173 Volkmer, Jane Anne, ret., *Song of the Chirimia: A Guatemalan Folktale*, illus. Jane Anne Volkmer, Carolrhoda Books, 1990 (hardcover), ISBN 0–87614–423–7, $18.75; (paper), ISBN 0–87614–592–6, $6.95, 40 pp. Ages 5–9, grades K–4.

In Spanish-English bilingual picture-book format, this book tells of the origin of the recorder-like flute of the Maya people. When Moonlight, daughter of Clear Sky the king, becomes despondent, her father desperately seeks advice from his counselors far and wide. The scribe who records marriages suggests that Moonlight is now a woman and might be happy again if she were married. Her father orders all single young men to present themselves for her choice. She shows no interest, however, until she hears Black Feather singing in a voice so sweet that it brings a smile to her lips. Still, she will not marry him until he can sing as sweetly as the birds. Granted three months to learn, Black Feather goes off by himself to the woods, where the Great Spirit gives him a hollow pipe with holes and shows him how to make music to rival any singing bird. The illustrations are boldly stylized in the manner of Maya sculpture with dark-skinned figures dressed in costumes of bright primary colors; the whole is decorated with designs using Guatemalan motifs.

174 Vuong, Lynette Dyer, ret., *Sky Legends of Vietnam*, illus. Vo-Dinh Mai, HarperCollins, 1993 (hardcover), ISBN 0–06–023000–2, $14.00, 128 pp. Ages 9 up, grades 4 up.

Of the six stories in this attractive book, four are explanatory myths: one of animal behavior, "Why the Rooster Crows at Sunrise" (1); two of constellations or star patterns, "The Weaver Fairy and the Buffalo Boy" (54) and "The Seven Weavers" (81); and one of the man in the moon, "The Miraculous Banyan Tree" (38). Another tells about the origin of the moon, "How the Moon Became Ivory" (9), and one concerns a heroic young hunter who becomes a corrupt king, "The Moon Fairy" (13). Although the term "fairy" usually occurs in folktale rather than in myth, Vuong points out in an interesting introduction that fairies are heavenly beings in the Taoist mythology in which these stories originate. An author's note at the end expands on the Taoist tradition. Also included is a translation of a Vietnamese song based on the Banyan Tree legend and a discussion of the Vietnamese language with a pronunciation glossary of names from the stories. Although printed in rather large type and not difficult, the legends are gracefully told, not in a simplified style. The dramatic full-page illustrations, one for each story, are unusual white scenes on black backgrounds.

Walker, Kath, ret. *See* Oodgeroo, no. 119.

175 Walker, Paul Robert, ret., *Big Men, Big Country: A Collection of American Tall Tales*, illus. James Bernardin, Harcourt, 1993 (hardcover), ISBN 0–15–207136–9, $16.95, 79 pp. Ages 8 up, grades 3 up.

Nine American work heroes are the subjects of these tall tales, all retold with appropriate humor and informal dialect. Most of them involve characters larger and stronger than life, although Gib Morgan (62), oilman, is more a trickster figure, distinguished by his intelligence and creativity. Some were actual people, like Davy Crockett (15), Big Mose (29), Ol' Gabe (42), whose real name was Jim Bridger, John Darling (37) of the Catskill Mountains, and probably John Henry (55), who dies after winning his contest with a steam drill. Others, like Pecos Bill (69), Paul Bunyan (49), and Old Stormalong (22), were undoubtedly fictional to start with, but all are the subject of outrageous hyperbole that grew in both oral and written versions. This book differs from several others that deal with the same material by following each tale with a short, factual section explaining what is known of the real character or the fictional beginnings and listing the main sources used by the reteller, a helpful addition. An annotated bibliography appears at the end. Illustrations include handsome, full-page color paintings, one for each story, and a few smaller black-and-white pencil drawings.

176 Walker, Paul Robert, ret., *Giants! Stories from Around the World*, illus. James Bernardin, Harcourt, 1995 (hardcover), ISBN 0–15–200883–7, $17.00, 73 pp. Ages 7–13, grades 2–8.

Strongly composed, deep-toned paintings that recall the work of Howard Pyle and his disciples introduce each of the forthrightly told stories about giants drawn from oral tradition from around the world. Of the seven stories, three are folktales; the others concern heroes from Hawaii, "Kana the Stretching Wonder" (17), in which the thin-as-a-rope hero rescues his kidnapped mother; from Greece, "The Cyclops" (35), whom Odysseus met and bested on his way home from Troy; from the Native Americans of the Pacific Northwest in a composite version from several groups, "Coyote and the Giant Sisters" (55), in which Coyote releases salmon whom the sisters have confined behind a dam; and from ancient Israel, "David and Goliath" (63), in which the youngest son of Jesse from Bethlehem assists King Saul by slaying the mighty champion of the Philistines. Concluding each tale is an italicized section containing information about sources and other commentary about the story. An author's note about the prevalence of giants in literature around the world and a fine bibliography complete the book, which, although intended for young and middle-grade readers, is dignified, respectful, and fast-moving enough to hold the attention of reluctant older readers.

177 Warner, Elizabeth, ret., *Heroes, Monsters and Other Worlds from Russian Mythology*, illus. Alexander Koshkin, Peter Bedrick, 1995 (hardcover), ISBN 0–87226–905–6, $22.50, 132 pp. Ages 10 up, grades 5 up.

This large collection from Russia is mostly folktale—stories of wizards and witches and of fabulous worlds of make believe—but among them are retellings of *bylinas*, hero tales of ancient Rus', most of them connected to the court of gentle Prince Vladimir in the tenth century. Among the heroes is Dunai (37) who, in seeking a bride for the prince, finds one for himself, then, in a fit of pride kills her and, in remorse, himself. Another of Vladimir's men is Sukhman (41) who saves the land from a great invading horde; when his report is not believed he rides away to the open steppe and dies of his wounds. In both these stories, rivers gush forth at the site of the hero's death. Three tales of the slaying of monsters are also connected with Vladimir's court: Dobrynya (69) kills a dragon; Alesha the priest's son (72) outwits and slays the crude, heathen creature Tugarin; and Il'ya of Murom (76) destroys a huge brigand called Nightingale. Sadko of Novgorod (44) is a poet and musician turned merchant who makes his fortune but nearly loses his life in his dealings with the Sea Tsar. A story of a later period is that of Mikula (21), whose strength and prowess so impress Prince Vol'ga that he is made a high official. Like other books in the Bedrick series, this is illustrated with both large, full-page or two-page paintings and, in this case, more interesting ink drawings, often in border strips, of figures and motifs from the stories. Each section is introduced with a discussion of the type, and the whole is preceded by an essay, "The Land of Old Russia." At the end is a list of sources and the Russian alphabet, its pronunciation, and its English transliteration.

178 West, John O., comp. and ed., *Mexican-American Folklore: Legends, Songs, Festivals, Proverbs, Crafts, Tales of Saints, of Revolutionaries, and More*, August House, 1988 (hardcover), ISBN 0–87483–060–5, $19.95, 315 pp.; 1988 (paper), ISBN 0–87484–059–1, $14.95, 242 pp. Ages 12 up, grades 7 up.

A very large compendium of miscellaneous folkloric material from the Mexican American community of the American Southwest, this books holds a wealth of entertaining literature, but almost nothing that can be termed mythological or heroic in the usual sense of these genres. Two Coyote stories appear that are of particular interest, however. The first, " 'Mana Sorra (Sister Fox) and 'Mano Coyote (Brother, or Br'er, Coyote)" (89), is a lively variant of the tar-baby story and presents Coyote as a fool several times over. In "Senor Coyote Acts as Judge" (91), on the other hand, Coyote displays great perspicacity in settling a dispute between a rattlesnake and a rabbit. The book resulted from fieldwork done by the compiler's students at the University of Texas at El Paso. A lengthy introduction, copious notes, tale-type and motif indexes, and a general index complete the book.

179 Williams, Sheron, ret., *And in the Beginning . . .* , illus. Robert Roth, Atheneum, 1992 (hardcover), ISBN 0–689–31650–X, $13.95, unp. Ages 5 up, grades K up.

In this black African account of the very beginning of things, Mahtmi, the Blessed One, having created the world in five days, ponders what likeness people shall have, sees his image in the primeval seas, and creates the first man of the "richest, darkest" earth from Kilimanjaro. He names the man Kwanza, which is Swahili for "the first one." The myth also explains the origin of prayer, loneliness, other races, parties, among other matters, and at the very end, the curly hair that many Africans have, curls fashioned by the Creator himself as a love token. Although the combination of colloquial and formal diction sometimes jars and the term "red" is unfortunately used to describe the first Native American Indian, the story has a gentle, warm, attractive humor and characterizes the Creator as fatherly and compassionate. Events are presented as though they were related in a story told by an aged grandmother to the writer. Powerful, expressive, often brooding watercolors make this picture-book version appropriate for all ages. The story is not attributed to any particular group of Africans.

Williamson, Roy A., ret. *See* Monroe, no. 113.

Wilson, Dorminster, ret. *See* Rohmer, no. 136.

180 Wisniewski, David, ret., *Sundiata: Lion King of Mali*, illus. David Wisniewski, Clarion, 1992 (hardcover), ISBN 0–395–61302–7, $16.95, unp. Ages 5 up, grades K up.

Vibrant, vigorous, three-dimensional cut-paper illustrations supplement the hero tale of Sundiata, the historical ruler of thirteenth-century C.E. Mali. In a powerfully and fluidly told narrative, with appropriate touches of archaic speech, a *griot* (African storyteller) relates how the greatest king of Mali was humbly born of a hunchbacked maiden. Lame, mute, and despised in his childhood, he eventually proves his right to the kingship by freeing his country from the tyranny of an evil sorcerer. A map of old Mali and an extensive note on the story's historicity and sources and the basis for the elements in the pictures complete this remarkably beautiful book. This is the most strikingly illustrated and the best short version of this important African hero tale available.

181 Wolkstein, Diane, ret., *Esther's Story*, illus. Juan Wijngaard, Morrow, 1996 (hardcover), ISBN 0–688–12128–6, $15.00, unp. Ages 7 up, grades 2 up.

Although Esther is generally regarded as a historical figure whether or not she actually lived, Wolkstein has combined with the Biblical material about the courageous ancient queen of Persia various "oral legends" from written and told sources. Fleshed out with Wolkstein's "own musings," the story of Esther's bravery in saving the lives of the Persian Jews in the face of great odds is presented as though in the form of diary entries written by Esther herself. They begin when Esther is eleven and continue through her betrothal and marriage to Ahasuerus, whose prime minister, Haman, treacherously issues an edict proscribing the Jews, through Esther's bravery in risking the king's anger to save them, then skips ahead to when she is seventy years of age and observes the Jews celebrating Purim, the festival that grew up as a tribute to her courage. Although the diary form seems awkward, the story is told with dignity, sympathy, and suspense, includes all the major details, and humanizes Esther believably. Overshadowing it are elegant full-color, full-page, framed paintings in deep, rich tones. They mostly catch the characters and create the sumptuous palace setting and only occasionally depict events. A pronunciation guide and note about sources appear at the beginning, and a short essay about Purim ends the book.

Wong, Hertha D., ed. *See* Elder, no. 43.

182 Wood, Audrey, ret., *The Rainbow Bridge*, illus. Robert Florczak, Harcourt, 1995 (hardcover), ISBN 0–15–265475–5, $16.00, unp. Ages 6 up, grades 1 up.

Magnificent, romantic, deep-toned, mostly double-spread paintings follow the dignified and respectful narrative of this Native American Indian creation myth from the Chumash of California and make it a book almost everyone can appreciate. The goddess Hutash, lonely in her island home off the coast of the North American continent, creates humans in her image. Sky Snake takes pity upon them and gives them fire so they can keep warm and cook their food. The story also explains how the Indians came to migrate to mainland California and how dolphins originated. An introductory note gives background on the legend and the people.

183 Yolen, Jane, ret., *Wings*, illus. Dennis Nolan, Harcourt, 1991 (hardcover), ISBN 0–15–297850–X, $15.95, unp. Ages 5 up, grades K up.

Elegant full-page and double-spread paintings with unusual perspectives and striking effects establish the setting of ancient Crete and augment the characterization and action of a familiar Greek and Graeco-Roman myth. On Crete, Daedalus, prototype craftsman and inventor, who designed the Labyrinth to confine the terrible Minotaur, fashions wings of feathers for himself and his young son, Icarus, in order to escape from the prison in which they have been confined by King Minos of Crete. Although repeatedly Daedalus warns him not to do so, Icarus flies too near the sun, whose heat melts the wax, and plunges to his death in the body of water now known as the Icarian Sea. Yolen skillfully combines various traditions with novelistic skill, adding details, creating suspense, and elaborating on motivations. An especially effective narrative feature, which emphasizes the story's theme of the price of hubris, or overweening pride, has the gods' reactions to the hero's actions noted in italicized, usually single-sentence summaries at appropriate intervals. Their emotions are shown in their faces, which appear mistily yet eloquently in the clouds above. The lyrical text employs distinctive images and turns of phrase, repetition, and an intimate storytelling voice. This is a handsome, sophisticated book with layered meanings in both text and pictures. An introduction gives sources, and a summary endnote adds details about the rest of Daedalus's life.

184 Young, Ed, ad., *Moon Mother: A Native American Creation Tale*, illus. Ed Young, HarperCollins, 1993 (hardcover), ISBN 0–06–021301–9, $15.00, 40 pp. Ages 8 up, grades 3 up.

A spirit person, coming upon the beautiful earth, decides to live here, but is lonesome. First he makes the animals, then, still longing for companionship, makes images of himself, warms them, and brings them to life, creating the first men. After living with them a long time he discovers a woman spirit person who also has come from the sky to live on earth. He joins her, and the men miss him. When they go seeking him, they find only a newborn girl baby, left for them when the woman spirit returned to the sky as the moon. The chief cares for the baby until she grows up, then takes her for his wife and initiates the human race. Although in oversize format with a minimum of words, the myth is retold seriously, and the beautiful illustrations are highly impressionistic, making the book more suitable for children older than the preschool to grade three audience for which it is marketed. In particular, the painting of a falling newborn silhouetted against the sky, still clearly revealing its umbilical cord, accompanied by the words, "... when a baby is born, he cries, because he has left the moon land and has lost his moon mother," is

sophisticated in both idea and visual impact, less disturbing and more mean-
ingful to older readers. No specific Native American group is listed as its
source.

Young, Judy Dockrey, coll., ed., and ret. *See* Young, Richard Alan,
nos. 185, 186, 187, and 188.

185 Young, Richard Alan, and Judy Dockrey Young, colls., eds., and
rets., *African-American Folktales for Young Readers*, illus. Kenneth Harris,
August House, 1993 (hardcover), ISBN 0–87483–308–6, $18.95;
(paper), ISBN 0–87483–309–4, $12.95, 176 pp. Ages 9 up, grades 4
up.

These thirty African-American stories can be classified into two main types:
folktales and hero tales. The latter encompass two kinds of heroes: the animal
tricksters Anansi the spider, Brother Rabbit, and Br'er Rabbit and the human
heroes John Henry (124), Annie Christmas (130), and Casey Jones, who was
white but was aided significantly by two African Americans (133). The trickster
tales are rollicking good narratives, vigorously told and filled with action and
dialogue so that they move quickly and colorfully. The human hero stories,
on the other hand, read more like the summaries one might find in a reference
book and include in undramatized narrative only the most important details
about the figures. Featuring Anansi are the following tales, all of which show
him as a fool: "Anansi Tries to Steal All the Wisdom in the World" (76), "Why
Anansi Has a Narrow Waist" (78), "Anansi and Turtle" (81), "Fling-A-Mile"
(87), and "Anansi and Candlefly" (93). The rabbit tales are all in the trickster
mode. About Brother Rabbit are "Brother Lion and Brother Man" (59), "Why
Brother Alligator Has a Rough Back" (103), "The Cabbage Inspector" (163),
and "Brother Possum and Brother Snake" (170). Br'er Rabbit figures in "How
Br'er Rabbit Outsmarted the Frogs" (66). The stories are preceded by material
introducing the collection, by introductions to the several sections, and by a
map; followed by notes about the tellers; and decorated with lively black-and-
white sketches that depict characters and situations. The stories are not only
good fun to read aloud or silently but also excellent sources for storytelling.

186 Young, Richard Alan, and Judy Dockrey Young, colls. and eds.,
Outlaw Tales: Legends, Myths, and Folklore from America's Middle Border,
August House, 1992 (paper), ISBN 0–87483–195–4, $10.95, 224 pp.
Ages 14 up, grades 9 up.

Folklorists and storytellers at Silver Dollar City near Branson, Missouri,
and natives of the area about which they write, the Youngs have compiled a

highly engaging collection of tales about historical outlaws and bad men and women of the American Middle Border (from Missouri to the Rockies) from about 1865 to the early 1900s. The stories are given in the edited words of the informants, many of whom recounted their recollections for the Works Progress Administration's (WPA) Writers' Project, while others were heard by the Youngs or gained from other written or oral sources, all of which are noted in the text or in the copious endnotes. The comments on the stories are also highly engaging and together with the tales make up a seamless whole of wonderfully entertaining reading. Here are stories of desperadoes, barflies, thieves, thugs, soldiers gone bad, hanging judges, and sundry villains, sometimes feared, occasionally loved, always the nucleus of yarns. Among them are the rousing, embroidered stories of Belle Starr (Myra Maybelle Shirley), "Belle and the Stuff of Legends" (21), "Belle at Devil's Den" (83), and "Belle at Marble Cave" (148); of Wild Bill Hickok (James Butler Hickok), "Wild Bill: The 'Prince of Pistoleers' " (45); of the James boys, "Jesse and Frank" (133); and of Calamity Jane (Martha Jane Cannary), "Angel of Mercy—II" (164), and "Angel of Mercy—III" (190), and "Calamity Jane Explains Her Name" (202). Mentioned variously also are such figures as the Daltons, the Youngers, John Wesley Hardin, Wyatt Earp, and many others less well known. Fine introductory material and endnotes are included.

187   Young, Richard, and Judy Dockrey Young, colls. and eds., *Race with Buffalo and Other Native American Stories for Young Readers*, illus. Wendell E. Hall, August House, 1994 (hardcover), ISBN 0–87483–343–4, $19.95, 172 pp. Ages 9 up, grades 4 up.

These thirty-one stories from Native American groups were all collected from oral retellings and, in most cases, further checked in printed or unpublished written compilations; each one is carefully documented in notes at the end. A few are folktales, but most have mythic elements or are hero tales of larger-than-life tricksters or monster slayers. A creation of the world story comes from the Crow (43). Explanatory stories of animal appearance come from the Cherokee (bats and flying squirrels, 105; possum, 143), the Seneca (bear, 111), the Iroquois (buzzard, 121; raccoon, 138), and the Kathlamet (birds' colors, 128). Explanatory stories of animal behavior come from the Cheyenne (buffalo's grazing, 47), the Cherokee (the wide distribution of animals, 117; the way possums play dead, 143), the Northern Pueblo (the bite of the mosquito, 85; coyote's baying at the moon, 114), and the Seneca (the way bear hangs his head, 91). Stories of the formation of constellations and star patterns come from the Kiowa (54), the Caddo (59), the Cherokee (108), and the Seneca (125). Fabulous animals appear in a number of stories, in particular those of the Flint Bird from the Acoma Pueblo (79) and the Bloodsucker from the Northern Pueblo people (85). A hero who slays monsters is Long Hair from the Acoma Pueblo (79); one who wins out through trickery is Skunnee Wundee from the Seneca (70). A trickster with supernatural powers is Kuloskap in a story from the Micmac (135). From the Choctaw comes "Grandmother Spider Steals the Fire" (37); from the Caddo is "The Twin Brothers" (23) about the origin of thunder and lightning; and from the Northern Pueblo people is "Blue Corn Maiden and the Coming of Winter" (51), explaining the change of seasons. A touching view of the world of the dead appears in "The Girl Who Married a Ghost" (155) from the Chinook. All are retold in a simple, unadorned storytelling style. Illustrations are attractive line drawings of scenes from the tales and end-pieces with Indian motifs. Despite some errors in editing (heroes misspelled in running heads, lie-lay confusions), this is a good collection, respectful and wide ranging. A glossary is included.

188 Young, Richard Alan, and Judy Dockrey Young, colls. and rets., *Stories from the Days of Christopher Columbus: A Multicultural Collection for Young Readers*, August House, 1992 (hardcover), ISBN 0–87483–199–7, $17.95; (paper), ISBN 0–87483–198–9, $8.95, 160 pp. Ages 6–14, grades 1–9.

The unifying theme of this collection, which consists mostly of folktales but also includes a few fables from Aesop, legends, and myths, is time: all the twenty-one tales were told during the late fifteenth century in Europe or by Native American Indians of the New World. The stories are presented in various imagined contexts, for example, as if told by Columbus's sailors aboard ship; the style is unadorned, direct, and respectful; pronunciations of difficult names are given in parentheses after the words; and conversation appears frequently. Simple line drawings add interest (the illustrator is not identified), introductions precede each section and individual stories, and notes on the stories and a glossary explaining terms and foreign and unfamiliar words concludes the book. "In the Taino Village" (33) is a simplified version of the Native American Taino creation story of the emergence type. "In the Aztec Palace: The Smoking Mountain" (55) tells how the Feathered Serpent god, Quetzalcoatl, enables two lovers to remain together by changing them into the two mountains that dominate the landscape near Mexico City. "The Tree of Life" (93) explains how the Carib Indians obtained various food plants from a tree established by the god Makunaima. "The Chests of Sand" (79) and "El Cid and the Lion" (88) are two episodes from the Spanish romance about the historical nobleman. Specific sources, that is, the translations from which the retellings were made, are not given. Although this is not an especially exciting collection, the tellings usefully give a good sample of oral literature of the period for young readers and listeners.

Zeitlin, Steve, ret. *See* Jaffe, no. 88.

189 Zeman, Ludmila, ret., *Gilgamesh the King*, illus. Ludmila Zeman, Tundra, 1992 (hardcover), ISBN 0–88776–283–2, $19.95, 24 pp. Ages 8 up, grades 3 up.

Lavishly illustrated in a style using motifs and designs from ancient Sumerian artifacts, this picture-book version of the Gilgamesh story tells only the first section of what is considered the earliest of all hero tales. Gilgamesh, part man and part god, has incredible strength and becomes a despotic ruler of Uruk, until the sun god answers the pleas of the oppressed people by creating a rival for him, Enkidu, who grows up among the animals of the forest. When word of this wild man reaches Gilgamesh, he sends beautiful Shamat to lure him to Uruk. There on the city wall they engage in a hand-to-hand combat that lasts for hours, until Gilgamesh slips and Enkidu grabs his hand to save him. Thereupon, they become close friends, and Gilgamesh reforms his harsh rule so that the people of Uruk thrive. The story is retold in simple sentences, not inappropriate for a translation from the clay tablets on which the earliest version is found. It is, however, somewhat cleaned up, probably in deference to the picture-book audience. Shamat, for instance, is simply a beauty who entices Enkidu with the music of her harp and her lovely voice, not a temple prostitute, as she is usually described. Zeman's second book dealing with the adventures of Gilgamesh is *The Revenge of Ishtar* (Tundra, 1995), in which Enkidu and Gilgamesh defeat the monster Humbaba, which has attacked the city and killed Shamat. When Gilgamesh spurns the goddess Ishtar, she rides the Bull of Heaven to Uruk, and together the friends defeat it. In revenge, Ishtar sends a wasting illness to kill Enkidu. In the third book of the series, *The Journey to the Underworld* (Tundra, 1996), Gilgamesh sets off to seek the secret of immortality, but he cannot bring it back from the underworld to his people.

Index of Stories by Types

TABLE OF CONTENTS OF TYPES

MYTHS

1. Origin of Humans
2. Origin of the World
3. Origin of the World and Humans
4. Floods and Similar Destructions
5. End of the World (Eschatological Stories)
6. Otherworlds and the World of the Dead
7. Seasons, Agriculture, and Fertility
8. Origin of Necessities and Realities

    A. Fire and Light

    B. Sun, Moon, Stars, Rainbows, Heavenly Phenomena, and Forces of Nature

    C. Geographical Features and Natural Phenomena

    D. Social Customs, Beliefs, Ceremonies, and Rituals

    E. Nations, Races, Cities, and States

    F. Animals

    G. Animal Appearance

    H. Animal Behavior

    I. Food and Drink

    J. Plants and Flowers

    K. Wisdom and Knowledge

    L. Literature, Stories, and Writing

    M. Music and Musical Instruments

    N. Arts and Crafts

O. Weapons and Work Implements

P. Troubles, Diseases, Hope, and the Like

Q. Death and Old Age

9. Gods' Adventures

TYPES THAT INCLUDE BOTH MYTHS AND HERO TALES

10. Goddesses and Important Female Figures

11. Searches and Quests

12. Tricksters: Gods, Humans, and Animals

HERO TALES

13. Fools and Buffoons

14. Bad Men and Outlaws

15. Lawmen and Judges

16. Holy Men, Teachers, Prophets, Spiritual Leaders, Lawgivers, and Wise Persons

17. Kings, Queens, and Rulers

18. Strong Men, Strong Women, and Monster Slayers

19. Warriors and Fighters

20. Figures of Romance and Chivalry

21. Voyagers and Adventurers

22. Poets, Bards, Singers, Storytellers, and Dancers

23. Magicians, Enchanters, and Enchanted Figures

24. Inventors

25. Athletes

26. Environmental Benefactors and Friends of Animals

27. Macho Lovers

28. Tall Tales

LIST OF STORIES BY TYPES

(Numerals refer to the book entries in the Guide. The culture is given in parentheses if it is not indicated in the title.)

MYTHS

1. Origin of Humans

"The Origin of Man" (India), 12

"Fox and the Parakeet Women" (Native American, Chorote), 13

"What Happened When Armadillo Dug a Hole in the Sky" (Native American, Cayapo), 13

"The Emergence of Ancestors" (Native American, Aztec), 18

"The Seeds of Humanity" (Native American, Guaymi), 18

"Atrahasis" (Mesopotamia), 40

"Coyote Makes a Texas Cowboy" (Native American), 44

"The Taming of Pecos Bill's Gal Sue" (United States), 44

"Men, Monkeys, and Mukulu" (Sub-Saharan Africa), 51

"Creation of Humankind" (Cuba), 56

"Oddudua and Oloddumare" (Cuba), 56

"The God Brings Fire to Man" (Greece), 67

"Khnum and the Theban Theogony" (Egypt), 71

"The Creation of People" (Native American, Crow), 82

"Creation of the Whites" (Native American, Yuchi), 96

"Mother Sun" (Native American, Yuchi), 96

"Origin of Races" (Native American, Seminole), 96

"Firstman" (Native American, Wampanoag), 105

"In the Beginning Pandora's Box" (Greece), 108

And the Earth Trembled: The Creation of Adam and Eve (Islam), 120

Iblis (Islam), 121

"The Gift of Fire" (Greece), 130

"Make Me a Man!" (Sub-Saharan Africa), 130

"The Plumed Serpent" (Native American, Aztec), 130

"The Sky World" (Indonesia), 130

"First People" (Inuit, Eskimo), 132

"Wolves" (Native American, Pueblo), 132

"The Beginning of History" (Native American, Ticuna, Brazil), 137

"The Creation of Human Beings: The Ages of Man" (Greece), 138

"The Flood Cycle" (Greece), 138

"Changing Woman" (Native American, Apache), 149

"Pandora: The First Woman?" (Greece), 155

"Bones in the Basket" (Native American, Modoc), 158

"Breath on the Mirror" (Native American, Maya), 160

"Part One (creation of humans)" (Native American, Maya), 161

"Part Four (creation of humans)" (Native American, Maya), 161

"First Fruits" (Burma), 165

"Coyote's Carving" (Native American), 170

"Mother Sun" (Native American, Creek), 171

And in the Beginning . . . (Sub-Saharan Africa), 179

The Rainbow Bridge (Native American, Chumash), 182

Moon Mother: A Native American Creation Tale, 184
"In the Taino Village" (Native American, Taino), 188

2. Origin of the World

"The Woman Who Fell from the Sky" (Native American, Mohawk), 3
"The Order of Creation" (Arabia), 4
"The Birth and Marriage of Siva" (India), 12
"How Lijaba Created the World" (India), 12
"Moon Was Tired of Walking on Air" (Native American, Chorote), 13
"In the Beginning" (Native American, Apache), 19
"In the Beginning" (Native American, Zuni), 19
"The Mind of *Wakonda*" (Native American, Winnebago), 19
"The Woman Who Fell from the Sky" (Native American, Iroquois), 19
"Creation by Thought" (Native American, Witoto, Colombia), 20
"Creation of the Self" (Native American, Mbya Guarani, Paraguay), 20
"The Creation" (Native American, Iroquois), 25
"The Earth on Turtle's Back" (Native American, Onondaga), 27
"Tunka-shila, Grandfather Rock" (Native American, Lakota), 27
"The Epic of Creation" (Mesopotamia), 40
"Theogony of Dunnu" (Mesopotamia), 40
"In the Beginning . . ." (Australian Aboriginal), 43
"*Kalevala*: The Mother of Water" (Finland), 43
"Baiame, the Great Spirit" (Australian Aboriginal), 51
"The Churning of the Sea of Milk" (Hindu), 51
"The Earth Diver" (Native American, Cheyenne), 51
"How Shiva Got His Blue Throat" (Hindu), 51
"Izanagi and Izanami" (Shinto), 51
"Old Spider and the Giant Clamshell" (Polynesia), 51
"Yin, Yang, and the Cosmic Egg" (China), 51
Owl Eyes (Native American, Mohawk), 52
"Creation of the Ground" (Cuba), 56
"Creation of the World" (Cuba), 56
"In the Beginning . . ." (Sub-Saharan Africa, Fon, Dahomey), 58
"The Coming of All Things" (Greece), 67
"Moon and Sun" (Sub-Saharan Africa, Fon, Dahomey), 67
"Separation of Earth and Sky" (India), 67
"Spider Ananse Finds *Something*" (Sub-Saharan Africa, Krachi, Togo), 67
"The Woman Who Fell from the Sky" (Native American, Huron), 67
"Michabo and the Flood" (Native American, Algonquin), 68
"Sif's Hair" (Norse), 70

"The Ogdoad of Hermopolis" (Egypt), 71

"Ptah of Memphis" (Egypt), 71

"The Sun God of Heliopolis" (Egypt), 71

"Indian Legend of the Deluge" (Native American, Ojibwa), 76

"Manabozho" (Native American, Ojibwa), 76

"Nenebojo and His Brother" (Native American, Ojibwa), 76

"Nenebuc, the Transformer" (Native American, Ojibwa), 76

"The 'Origin Legend' (King Version)" (Native American, Ojibwa), 76

"The Story of Nana-Bo-Zhoo and His Brother" (Native American, Ojibwa), 76

"Winabijou Looks for the Wolf" (Native American, Ojibwa), 76

"The Beginning of Earth" (Inuit), 82

"The Moon and the Heavenly Nectar" (India), 89

"Earth-Diver" (Native American, Yuchi), 96

All of You Was Singing (Native American, Aztec), 102

"Sky Woman and the Twins" (Native American, Wampanoag), 105

"The Song of Creation" (Native American, Wampanoag), 105

"The Myth of Tlaltecuhtli" (Native American, Aztec), 106

"First Creator and Lone Man" (Native American, Mandan), 130

"Vainamoinen" (Finland), 130

"The Creation, Death, and Rebirth of the Universe, Gods, and Human Beings" (Norse), 138

"The Creation of the Titans and the Gods" (Greece), 138

"The Creation of the Universe, Gods, and Japan," 138

"The Story of the Mountain Spirits" (Native American, Apache), 149

"Battles: Mesopotamia," 150

"The Birth of Japan," 150

"Creating the World: Egypt," 150

"Creating the World: North America" (Native American, Onondaga), 150

"Creating the World: Scandinavia" (Norse), 150

"Rangi and Papa" (New Zealand, Maori), 150

"How the World Began: The Greek Version," 155

"From Darkness to Light" (Native American, Mandan), 158

"Part One (creation of the world)" (Native American, Maya), 161

"Fall of the Sky Maiden" (Native American, Iroquois), 165

"The Water-Mother" (Finland), 165

"Coyote's Cave" (Native American), 170

"The Earth on Turtle's Back" (Native American, Lenape), 171

"Old Man at the Beginning" (Native American, Crow), 187

3. Origin of the World and Humans

"The Beginning and the End of the World" (Native American, Okanagan), 3

The Origin of Life on Earth: An African Creation Myth (Sub-Saharan Africa), 5

"The Garden of Eden" (ancient Israel), 9

"Creation Tales" (Eskimo), 19

"Creation Tales" (Native American, Nunivak), 19

"Elder Brother" (Native American, Pima), 19

"The House of Myths" (Native American, Kwakiutl), 19

"Toads and Frogs" (Native American, Gabrielino/Luiseno), 19

"The *Walam Olum*" (Native American, Delaware), 19

"Alone in the Darkness" (Native American, Tariana, Brazil), 20

"Myths of the Kogi" (Native American, Colombia), 20

"The Twin Myth" (Native American, Waiwai, Guiana), 20

"Wirakocha" (Native American, Inca, Peru), 20

The Woman Who Fell from the Sky: The Iroquois Story of Creation (Native American), 22

"The Coming of Gluscabi" (Native American, Abenaki), 27

"Four Worlds: The Dine Story of Creation," (Native American, Navajo), 27

"Formation of the Earth" (Sub-Saharan Africa, Yoruba, Brazil, Cuba, Haiti), 42

"The Creation" (Native American, Mohawk), 43

"The Emergence" (Native American, Navajo), 43

"How Moon Fathered the World" (Sub-Saharan Africa, Wakaranga, Zimbabwe), 43

"Tangaroa, Maker of All Things" (Tahiti), 43

"Inca Ancestors" (Native American), 51

"In the Beginning" (ancient Israel), 51

"In the Beginning" (Sub-Saharan Africa, Bushman), 57

"In the Beginning" (Sub-Saharan Africa, Swazi), 57

"In the Beginning . . ." (Sub-Saharan Africa, Pygmy), 58

Cry of the Benu Bird: An Egyptian Creation Story, 61

"The Angry Gods" (Tahiti), 67

"Bandicoots Come from His Body" (Australian Aboriginal), 67

"Bursting from the Hen's Egg" (China), 67

"An Endless Sea of Mud" (Sub-Saharan Africa, Kono, Guinea), 67

"Finding Night" (Melanesia), 67

"First Man Becomes the Devil" (Russian Altaic), 67

"First Man, First Woman" (ancient Israel), 67

"Four Creations to Make a Man" (Native American, Maya), 67

"The Frost Giant" (Norse), 67

"In the Beginning" (ancient Israel), 67

"Man Copies God" (Sub-Saharan Africa, Lozi, Zambia), 67

"Marduk, God of Gods" (Mesopotamia), 67

"Owner of the Sky" (Sub-Saharan Africa, Yoruba, Nigeria), 67

"The Pea-Pod Man" (Inuit, Eskimo), 67

"The Sun-God and the Dragon" (Egypt), 67

"Sun, Life, Wind, and Death" (Micronesia), 67

"Traveling to Form the World" (Native American, Blackfeet), 67

"Turtle Dives to the Bottom of the Sea" (Native American, Maidu), 67

"Tirawa Creates the People" (Native American, Pawnee), 68

The Creation (ancient Israel), 90

"Introduction" (Native American, Ojibway), 91

Why There Is No Arguing in Heaven: A Mayan Myth (Native American), 99

"Maushop Builds Turtle Island" (Native American, Wampanoag), 105

"The Birth of All of Heaven and Earth" (Native American, Maya), 106

"The Creation of the World" (Native American, Aztec), 106

"The Mixtec Creation Myth" (Native American), 106

"Myths of the Suns and the Toltec-Chichimec Origins of the Mexica People" (Native American), 106

"The Creation" (ancient Israel), 114

"The Garden of Eden" (ancient Israel), 114

"The Beginning of Life" (Australian Aboriginal), 119

"Creation: The Nine Worlds" (Norse), 124

"Beginnings, Middles and Ends" (Norse), 128

"Children of the Sun God" (Native American, Navajo), 130

"The Cosmic Egg" (China), 130

"The Dreamtime" (Australian Aboriginal), 130

"An Earthly Paradise" (Iran), 130

"First Things" (Egypt), 130

"The Floating World" (Japan), 130

"Made from Mud" (Siberia), 130

"The Old Man of the Ancients" (Native American, Modoc), 130

"Out of the Ice" (Norse), 130

"The Sweat of His Brow" (Serbia), 130

"Other Animals" (Native American, Cherokee), 132

"Wolf Star" (Native American, Pawnee), 132

"Iyadola's Babies" (Sub-Saharan Africa), 133

"The Creation, Death, and Rebirth of the Universe, Gods, and Human Beings" (Norse), 138

"The Creation of Ireland: The Ages of the World" (Ireland/Scotland), 138

"The Creation of the Navajo People: The Five Worlds" (Native American), 138

"The Creation of the Universe" (Native American, Toltec/Aztec, Mexico), 138

"The Creation of the Universe and Human Beings" (China), 138

"The Creation of the Universe and Human Beings" (Native American, Maya, Guatemala), 138

"The Creation of the Universe and Human Beings" (Native American, Tiahuanaco, pre-Inca, Peru), 138

"The Creation of the Universe, Gods, and Human Beings" (Mesopotamia), 138

"The Creation of the Universe, Ife, and Human Beings" (Sub-Saharan Africa, Yoruba, Nigeria), 138

"Creating the World: Guatemala" (Native American, Maya), 150

"Ta'aroa" (Tahiti), 150

"Before All Things Began" (Native American, Zuni), 158

"Big Raven Creates the World" (Siberia, Chuckchee), 158

"Creation" (Native American, Mohawk), 158

"A Place to Have Children" (Native American, Osage), 158

"The Primal Potter" (India), 165

"A Terrestrial Paradise" (China), 165

And in the Beginning . . . (Sub-Saharan Africa), 179

4. Floods and Similar Destructions

Llama and the Great Flood: A Folktale from Peru (Native American, Quechua), 2

"Myths and Legends of the Extinct Arabs," 4

"The Queen Priestess and the Dyke of Ma'rib" (Arabia), 4

"The Vengeance of God" (Arabia), 4

"The Flood" (ancient Israel), 9

"When Orekeke Wrestled Tornado" (Native American, Teheulces), 13

The Tree That Rains: The Flood Myth of the Huichol Indians of Mexico, 15

"The Flood Myth" (Native American, Mixe), 18

"The Loss of the Ancients" (Native American, Tarahumara), 18

"The Tree and the Flood" (Native American, Cabecar), 18

"Elder Brother" (Native American, Pima), 19

"Mink" (Native American, Kwakiutl), 19

"The *Walam Olum*" (Native American, Delaware), 19

"Cold" (Native American, Toba, Argentina), 20

"Darkness" (Native American, Toba, Argentina), 20

"Fire" (Native American, Mataco, Argentina), 20

"Tokwah, Lord of the Dead" (Native American, Mataco, Argentina), 20

"Grand Canyon" (Native American, Hopi), 24

"Atrahasis" (Mesopotamia), 40

"The Epic of Gilgamesh" (Mesopotamia), 40

"Halibu the Hunter" (Mongolia), 43

"Ea, Ziusdra, and the Great Flood" (Mesopotamia), 51

"Fire, Ice, and Flood" (Native American, Aztec), 51

"Fire, Ice, and Flood" (Native American, Hopi), 51

"How the Fish Saved Manu" (Hindu), 51

"The Lie and Evil Enter the Ark" (Jewish), 51

"Olokun" (Cuba), 56

"In the Beginning . . ." (Sub-Saharan Africa, Pygmy), 58

"Four Creations to Make a Man" (Native American, Maya), 67

"Michabo and the Flood" (Native American, Algonquin), 68

"The Great Flood" (Native American, Navajo), 74

"Indian Legend of the Deluge" (Native American, Ojibwa), 76

"Manabozho" (Native American, Ojibwa), 76

"Nenebojo and His Brother" (Native American, Ojibwa), 76

"Nenebuc, the Transformer" (Native American, Ojibwa), 76

"The 'Origin Legend' (King Version)" (Native American, Ojibwa), 76

"The Story of Nana-Bo-Zhoo and His Brother" (Native American, Ojibwa), 76

"Winabijou Looks for the Wolf" (Native American, Ojibwa), 76

The Epic of Gilgamesh (Mesopotamia), 86

"Introduction" (Native American, Ojibway), 91

"Muzzu-Kummik-Quae: Mother Earth" (Native American, Ojibway), 91

"The Flood" (Native American, Alabama), 96

"The Flood" (Native American, Caddo), 96

"The Great Migration and Old Man Winter" (Native American, Wampanoag), 105

"The Birth of All of Heaven and Earth" (Native American, Maya), 106

"The Creation of the World" (Native American, Maya), 106

"The Mixtec Creation Myth" (Native American), 106

"Myths of the Suns and the Toltec-Chichimec Origins of the Mexica People" (Native American), 106

"The Lord Speaks to Noah" (ancient Israel), 114

"Noah and the Ark" (ancient Israel), 114

"Sodom and Gomorrah" (ancient Israel), 114

"The Mysterious Visitors: The Story of Baucis and Philemon" (Graeco-Roman), 123

"Beginnings, Middles and Ends" (Norse), 128

"Atlantis" (Greece), 130

"Earth-maker and Coyote" (Native American, Maidu), 130

"Gilgamesh" (Mesopotamia), 130

"The Great Flood" (Serbia), 130

"Water, Moon, and Sun" (Sub-Saharan Africa, Nigeria), 133

"The Creation, Death, and Rebirth of the Universe" (India), 138

"The Creation of Human Beings: The Ages of Man" (Greece), 138

"The Creation of Ireland: The Ages of the World" (Ireland/Scotland), 138

"The Creation of the Navajo People: The Five Worlds" (Native American), 138

"The Creation of the Universe" (Native American, Toltec/Aztec, Mexico), 138

"The Creation of the Universe and Human Beings" (Native American, Maya, Guatemala), 138

"The Creation of the Universe and Human Beings" (Native American, Tiahuanaco, pre-Inca, Peru), 138

"The Creation of the Universe, Ife, and Human Beings" (Sub-Saharan Africa, Yoruba, Nigeria), 138

"The Flood Cycle" (Greece), 138

"*Gilgamesh*" (Mesopotamia), 138

"The Wonderful Head" (Ireland), 139

"Battles: North America" (Native American, Mandan), 150

"The Forces of Nature: Central America" (Native American, Maya), 150

"Matsya" (Hindu), 150

"The Raft" (Native American, Cree), 158

"Part One (floods and destruction)" (Native American, Maya), 161

"Lake Te Anau" (New Zealand, Maori), 162

"Noah's Miraculous Voyage" (Jewish), 165

"A Terrestrial Paradise" (China), 165

"The Long Winter" (Native American, Slavey), 171

5. End of the World (Eschatological Stories)

"The Beginning and the End of the World" (Native American, Okanagan), 3

"Why the World Doesn't End" (Native American, Lenape), 21

"In the Beginning . . ." (Sub-Saharan Africa, Fon, Dahomey), 58

"Ragnarok" (Norse), 70

"Twilight of the Gods" (Norse), 124

"Beginnings, Middles and Ends" (Norse), 128

"Atlantis" (Greece), 130

"First Things" (Egypt), 130

"Ragnarok" (Norse), 130

"The Rainbow Serpent" (Sub-Saharan Africa, Fon), 130

"The Purifying Stream" (Iran), 130

"The Death of Baldur" (Norse), 133

"The Creation, Death, and Rebirth of the Universe" (India), 138

"The Creation, Death, and Rebirth of the Universe, Gods, and Human Beings" (Norse), 138

"Battles: Scandinavia" (Norse), 150

"How the World Will End" (Native American, Cheyenne), 159

6. Otherworlds and the World of the Dead

"The Rock of Khlop on Satawal" (Micronesia), 8

"The Ancestors Are All around Us" (Native American, Selkam), 13

"Ghosts and Souls" (Native American, Tapirape), 13

"The Dead Wife" (Native American, Miskito), 18

"Coyote as Orpheus" (Native American, Chinook), 19

"The Story of Odysseus" (Greece), 26

"The Descent of Ishtar to the Underworld" (Mesopotamia), 40

"The Epic of Gilgamesh" (Mesopotamia), 40

"Nergal and Ereshkigal" (Mesopotamia), 40

"T'appin (Terrapin)" (African American), 43

"Izanagi and Izanami" (Shinto), 51

"Yama, the God of Death" (India), 65

"Sun, Life, Wind, and Death" (Micronesia), 67

"The Girl Who Married a Ghost" (Native American, Nisqualli), 68

"Baldur" (Norse), 70

"The Myth of Kingship" (Egypt), 71

"Nanabush and the Young Man and Wife" (Native American, Ojibwa), 76

"The 'Origin Legend' (Judge Version)" (Native American, Ojibwa), 76

"The 'Origin Legend' (King Version)" (Native American, Ojibwa), 76

"Paradise" (Native American, Ojibwa), 76

"The Last Journey" (Native American, Skidi Pawnee), 82

The Epic of Gilgamesh (Mesopotamia), 86

The Precious Gift: A Navaho Creation Myth (Native American), 87

"Cheeby-aub-oozoo: The Ghost of Rabbit" (Native American, Ojibway), 91

"The Daughter of the Sun" (Native American, Cherokee), 96

"Journey to the Sky" (Native American, Alabama), 96

"Orpheus" (Native American, Yuchi), 96

"How Death Came into the World" (Native American, Wampanoag), 105

"The Hero Journey of the Hero Twins" (Native American, Maya), 106

"Myths of the Suns and the Toltec-Chichimec Origins of the Mexica People" (Native American), 106

"Brave Quest" (Native American, Blackfeet), 107

"Orpheus and Eurydice" (Greece), 108

"Persephone and the Pomegranate Seeds" (Greece), 108

"The Land of the Dead" (Native American, Gabrielino), 113

"The Girl and the Ghost" (Native American, Nisqually), 115

"Daughter of the Sun" (Native American, Cherokee), 116

"Curlew" (Australian Aboriginal), 119

"Journey to the Underworld: The Story of Orpheus and Eurydice" (Graeco-Roman), 123

"The Kidnapping: The Story of Ceres and Proserpina" (Graeco-Roman), 123

"The Death of Balder" (Norse), 124

"Baldr and Loki" (Norse), 128

"Beginnings, Middles and Ends" (Norse), 128

"Aeneas in the Underworld" (Rome), 130

"The Death of Balder" (Norse), 130

"Izanami and Izanagi" (Japan), 130

"The Old Man of the Ancients" (Native American, Modoc), 130

"Orpheus and Eurydice" (Greece), 130

"Sedna" (Inuit, Eskimo), 130

"The Voyage of Bran" (Ireland), 130

Mother Scorpion Country/La Tierra de la Madre Escorpion (Native American, Miskito), 136

"The *Aeneid* of Virgil" (Rome), 138

"The Creation, Death, and Rebirth of the Universe, Gods, and Human Beings" (Norse), 138

"The Creation of the Universe, Gods, and Japan," 138

"The Death of Baldur" (Norse), 138

"Demeter and Persephone" (Greece), 138

"*Gilgamesh*" (Mesopotamia), 138

"*Mwindo*" (Sub-Saharan Africa, Nyanga, Zaire), 138

"The *Odyssey* of Homer" (Greece), 138

"Osiris, Isis, and Horus" (Egypt), 138

"The Land of the Dead" (Greece), 154

"Adonis" (Greece), 155

"Hades" (Greece), 155

"Orpheus and Eurydice" (Greece), 155

"Hutu and Pare" (New Zealand, Maori), 162

"Mataora and Niwareka in the Underworld" (New Zealand, Maori), 162

"Putawai" (New Zealand, Maori), 162

"Pwyll, Prince of Dyfed" (Wales), 163

"Dark Dramas of the Firmament" (Native American, Naskapi), 165

"Dark Dramas of the Firmament" (Siberia), 165

"Fall of the Sky Maiden" (Native American, Iroquois), 165

"The Countess of the Fountain" (England), 166

"Daring the Dark" (Rome), 166

"Journeys into Wonder" (Ireland), 166

"A Man among Gods" (Norse), 166

"A Parting of Worlds" (Ireland), 166

"Realms of Eternal Night" (Mesopotamia), 166

"Realms of Eternal Night" (Norse), 166

"The God of Fire and Thunder" (Japan), 169

"The Long Winter" (Native American, Slavey), 171

"The Girl Who Married a Ghost" (Native American, Chinook), 187

7. Seasons, Agriculture, and Fertility

"Evil Kachina Steals Yellow Woman" (Native American, Cochiti), 3

"Sun Steals Yellow Woman" (Native American, Cochiti), 3

"Whirlwind Man Steals Yellow Woman" (Native American, Laguna), 3

"Cybele and Attis" (Anatolia, Phrygia), 6

"The Rain Prince's Bride" (India), 12

"Daughter of Rain" (Native American, Cayapo), 13

"How Averiri Made the Night and the Seasons" (Native American, Campas), 13

"Snow Boy" (Native American, Lenape), 21

"Telling about Coyote" (Native American, Pueblo), 23

"The Hunting of the Great Bear" (Native American, Iroquois), 25

"The Two Brothers" (Native American, Iroquois), 25

"Introduction (Demeter and Persephone)" (Greece), 26

"How Fisher Went to the Skyland: The Origin of the Big Dipper" (Native American, Anishinabe), 27

"Spring Defeats Winter" (Native American, Seneca), 27

Stolen Thunder: A Norse Myth, 32

"The Descent of Ishtar to the Underworld" (Mesopotamia), 40

"Nergal and Ereshkigal" (Mesopotamia), 40

"Coyote Steals Spring" (Native American, Pacific Northwest), 41

"How Gluskabe Brought the Summer" (Native American, Abenaki), 43

"The Apples of Iduna" (Norse), 70

"Baldur" (Norse), 70

"The Myth of Kingship" (Egypt), 71

"The Gift of Corn; or, Mondamin, the Red Plume" (Native American, Ojibwa), 76

"Legend About Tobacco" (Native American, Ojibwa), 76

"The Legend of the Three Sisters" (Native American, Ojibwa), 76

"The Seasons" (Native American, Ojibwa), 76

"Winter and Spring" (Native American, Iroquois), 82

Ahaiyute and Cloud Eater (Native American, Zuni), 83

"The Girl Who Had Seven Brothers" (India), 89

"The King Without an Heir" (India), 89

"Lakshmi and the Clever Washerwoman" (India), 89

"The Manitous of the Forests and Meadows" (Native American, Ojibway), 91

Peboan and Seegwun (Native American, Ojibwa), 97

"The Great Migration and Old Man Winter" (Native American, Wampanoag), 105

"The Birth of Huitzilopochtli" (Native American, Aztec), 106

"The Myth of Mayahuel" (Native American, Aztec), 106

"The Myth of Tlaltecuhtli" (Native American, Aztec), 106

"John Barleycorn" (United States), 107

"Chinook Wind Wrestles Cold Wind" (Native American, Wasco), 113

"The Kidnapping: The Story of Ceres and Proserpina" (Graeco-Roman), 123

"The Death of Balder" (Norse), 124

"The Fairest Feet" (Norse), 124

"The Giant's Bride" (Norse), 124

"The Golden Apples" (Norse), 124

"The Magic Stallion" (Norse), 124

"Marriage of the Ice Maiden" (Norse), 124

"Aesir, Vanir and a Few Kings" (Norse), 128

"Baldr and Loki" (Norse), 128

"Where to Find Norse Myths," 128

"The Apples of Youth" (Norse), 130

"The Cat Goddess" (Egypt), 130

"The Holy Grail" (England), 130

"Isis and Osiris" (Egypt), 130

"Mother of Life and Death" (India), 130

"Persephone" (Greece), 130

"The Plumed Serpent" (Native American, Aztec), 130

"Telepinu" (Hittite), 130

"World Without Sun" (Japan), 130

"Persephone" (Greece), 133

"Why the Sun Forsook the Tundra" (Siberia), 134

"Ahaiyute and the Cloud-Eater" (Native American, Zuni), 138

"Ama-terasu" (Japan), 138

"Dagda the Good" (Ireland/Scotland), 138

"The Death of Baldur" (Norse), 138

"Demeter and Persephone" (Greece), 138

"Indra and the Dragon" (India), 138

"Osiris, Isis, and Horus" (Egypt), 138

"The Quarrel between Sagbata and Sogbo" (Sub-Saharan Africa, Fon, Dahomey), 138

"Telepinu" (Hittite), 138

"The Theft of Idun's Apples" (Norse), 138

"Yi the Archer and the Ten Suns" (China), 138

"Discoveries: Madagascar," 150

"Discoveries: North America" (Native American, Chippewa), 150

"The Forces of Nature: Greece," 150

"Shen Nung" (China), 150

"Adonis" (Greece), 155

"Persephone in Hades" (Greece), 155

"How Snowmaker Was Taught a Lesson" (Native American, Micmac), 159

"Mouse and Tapir" (South America), 164

"Realms of Eternal Night" (Norse), 166

"Realms of Eternal Night" (Mesopotamia), 166

How the Seasons Came: A North American Indian Folk Tale (Native American, Algon-quin), 168

"The Long Winter" (Native American, Slavey), 171

"Blue Corn Maiden and the Coming of Winter" (Native American, Northern Pueblo), 187

8. Origin of Necessities and Realities

8.A. Fire and Light (See also category 8.B.)

"The Coffin of God's Daughter" (Sub-Saharan Africa, Twi, Ghana), 16

"Blue Sun" (Native American, Maya), 17

"Opossum Steals Fire" (Native American, Mazatec), 18

"The Sun and Fire" (Native American, Huichol), 18

"The Sun and His Brothers" (Native American, Tzotzil), 18

"The Raven Cycle" (Native American, Tsimshian), 19

"The Bird Nester and the Jaguar" (Native American, Ge, Brazil), 20

"Tokwah, Lord of the Dead" (Native American, Mataco, Argentina), 20

"The Yoaloh Brothers" (Native American, Yamana, Chile), 20

"The Big Fish and the Sun" (Native American, Lenape), 21

The Woman Who Fell from the Sky: The Iroquois Story of Creation (Native American), 22

"Coyote Steals Fire" (Native American, Karuk), 23

"Loo-Wit, The Fire-Keeper" (Native American, Nisqually), 27

How Iwariwa the Cayman Learned to Share (Native American, Yanomami), 36

"How Moon Fathered the World" (Sub-Saharan Africa, Wakaranga, Zimbabwe), 43

"The Foolishness of the Ostrich" (Sub-Saharan Africa, Bushman), 57

"How Manabozho Stole Fire" (Native American, Chippewa), 60

"The God Brings Fire to Man" (Greece), 67

"Heavenly Fire Gained and Lost" (Native American, Ojibwa), 76

"The Manitous of the Forests and Meadows" (Native American, Ojibway), 91

"Bears and Fire" (Native American, Alabama), 96

"The Theft of Fire" (Native American, Hitchiti), 96

Fire Race: A Karuk Coyote Tale (Native American), 104

"Maushop and Grandfather Sun" (Native American, Wampanoag), 105

"Story of the Sweat Lodge" (Native American, Wampanoag), 105

"The Creation of the World" (Native American, Aztec), 106

"In the Beginning Pandora's Box" (Greece), 108

"Fire and the Opossum" (Native American, Mazateco, Mexico), 117

"The Gift of Fire" (Greece), 130

"Maui-of-a-Thousand Tricks" (Polynesia), 130

"World Without Sun" (Japan), 130

"How Maui Stole Fire from the Gods" (Pacific Islands), 133

"Mistress of Fire" (Siberia), 134

"The Flood Cycle" (Greece), 138

"Discoveries: South America" (Native American, Amazon Kayapo), 150

"The Divine Archer" (China), 150

"Prometheus: The First of the Great Heroes" (Greece), 155

"The Great Eastern City" (Native American, Maya), 160

"White Sparkstriker" (Native American, Maya), 160

"Part Four (fire)" (Native American, Maya), 161

"A Terrestrial Paradise" (China), 165

"How Beaver Stole Fire" (Native American, Nez Perce), 171

"Mother Sun" (Native American, Creek), 171

Rainbow Crow: A Lenape Tale (Native American), 172

The Rainbow Bridge (Native American, Chumash), 182

"Grandmother Spider Steals the Fire" (Native American, Choctaw), 187

"The Twin Brothers" (Native American, Caddo), 187

8.B. Sun, Moon, Stars, Rainbows, Heavenly Phenomena, and Forces of Nature (See also category 8.A.)

"The Flood" (ancient Israel), 9

"Moon Splits Hare's Lip (Nose)," 10
>   Story 1 (African American, Georgia)
>   Story 3 (Sub-Saharan Africa, Hausa, Nigeria)
>   Stories 6–10 (Sub-Saharan Africa, Bushman, Botswana)
>   Stories 21–27 (Sub-Saharan Africa, Hottentot, South Africa)

"The Traveling Sky Baskets" (Native American, Apanyekra), 13

"Why Rainbow Is Bent" (Native American, Selkam), 13

"Why Sun Has a Headdress and Moon Has None" (Native American, Ramkokamekra), 13

"Blue Sun" (Native American, Maya), 17

"The Lord Sun's Bride" (Native American, Maya), 17

"The Childhood of Sun and Moon" (Native American, Chatino), 18

"The Sun and Fire" (Native American, Huichol), 18

"The Sun and His Brothers" (Native American, Tzotzil), 18

"Toads and Frogs" (Native American, Garielino/Luiseno), 19

"Moon and His Sister" (Native American, Barasana, Brazil), 20

"The Origin of Night" (Native American, Bororo, Brazil), 20

"Coyote Places the Stars" (Native American, Hopi), 23

"Ne-ah-ga (Niagara)" (Native American, Seneca), 24

"The Hunting of the Great Bear" (Native American, Iroquois), 25

"The Wife of Thunderer" (Native American, Iroquois), 25

"Gluscabi and the Wind Eagle" (Native American, Abenaki), 27

"How Fisher Went to the Skyland: The Origin of the Big Dipper" (Native American, Anishinabe), 27

"How Raven Made the Tides" (Native American, Tsimshian), 27

"The Spider Brothers Make the Rainbow" (Native American, Achomawi), 31

"First Encounter Between Oggun and Shango" Sub-Saharan Africa, Yoruba), 42

"Formation of the Earth" (Sub-Saharan Africa, Yoruba), 42

"Oddua and Yembo's Love" (Sub-Saharan Africa, Yoruba), 42

"Anansi's Rescue from the River" (Sub-Saharan Africa, Ashanti, Ghana), 43

"The Creation" (Native American, Mohawk), 43

"Juruna Kills the Sun" (Native American, Juruna, Brazil), 43

"The Stealing of the Sun" (Native American, Kato), 43

"Sun and Moon" (Native American, Nivakle, Paraguay), 43

"Sun's Arrival in the Sky" (Native American, Miwok), 43

"Izanagi and Izanami" (Shinto), 51

The Lost Children (Native American, Blackfeet), 55

"The Giraffe in the Sky" (Sub-Saharan Africa, Bushman), 57

"In the Beginning . . ." (Sub-Saharan Africa, Fon), 58

The Fifth and Final Sun: An Ancient Aztec Myth of the Sun's Origin (Native American), 62

"Finding Night" (Melanesia), 67

"The First Eclipse" (Japan), 81

"Thunderbird" (Native American, Pawnee/Blackfeet/Tlingit/Kwakiutl), 82

"The Moon and the Heavenly Nectar" (India), 89

"Lightning and the People" (Native American, Caddo), 96

"How the Sun Was Made" (Australian Aboriginal), 100

"Maushop and Grandfather Sun" (Native American, Wampanoag), 105

"The Birth of All of Heaven and Earth" (Native American, Maya), 106

"The Creation of the Sun and the Moon" (Native American, Aztec), 106

"The Creation of the World" (Native American, Aztec), 106

"The Hero Journey of the Hero Twins" (Native American, Maya), 106

"Myths of the Suns and the Toltec-Chichimec Origins of the Mexica People" (Native American), 106

"Admirable Hare" (Ceylon), 107

"Saving Time" (Polynesia), 107

"Shooting the Sun" (China), 107

"Orpheus and Eurydice" (Greece), 108

"The Twelve Labors of Heracles" (Greece), 108

Raven: A Trickster Tale from the Pacific Northwest (Native American), 110

"Anitsutsa—The Boys" (Native American, Cherokee), 113

"Baakil and His Five Wives" (Native American, Tachi Yokuts), 113

"Black God and His Stars" (Native American, Navajo), 113

"Bright Shining Old Man" (Native American, Onondaga), 113

"The Celestial Bear" (Native American, Micmac), 113

"The Celestial Canoe" (Native American, Alabama), 113

"Coyote Scatters the Stars" (Native American, Cochiti Pueblo), 113

"The Dove Maidens" (Native American, Picuris Pueblo), 113

"Eight Wise Men" (Native American, Chumash), 113

"The Elk Hunters" (Native American, Snohomish), 113

"The Elkskin" (Native American, Quileute), 113

"The Fixed Star" (Native American, Blackfeet), 113

"Grizzly Bear Brother-in-Law" (Native American, Coeur d'Alene), 113

"How Coyote Arranged the Night Sky" (Native American, Wasco), 113

"How Rattlesnake Had His Revenge" (Native American, Luiseno), 113

"The Little Girl Who Scatters the Stars" (Native American, Cochiti Pueblo), 113

"Raccoon's Children and Baby Coyote" (Native American, Shasta), 113

"The Seven Boys-Turned-Geese" (Native American, Chumash), 113

"The Seven Sisters" (Native American, Luiseno), 113

"The Seven Stars" (Native American, Assiniboin), 113

"The Seventh Star" (Native American, Skidi Pawnee), 113

"Stone God" (Native American, Skidi Pawnee), 113

"Where the Dog Ran" (Native American, Cherokee), 113

"Wild Onion Women" (Native American, Monache), 113

"The Wolf and the Crane" (Native American, Tachi Yokuts), 113

"Noah Hears God's Promise" (ancient Israel), 114

"The Three Suns" (Native American, Zincantec), 117

The Fish Skin (Native American, Cree), 118

"Mirrabooka" (Australian Aboriginal), 119

"Davy Crockett" (United States), 122

"The Great Bear: The Story of Callisto and Arcus" (Graeco-Roman), 123

"Lost at Sea: The Story of Ceyx and Alcyone" (Graeco-Roman), 123

How the Stars Fell into the Sky: A Navajo Legend (Native American), 126

"Hunting the Sun" (Australian Aboriginal), 130

"Maui-of-a-Thousand Tricks" (Polynesia), 130

"World Without Sun" (Japan), 130

"Bearskin-Woman" (Native American, Blackfeet), 132

"How Maui Stole Fire from the Gods" (Pacific Islands), 133

"Naming the Winds" (Native American, Iroquois), 133

"Daughter of the Moon, Son of the Sun" (Siberia), 134

"The Girl and the Moon Man" (Siberia), 134

"How the Sun Was Rescued" (Siberia), 134

"The Silver Maid" (Siberia), 134

"The Sun Maiden and the Crescent Moon" (Siberia), 134

"The Two Suns" (Siberia), 134

"The Creation of the Universe" (Native American, Toltec/Aztec, Mexico), 138

"Raven and the Sources of Light" (Native American, Haida/Tlingit, Canada), 138

"The Forces of Nature: Indonesia" (Sulawesi), 150

"The Forces of Nature: Scandinavia" (Norse), 150

"The Sun, the Moon, and the Stars: Japan," 150

"The Sun, the Moon, and the Stars: Mexico" (Native American, Aztec), 150

"The Sun, the Moon, and the Stars: North America" (Native American, Micmac), 150

"The Birth of Niagara Falls" (Native American, Algonquin), 159

"The First Tornado" (Native American, Kiowa), 159

"Part Four (origin of the sun)" (Native American, Maya), 161

"Part Two (constellations)" (Native American, Maya), 161

"Maui Tames the Sun" (New Zealand, Maori), 162

"Rona and the Legend of the Moon" (New Zealand, Maori), 162

"Bear and Coyote" (Western Canada), 164

"Dark Dramas of the Firmament" (Burma), 165

"Dark Dramas of the Firmament" (Sub-Saharan Africa), 165

"Hieroglyphics of the Heavens" (Greece), 165

"Lindu's Astral Veil" (Estonia), 165

"Lunar Denizens" (Buddhist), 165

"Phaethon's Folly" (Greece), 165

"The Twin Luminants" (Korea), 165

"The Story of Lightning and Thunder" (Sub-Saharan Africa, Efik Ibibio), 167

"Why the Sun and Moon Live in the Sky" (Sub-Saharan Africa, Efik Ibibio), 167

"The Long Winter" (Native American, Slavey), 171

"How the Moon Became Ivory" (Vietnam), 174

"The Miraculous Banyan Tree" (Vietnam), 174

"The Seven Weavers" (Vietnam), 174

"The Weaver Fairy and the Buffalo Boy" (Vietnam), 174

"Bears' Lodge" (Native American, Kiowa), 187

"The Evening Star" (Native American, Caddo), 187

"The Seven Star Brothers" (Native American, Seneca), 187

"Where the Dog Ran Across the Sky" (Native American, Cherokee), 187

8.C. Geographical Features and Natural Phenomena

"What Happened When Fox Opened the Bottle Tree" (Native American, Chorote), 13

"Why the Sky Is High" (Sub-Saharan Africa, Ga, Ghana), 16

"The Tree and the Flood" (Native American, Cabecar), 18

"The Tree and the Flood" (Native American, South America), 20

"El Capitan" (Native American, Navajo), 24

"Great Smokies" (Native American, Cherokee), 24

"Lake Champlain" (Native American, Abenaki), 24

"Mau-shop (Gay Head)" (Native American, Wampanoag), 24

"The Wife of the Thunderer" (Native American, Iroquois), 25

"How Thunder and Earthquake Made Ocean" (Native American, Yurok), 27

How the Sea Began: A Taino Myth (Native American), 37

"Izanagi and Izanami" (Shinto), 51

The Legend of the Cranberry: A Paleo-Indian Tale (Native American, Delaware), 59

"Legend of the Creation of the Islands" (Native American, Ojibwa), 76

"Legend of the Great Lakes" (Native American, Ojibwa), 76

"Nanabush and the Ducks" (Native American, Ojibwa), 76

"Sugarloaf Rock" (Native American, Ojibwa), 76

"Wife Is Turned to Stone" (Native American, Ojibwa), 76

"Rainbow Snake" (Australian Aboriginal), 107

"Echo and Narcissus" (Greece), 108

"Coyote Loves a Star" (Native American, Klamath), 113

"The Face in the Pool: The Story of Echo and Narcissus" (Graeco-Roman), 123

"The Fall of Icarus" (Greece), 130

"Vainamoinen" (Finland), 130

"The Creation of the Universe, Gods, and Japan," 138

"The House of Origin" (Native American, Inca, Peru), 138

"The Naming of Places" (Ireland), 139

"Flint Visits Rabbit" (Native American, Cherokee), 140

"Typhon and Zeus" (Greece), 150

"Narcissus and Echo" (Greece), 155

"The Birth of Niagara Falls" (Native American, Algonquin), 159

"How Eagle Man Created the Islands of the Pacific Coast" (Native American, Bella Coola), 159

"Kupe's Discovery of Aotearoa" (New Zealand, Maori), 162

"Maui and the Great Fish" (New Zealand, Maori), 162

"Fiery Lairs of Gods and Monsters" (Graeco-Roman), 165

"A Hog's Itch" (Celebes, South Seas), 165

"Phaethon's Folly" (Greece), 165

"A Restless Frog" (Mongolia), 165

"The Trembling Earth" (Sub-Saharan Africa), 165

"Princess Glory" (Japan), 169

"Raven, the River Maker" (Native American, Tlingit), 171

"Dunai and Nastas'ya" (Russia), 177

"Sukhman" (Russia), 177

Wings (Greece), 183

"In the Aztec Palace: The Smoking Mountain" (Native American, Aztec), 188

8.D. Social Customs, Beliefs, Ceremonies, and Rituals

"Lord Siva and the Satwaras" (India), 12

"The Youngest Daughter-in-law" (India), 12

"The Red Swan" (Native American, Winnebago), 19

"The Origin of Male Domination" (Native American, Mundurucu, Brazil), 20

"The White Buffalo Calf Woman and the Sacred Pipe" (Native American, Lakota, Sioux), 27

"Woman and Man Started Even" (African American), 66

"Sun, Life, Wind, and Death" (Micronesia), 67

"Cheeby-aub-oozoo: The Ghost of Rabbit" (Native American, Ojibway), 91

"Kanati and Selu" (Native American, Cherokee), 96

"Maushop and Grandfather Sun" (Native American, Wampanoag), 105

"Story of the Sweat Lodge" (Native American, Wampanoag), 105

"How Men and Women Finally Agreed" (Sub-Saharan Africa, Kikuyu, Kenya), 107

"Whose Footprints?" (Sub-Saharan Africa, Fon, Benin), 107

"The Sacred Pole" (Native American, Omaha), 113

"Seneca Medicine" (Native American), 132

"How the Chukchi People Became Friends" (Siberia), 134

"The Little Whale" (Siberia), 134

"Mataora and Niwareka in the Underworld" (New Zealand, Maori), 162

"A Terrestrial Paradise" (China), 165

And in the Beginning . . . (Sub-Saharan Africa), 179

8.E. Nations, Races, Cities, and States

"The Demiurge Builders of Nan Madol" (Micronesia), 8

"The Tower" (ancient Israel), 9

"The Twin Myth" (Native American, Waiwai, Guiana), 20

Nyumba ya Mumbi: The Gikuyu Creation Myth (Sub-Saharan Africa), 50

"Inca Ancestors" (Native American), 51

"Emergence" (Native American, Choctaw), 96

"The Origin of Animals (Clans)" (Native American, Creek), 96

"The Coming of the Golden Stool" (Sub-Saharan Africa, Ashanti, Ghana), 98

"The Horse with the Golden Horn" (Sub-Saharan Africa, Hausa, Ghana), 98

"The Finding and Founding of Tenochtitlan" (Native American, Aztec), 106

"How Men and Women Finally Agreed" (Sub-Saharan Africa, Kikuyu, Kenya), 107

"The Tower of Babel" (ancient Israel), 114

"Buffalo-Maiden" (Native American, Arikara), 132

"The Children of the Sun" (Native American, Inca, Peru), 138

"Romulus and Remus" (Rome), 138

"A Beginning" (Jewish), 144

"Romulus and Remus" (Rome), 150

"Phaethon's Folly" (Greece), 165

8.F. Animals (See also categories 8.G and 8.H.)

"The Origin of Man" (India), 12

"Blue Sun" (Native American, Maya), 17

"The Lord Sun's Bride" (Native American, Maya), 17

"The Seeds of Humanity" (Native American, Guaymi), 18

"The Sun and His Brothers" (Native American, Tzotzil), 18

"The Mother of Animals" (Eskimo), 19

"The Giant Squirrel" (Native American, Lenape), 21

"The White Deer" (Native American, Lenape), 21

"The Two Brothers" (Native American, Iroquois), 25

"Sedna, the Woman Under the Sea" (Native American, Inuit), 27

"Sixth Child—Osain" (Sub-Saharan Africa, Yoruba), 42

"Juruna Kills the Sun" (Native American, Juruna, Brazil), 43

"The Lustful Raven" (Inuit), 43

"The Origin of Different Water Animals" (India), 43

"The Origin of Fishes" (Sub-Saharan Africa, Fon, Benin), 43

"Kidnapped by a Flea" (United States), 44

"Men, Monkeys, and Mukulu" (Sub-Saharan Africa), 51

"Miz Hattie Gets Some Company" (African American), 66

"The First Robin" (Native American, Ojibwa), 76

"The Woodpecker" (Native American, Ojibwa), 76

"Nana'b'oozoo" (Native American, Ojibway), 91

"The Daughter of the Sun" (Native American, Cherokee), 96

"Kanati and Selu" (Native American, Cherokee), 96

"The Origin of Animals (Clans)" (Native American, Creek), 96

"Owner of the Animals" (Native American, Caddo), 96

"Maushop and the Porpoises" (Native American, Wampanoag), 105

"Maushop Builds Turtle Island" (Native American, Wampanoag), 105

"Rainbow Snake" (Australian Aboriginal), 107

"Arachne the Spinner" (Greece), 108

"In the Beginning Pandora's Box" (Greece), 108

"Daughter of the Sun" (Native American, Cherokee), 116

"The Three Suns" (Native American, Zincantec, Mexico), 117

"Curlew" (Australian Aboriginal), 119

"Lost at Sea: The Story of Ceyx and Alcyone" (Graeco-Roman), 123

"The Weaving Contest: The Story of Arachne and Minerva" (Graeco-Roman), 123

"First Creator and Lone Man" (Native American, Mandan), 130

"The Origin of the Ox" (China), 130

"Buffalo-Maiden" (Native American, Arikara), 132

"Magic Beasts" (Native American, Comanche), 132

"Other Animals" (Native American, Cherokee), 132

"Wolves" (Inuit, Eskimo), 132

Dance of the Sacred Circle: A Native American Tale (Native American, Blackfeet), 135

"Sedna" (Inuit), 150

"Big Raven Creates the World" (Siberia), 158

"Bones in the Basket" (Native American, Modoc), 158

"How Horses Came into the World" (Native American, Blackfeet), 159

"Part One (origin of animals)" (Native American, Maya), 161

"The Braggart's Bungle" (Mongolia), 165

"Fall of the Sky Maiden" (Native American, Iroquois), 165

"First Fruits" (Burma), 165

"The Garden of the Gods" (Greece), 165

"A Muddy Metamorphosis" (Greece), 165

"Noah's Miraculous Voyage" (Jewish), 165

"The Primal Potter" (India), 165

"How All Animals Came on Earth" (Sub-Saharan Africa, Ekoi, Nigeria), 167

"Coyote's Cave" (Native American), 170

The Rainbow Bridge (Native American, Chumash), 182

Moon Mother: A Native American Creation Tale, 184

"In the Taino Village" (Native American, Taino), 188

8.G. Animal Appearance (See also categories 8.F and 8.H.)

"Trickster Seeks Endowments; Measuring the Snake; Challenging Birds (Insects) to Fill a Container; Milking a Cow (Deer) Stuck in a Tree," 10

> Story 7 (Sub-Saharan Africa, Liberia)
> Story 14 (Sub-Saharan Africa, Ghana)
> Story 22 (Sub-Saharan Africa, Ashanti, Ghana)
> Story 30 (Native American, Hitchiti, Oklahoma)
> Stories 38–45 (African American, South Carolina)

Story 60 (Mexico)
Story 61 (Native American, Chuh, Guatemala)
Story 68 (African, Marie Galante)
Story 73 (African, Martinique)
Story 76 (African, Trinidad)
Story 77 (Native American, Warao, Venezuela)

"Moon Splits Hare's Lip (Nose)," 10
Story 1 (African American, Georgia)
Stories 4–10 (Sub-Saharan Africa, Bushman, Botswana)
Stories 11–15 (Sub-Saharan Africa, Bushman, South Africa)
Stories 18–30 (Sub-Saharan Africa, Hottentot, South Africa)
Stories 31–32 (Sub-Saharan Africa, Hottentot, Namibia)

"How the Birds Got New Beaks and Men Got Teeth" (Native American, Bororo), 13

"Ananse Meets His Measure" (Sub-Saharan Africa), 14

"The Opposite Party" (Sub-Saharan Africa), 14

"Adene and the Pineapple Child" (Sub-Saharan Africa, Ga, Ghana), 16

"Ata and the Messenger Bird" (Sub-Saharan Africa, Krobo, Ghana), 16

"The Bag of Salt" (Sub-Saharan Africa, Ga, Ghana), 16

"The Gluttonous Monkey" (Sub-Saharan Africa, Avatime, Ghana), 16

"How Crab Got His Shell" (Sub-Saharan Africa, Northern Ghana), 16

"The Price of Eggs" (Sub-Saharan Africa, Sefwi, Ghana), 16

"The Quarrel Between Heaven and Earth" (Sub-Saharan Africa, Yoruba, Nigeria), 16

"Tortoise and the Stew Bowl" (Sub-Saharan Africa, Ga, Ghana), 16

"Tortoise Buys a House" (Sub-Saharan Africa, Yoruba, Nigeria), 16

"Tortoise Disobeys" (Sub-Saharan Africa, Yoruba, Nigeria), 16

"The Vultures and the Liver Cave" (Sub-Saharan Africa, Krio, Sierra Leone), 16

"Why Bush Pig Has a Red Face" (Sub-Saharan Africa, Ga, Ghana), 16

"Why Spider Is Bald" (Sub-Saharan Africa, Ga, Ghana), 16

"Why the Mason Wasp Has a Narrow Waist" (Sub-Saharan Africa, Krobo, Ghana), 16

"The Yam Farm and the Problem Tongue" (Sub-Saharan Africa, Ga, Ghana), 16

"Coyote Continues Upriver" (Native American, Karuk), 23

"Coyote on the Beach" (Native American, Karuk), 23

"Telling about Coyote" (Native American, Pueblo), 23

"Chipmunk and Bear" (Native American, Iroquois), 25

"How Bear Lost His Tail" (Native American, Iroquois), 25

"How Buzzard Got His Feathers" (Native American, Iroquois), 25

"Rabbit and the Willow Tree" (Native American, Iroquois), 25

"Turtle Makes War on Men" (Native American, Iroquois), 25

"How Turtle Flew South for the Winter" (Native American, Dakota, Sioux), 27

"The Monkey Bridge to Lanka" (Hindu), 29

"How the Rabbit Lost Its Tail" (Native American, Sioux), 34

"Old Man and the Bobcat" (Native American, Blackfeet), 34

"Grandfather Spider's Feast" (Sub-Saharan Africa), 41

Owl Eyes (Native American, Mohawk), 52

"The First Zebra" (Sub-Saharan Africa, Angoni), 57

"How Jackal Got His Markings" (Sub-Saharan Africa, Hottentot), 57

"How Tsessebe Got His Peculiar Horns" (Sub-Saharan Africa, Bushman), 57

"Chameleon and the Greedy Spider" (Sub-Saharan Africa, Bushman), 58

"Why Pangolin Has Scales" (Sub-Saharan Africa, Angoni), 58

"How Manabozho Saved the Rose" (Native American, Chippewa), 60

Great Rabbit and the Long-Tailed Wildcat (Native American, Passamaquoddy), 63

"Coyote's New Coat" (Native American, Navajo), 74

"How Nanbush Fixed the Eye of the Owl" (Native American, Ojibwa), 76

"How the Turtle Got Its Shell" (Native American, Ojibwa), 76

"Manabozho" (Native American, Ojibwa), 76

"Nanbush and the Mud Turtle" (Native American, Ojibwa), 76

"Nenebojo and His Brother" (Native American, Ojibwa), 76

"Nenebojo Goes Hunting" (Native American, Ojibwa), 76

"Nenebuc, the Transformer" (Native American, Ojibwa), 76

"The Story of Nana-Bo-Zhoo and His Brother" (Native American, Ojibwa), 76

"Why Roses Have Thorns" (Native American, Ojibwa), 76

"Why the Buffalo Has a Hump" (Native American, Ojibwa), 76

"Why the Porcupine Has Quills" (Native American, Ojibwa), 76

"Winabijou Looks for the Wolf" (Native American, Ojibwa), 76

"How the Turtle Cracked His Shell" (Native American, Cherokee), 80

"Bluebird and Coyote" (Native American, Pima), 82

The Precious Gift: A Navaho Creation Myth (Native American), 87

Sally Ann Thunder Ann Whirlwind Crockett (United States), 92

"The Celestial Bear" (Native American, Micmac), 113

"Possum, Turtle, and the Wolves" (Native American, Cherokee), 115

"The Brave Little Parrot" (Buddhist), 116

"Fire and the Opossum" (Native American, Mazateco, Mexico), 117

"The Rabbit's Ears" (Native American, Maya, Mexico), 117

"Aioga" (Siberia), 134

"Ankakumikaityn the Nomad Wolf" (Siberia), 134

"The Raven and the Owl" (Siberia), 134

"Why Hares Have Long Ears" (Siberia), 134

"Flint Visits Rabbit" (Native American, Cherokee), 140

"How Deer Won His Antlers" (Native American, Cherokee), 140

"How Rabbit Tricked Otter" (Native American, Cherokee), 140

"Why Deer's Teeth Are Blunt" (Native American, Cherokee), 140

"Why Possum's Tail Is Bare" (Native American, Cherokee), 140

How Turtle's Back Was Cracked: A Traditional Cherokee Tale (Native American), 141

"The Star Maiden" (Native American, Chippewa), 145

"Indra and the Peacock" (India), 150

"Plants and Animals: Canada" (Inuit), 150

"Plants and Animals: Sierra Leone" (Sub-Saharan Africa), 150

Rabbit Wishes (Cuba), 152

"Why Rabbits and Owls Look the Way They Do" (Native American, Mohawk), 159

"The Tails of Animals" (Native American, Maya), 161

"Maui and the Birds" (New Zealand, Maori), 162

"Crane and Crow" (Australia), 164

"Fox and Bear" (Northern Europe), 164

"Tortoise and Crane" (China), 164

"A Feathered Heraldry" (India), 165

"A Feathered Heraldry" (Latvia), 165

"How the Elephant Lost Its Wings" (India), 165

"Coyote and the Crow Buffalo-Ranchers" (Native American), 170

"How Possum Got His Skinny Tail" (Native American, Cherokee), 171

"Rabbit and the Willow" (Native American, Seneca), 171

"Raven, the River Maker" (Native American, Tlingit), 171

Rainbow Crow: A Lenape Tale (Native American), 172

"Why Anansi Has a Narrow Waist" (African American), 185

"Why Brother Alligator Has a Rough Back" (African American), 185

"The Ballgame Between the Animals and the Birds" (Native American, Cherokee), 187

"How Bear Lost His Tail" (Native American, Seneca), 187

"How Buzzard Got His Clothing" (Native American, Iroquois), 187

"How the Animals Came to Be of Many Colors" (Native American, Kathlamet), 187

"Possum's Beautiful Tail" (Native American, Cherokee), 187

"Raccoon and the Crabs" (Native American, Iroquois), 187

8.H. Animal Behavior (See also categories 8.F and 8.G.)

"A Debt Made Profit, Or, Why Monkeys Live in Trees" (Sub-Saharan Africa), 14

"Aja and the Enchanted Beast" (Sub-Saharan Africa, Krobo, Ghana), 16

"Ananse Is Put in His Place" (Sub-Saharan Africa, Sefwi, Ghana), 16

"Crab and Guinea Fowl Part Ways" (Sub-Saharan Africa, Yoruba, Ghana), 16

"The Fairies and the Flute" (Sub-Saharan Africa, Anengme, Ghana), 16

"The Most Powerful Name" (Sub-Saharan Africa, Avatime, Ghana), 16

"The Nefarious Fly" (Sub-Saharan Africa, Sefwi, Ghana), 16

"The Return of Ananse" (Sub-Saharan Africa, Sefwi, Ghana), 16

"The Scarecrow" (Sub-Saharan Africa, Ga, Ghana), 16

"Spider and the Nightjar" (Sub-Saharan Africa, Sefwi, Ghana), 16

"Spider the Artist" (Sub-Saharan Africa, Ga, Ghana), 16

"Why Fowls Scratch" (Sub-Saharan Africa, Twi, Ghana), 16

"Why Hippo Wears No Coat" (Sub-Saharan Africa, Krobo, Ghana), 16

"Why Lizard Bobs His Head" (Sub-Saharan Africa, Ga, Ghana), 16

"Coyote and Badger" (Native American, Kathlamet Chinook), 23

"The Race" (Native American, Cheyenne), 24

"How Buzzard Got His Feathers" (Native American, Iroquois), 25

"Raccoon and the Crayfish" (Native American, Iroquois), 25

"The Two-headed Snake" (Native American, Iroquois), 25

"Koluscap and the Water Monster" (Native American, Micmac, Maliseet), 27

"Arachne's Gift" (Greece), 31

"Anansi Plays Dead" (Sub-Saharan Africa, Ashanti, Ghana), 43

"The Song of the Birds" (Native American, Mohawk), 43

"The Elephant and the Rain" (Sub-Saharan Africa, Bushman), 57

"How Cheetah Got His Speed" (Sub-Saharan Africa, Bushman), 57

"The Living Stones" (Sub-Saharan Africa, Swazi), 57

"No Fish for Hippo" (Sub-Saharan Africa, Bushman), 57

"The Birds' Great Race" (Sub-Saharan Africa, Bushman), 58

"Chameleon and First Man" (Sub-Saharan Africa, Ndebele), 58

"Chameleon and the Greedy Spider" (Sub-Saharan Africa, Bushman), 58

"Dung Beetle's Burden" (Sub-Saharan Africa, Ghana), 58

"Why Guinea Fowl Calls at Dawn (and Why Flies Buzz)" (Sub-Saharan Africa, Ekoi, Nigeria), 58

"Why Pangolin Has Scales" (Sub-Saharan Africa, Angoni), 58

"Why Python Can Shed His Skin" (Sub-Saharan Africa, Mende), 58

"Legend About Tobacco" (Native American, Ojibwa), 76

"Nanabush and Manitou" (Native American, Ojibwa), 76

"Why the Buffalo Has a Hump" (Native American, Ojibwa), 76

"Why the Cat Falls on Her Feet" (Native American, Ojibwa), 76

"Why the Geese Fly in a Line" (Native American, Ojibwa), 76

"Why the Squirrel Coughs" (Native American, Ojibwa), 76

"Rabbit and Possum Hunt for a Wife" (Native American, Cherokee), 80

"Why Wolves Chase Deer" (Native American, Tsimshian), 82

The Precious Gift: A Navaho Creation Myth (Native American), 87

"How the Sun Was Made" (Australian Aboriginal), 100

"Skinning Out" (Ethiopia), 107

"Coyote Scatters the Stars" (Native American, Cochiti Pueblo), 113

"The Cuckoo" (Siberia), 134

"How Deer Won His Antlers" (Native American, Cherokee), 140

"How Rabbit Tricked Otter" (Native American, Cherokee), 140

"Rabbit Goes Duck Hunting" (Native American, Cherokee), 140

"Why Possum's Tail Is Bare" (Native American, Cherokee), 140

"Why Butterflies Cannot Sing" (Native American, Tohono O'Odhan, Papago), 159

"Why the Dog Is Our Best Friend" (Native American, Oneida), 159

"Crane and Crow" (Australia), 164

"Rubber Girl" (Sub-Saharan Africa, Yoruba), 167

"Why Hippo Lives in Water" (Sub-Saharan Africa, Efik Ibibio), 167

"Coyote and Sun" (Native American), 170

"How Possum Got His Skinny Tail" (Native American, Cherokee), 171

"How Spider Caught Flies" (Native American, Wishosk), 171

"Why the Rooster Crows at Sunrise" (Vietnam), 174

"Bear's Race with Turtle" (Native American, Seneca), 187

"The Bloodsucker" (Native American, Northern Pueblo), 187

"Coyote's Sad Song to the Moon" (Native American, Northern Pueblo), 187

"Kanati the Hunter and the Cave of Animals" (Native American, Cherokee), 187

"Possum's Beautiful Tail" (Native American, Cherokee), 187

"Race with Buffalo" (Native American, Cheyenne), 187

8.I. Food and Drink

"The First Sakau on Pohnpei" (Micronesia), 8

"The Man of Crops" (Native American, Jicaque), 18

"Coyote Releases Salmon" (Native American, Salish), 19

"The Star Woman" (Native American, Ge, Brazil), 20

"The Twin Myth" (Native American, Waiwai, Guiana), 20

"The Coming of Corn" (Native American, Cherokee), 27

"Manabozho and the Maple Trees" (Native American, Anishinabe), 27

How the Sea Began: A Taino Myth (Native American), 37

"Coyote Makes a Texas Cowboy" (Native American), 44

The Legend of the Cranberry: A Paleo-Indian Tale (Native American, Delaware), 59

"How Manabozho Found Rice" (Native American, Chippewa), 60

"The Gift of Corn; or Mondamin, the Red Plume" (Native American, Ojibwa), 76

"The Legend of the Three Sisters" (Native American, Ojibwa), 76

"The Manitous of the Forests and Meadows" (Native American, Ojibway), 91

"The Spirit of Maundau-meen (Maize)" (Native American, Ojibway), 91

"Journey to the Sky" (Native American, Alabama), 96

"Kanati and Selu" (Native American, Cherokee), 96

"The Origin of Maize" (Native American, Abnaki), 96

"The Origin of Maize" (Native American, Creek), 96

"The Great Migration and Old Man Winter" (Native American, Wampanoag), 105

"The Creation of the World" (Native American, Aztec), 106

"The Myth of Mayahuel" (Native American, Aztec), 106

"Myths of the Suns and the Toltec-Chichimec Origins of the Mexica People" (Native American, Toltec), 106

"First Snow" (Native American), 107

"The Legend of Obi Obi Gui" (Sub-Saharan Africa, Yoruba, Nigeria), 116

"First Creator and Lone Man" (Native American, Mandan), 130

"The Great Flood" (Serbia), 130

"The Plumed Serpent" (Native American, Aztec), 130

"The Creation of the Universe" (Native American, Toltec/Aztec, Mexico), 138

"Paraparawa and Waraku" (Native American, Trio, Brazil), 138

"Discoveries: Madagascar," 150

"Discoveries: North America" (Native American, Chippewa), 150

"Bequest of a Golden Stranger" (Native American, Iroquois), 165

"The Tree of Life" (Native American, Carib), 188

8.J. Plants and Flowers

"The Warrior Maiden" (Native American, Oneida), 3

"Spider Learns to Listen" (Sub-Saharan Africa, Sefwi, Ghana), 16

"The Wisdom of Aja" (Sub-Saharan Africa, Krobo, Ghana), 16

"Sixth Child—Osain" (Sub-Saharan Africa, Yoruba, Brazil, Cuba, Haiti), 42

"How Manabozho Saved the Rose" (Native American, Chippewa), 60

"The Duck Dinner" (Native American, Ojibwa), 76

"Nanabush and the Ducks" (Native American, Ojibwa), 76

"Why Roses Have Thorns" (Native American, Ojibwa), 76

"Why the Birch Bark Is Spotted" (Native American, Ojibwa), 76

"The Manitous of the Forests and Meadows" (Native American, Ojibway), 91

"The Origin of Tobacco" (Native American, Yuchi), 96

"The Birth of All of Heaven and Earth" (Native American, Maya), 106

"Apollo and Daphne" (Greece), 108

"Echo and Narcissus" (Greece), 108

"Apollo's Tree: The Story of Daphne and Apollo" (Graeco-Roman), 123

"The Face in the Pool: The Story of Echo and Narcissus" (Graeco-Roman), 123

"Plants and Animals: Greece," 150

"Adonis" (Greece), 155

"Hyacinth" (Greece), 155

"Narcissus and Echo" (Greece), 155

"Origin of the Calabash Tree" (Native American, Maya), 161

"The Garden of the Gods" (Greece), 165

"Rabbit and the Willow" (Native American, Seneca), 171

8.K. Wisdom and Knowledge

"Spider and the Calabash of Knowledge" (Sub-Saharan Africa, Twi, Ghana), 16

"The Gifts of the Little People" (Native American, Iroquois), 25

"The Elephant-Headed God" (Hindu), 29

"Adapa" (Mesopotamia), 40

"Ninth Child—Oba Nani (Wisdom and Teacher of the World)" (Sub-Saharan Africa, Yoruba, Brazil, Cuba, Haiti), 42

"Seventh Child and First Female—Dada (Brain)" (Sub-Saharan Africa, Yoruba, Brazil, Cuba, Haiti), 42

"The God Brings Fire to Man" (Greece), 67

"Plutarch's Version" (Egypt), 71

"The Midewewin" (Native American, Ojibwa), 76

"The 'Origin Legend' (Judge Version)" (Native American, Ojibwa), 76

"How Wisdom Came to the Tribe" (Sub-Saharan Africa, Ashanti, Ghana), 98

"Cheepii Keeps Himself Safe" (Native American, Wampanoag), 105

"Firstman" (Native American, Wampanoag), 105

"Maushop Builds Turtle Island" (Native American, Wampanoag), 105

"Basket Woman, Mother of the Stars" (Native American, Skidi Pawnee), 113

"The Sun Dance Wheel" (Native American, Arapaho), 113

"White Elk, the Bear Man" (Native American, Pitahawirata Pawnee), 113

"Odin's Three Quests" (Norse), 124

"The Food of Life" (Mesopotamia), 130

"The Gift of Fire" (Greece), 130

"The Plumed Serpent" (Native American, Aztec), 130

"The Tree of Life" (Norse), 130

"The Creation of the Universe and Human Beings" (Native American, Tiahuanaco, pre-Inca, Peru), 138

"Quetzalcoatl" (Native American, Toltec/Aztec, Mexico), 138

"Frigg and Odin" (Norse), 150

"Osiris and Isis" (Egypt), 150

"Anansi Tries to Steal All the Wisdom in the World" (African American), 185

8.L. Literature, Stories, and Writing

"Spider's Bargain with God" (Sub-Saharan Africa, Sefwi, Ghana), 16

"Why We Tell Stories About Spider" (Sub-Saharan Africa, Ga, Ghana), 16

"How the First Stories Came Out of the Earth" (Native American, Lenape), 21

"The Coming of Legends" (Native American, Iroquois), 25

"Of Science and Indian Myths" (Native American, Seneca), 27

"Anansi Owns All Tales That Are Told" (Sub-Saharan Africa, Ashanti, Ghana), 43

"Maudjee-kawiss: The First Son" (Native American, Ojibway), 91

"The Tasks of the Trickster" (Sub-Saharan Africa, Ashanti, Gold Coast), 96

"Where to Find Norse Myths," 128

"The Sky God's Stories" (Sub-Saharan Africa, Ashanti), 130

"A Terrestrial Paradise" (China), 165

"How Stories Came into the World" (Sub-Saharan Africa, Ekoi, Nigeria), 167

8.M. Music and Musical Instruments

"The First Love Music" (Native American, Lakota Sioux), 82

"Cheeby-aub-oozoo: The Ghost of Rabbit" (Native American, Ojibway), 91

"Pukawiss: The Disowned" (Native American, Ojibway), 91

All of You Was Singing (Native American, Aztec), 102

"How Music Was Fetched out of Heaven" (Native American, Aztec), 107

"Odin's Three Quests" (Norse), 124

"King Midas's Ears" (Greece), 130

"How Happiness Came" (Siberia), 134

"The Creation of the Universe" (Native American, Toltec/Aztec, Mexico), 138

"A Terrestrial Paradise" (China), 165

Song of the Chirimia: A Guatemalan Folktale (Native American, Maya), 173

8.N. Arts and Crafts

"The God Brings Fire to Man" (Greece), 67

"Firstman" (Native American, Wampanoag), 105

"The Great Migration and Old Man Winter" (Native American, Wampanoag), 105

"Maushop and Grandfather Sun" (Native American, Wampanoag), 105

"Maushop Builds Turtle Island" (Native American, Wampanoag), 105

The Magic Weaver of Rugs: A Tale of the Navajo (Native American), 127

"The Gift of Fire" (Greece), 130

"The Plumed Serpent" (Native American, Aztec), 130

"How Happiness Came" (Siberia), 134

"The Children of the Sun" (Native American, Inca, Peru), 138

"Quetzalcoatl" (Native American, Toltec/Aztec, Mexico), 138

8.O. Weapons and Work Implements

"The Yoalah Brothers" (Native American, Yamana, Chile), 20

"Animal Gods: Australian" (Binbinga Aboriginal), 150

8.P. Troubles, Diseases, Hope, and the Like

"The Garden of Eden" (ancient Israel), 9

"Coyote Gives Birth" (Native American, Southern Paiute), 23

"The Two Brothers" (Native American, Iroquois), 25

"First Encounter Between Oggun and Shango" (Sub-Saharan Africa, Yoruba, Brazil, Cuba, Haiti), 42

"Second Child—Oggun (Metals)" (Sub-Saharan Africa, Yoruba, Brazil, Cuba, Haiti), 42

"Tenth Child—Oya (The Air We Breathe)" (Sub-Saharan Africa, Brazil, Cuba, Haiti), 42

"The Creation" (Native American, Mohawk), 43

"The Lie and Evil Enter the Ark" (Jewish), 51

"The Orishas in the World" (Cuba), 56

"Bursting from the Hen's Egg" (China), 67

"First Man Becomes the Devil" (Russian Altaic), 67

"Pandora" (Greece), 67

"Sky Woman and the Twins" (Native American, Wampanoag), 105

"Story of the Sweat Lodge" (Native American, Wampanoag), 105

"In the Beginning Pandora's Box" (Greece), 108

"Cain and Abel" (ancient Israel), 114

"The Forbidden Fruit" (ancient Israel), 114

"Baiami and Bunyip" (Australian Aboriginal), 119

Iblis (Islam), 121

"An Earthly Paradise" (Iran), 130

"The Gift of Fire" (Greece), 130

"Father of Sickness" (Siberia), 134

"The Little Whale" (Siberia), 134

"Pandora's Jar" (Greece), 150

"Pandora: The First Woman?" (Greece), 155

"Fall of the Sky Maiden" (Native American, Iroquois), 165

"Coyote and the Blackbirds" (Native American, Tewa), 171

8.Q. Death and Old Age

"Moon Splits Hare's Lip (Nose)," 10

       Story 2 (Native American, Chitimacha, Louisiana)

       Story 3 (Sub-Saharan Africa, Hausa, Nigeria)

       Stories 4–10 (Sub-Saharan Africa, Bushman, Botswana)

       Stories 11–16 (Sub-Saharan Africa, Bushman, South Africa)

       Story 17 (Sub-Saharan Africa, Bushman, Namibia)

       Stories 18–30 (Sub-Saharan Africa, Hottentot, South Africa)

       Stories 31–32 (Sub-Saharan Africa, Hottentot, Namibia)

"The Opposite Party" (Sub-Saharan Africa), 14

"Why the Earth Eats the Dead" (Native American, Bribri), 18

"Coyote as Orpheus" (Native American, Chinook), 19

"The Raven Cycle" (Native American, Tsimshian), 19

"Toads and Frogs" (Native American, Gabrielino/Luiseno), 19

"The Plant from the Grave" (Native American, Yuracare, Bolivia), 20

"Tokwah, Lord of the Dead" (Native American, Mataco, Argentina), 20

"The Yoaloh Brothers" (Native American, Yamana, Chile), 20

"First Woman Invents Compassion" (Native American, Blackfeet), 23

"Sex, Fingers, and Death" (Native American, Yana), 23

"The Origin of Death" (Native American, Siksika, Blackfeet), 27

"Adapa" (Mespotamia), 40

"The Epic of Gilgamesh" (Mesopotamia), 40

"Birth of Orula" (Sub-Saharan Africa, Yoruba, Brazil, Cuba, Haiti), 42

"Jeggua's Punishment" (Sub-Saharan Africa, Yoruba, Brazil, Cuba, Haiti), 42

"The Chameleon and the Lizard" (Sub-Saharan Africa, Margi), 43

"The Origin of Death" (Sub-Saharan Africa, Hottentot), 43

"The Toad" (Sub-Saharan Africa, Ibo, Nigeria), 43

"Chameleon and First Man" (Sub-Saharan Africa, Ndebele), 58

"Why Python Can Shed His Skin" (Sub-Saharan Africa, Mende), 58

"The Angry Gods" (Tahiti), 67

"An Endless Sea of Mud" (Sub-Saharan Africa, Kono, Guinea), 67

"Finding Night" (Melanesia), 67

"Sun, Life, Wind, and Death" (Micronesia), 67

"Traveling to Form the World" (Native American, Blackfeet), 67

"The Woman Who Fell from the Sky" (Native American, Huron), 67

The Epic of Gilgamesh (Mesopotamia), 86

The Precious Gift: A Navaho Creation Myth (Native American), 87

"The Daughter of the Sun" (Native American, Cherokee), 96

"How Death Came into the World" (Native American, Wampanoag), 105

"The Man Who Almost Lived Forever" (Mesopotamia), 107

"Skinning Out" (Ethiopia), 107

"In the Beginning Pandora's Box" (Greece), 108

"The Forbidden Fruit" (ancient Israel), 114

"Daughter of the Sun" (Native American, Cherokee), 116

"Curlew" (Australian Aboriginal), 119

"Earth-maker and Coyote" (Native American, Maidu), 130

"The Food of Life" (Mesopotamia), 130

"Gilgamesh" (Mesopotamia), 130

"Why Do We Die?" (Sub-Saharan Africa, Ibo), 130

"Snakes" (Native American, Arawak, Guiana), 132

"The Creation of the Universe, Gods, and Japan," 138

"Gilgamesh" (Mesopotamia), 138

"Great Deities: Burundi" (Sub-Saharan Africa), 150

"The Death of Death" (Native American, Maya), 160

"Mataora and Niwareka in the Underworld" (New Zealand, Maori), 162

9. Gods' Adventures

"The Birth and Marriage of Siva" (India), 12

"Lord Krishna's Wives" (India), 12

"Lord Siva and the Satwaras" (India), 12

"Vayanatu Kulavan" (India), 12

"Chac" (Native American, Maya), 17

"The Lord Sun's Bride" (Native American, Maya), 17

"Introduction" (Ares, Aphrodite, Hephaistos), (Greece), 26

"Oedipus and the Theban Cycle" (Greece), 26

"Shiva and the Mountain" (Hindu), 29

Stolen Thunder: A Norse Myth, 32

Cupid and Psyche (Graeco-Roman), 35

"Anzu" (Mesopotamia), 40

"Erra and Ishum" (Mesopotamia), 40

"The Blue God's Birth" (Hindu), 51

"How Dayamanti Chose Her Husband" (Hindu), 51

"How Ganesh Got His Elephant Head" (Hindu), 51

"Fenris, the Wolf" (Norse), 65

"Yama, the God of Death" (India), 65

The Curse of the Ring (Norse), 69

"Geirrod" (Norse), 70

"Utgard" (Norse), 70

"The Wall of Asgard" (Norse), 70

"How Ganesh Got His Elephant Head" (India), 89

"Stealing Heaven's Thunder" (Norse), 107

"Chariot of the Sun God: The Story of Phaeton and Helios" (Graeco-Roman), 123

"The Four Tasks: The Story of Cupid and Psyche" (Graeco-Roman), 123

"Lost at Sea: The Story of Ceyx and Alcyone" (Graeco-Roman), 123

"The Mysterious Visitors: The Story of Baucis and Philemon" (Graeco-Roman), 123

"The Giant's Bride" (Norse), 124

"The Giant's Cauldron" (Norse), 124

"The Golden Apples" (Norse), 124

"How Thor Got His Hammer" (Norse), 124

"Loki's Children" (Norse), 124

"The Magic Stallion" (Norse), 124

"Spell of the Giant King" (Norse), 124

"Thor and the Clay Giant" (Norse), 124

"Aesir, Vanir and a Few Kings" (Norse), 128

"Baldr and Loki" (Norse), 128

"Odin and Thor" (Norse), 128

"Where to Find Norse Myths," 128

"The Apples of Youth" (Norse), 130

"The Elephant God" (India), 130

"Thor in the Land of the Giants" (Norse), 130

"The Theft of Thor's Hammer" (Norse), 138

"The Arrival of the Gods" (Ireland), 139

"Part Two (adventures of gods)" (Native American, Maya), 161

"Part Three (adventures of gods)" (Native American, Maya), 161

"Phaethon's Folly" (Greece), 165

TYPES THAT INCLUDE BOTH MYTHS AND HERO TALES

10. Goddesses and Important Female Figures

"The Two Kings, Shah Shahryar and Shah Zaman, and the Wazir's Daughter Sheherezade" (Arabia), 1

"The Beginning and the End of the World" (Native American, Okanagon), 3

"Evil Kachina Steals Yellow Woman" (Native American, Cochiti), 3

"Sun Steals Yellow Woman" (Native American, Cochiti), 3

"The Warrior Maiden" (Native American, Oneida), 3

"Whirlwind Man Steals Yellow Woman" (Native American, Laguna), 3

"The Woman Who Fell from the Sky" (Native American, Mohawk), 3

"The Arabian Nights" (Arabia), 4

"Queen Balqis and King Sulayman" (Arabia), 4

"The Story of Queen Zabba and King Jadhima" (Arabia), 4

"The Woman with the Wonderful Sight" (Arabia), 4

"Cybele and Attis" (Anatolia, Phrygia), 6

"Joan of Arc" (France), 7

"The Adventures of Samson" (ancient Israel), 9

"Deborah, Judge over Israel" (ancient Israel), 9

"The Garden of Eden" (ancient Israel), 9

"Moses' Ark" (ancient Israel), 9

"The Promised Land" (ancient Israel), 9

"The Wisdom of Solomon" (ancient Israel), 9

"Oba's Ear: A Yoruba Myth in Cuba and Brazil," 10

"Annie Oakley Makes Her Name" (United States), 11

"Calamity's Bet" (United States), 11

"How Daniel Boone Found His Wife" (United States), 11

"The Queen of the Bull-Whackers" (United States), 11

"The Birth and Marriage of Siva" (India), 12

"The Goddess of Mahi River" (India), 12

"Lord Krishna's Wives" (India), 12

"The Rain Prince's Bride" (India), 12

"Siva and Parvati" (India), 12

"The Youngest Daughter-in-Law" (India), 12

"The Dead Wife" (Native American, Miskito), 18

"Creation Tales" (Eskimo), 19

"The Mother of Animals" (Eskimo), 19

"Alone in the Darkness" (Native American, Tariana, Brazil), 20

"Myths of the Kogi" (Native American, Kogi, Colombia), 20

"The Yoaloh Brothers" (Native American, Yamana, Chile), 20

"The Brave Woman and the Flying Head" (Native American, Iroquois), 25

"The Girl Who Was Not Satisfied with Simple Things" (Native American, Iroquois), 25

"The Stone Coat Woman" (Native American, Iroquois), 25

"The Two Daughters" (Native American, Iroquois), 25

"Introduction" (Demeter and Persephone), (Greece), 26

"Introduction" (Ares, Aphrodite, and Hephaistos), (Greece), 26

"Jason, Medea and the Golden Fleece" (Greece), 26

"Oedipus and the Theban Cycle" (Greece), 26

"The Story of Odysseus" (Greece), 26

"Sedna, the Woman Under the Sea" (Inuit), 27

"The White Buffalo Calf Woman and the Sacred Pipe" (Native American, Lakota Sioux), 27

"For Love of Urvashi" (Hindu), 29

"Kunti's Secret Son" (Hindu), 29

Atalanta's Race (Greece), 30

"Arachne's Gift" (Greece), 31

The Mud Pony (Native American, Pawnee), 33

Cupid and Psyche (Graeco-Roman), 35

"The Descent of Ishtar to the Underworld" (Mesopotamia), 40

"The Epic of Gilgamesh" (Mesopotamia), 40

"Nergal and Ereshkigal" (Mesopotamia), 40

"Coyote Steals Spring" (Native American, Pacific Northwest), 41

"Birth of Orula" (Sub-Saharan Africa, Yoruba, Brazil, Cuba, Haiti), 42

"Jeggua's Punishment" (Sub-Saharan Africa, Yoruba, Brazil, Cuba, Haiti), 42

"Ninth Child—Oba Nani (Wisdom and Teacher of the World)" (Sub-Saharan Africa, Yoruba, Brazil, Cuba, Haiti), 42

"Seventh Child and First Female—Dada (Brain)" (Sub-Saharan Africa, Yoruba, Brazil, Cuba, Haiti), 42

"The Creation" (Native American, Mohawk), 43

"*Kalevala*: The Mother of Water" (Finland), 43

"Born Before Her Time" (United States), 44

"Calamity Jane Meets a Long-Lost Lover" (United States), 44

"Deadwood Dick and the Grizzly" (United States), 44

"How Old Calam Got Her Name" (United States), 44

"Like Father, Like Daughter" (United States), 44

"Lover Boy of the Prairies" (United States), 44

"She Fought Her Weight in She-B'ars" (United States), 44

"The Taming of Pecos Bill's Gal Sue" (United States), 44

"The Warrior Woman" (United States), 44

"The Blue God's Birth" (Hindu), 51

"The First Christmas" (Christian), 51

"Hanuman and the Search for Sita" (India), 51

"How Dayamanti Chose Her Husband" (Hindu), 51

"Izanagi and Izanami" (Shinto), 51

"Old Spider and the Giant Clamshell" (Polynesia), 51

"The Story of Maryam's Son" (Islam), 51

"How Manabozho Found Rice" (Native American, Chippewa), 60

"How Manabozho Saved the Rose" (Native American, Chippewa), 60

"How Manabozho Stole Fire" (Native American, Chippewa), 60

"Everlasting Life" (China), 65

"The Angry Gods" (Tahiti), 67

"Moon and Sun" (Sub-Saharan Africa, Fon, Dahomey), 67

"The Woman Who Fell from the Sky" (Native American, Huron), 67

The Curse of the Ring (Norse), 69

"Baldur" (Norse), 70

"The Myth of Kingship" (Egypt), 71

"Plutarch's Version" (Egypt), 71

The Kitchen Knight: A Tale of King Arthur (England), 78

"Of Guinevere and the Round Table" (England), 79

"Of Swords and Sorcerers" (England), 79

"The Ten Fingers of Sedna" (Eskimo), 81

"The Wishes of Savitri" (India), 81

Perseus (Greece), 85

The Epic of Gilgamesh (Mesopotamia), 86

"The Girl in the Forest" (India), 89

"How Ganesh Got His Elephant Head" (India), 89

"How Ram Defeated the Demon King Ravan" (India), 89

"The King Without an Heir" (India), 89

"Introduction" (Native American, Ojibway), 91

"The Manitous of the Forests and Meadows" (Native American, Ojibway), 91

Sally Ann Thunder Ann Whirlwind Crockett (United States), 92

Rimonah of the Flashing Sword: A North African Tale (Egypt), 94

"Sky Woman and the Twins" (Native American, Wampanoag), 105

"The Birth of Huitzilopochtli" (Native American, Aztec), 106

"The Myth of Mayahuel" (Native American, Aztec), 106

"The Myth of Tlaltecuhtli" (Native American, Aztec), 106

"The Singer Above the River" (Germany), 107

"Arachne the Spinner" (Greece), 108

"Atalanta's Race" (Greece), 108

"Echo and Narcissus" (Greece), 108

"In the Beginning Pandora's Box" (Greece), 108

"Odysseus" (Greece), 108

"Orpheus and Eurydice" (Greece), 108

"Persephone and the Pomegranate Seeds" (Greece), 108

"Theseus and the Minotaur" (Greece), 108

"The Wooden Horse" (Greece), 108

"Esther Becomes Queen" (ancient Israel), 114

"The Forbidden Fruit" (ancient Israel), 114

"Isaac and Rebekah" (ancient Israel), 114

"Jacob and Esau" (ancient Israel), 114

"The Queen of Sheba" (ancient Israel), 114

"Rachel and Leah" (ancient Israel), 114

"Ruth and Naomi" (ancient Israel), 114

"Samson and Delilah" (ancient Israel), 114

"The Walls of Jericho" (ancient Israel), 114

"Daughter of the Sun" (Native American, Cherokee), 116

"Medusa" (Greece), 116

"The Beginning of Life" (Australian Aboriginal), 119

"Pecos Bill" (United States), 122

"Sally Ann Thunder Ann Whirlwind" (United States), 122

"The Face in the Pool: The Story of Echo and Narcissus" (Graeco-Roman), 123

"The Golden Apples: The Story of Atalanta and Hippomenes" (Graeco-Roman), 123

"The Great Bear: The Story of Callisto and Arcus" (Graeco-Roman), 123

"Journey to the Underworld: The Story of Orpheus and Eurydice" (Graeco-Roman), 123

"The Kidnapping: The Story of Ceres and Proserpina" (Graeco-Roman), 123

"Lost at Sea: The Story of Ceyx and Alcyone" (Graeco-Roman), 123

"The Weaving Contest: The Story of Arachne and Minerva" (Graeco-Roman), 123

"The Death of Balder" (Norse), 124

"The Fairest Feet" (Norse), 124

"The Golden Apples" (Norse), 124

"Marriage of the Ice Maiden" (Norse), 124

How the Stars Fell into the Sky: A Navajo Legend (Native American), 126

"Aesir, Vanir and a Few Kings" (Norse), 128

"Baldr and Loki" (Norse), 128

"Gods and Heroes" (Norse), 128

"Where to Find Norse Myths," 128

"The Apples of Youth" (Norse), 130

"The Cat Goddess" (Egypt), 130

"The Elephant God" (India), 130

"Isis and Osiris" (Egypt), 130

"Mother of Life and Death" (India), 130

"Persephone" (Greece), 130

"Sedna" (Inuit, Eskimo), 130

"World Without Sun" (Japan), 130

"Kotura, Lord of the Winds" (Siberia), 134

"The *Aeneid* of Virgil" (Rome), 138

"Ama-terasu" (Japan), 138

"The Creation of the Universe, Gods, and Japan," 138

"Demeter and Persephone" (Greece), 138

"*Gilgamesh*" (Mesopotamia), 138

"Osiris, Isis, and Horus" (Egypt), 138

"The *Ramayana*" (India), 138

"The *Saga of Sigurd the Volsung*," (Norse), 138

"The Theft of Idun's Apples" (Norse), 138

"The Children of Lir" (Ireland), 139

"Annie Christmas" (African American), 145

"Hekeke" (Native American, Miowok), 145

"Hiiaka" (Hawaii), 145

"Otoonah" (Eskimo), 145

"Pale-Faced Lightning" (Native American, Pueblo), 145

"Pohaha" (Native American, Tewa Pueblo), 145

"Sal Fink" (United States), 145

"The Star Maiden" (Native American, Chippewa), 145

"Aphrodite: Goddess of Love" (Greece), 147

"Atalanta: The Fleet-footed Huntress" (Greece), 147

"Athena: Warrior Goddess of Wisdom" (Greece), 147

"Bilqis: The Queen of Sheba" (Arabia), 147

"Boadicea: Queen of the Iceni" (British Isles), 147

"Circe: The Enchantress" (Greece), 147

"Demeter: Goddess of the Grain" (Greece), 147

"Esther: The Champion of Her People" (ancient Israel), 147

"Guanyin: The Goddess of Mercy" (China), 147

"The Hunter Maiden of the Zuni People" (Native American), 147

"Joan of Arc" (France), 147

"Judith and Holofernes" (ancient Israel), 147

"Mary Bryant" (Australia), 147

"Medea: A Cruel and Savage Witch" (Greece), 147

"Pocahontas" (Native American, Algonkion), 147

"Rehab and the Fall of Jericho" (ancient Israel), 147

"Scheherazade" (Arabia), 147

"Battles: India," 150

"Great Warriors: Russia," 150

"Sedna" (Inuit), 150

Black Ships Before Troy: The Story of THE ILIAD (Greece), 153

"The Enchantress" (Greece), 154

"Farewell to Calypso" (Greece), 154

"The King's Daughter" (Greece), 154

"The Slaying of the Suitors" (Greece), 154

"The Adventures of Odysseus" (Greece), 155

"Antigone: A Hero Can Also Be a Woman" (Greece), 155

"The Golden Fleece, Jason, and Medea" (Greece), 155

"The House of Atreus: Murder, Vengeance, and Forgiveness," (Greece), 155

"Pandora: The First Woman?" (Greece), 155

"Persephone in Hades" (Greece), 155

"Perseus and the Medusa: Everybody's Fairy Tale" (Greece), 155

"The Trojan War" (Greece), 155

King Arthur and the Round Table (England), 156

"Part Four (the first prostitutes)" (Native American, Maya), 161

"Putawai" (New Zealand, Maori), 162

"Branwen, Daughter of Llyr" (Wales), 163

"Math, Son of Mathonwy" (Wales), 163

"Fall of the Sky Maiden" (Native American, Iroquois), 165

"Lindu's Astral Veil" (Estonia), 165

"A Terrestrial Paradise" (China), 165

"Realms of Eternal Night" (Mesopotamia), 166

"Princess Glory" (Japan), 169

"Coyote and the Giant Sisters" (Native American, Pacific Northwest), 176

Esther's Story (ancient Israel), 181

The Rainbow Bridge (Native American, Chumash), 182

"Annie Christmas" (African American), 185

"Angel of Mercy—II" (United States), 186

"Angel of Mercy—III" (United States), 186

"Belle and the Stuff of Legends" (United States), 186

"Belle at Devil's Den" (United States), 186

"Belle at Marble Cave" (United States), 186

"Calamity Jane Explains Her Name" (United States), 186

11. Searches and Quests

"Evil Kachina Steals Yellow Woman" (Native American, Cochiti), 3

"Sun Steals Yellow Woman" (Native American, Cochiti), 3

"The City of Brass" (Arabia), 4

"The Promised Land" (ancient Israel), 9

"The Dead Wife" (Native American, Miskito), 18

"Hodadenon: The Last One Left and the Chestnut Tree" (Native American, Iroquois), 25

"The Descent of Ishtar to the Underworld" (Mesopotamia), 40

"The Epic of Gilgamesh" (Mesopotamia), 40

"How Gluskabe Brought the Summer" (Native American, Abenaki), 43

"T'appin (Terrapin)" (African American), 43

Jason and the Golden Fleece (Greece), 47

"Hanuman and the Search for Sita" (India), 51

"How Rama Defeated Ravana" (India), 51

"The Merchant and the Five Hundred Gold Coins" (Sikh), 51

"How the World Was Saved" (Native American, Navajo), 68

"The Apples of Iduna" (Norse), 70

"Baldur" (Norse), 70

"Sif's Hair" (Norse), 70

"The Myth of Kingship" (Egypt), 71

"Plutarch's Version" (Egypt), 71

"Manabozho" (Native American, Ojibwa), 76

"Nanabush Kitche Manitou's Emissary" (Native American, Ojibwa), 76

"The Twelve Labors of Hercules" (Graeco-Roman), 80

"Geriguiaguiatugo" (Native American, Bororo), 81

Ahaiyute and Cloud Eater (Native American, Zuni), 83

Perseus (Greece), 85

The Epic of Gilgamesh (Mesopotamia), 86

"How Ram Defeated the Demon King Ravan" (India), 89

"The Manitous of the Forests and Meadows" (Native American, Ojibway), 91

"Nana'b'oozoo" (Native American, Ojibway), 91

"The Daughter of the Sun" (Native American, Cherokee), 96

"Orpheus" (Native American, Yuchi), 96

All of You Was Singing (Native American, Aztec), 102

"The Great Migration and Old Man Winter" (Native American, Wampanoag), 105

"The Hero Journey of the Hero Twins" (Native American, Maya), 106

"Brave Quest" (Native American, Blackfeet), 107

"Jason and the Golden Fleece" (Greece), 108

"Odysseus" (Greece), 108

"Orpheus and Eurydice" (Greece), 108

"Persephone and the Pomegranate Seeds" (Greece), 108

"Perseus" (Greece), 108

"Theseus and the Minotaur" (Greece), 108

"The Twelve Labors of Heracles" (Greece), 108

"Medusa" (Greece), 116

"The Four Tasks: The Story of Cupid and Psyche" (Graeco-Roman), 123

"Journey to the Underworld: The Story of Orpheus and Eurydice" (Graeco-Roman), 123

"The Kidnapping: The Story of Ceres and Proserpina" (Graeco-Roman), 123

"The Death of Balder" (Norse), 124

"The Giant's Bride" (Norse), 124

"The Golden Apples" (Norse), 124

"How Thor Got His Hammer" (Norse), 124

"Marriage of the Ice Maiden" (Norse), 124

"Odin's Three Quests" (Norse), 124

"Aesir, Vanir and a Few Kings" (Norse), 128

"Baldr and Loki" (Norse), 128

"Where to Find Norse Myths" (Norse), 128

"Aeneas in the Underworld" (Rome), 130

"Gilgamesh" (Mesopotamia), 130

"The Holy Grail" (England), 130

"Isis and Osiris" (Egypt), 130

"The Labors of Heracles" (Greece), 130

"Persephone" (Greece), 130

"Theseus and the Minotaur" (Greece), 130

"The Winged Horse" (Greece), 130

"Bold Yatto and His Sister Tayune" (Siberia), 134

"Brave Azmun" (Siberia), 134

"How Anga Fetched a Serpent's Skin and a Bear's Fur" (Siberia), 134

"The *Aeneid* of Virgil" (Rome), 138

"Demeter and Persephone" (Greece), 138
"*Gilgamesh*" (Mesopotamia), 138
"The *Odyssey* of Homer" (Greece), 138
"The Quest for the Sun" (China), 138
"The *Ramayana*" (India), 138
"Telepinu" (Hittite), 138
"Great Deities: Phoenecia," 150
"Osiris and Isis" (Egypt), 150
"Telemachus Seeks His Father" (Greece), 154
"Adonis" (Greece), 155
"The Adventures of Odysseus" (Greece), 155
"The Golden Fleece, Jason, and Medea" (Greece), 155
"Orpheus and Eurydice" (Greece), 155
"Persephone in Hades" (Greece), 155
"Perseus and the Medusa: Everybody's Fairy Tale" (Greece), 155
"Hutu and Pare" (New Zealand, Maori), 162
"Kupe's Discovery of Aotearoa" (New Zealand, Maori), 162
"Mataora and Niwareka in the Underworld" (New Zealand, Maori), 162
"Daring the Dark" (Rome), 166
"A Parting of Worlds" (Ireland), 166
"Realms of Eternal Night" (Mesopotamia), 166
"Realms of Eternal Night" (Norse), 166
"How Beaver Stole Fire" (Native American, Nez Perce), 171
"The Long Winter" (Native American, Slavey), 171
"Raven, the River Maker" (Native American, Tlingit), 171
"Kana the Stretching Wonder" (Hawaii), 176

12. Tricksters: Gods, Humans, and Animals

"Coyote Kills Owl-Woman" (Native American, Okanagan), 3
"Trickster Seeks Endowments; Measuring the Snake; Challenging Birds (Insects) to
    Fill a Container; Milking a Cow (Deer) Stuck in a Tree," 10
        Stories 1–2 (Sub-Saharan Africa, Mandinka, Gambia)
        Stories 3–5 (Sub-Saharan Africa, Temne, Sierra Leone)
        Stories 6–7 (Sub-Saharan Africa, Liberia)
        Story 8 (Sub-Saharan Africa, De, Liberia)
        Story 9 (Sub-Saharan Africa, Wobe, Ivory Coast)
        Story 10 (Sub-Saharan Africa, Fulani, Mali)
        Story 11 (Sub-Saharan Africa, Malinke, Mali)
        Stories 12–13 (Sub-Saharan Africa, Mosi, Upper Volta)
        Stories 14–17 (Sub-Saharan Africa, Ghana)
        Stories 18–22 (Sub-Saharan Africa, Ashanti, Ghana)
        Story 23 (Sub-Saharan Africa, Ewe, Ghana)

Stories 24–26 (Sub-Saharan Africa, Hausa, Nigeria)
Story 27 (Sub-Saharan Africa, Bura, Nigeria)
Story 28 (Sub-Saharan Africa, Igbo, Nigeria)
Story 29 (Sub-Saharan Africa, Mbala, Zaire)
Story 30 (Native American, Hitchiti, Oklahoma)
Story 31 (Native American, Natchez, Oklahoma)
Story 32 (Native American, Chitimacha, Louisiana)
Story 33 (African American, Mississippi)
Stories 34–35 (African American, Alabama)
Story 36 (African American, Virginia)
Stories 37–48 (African American, South Carolina)
Stories 49–56 (African American, Georgia)
Stories 57–58 (Native American,, Creek, Georgia)
Story 59 (Native American, Seminole, Florida)
Story 60 (Mexico)
Story 61 (Native American, Chuh, Guatemala)
Story 62 (African, Bahamas)
Story 63 (African, Dominican Republic)
Stories 64–67 (African, Guadaloupe)
Story 68 (African, Marie Galante)
Stories 69–70 African, Les Saintes)
Stories 71–72 (African, Dominica)
Story 73 (African, Martinique)
Story 74 (African, Saint Lucia)
Story 75 (African, Grenada)
Story 76 (African, Trinidad)
Story 77 (Native American, Warao, Venezuela)
Story 78 (Colombia)

"Moon Splits Hare's Lip (Nose)," 10
Story 1 (African American, Georgia)
Story 2 (Native American, Chitimacha, Louisiana)
Story 3 (Sub-Saharan Africa, Hausa, Nigeria)
Stories 6–10 (Sub-Saharan Africa, Bushman, Botswana)
Stories 11–16 (Sub-Saharan Africa, Bushman, South Africa)
Story 17 (Sub-Saharan Africa, Bushman, Namibia)
Stories 18–30 (Sub-Saharan Africa, Hottentot, South Africa)
Stories 31–32 (Sub-Saharan Africa, Hottentot, Namibia)

"Crockett Gets the Votes" (United States), 11

"Coyote Turns into a Buffalo" (Native American, Pawnee), 11

"How Mr. Rabbit Was Too Sharp for Mr. Fox" (African American), 11

"The Wonderful Tar-Baby Story" (African American), 11

"Siva and Parvati" (India), 12

"Ananse's Harvest" (Sub-Saharan Africa), 14

"A Debt Made Profit, Or, Why Monkeys Live in Trees" (Sub-Saharan Africa), 14

"The Glue of Greed" (Sub-Saharan Africa), 14

"Head Over Heart" (Sub-Saharan Africa), 14

"The Monster at the Stream" (Sub-Saharan Africa), 14

"The Opposite Party" (Sub-Saharan Africa), 14

"Ananse and God's Business" (Sub-Saharan Africa, Larteh, Twi, Ghana), 16

"The Cloud Mother" (Sub-Saharan Africa, Krio, Sierra Leone), 16

"Dog Is Betrayed" (Sub-Saharan Africa, Yoruba, Nigeria), 16

"How Tortoise Got Water" (Sub-Saharan Africa, Yoruba, Nigeria), 16

"The Return of Ananse" (Sub-Saharan Africa, Sefwi, Ghana), 16

"Spider Finds a Fool" (Sub-Saharan Africa, Ga, Ghana), 16

"Spider's Bargain with God" (Sub-Saharan Africa, Sefwi, Ghana), 16

"Spider the Swindler" (Sub-Saharan Africa, Sefwi, Ghana), 16

"The Stone with Whiskers" (Sub-Saharan Africa, Krio, Sierra Leone), 16

"Tortoise and the Singing Crab" (Sub-Saharan Africa, Vane Avatime, Ghana), 16

"Tortoise Sheds a Tear" (Sub-Saharan Africa, Yoruba, Nigeria), 16

"The Yam Farm and the Problem Tongue" (Sub-Saharan Africa, Ga, Ghana), 16

"Rabbit and Coyote" (Native American, Maya), 17

"Rabbit and Puma" (Native American, Maya), 17

"Rabbit Gets Married" (Native American, Maya), 17

"The Bird Nester" (Native American, Apache), 19

"Coyote as Orpheus" (Native American, Chinook), 19

"Coyote Releases Salmon" (Native American, Salish), 19

"Mink" (Native American, Kwakiutl), 19

"The Raven Cycle" (Native American, Tsimshian), 19

"Tokwah, Lord of the Dead" (Native American, Mataco, Argentina), 20

"More Wehixamukes" (Native American, Lenape), 21

"Six Stories About Wehixamukes" (Native American, Lenape), 21

"Coyote and the Prairie Dogs" (Native American, Navajo), 23

"Coyote Marries His Own Daughter" (Native American, Karuk), 23

"Coyote Steals Fire" (Native American, Karuk), 23

"Coyote Tricks Grey Fox" (Native American, Apache), 23

"Coyote Turns into Driftwood" (Native American, Karuk), 23

"How Her Teeth Were Pulled" (Native American, Northern Paiute), 23

"Two Coyotes" (Native American, Nez Perce), 23

"How Bear Lost His Tail" (Native American, Iroquois), 25

"The Hungry Fox and the Boastful Suitor" (Native American, Iroquois), 25

"Rabbit and Fox" (Native American, Iroquois), 25

"Skunny-Wundy and the Stone Giant" (Native American, Iroquois), 25

"Turtle's Race with Bear" (Native American, Iroquois), 25

"Turtle's Race with Beaver" (Native American, Iroquois), 25

"Gluscabi and the Game Animals" (Native American, Abenaki), 27

"Kokopilan, the Hump-Backed Flute Player" (Native American, Hopi), 27

"Old Man Coyote and the Rock" (Native American, Pawnee), 27

"Ashes to Ashes" (Hindu), 29

"The Dwarf's Three Steps" (Hindu), 29

"Old Man and the Bobcat" (Native American, Blackfeet), 34

Robin Hood and His Merry Men (England), 38

Robin Hood in the Greenwood (England), 39

"Coyote Steals Spring" (Native American, Pacific Northwest), 41

"Grandfather Spider's Feast" (Sub-Saharan Africa), 41

"Hungry Spider" (Sub-Saharan Africa, Ashanti), 41

"Anansi Owns All Tales That Are Told" (Sub-Saharan Africa, Ashanti, Ghana), 43

"Anansi Plays Dead" (Sub-Saharan Africa, Ashanti, Ghana), 43

"Anansi's Rescue from the River" (Sub-Saharan Africa, Ashanti, Ghana), 43

"Coyote Juggles His Eyes" (Native American, Sioux), 43

"How Ijapa, Who Was Short, Became Long" (Sub-Saharan Africa, Yoruba, Nigeria), 43

"Ijapa Cries for His Horse" (Sub-Saharan Africa, Yoruba, Nigeria), 43

"The Jackal and the Hen" (Kabyle, Algeria), 43

"The Jackal and the Lion" (Kabyle, Algeria), 43

"The Lustful Raven" (Inuit), 43

"The Monkey-Son" (Tamiladu, India), 43

"The Raven and the Hunter" (Inuit), 43

"The Raven and the Whale" (Inuit), 43

"Sheer Tops" (African American), 43

"The Stealing of the Sun" (Native American, Kato), 43

"Sun's Arrival in the Sky" (Native American, Miwok), 43

"T'appin (Terrapin)" (African American), 43

"The Winnebago Trickster Cycle" (Native American), 43

"Coyote Makes a Texas Cowboy" (Native American), 44

"Hare and the White Man" (Sub-Saharan Africa, Tswana), 45

Brer Tiger and the Big Wind (African American), 46

"Chameleon and the Greedy Spider" (Sub-Saharan Africa, Bushman), 58

"Dung Beetle's Burden" (Sub-Saharan Africa, Ghana), 58

"The Free Spirits, Bouki and Malice" (Haiti), 65

"Manabozo" (Native American), 65

"Little Girl and Buh Rabby" (African American), 66

"The Pea-Pod Man" (Inuit), 67

"Spider Ananse Finds *Something*" (Sub-Saharan Africa, Krachi, Togo), 67

"Traveling to Form the World" (Native American, Blackfeet), 67

"Turtle Dives to the Bottom of the Sea" (Native American, Maidu), 67

The Curse of the Ring (Norse), 69

"The Apples of Iduna" (Norse), 70

"Baldur" (Norse), 70

"Sif's Hair" (Norse), 70

"The Day Magpie Tricked Coyote" (Native American, Navajo), 74

"First Angry" (Native American, Navajo), 74

"The Guardian of the Corn" (Native American, Navajo), 74

Robin Hood (England), 75

"Bagging Geese" (Native American, Ojibwa), 76

"The Duck Dinner" (Native American, Ojibwa), 76

"How Manabozho Disguised Himself as a Woman" (Native American, Ojibwa), 76

"Indian Legend of the Deluge" (Native American, Ojibwa), 76

"Manabozho" (Native American, Ojibwa), 76

"Menaboju's Marriage" (Native American, Ojibwa), 76

"Nanabush and the Ducks" (Native American, Ojibwa), 76

"Ne-naw-bo-zhoo Spoils the Sugar Trees" (Native American, Ojibwa), 76

"Nenebojo and the Deer" (Native American, Ojibwa), 76

"Why the Squirrel Coughs" (Native American, Ojibwa), 76

"Catching the Sun" (Polynesia), 81

"The Monkey Who Would Be King" (China), 81

"Nana'b'oozoo" (Native American, Ojibway), 91

"Pukawiss: The Disowned" (Native American, Ojibway), 91

"The Bandit" (Jewish), 93

"The Candlesticks" (Jewish), 93

"The Cow" (Jewish), 93

"The Goose's Foot" (Jewish), 93

"Hershel Goes to Heaven" (Jewish), 93

"An Incredible Story" (Jewish), 93

"The Miracle" (Jewish), 93

"Money from a Table" (Jewish), 93

"Potatoes!" (Jewish), 93

"What Hershel's Father Did" (Jewish), 93

"Owner of the Animals" (Native American, Caddo), 96

"The Tasks of the Trickster" (Sub-Saharan Africa, Ashanti, Gold Coast), 96

"The Theft of Fire" (Native American, Hitchiti), 96

"A Tug of War" (Native American, Creek), 96

"How Wisdom Came to the Tribe" (Sub-Saharan Africa, Ashanti, Ghana), 98

"The Nkorowa Dance" (Sub-Saharan Africa, Ashanti, Ghana), 98

"The Spider and the Terrible Great Ones" (Sub-Saharan Africa, Hausa, Ghana), 98

The Story of Robin Hood (England), 101

"Maushop and Grandfather Sun" (Native American, Wampanoag), 105

"Anansi and the Mind of God" (West Indies), 107

"First Snow" (Native American), 107

"Robin Hood and the Golden Arrow" (England), 107

"Saving Time" (Polynesia), 107

"Odysseus" (Greece), 108

"The Wooden Horse" (Greece), 108

Raven: A Trickster Tale from the Pacific Northwest (Native American), 110

"Jacob and Esau" (ancient Israel), 114

"Possum, Turtle, and the Wolves" (Native American, Cherokee), 115

"Br'er Rabbit Builds a Home" (African American), 116

"Gluscabi and the Wind Eagle" (Native American, Abenaki), 116

"The Death of Balder" (Norse), 124

"The Golden Apples" (Norse), 124

"How Thor Got His Hammer" (Norse), 124

"The Magic Stallion" (Norse), 124

"Baldr and Loki" (Norse), 128

"Where to Find Norse Myths," 128

Monkey Creates Havoc in Heaven (China), 129

"The Apples of Youth" (Norse), 130

"The Death of Balder" (Norse), 130

"Earth-maker and Coyote" (Native American, Maidu), 130

"Going to the Palace" (Haiti), 130

"The Great Flood" (Serbia), 130

"Loki the Trickster" (Norse), 130

"Maui-of-a-Thousand Tricks" (Polynesia), 130

"Ankakumikaityn the Nomad Wolf" (Siberia), 134

"Coot and the Fox" (Siberia), 134

"The Death of Baldur" (Norse), 138

"Quetzalcoatl" (Native American, Toltec/Aztec, Mexico), 138

"Raven and the Sources of Light" (Native American, Haida/Tlingit, Canada), 138

"The Theft of Idun's Apples" (Norse), 138

"The Theft of Thor's Hammer" (Norse), 138

"How Rabbit Tricked Otter" (Native American, Cherokee), 140

How Turtle's Back Was Cracked: A Traditional Cherokee Tale (Native American), 141

"Odysseus: Agile of Body and Mind" (Greece), 148

"Animal Gods: North America" (Native American, Haida, Tlingit, Tsimshian), 150

"Cagn" (Sub-Saharan Africa, San, Bushman), 150

Muwin and the Magic Hare (Native American, Passamaquoddy), 151

"The Beggar in the Corner" (Greece), 154

"The Cyclops" (Greece), 154

"The Birth of Maui" (New Zealand, Maori), 162

"Maui and the Great Fish" (New Zealand, Maori), 162

"Fox and Bear" (Northern Europe), 164

"Coyote and the Crow Buffalo-Ranchers" (Native American), 170

"Coyote Learns a Lesson" (Native American), 170

"Coyote's Eyes" (Native American), 170

"Coyote's Revenge" (Native American), 170

"How Beaver Stole Fire" (Native American, Nez Perce), 171

"How Possum Got His Skinny Tail" (Native American, Cherokee), 171

"Raven, the River Maker" (Native American, Tlingit), 171

"A Tug of War" (Native American, Creek), 171

Rainbow Crow: A Lenape Tale (Native American), 172

"Gib Morgan Brings in the Well" (United States), 175

"Coyote and the Giant Sisters" (Native American, Pacific Northwest), 176

"The Cyclops" (Greece), 176

"Senor Coyote Acts as Judge" (Mexican American), 178

"Anansi Tries to Steal All the Wisdom in the World" (African American), 185

"Brother Lion and Brother Man" (African American), 185

"Brother Possum and Brother Snake" (African American), 185

"The Cabbage Inspector" (African American), 185

"How Br'er Rabbit Outsmarted the Frogs" (African American), 185

"Why Brother Alligator Has a Rough Back" (African American), 185

"Kuloskap and the Three Wishes" (Native American, Micmac), 187

"Skunnee Wundee and the Stone Giant" (Native American, Seneca), 187

HERO TALES

13. Fools and Buffoons

"Trickster Seeks Endowments; Measuring the Snake; Challenging Birds (Insects) to
    Fill a Container; Milking a Cow (Deer) Stuck in a Tree," 10
        Stories 15–17 (Sub-Saharan Africa, Ghana)
        Story 22 (Sub-Saharan Africa, Ashanti, Ghana)
        Story 30 (Native American, Hitchiti, Oklahoma)
        Story 31 (Native American, Natchez, Oklahoma)
        Story 35 (African American, Alabama)
        Stories 38–45 (African American, South Carolina)
        Story 75 (African, Grenada)

"Moon Splits Hare's Lip (Nose)," 10
        Story 2 (Native American, Chitimacha, Louisiana)
        Stories 4–10 (Sub-Saharan Africa, Bushman, Botswana)
        Stories 11–16 (Sub-Saharan Africa, Bushman, South Africa)
        Story 17 (Sub-Saharan Africa, Bushman, Namibia)

Stories 21–30 (Sub-Saharan Africa, Hottentot, South Africa)

Stories 31–32 (Sub-Saharan Africa, Hottentot, Namibia)

"Coyote Turns into a Buffalo" (Native American, Pawnee), 11

"Ananse's Harvest" (Sub-Saharan Africa), 14

"The Glue of Greed" (Sub-Saharan Africa), 14

"Spider Finds a Fool" (Sub-Saharan Africa, Ga, Ghana), 16

"The Yam Farm and the Problem Tongue" (Sub-Saharan Africa, Ga, Ghana), 16

"Crazy Jack Puts His Nose to the Ground" (Native American, Lenape), 21

"Jack Babysits" (Native American, Lenape), 21

"Six Stories About Wehixamukes" (Native American, Lenape), 21

"Wehixamukes Story" (Native American, Lenape), 21

"Coyote Marries His Own Daughter" (Native American, Karuk), 23

"Coyote in the Cedar Tree" (Native American, Chinook), 34

"Old Man and the Bobcat" (Native American, Blackfeet), 34

"Anansi Plays Dead" (Sub-Saharan Africa, Ashanti, Ghana), 43

"Coyote Juggles His Eyes" (Native American, Sioux), 43

"Ijapa Cries for His Horse" (Sub-Saharan Africa, Yoruba, Nigeria), 43

"The Jackal and the Hen" (Kabyle, Algeria), 43

"The Lustful Raven" (Inuit), 43

"The Raven and the Whale" (Inuit), 43

"T'appin (Terrapin)" (African American), 43

"The Winnebago Trickster Cycle" (Native American, Winnebago), 43

"Hare and His Friends" (Sub-Saharan Africa, Luo), 45

"The Golden Shoes" (Russian Jewish), 53

"Coyote's New Coat" (Native American, Navajo), 74

"The Day Magpie Tricked Coyote" (Native American, Navajo), 74

"First Angry" (Native American, Navajo), 74

"The Guardian of the Corn" (Native American, Navajo), 74

"The Duck Dinner" (Native American, Ojibwa), 76

"Manabozho" (Native American, Ojibwa), 76

"Nanabush and the Ducks" (Native American, Ojibwa), 76

"Nanibozho Visits the Woodpecker" (Native American, Ojibwa), 76

"Nenebojo Dives for Berries and Peaches" (Native American, Ojibwa), 76

"Nenebojo Makes Ice Music" (Native American, Ojibwa), 76

"Nenebojo Visits Black Duck" (Native American, Ojibwa), 76

"Nenebuc, the Transformer" (Native American, Ojibwa), 76

"Muckachuck" (Native American, Wampanoag), 105

"Chariot of the Sun God: The Story of Phaeton and Helios" (Graeco-Roman), 123

How the Stars Fell into the Sky: A Navajo Legend (Native American), 126

Monkey Creates Havoc in Heaven (China), 129

"Glooskap and the Wasis" (Native American, Algonquin), 130

"A Beginning" (Jewish), 144

"Coyote's Eyes" (Native American), 170

"Coyote Learns a Lesson" (Native American), 170

"Coyote and the Blackbirds" (Native American, Tewa), 171

"Rabbit and the Willow" (Native American, Seneca), 171

"'Mana Sorra (Sister Fox) and 'Mano Coyote (Brother, or Br'er, Coyote)" (Mexican American), 178

"Anansi and Candlefly" (African American), 185

"Anansi and Turtle" (African American), 185

"Fling-A-Mile" (African American), 185

"Why Anansi Has a Narrow Waist" (African American), 185

14. Bad Men and Outlaws

Robin Hood and His Merry Men (England), 38

Robin Hood in the Greenwood (England), 39

"El Chivato" (United States), 44

"El Keed" (United States), 44

"He Rose from the Grave" (United States), 44

"No-Head Joaquin and Three-Fingered Jack" (United States), 44

"Renaud the Rebel" (France), 49

Robin Hood (England), 75

The Story of Robin Hood (England), 101

"Robin Hood and the Golden Arrow" (England), 107

"The House of Atreus: Murder, Vengeance, and Forgiveness" (Greece), 155

"Il'ya of Murom and Nightingale, the Brigand" (Russia), 177

"Angel of Mercy—II" (United States), 186

"Angel of Mercy—III" (United States), 186

"Belle and the Stuff of Legends" (United States), 186

"Belle at Devil's Den" (United States), 186

"Belle at Marble Cave" (United States), 186

"Calamity Jane Explains Her Name" (United States), 186

"Jesse and Frank" (United States), 186

"Wild Bill: The 'Prince of Pistoleers'" (United States), 186

15. Lawmen and Judges

"Ah Ling's Hommyside" (United States), 44

"Fining the Deceased" (United States), 44

"The Hanging of Carlos Robles" (United States), 44

"The King of the Pistoleers" (United States), 44

"The Law West of the Pecos" (United States), 44

"Roy Bean's Pet Bear" (United States), 44

16. Holy Men, Teachers, Prophets, Spiritual Leaders, Lawgivers, and Wise Persons

"Francis of Assisi" (Italy), 7

"Deborah, Judge over Israel" (ancient Israel), 9

"Elijah, the Prophet of God" (ancient Israel), 9

"The Exodus" (ancient Israel), 9

"The Flood" (ancient Israel), 9

"Moses' Ark" (ancient Israel), 9

"The Promised Land" (ancient Israel), 9

Exodus (ancient Israel), 28

"The Blossom Tree" (Tibet), 43

"Abraham and the Idols" (Jewish), 51

"The Battles of Badr and Uhud" (Islam), 51

"The First Christmas" (Christian), 51

"The Great Bronze Buddha and the Whale" (Buddhist), 51

"The Hare and the Earthquake" (Buddhist), 51

"Jesus' Last Days" (Christian), 51

"The Life of Guru Nanak" (Sikh), 51

"The Life of the Buddha" (Buddhist), 51

"The Merchant and the Five Hundred Gold Coins" (Sikh), 51

"Muhammed Escapes from Mecca" (Islam), 51

"The Prince and the Guru's Cloak" (Sikh), 51

"The Story of Maryam's Son" (Islam), 51

"The Ten Plagues of Egypt" (ancient Israel), 51

"The Valley of the Ants" (Islam), 51

"Bavasi's Feast" (Russian Jewish), 53

The Shadow of a Flying Bird: A Legend from the Kurdistani Jews, 54

"The Case of the Boiled Egg" (Jewish), 88

"Cheeby-aub-oozoo: The Ghost of Rabbit" (Native American, Ojibway), 91

"Admirable Hare" (Ceylon), 107

The Buddha: His Life Retold (India), 112

"Abraham" (ancient Israel), 114

"The Birth of Moses" (ancient Israel), 114

"The Coat of Many Colors" (ancient Israel), 114

"The Death of Moses" (ancient Israel), 114

"Handwriting on the Wall" (ancient Israel), 114

"Isaac and Rebekah" (ancient Israel), 114
"Jacob and Esau" (ancient Israel), 114
"Jacob's Ladder" (ancient Israel), 114
"Jonah and the Whale" (ancient Israel), 114
"King Solomon's Wisdom" (ancient Israel), 114
"The Lord's Message to Moses" (ancient Israel), 114
"The Lord Speaks to Noah" (ancient Israel), 114
"Noah and the Ark" (ancient Israel), 114
"Noah Hears God's Promise" (ancient Israel), 114
"The Prophet Elijah" (ancient Israel), 114
"Rachel and Leah" (ancient Israel), 114
"Sodom and Gomorrah" (ancient Israel), 114
"Solomon's Dream" (ancient Israel), 114
"The Ten Commandments" (ancient Israel), 114
"The Golden Idol" (Ireland), 139
"The Land of Promise" (Ireland), 139
Buddha, 142
"Moses the Lawgiver" (ancient Israel), 148
"Lunar Denizens" (Buddhist), 165
"Noah's Miraculous Voyage" (Jewish), 165
"Come to My Kasaga Mountain" (Japan), 169
"The God of Fire and Thunder" (Japan), 169
"Gyogi and Baraman" (Japan), 169
"Kobo Daishi" (Japan), 169
"The Old Mackerel Peddler" (Japan), 169
"Very High in the Mountains" (Japan), 169
"The Wizard of the Mountains" (Japan), 169
"Senor Coyote Acts as Judge" (Mexican American), 178

17. Kings, Queens, and Rulers

"Iran of the Tall Columns" (Arabia), 4
"Queen Balqis and King Sulayman" (Arabia), 4
"The Story of Queen Zabba and King Jadhima" (Arabia), 4
"The Wisdom of Solomon" (ancient Israel), 9
"Bhimnath Mahadev" (India), 12
"Oedipus and the Theban Cycle" (Greece), 26
"The Story of Odysseus" (Greece), 26
"Theseus of Athens" (Greece), 26
"Krishna—Man and God" (India), 29
"The Monkey Bridge to Lanka" (India), 29

"The Epic of Gilgamesh" (Mesopotamia), 40

"Etana" (Mesopotamia), 40

"Arthur" (England), 49

"Charlemagne" (France), 49

"Queen Guinevere" (England), 49

"Hanuman and the Search for Sita" (India), 51

"How Rama Defeated Ravana" (India), 51

The Story of Yuriwaka (Japan), 73

Excalibur (England), 77

"Of Castles and Dragons" (England), 79

"Of Guinevere and the Round Table" (England), 79

"Of Swords and Sorcerers" (England), 79

"Of the Last Battle" (England), 79

"Nidud the Cruel" (Norse), 81

The Epic of Gilgamesh (Mesopotamia), 86

"The Case of the Boiled Egg" (Jewish), 88

"How Ram Defeated the Demon King Ravan" (India), 89

The Legends of King Arthur (England), 103

"Quetzalcoatl's Hero Journey" (Native American, Aztec), 106

"The Golden Wish" (Greece), 107

"King Midas" (Greece), 108

"Odysseus" (Greece), 108

"Esther Becomes Queen" (ancient Israel), 114

"Mordecai and Haman" (ancient Israel), 114

"Pharaoh's Dreams" (ancient Israel), 114

"The Queen of Sheba" (ancient Israel), 114

"The Golden Touch: The Story of Bacchus and King Midas" (Graeco-Roman), 123

"Gods and Heroes" (Norse), 128

"Aeneas in the Underworld" (Rome), 130

"Cadmus and the Sown Men" (Greece), 130

"The Death of King Arthur" (Celts), 130

"Gilgamesh" (Mesopotamia), 130

"The Golden Touch" (Greece), 130

"The Holy Grail" (Celts), 130

"King Midas's Ears" (Greece), 130

"The Plumed Serpent" (Native American, Aztec), 130

"Romulus and Remus" (Rome), 130

"The Sword in the Stone" (Celts), 130

The Tale of Sir Gawain (England), 131

"King Midas" (Greece), 133

"The *Aeneid* of Virgil" (Rome), 138

"*Gilgamesh*" (Mesopotamia), 138

"*King Arthur*" (England), 138

"*Mwindo*" (Sub-Saharan Africa, Nyanga, Zaire), 138

"The *Odyssey* of Homer" (Greece), 138

"Quetzalcoatl" (Native American, Toltec/Aztec, Mexico), 138

"The *Ramayana*" (India), 138

"Romulus and Remus" (Rome), 138

"Branwen, Daughter of Llyr" (Wales), 139

"The Four Branches of The Mabinogion" (Wales), 139

"The Land of Promise" (Ireland), 139

"The Legend of King Arthur" (England), 139

"Manawydan, Son of Llyr" (Wales), 139

Arthur and the Sword (England), 143

"Bilqis: The Queen of Sheba" (Arabia), 147

"Boadicea: Queen of the Iceni" (British Isles), 147

"Gilgamesh: The Epic Hero of the Sumerians" (Mesopotamia), 148

"King Arthur: The Stuff of Heroes" (England), 148

"Moses the Lawgiver" (ancient Israel), 148

"Gilgamesh" (Mesopotamia), 150

"Romulus and Remus" (Rome), 150

Black Ships Before Troy: The Story of THE ILIAD (Greece), 153

"The Slaying of the Suitors" (Greece), 154

"The Adventures of Odysseus" (Greece), 155

"Midas" (Greece), 155

"Oedipus: The Tragic Hero Who Might Have Asked 'Why Me?'" (Greece), 155

"Theseus: The Favorite Hero of Athens" (Greece), 155

King Arthur and the Round Table (England), 156

King Arthur: The Sword in the Stone (England), 157

"Branwen, Daughter of Llyr" (Wales), 163

"Pwyll, Prince of Dyfed" (Wales), 163

"Daring the Dark" (Rome), 166

"The Moon Fairy" (Vietnam), 174

"The Cyclops" (Greece), 176

"David and Goliath" (ancient Israel), 176

Esther's Story (ancient Israel), 181

Gilgamesh the King (Mesopotamia), 189

18. Strong Men, Strong Women, and Monster Slayers

"George" (England), 7

"The Adventures of Samson" (ancient Israel), 9

"How Paul Bunyan Cleared North Dakota" (United States), 11

"John Henry, the Steel Driving Man" (African American), 11

"Tony Beaver Meets Paul Bunyan" (United States), 11

"Why the Great Lakes Have No Whales" (United States), 11

"Star Boy" (Native American, Crow, Arapaho, Blackfeet, Kiowa), 19

"Ball Player" (Native American, Lenape), 21

"The Big Fish and the Sun" (Native American, Lenape), 21

"The Dogs Who Saved Their Master" (Native American, Iroquois), 25

"The Story of Okteondon or the Workers of Evil" (Native American, Iroquois), 25

"The Two-headed Snake" (Native American, Iroquois), 25

"Jason, Medea and the Golden Fleece" (Greece), 26

"The Labours of Herakles" (Greece), 26

"Oedipus and the Theban Cycle" (Greece), 26

"Perseus and Medusa" (Greece), 26

"Theseus of Athens" (Greece), 26

"The Hero Twins and the Swallower of Clouds" (Native American, Zuni), 27

"Bhima and the Monkey's Tail" (India), 29

"The Epic of Gilgamesh" (Mesopotamia), 40

"Deadwood Dick and the Grizzly" (United States), 44

"Kit Carson and the Grizzlies" (United States), 44

"Paul Bunyan and His Little Blue Ox" (United States), 44

"Paul Bunyan Helps to Build a Railroad" (United States), 44

"The Saga of Pecos Bill" (United States), 44

"The Taming of Pecos Bill's Gal Sue" (United States), 44

"Thunder Bay" (United States), 44

Jason and the Golden Fleece (Greece), 47

"Hanuman and the Search for Sita" (India), 51

"How Rama Defeated Ravana" (India), 51

"Perseus and Andromeda" (Greece), 64

"Sigurd and Fafnir" (Norse), 64

"St. George and the Dragon" (England), 64

"Childe Rowland and Burd Ellen" (England), 65

"Manabozo" (Native American), 65

"Medusa" (Greece), 65

"Rolling Rio, the Gray Man, and Death" (African American), 65

"Annie Christmas" (African American), 66

"How the World Was Saved" (Native American, Navajo), 68

The Curse of the Ring (Norse), 69

The Story of Yuriwaka (Japan), 73

"The Birth of Nenebojo" (Native American, Ojibwa), 76

"Manabozho" (Native American, Ojibwa), 76

"Manabozho Visits the Man Whom the People Are Afraid Of" (Native American, Ojibwa), 76

"Nanabush Kitche Manitou's Emissary" (Native American, Ojibwa), 76

The Kitchen Knight: A Tale of King Arthur (England), 78

"The Twelve Labors of Hercules" (Graeco-Roman), 80

"The Dragon and Saint George" (England), 81

"The Grendel" (England), 81

Perseus (Greece), 85

The Epic of Gilgamesh (Mesopotamia), 86

"The Birth of Krishna, the Blue God" (India), 89

"Krishna and the Demon Nurse" (India), 89

"The Serpent King" (India), 89

Sally Ann Thunder Ann Whirlwind Crockett (United States), 92

"George and the Dragon" (Persia), 107

"Saving Time" (Polynesia), 107

"Jason and the Golden Fleece" (Greece), 108

"Perseus" (Greece), 108

"Theseus and the Minotaur" (Greece), 108

"The Twelve Labors of Heracles" (Greece), 108

Saint George and the Dragon (England), 109

"David and Goliath" (ancient Israel), 114

"Samson" (ancient Israel), 114

"Samson and Delilah" (ancient Israel), 114

"Medusa" (Greece), 116

"Davy Crockett" (United States), 122

"John Henry" (African American), 122

"Mose" (United States), 122

"Paul Bunyan" (United States), 122

"Pecos Bill" (United States), 122

"Sally Ann Thunder Ann Whirlwind" (United States), 122

"Stormalong" (United States), 122

"Beowulf" (British Isles), 130

"Gilgamesh" (Mesopotamia), 130

"The Labors of Heracles" (Greece), 130

"Theseus and the Minotaur" (Greece), 130

"The Giants Who Couldn't Swim" (Ireland), 133

"How Perseus Killed the Gorgon" (Greece), 133

"Little Oonyani" (Siberia), 134

"Net-Pos-Hu the Archer" (Siberia), 134

"Ahaiyuta and the Cloud-Eater" (Native American, Zuni), 138

"*Beowulf*" (England, Scandinavia), 138

"*Gilgamesh*" (Mesopotamia), 138

"The Labors and Death of Heracles" (Greece), 138

"Lodge-Boy and Thrown-Away" (Native American, Crow), 138

"The Quest for the Sun" (China), 138

"The *Ramayana*" (India), 138

"The *Saga of Sigurd the Volsung*" (Norse), 138

"The Story of CuChulainn" (Ireland), 139

"The Story of Fionn" (Ireland), 139

"The Wonderful Head" (Ireland), 139

"Annie Christmas" (African American), 145

"Sal Fink" (United States), 145

"John Henry: The Steel-Driving Man" (African American), 146

"Old Stormalong: The Deep-Water Sailor" (United States), 146

"Paul Bunyan and Babe the Blue Ox" (United States), 146

"Slue-Foot Sue and Pecos Bill" (United States), 146

"Strap Buckner: The Texas Fighter" (United States), 146

"Beowulf the Dragon Slayer" (England), 148

"Cuchulain the Champion" (Ireland), 148

"Gilgamesh: The Epic Hero of the Sumerians" (Mesopotamia), 148

"Heracles the Strong One" (Greece), 148

"Perseus the Fearless" (Greece), 148

"Samson the Nazirite" (ancient Israel), 148

"Sigurd of the Volsungs" (Norse), 148

"Theseus the Daring and the Bold" (Greece), 148

"Gilgamesh" (Mesopotamia), 150

"Great Warriors: Greece," 150

"Great Warriors: North America" (Native American, Navajo), 150

"Quetzalcoatl" (Native American, Aztec), 150

"The Cyclops" (Greece), 154

"The Golden Fleece, Jason, and Medea" (Greece), 155

"Hercules: The Strongest Man on Earth" (Greece), 155

"Perseus and the Medusa: Everybody's Fairy Tale" (Greece), 155

"Theseus: The Favorite Hero of Athens" (Greece), 155

"Maui and the Great Fish" (New Zealand, Maori), 162

"Maui Tames the Sun" (New Zealand, Maori), 162

"Branwen, Daughter of Llyr" (Wales), 163

"Hieroglyphics of the Heavens" (Greece), 165

"Big Mose and the Lady Washington" (United States), 175

"Davy Crockett Teaches the Steamboat a Leetle Patriotism" (United States), 175

"John Darling and the Skeeter Chariot" (United States), 175

"John Henry Races the Steam Drill" (African American), 175

"Old Stormalong Finds a Man-Sized Ship" (United States), 175

"Ol' Gabe in the Valley of the Yellowstone" (United States), 175

"Paul Bunyan and the Winter of the Blue Snow" (United States), 175

"Pecos Bill Finds a Ranch but Loses a Wife" (United States), 175

"David and Goliath" (ancient Israel), 176

"Alesha the Priest's Son and Tugarin" (Russia), 177

"Dobrynya and the Dragon" (Russia), 177

"Il'ya of Murom and Nightingale, the Brigand" (Russia), 177

"Mikula Selyaninovich the Peasant's Son and Vol'ga" (Russia), 177

"Annie Christmas" (African American), 185

"John Henry" (African American), 185

"Long Hair and Flint Bird" (Native American, Acoma Pueblo), 187

Gilgamesh the King (Mesopotamia), 189

19. Warriors and Fighters

"The Warrior Maiden" (Native American, Oneida), 3

"The Promised Land" (ancient Israel), 9

"The Death of Crockett" (United States), 11

"Mose Humphries, the Fighting Fireman" (United States), 11

"Bhimnath Mahadev" (India), 12

"The Twin Myth" (prototype story; Native American, South America), 20

"The Trojan War" (Greece), 26

"Krishna—Man and God" (India), 29

The Mud Pony (Native American, Pawnee), 33

"How Gluskabe Brought the Summer" (Native American, Abenaki), 43

"Calamity Jane Meets a Long-Lost Lover" (United States), 44

"Deadwood Dick to the Rescue" (United States), 44

"How Old Calam Got Her Name" (United States), 44

"The Irrepressible Backwoodsman and Original Humorist" (United States), 44

"Jim Bowie and His Big Knife" (United States), 44

"Jim Bowie Takes a Hand" (United States), 44

"The King of the Pistoleers" (United States), 44

"Like Father, Like Daughter" (United States), 44

"Little Big Man" (United States), 44

"Lover Boy of the Prairies" (United States), 44

"Old Solitaire" (United States), 44

"She Fought Her Weight in She-B'ars" (United States), 44

"Swallowing a Scalping Knife" (United States), 44

"Tarzan Boone" (United States), 44

"The Warrior Woman" (United States), 44

William Tell (Switzerland), 48

The Curse of the Ring (Norse), 69

The Story of Yuriwaka (Japan), 73

The Kitchen Knight: A Tale of King Arthur (England), 78

Ahaiyute and Cloud Eater (Native American, Zuni), 83

"How Krishna Killed the Wicked King Kans" (India), 89

"Maudjee-kawiss: The First Son" (Native American, Ojibway), 91

"Muzzu-Kimmik-Quae: Mother Earth" (Native American, Ojibway), 91

"Nana'b'oozoo" (Native American, Ojibway), 91

Rimonah of the Flashing Sword: A North African Tale (Egypt), 94

El Cid (Spain), 95

"The Hero Journey of the Hero Twins" (Native American, Maya), 106

"Brave Quest" (Native American, Blackfeet), 107

"The Death of El Cid" (Spain), 107

"Juno's Roman Geese," 107

Saint George and the Dragon (England), 109

"Gideon's Trumpet" (ancient Israel), 114

"The Walls of Jericho" (ancient Israel), 114

Finn Mac Cool and the Small Men of Deeds (Ireland, Scotland), 125

"Gods and Heroes" (Norse), 128

"Beowulf" (England), 130

"Cuchulain" (Ireland), 130

"The Winged Horse" (Greece), 130

"Beowulf" (England, Scandinavia), 138

"The *Iliad* of Homer" (Greece), 138

"Kotan Utunnai: The Ainu Epic Hero" (Japan), 138

"The *Ramayana*" (India), 138

"The *Saga of Sigurd the Volsung*" (Norse), 138

"The Second Battle of Moytura" (Celts), 139

"The Sorrows of Storytelling" (Celts), 139

"The Story of CuChulainn" (Ireland), 139

"Strap Buckner: The Texas Fighter" (United States), 146

"Joan of Arc" (France), 147

"El Cid Campeador of Spain," 148

"Roland, Hero of France," 148
"Sigurd of the Volsungs" (Norse), 148
"Great Warriors: China," 150
"Great Warriors: Ireland," 150
"The Trojan War" (Greece), 150
Black Ships Before Troy: The Story of THE ILIAD (Greece), 153
"The Slaying of the Suitors" (Greece), 154
"The Trojan War" (Greece), 155
"The Countess of the Fountain" (England), 166
"Journeys into Wonder" (Ireland), 166
"A Man among Gods" (Norse), 166
"A Parting of Worlds" (Ireland), 166
"Realms of Eternal Night" (Norse), 166
"David and Goliath" (ancient Israel), 176
"Kana the Stretching Wonder" (Hawaii), 176
"Sukhman" (Russia), 177
Sundiata: Lion King of Mali (Sub-Saharan Africa), 180
"Casey Jones and His Friends" (African American), 185
"Wild Bill: The 'Prince of Pistoleers' " (United States), 186
"The Chests of Sand" (Spain), 188
"El Cid and the Lion" (Spain), 188

20. Figures of Romance and Chivalry

"Arthur" (England), 49
"The Deeds of Tristan" (England), 49
"Hasty Huon" (France), 49
"The Holy Grail" (England), 49
"The Knight of Lion" (England), 49
"Mission Impossible" (France), 49
"Ogier the Dane" (France), 49
"Oliver" (France), 49
"Percival of Wales" 49
"Queen Guinevere" (England), 49
"The Round Table" (England), 49
"Sir Lancelot of the Lake" (England), 49
"The Stormy Fountain" (England), 49
"Tristan and Iseult" (England), 49
"William Short-Nose" (France), 49
"Young Roland" (France), 49
Sir Gawain and the Loathly Lady (England), 72

Excalibur (England), 77

"Of Castles and Dragons" (England), 79

"Of Guinevere and the Round Table" (England), 79

"Of Swords and Sorcerers" (England), 79

"Of the Boy Who Would Be a Knight" (England), 79

"Of the Coming of Sir Galahad" (England), 79

"Of the Last Battle" (England), 79

"Of the Quest for the Holy Grail" (England), 79

"Of the Sword Bridge" (England), 79

"Of True Love" (England), 79

"The Ugly Wife" (England), 81

The Legends of King Arthur (England), 103

The Tale of Sir Gawain (England), 131

"*King Arthur*" (England), 138

"The Legend of King Arthur" (England), 139

"King Arthur: The Stuff of Heroes" (England), 148

"Roland, Hero of France," 148

King Arthur and the Round Table (England), 156

"The Countess of the Fountain" (England), 166

21. Voyagers and Adventurers

"Jason, Medea, and the Golden Fleece" (Greece), 26

"The Story of Odysseus" (Greece), 26

"Yuhishtira's Journey" (Hindu), 29

"The Epic of Gilgamesh" (Mesopotamia), 40

Jason and the Golden Fleece (Greece), 47

The Story of Yuriwaka (Japan), 73

Leif's Saga: A Viking Tale (Norse), 84

The Epic of Gilgamesh (Mesopotamia), 86

"The Hero Journey of the Hero Twins" (Native American, Maya), 106

"Brave Quest" (Native American, Blackfeet), 107

"Jason and the Golden Fleece" (Greece), 108

"Odysseus" (Greece), 108

"Maui-of-a-Thousand-Tricks" (Polynesia), 130

"The *Odyssey* of Homer" (Greece), 138

"Mary Bryant" (Australia), 147

"Jason the Voyager" (Greece), 148

"Odysseus: Agile of Body and Mind" (Greece), 148

"Farewell to Calypso" (Greece), 154

"The Lord of the Winds" (Greece), 154

"Sea Perils" (Greece), 154

"The Adventures of Odysseus" (Greece), 155

"The Golden Fleece, Jason, and Medea" (Greece), 155

"Kupe's Discovery of Aotearoa" (New Zealand, Maori), 162

"How Sadko Angered the Sea Tsar" (Russia), 177

22. Poets, Bards, Singers, Storytellers, and Dancers

"The Two Kings, Shah Shahryar and Shah Zaman, and the Wazir's Daughter Sheh-
    erezade" (Arabia), 1

"The Arabian Nights," 4

Kalevala: Song of the Bear" (Finland), 43

"Childe Rowland and Burd Ellen" (England), 65

"The Death of Nornagest" (Norse), 81

"Pukawiss: The Disowned" (Native American, Ojibway), 91

"Orpheus and Eurydice" (Greece), 108

"How Caedmon Got His Hymn" (England), 115

"Journey to the Underworld: The Story of Orpheus and Eurydice" (Graeco-Roman),
    123

"Taliesin" (Wales), 130

Gassire's Lute" (Sub-Saharan Africa, Soninke, Faraka), 138

"Scheherazade" (Arabia), 147

"Vainamoinen: Hero, Singer and Enchanter" (Finland), 148

"Orpheus and Eurydice" (Greece), 155

"Sadko of Novgorod" (Russia), 177

23. Magicians, Enchanters, and Enchanted Figures

"Arthur" (England), 49

"Magician and Rogue" (France), 49

"Merlin and Viviane" (England), 49

"Nanabush and the Four Men" (Native American, Ojibwa), 76

"Sugarloaf Rock" (Native American, Ojibwa), 76

"Of Castles and Dragons" (England), 79

"Of Swords and Sorcerers" (England), 79

The Legends of King Arthur (England), 103

The Children of Lir (Ireland), 111

"The Children of Lir" (Ireland), 139

"The Isle of Man" (Ireland), 139

"Magic Birds and Enchanted Animals" (Ireland), 139

"Math, Son of Mathonwy" (Wales), 139

"Circe: The Enchantress" (Greece), 147

"Medea: A Cruel and Savage Witch" (Greece), 147

"The Enchantress" (Greece), 154

"Manawydan, Son of Llyr" (Wales), 163

"Math, Son of Mathonwy" (Wales), 163

"Pwyll, Prince of Dyfed" (Wales), 163

24. Inventors

"Febold Feboldson, the Most Inventingest Man" (United States), 11

"How Gib Invented Rubber Boots" (United States), 11

"The Fall of Icarus" (Greece), 130

Wings (Greece), 183

25. Athletes

Atalanta's Race (Greece), 30

"Atalanta's Race" (Greece), 108

"The Golden Apples: The Story of Atalanta and Hippomenes" (Graeco-Roman), 123

"Atalanta: The Fleet-footed Huntress" (Greece), 147

26. Environmental Benefactors and Friends of Animals

"Francis of Assisi" (Italy), 7

"How Johnny Appleseed Brought Apple Blossoms to the West" (United States), 11

"Johnny Appleseed" (United States), 122

27. Macho Lovers

"The King of the Pistoleers" (United States), 44

"Lover Boy of the Prairies" (United States), 44

28. Tall Tales

"Annie Oakley Makes Her Name" (United States), 11

"Babe, Paul Bunyan's Blue Ox" (United States), 11

"Calamity's Bet" (United States), 11

"Crockett Gets the Votes" (United States), 11

"Crockett Pops the Question" (United States), 11

"Daniel Boone's Tale of the Three Notches" (United States), 11

"Davy Crockett Meets His Match" (United States), 11

"Febold Feboldson, the Most Inventingest Man" (United States), 11

"Gib Morgan and the Whickles" (United States), 11

"Gib's Biggest Rig" (United States), 11

"How Daniel Boone Found His Wife" (United States), 11

"How Gib Invented Rubber Boots" (United States), 11

"How Gib Saved His Tool Dresser" (United States), 11

"How Johnny Appleseed Brought Apple Blossoms to the West" (United States), 11

"How Mike Fink Beat Davy Crockett in a Shooting Match" (United States), 11

"How Paul Bunyan Cleared North Dakota" (United States), 11

"Mike Fink and the Deacon's Bull" (United States), 11

"Mose Humphries, the Fighting Fireman" (United States) 11

"Paul Bunyan's Birth" (United States), 11

"The Queen of the Bull-Whackers" (United States), 11

"The Round Drive" (United States), 11

"The Saga of Pecos Bill" (United States), 11

"Sam Patch, the Jumping Man" (United States), 11

"Tony Beaver Meets Paul Bunyan" (United States), 11

"Why the Great Lakes Have No Whales" (United States), 11

"Ah Ling's Hommyside" (United States), 44

"Born Before Her Time" (United States), 44

"Calamity Jane Meets a Long-Lost Lover" (United States), 44

"A Damn Good Jump" (United States), 44

"Davy Crockett on the Stump" (United States), 44

"Deadwood Dick and the Grizzly" (United States), 44

"Deadwood Dick to the Rescue" (United States), 44

"Did Such a Helliferocious Man Ever Live?" (United States), 44

"The Drinks Are on Me, Gentlemen" (United States), 44

"El Chivato" (United States), 44

"Fining the Deceased" (United States), 44

"Grinning the Bark off a Tree" (United States), 44

"The Hanging of Carlos Robles" (United States), 44

"He Rose from the Grave" (United States), 44

"How Old Calam Got Her Name" (United States), 44

"The Irrepressible Backwoodsman and Original Humorist" (United States), 44

"Jim Bowie and His Big Knife" (United States), 44

"Kidnapped by a Flea" (United States), 44

"The King of the Pistoleers" (United States), 44

"Kit Carson and the Grizzlies" (United States), 44

"Like Father, Like Daughter" (United States), 44

"Little Big Man" (United States), 44

"Lover Boy of the Prairies" (United States), 44

"No-Head Joaquin and Three-Fingered Jack" (United States), 44

"Old Solitaire" (United States), 44

"Paul Bunyan and His Little Blue Ox" (United States), 44

"Paul Bunyan Helps to Build the Railroad" (United States), 44

"Pegleg Smith and Headless Harry" (United States), 44

"Roy Bean's Pet Bear" (United States), 44

"The Saga of Pecos Bill" (United States), 44

"She Fought Her Weight in She-B'ars" (United States), 44

"A Shooting Match" (United States), 44

"Swallowing a Scalping Knife" (United States), 44

"The Taming of Pecos Bill's Gal Sue" (United States), 44

"Thunder Bay" (United States), 44

"The Warrior Woman" (United States), 44

"Rolling Rio, the Gray Man, and Death" (African American), 65

"Annie Christmas" (African American), 66

"Davy Crockett" (United States), 122

"Febold Feboldson" (United States), 122

"John Henry" (African American), 122

"Johnny Appleseed" (United States), 122

"Mose" (United States), 122

"Paul Bunyan" (United States), 122

"Pecos Bill" (United States), 122

"Sally Ann Thunder Ann Whirlwind" (United States), 122

"Stormalong" (United States), 122

"Sal Fink" (United States), 145

"John Henry: The Steel-Driving Man" (African American), 146

"Old Stormalong: The Deep-Water Sailor" (United States), 146

"Paul Bunyan and Babe the Blue Ox" (United States), 146

"Slue-Foot Sue and Pecos Bill" (United States), 146

"Strap Buckner: The Texas Fighter" (United States), 146

"Big Mose and the Lady Washington" (United States), 175

"Davy Crockett Teaches the Steamboat a Leetle Patriotism" (United States), 175

"Gib Morgan Brings in the Well" (United States), 175

"John Darling and the Skeeter Chariot" (United States), 175

"John Henry Races the Steam Drill" (African American), 175

"Old Stormalong Finds a Man-Sized Ship" (United States), 175

"Ol' Gabe in the Valley of the Yellowstone" (United States), 175

"Paul Bunyan and the Winter of the Blue Snow" (United States), 175

"Pecos Bill Finds a Ranch but Loses a Wife" (United States), 175

"Annie Christmas" (African American), 185

"John Henry" (African American), 185

"Belle and the Stuff of Legends" (United States), 186

Index of Cultures

(Numerals refer to entry numbers in the Guide of books in which at least one, sometimes all, of the stories come from the culture indicated.)

Abenaki; Abnaki (Native American), 24, 27, 43, 96, 116

Aboriginal (Australian), 43, 51, 67, 100, 107, 119, 130, 150

Achomawi (Native American), 31

Acoma Pueblo (Native American), 187

Africa (no group specified), 41, 51, 165, 179

Africa, North, 43, 61, 67, 71, 94, 107, 130, 138, 150

Africa, Sub-Saharan, 5, 10, 14, 16, 41, 42, 43, 45, 50, 51, 57, 58, 67, 96, 98, 107, 116, 130, 133, 138, 150, 165, 167, 179, 180

African American, 10, 11, 43, 46, 65, 66, 116, 145, 146, 175, 185

Alabama (Native American), 96, 113

Algeria (North Africa), 43

Algonquin; Algonkian (Native American), 68, 130, 147, 159, 168

Altaic (Russia), 67

Amazon Kayapo (Native American), 150

Anatolia (Phrygia), 6

Ancient Israel, 9, 28, 51, 67, 90, 114, 147, 148, 176, 181

Anengme (Sub-Saharan Africa), 16

Anglo-Saxon, 81, 115, 130, 131, 148

Angoni (Sub-Saharan Africa), 57, 58

Anishinabe; Anishnabeg (Native American), 27, 76

Apache (Native American), 19, 23, 149

Apanyekra (Native American), 13

Arabia, 1, 4, 120, 121, 147

Arapaho (Native American), 19, 113

Arawak (Native American), 132

Argentina (Native American), 20

Arikara (Native American), 132

Ashanti (Sub-Saharan Africa), 10, 41, 43, 96, 98, 130

Asia, 12, 29, 43, 51, 65, 67, 73, 81, 89, 107, 112, 116, 129, 130, 134, 138, 142, 147, 150, 164, 165, 169, 174

Assiniboin (Native American), 113

Australia, 43, 51, 67, 100, 107, 119, 130, 147, 150, 164

Australia and New Zealand, 150

Avatime (Sub-Saharan Africa), 16

Aztec (Native American), 18, 51, 62, 102, 106, 107, 130, 138, 150, 188

Babylon. *See* Mesopotamia

Bagando (Sub-Saharan Africa), 130

Bahamas, 10

Barasana (Native American), 20

Bast (North Africa), 130

Bella Coola (Native American), 159

Benin (Sub-Saharan Africa), 43, 107
Biloxi (Native American), 96
Binbinga (Australian Aboriginal), 150
Blackfeet (Native American), 19, 23, 27,
    34, 55, 67, 82, 107, 113, 132, 135, 159
Bolivia (Native American), 20
Bororo (Native American), 13, 20, 81
Botswana (Sub-Saharan Africa), 10
Brazil, 10, 20, 42, 43, 137, 138
Bribri (Native American), 18
British Isles, 7, 38, 39, 49, 64, 65, 72,
    75, 77, 78, 79, 81, 101, 103, 107, 109,
    111, 115, 125, 130, 131, 133, 138, 139,
    143, 147, 148, 150, 156, 157, 163, 166
Buddhist, 51, 112, 116, 142, 165
Bura (Sub-Saharan Africa), 10
Burma, 165
Burundi (Sub-Saharan Africa), 150
Bushman (Sub-Saharan Africa), 10, 57,
    58, 150

Cabecar (Native American), 18
Caddo (Native American), 96, 187
Campas (Native American), 13
Canada, Western, 138, 150, 164
Carib (Native American), 188
Cayapo (Native American), 13
Celebes (Sulawesi), 165
Celtic. See British Isles
Ceylon (Sri Lanka), 107
Chatino (Native American), 18
Cherokee (Native American), 24, 27, 80,
    96, 113, 115, 116, 132, 140, 141, 171,
    187
Cheyenne (Native American), 24, 51,
    159, 187
Chichimec (Native American), 106
Chickasaw (Native American), 96
Chile (Native American), 20
China, 51, 65, 67, 81, 107, 129, 130,
    138, 147, 150, 164, 165
Chinook (Native American), 19, 34, 187
Chippewa; Ojibwa (Native American),
    60, 76, 91, 97, 145, 150
Chitimacha (Native American), 10
Choctaw (Native American), 96, 187
Chorote (Native American), 13
Christian, 51

Chuckchee (Native American), 158
Chuh (Native American), 10
Chukchi (Siberia), 134
Chumash (Native American), 113, 182
Cochiti (Native American), 3, 113
Coeur d'Alene (Native American), 113
Colombia, 10, 20
Comanche (Native American), 132
Cree (Native American), 118, 158
Creek (Native American), 10, 96, 171
Crow (Native American), 19, 82, 138,
    187
Cuba, 10, 42, 56, 152

Dahomey (Sub-Saharan Africa), 58, 67,
    138
Dakota (Native American), 27
De (Sub-Saharan Africa), 10
Delaware; Lenape (Native American),
    19, 21, 59, 171, 172
Dine (Native American), 27
Dominica (African), 10
Dominican Republic, 10

Efik Ibibio (Sub-Saharan Africa), 167
Egypt, 61, 67, 71, 94, 130, 138, 150
Ekoi (Sub-Saharan Africa), 58, 167
England, 7, 38, 39, 49, 64, 65, 72, 75,
    77, 78, 79, 81, 101, 103, 107, 109,
    115, 130, 131, 138, 139, 143, 147, 148,
    156, 157, 166
Eskimo; Inuit, 19, 27, 43, 67, 81, 82,
    130, 132, 134, 145, 150
Estonia, 165
Ethiopia (North Africa), 107
Europe, Continental, 7, 26, 30, 31, 32,
    35, 43, 47, 48, 49, 53, 64, 65, 67, 69,
    70, 80, 81, 84, 85, 88, 93, 95, 107,
    108, 116, 123, 124, 128, 130, 133, 138,
    144, 147, 148, 150, 153, 154, 155, 164,
    165, 166, 176, 177, 183, 188
Evenk (Siberia), 134
Ewe (Sub-Saharan Africa), 10

Faraka (Sub-Saharan Africa), 138
Finland, 43, 130, 148, 165
Fon (Sub-Saharan Africa), 43, 58, 67,
    107, 130, 138

France, 7, 49, 147, 148
Fulani (Sub-Saharan Africa), 10

Ga (Sub-Saharan Africa), 16
Gabrielino (Native American), 19, 113
Gambia (Sub-Saharan Africa), 10
Ge (Native American), 20
Germany, 107
Ghana (Sub-Saharan Africa), 10, 16, 58,
    98
Gikuyu; Kikuyu (Sub-Saharan Africa), 50,
    107
Gold Coast (Sub-Saharan Africa), 96
Graeco-Roman, 35, 80, 123, 165
Greece, 26, 30, 31, 47, 64, 65, 67, 85,
    107, 108, 116, 123, 130, 133, 138, 147,
    148, 150, 153, 154, 155, 165, 176, 183
Grenada, 10
Guadeloupe, 10
Guatemala (Native American), 138, 150,
    160, 161, 173
Guaymi (Native American), 18
Guiana (Native American), 20, 132
Guinea (Sub-Saharan Africa), 67
Gujarat (India), 12

Haida (Native American), 138, 150
Haiti, 42, 65, 130
Hausa (Sub-Saharan Africa), 10, 98
Hawaii, 145, 176
Hindu, 29, 51, 150
Hitchiti (Native American), 10, 96
Hittite (Middle East), 130, 138
Hopi (Native American), 23, 24, 27, 51
Hottentot (Sub-Saharan Africa), 10, 43,
    57
Huichol (Native American), 15, 18
Huron (Native American), 67

Ibo (Sub-Saharan Africa), 43, 130
Igbo (Sub-Saharan Africa), 10
Inca (Native American), 20, 51, 138
India, 12, 29, 43, 51, 65, 67, 81, 89, 112,
    130, 138, 142, 150, 165
Indonesia, 130, 150, 165
Inuit; Eskimo, 19, 27, 43, 67, 81, 82,
    130, 132, 134, 145, 150
Iran, 130

Ireland, 111, 125, 130, 133, 138, 139,
    148, 150, 166
Iroquois (Native American), 3, 19, 22,
    25, 82, 133, 150, 165, 187
Islam, 51, 120, 121
Israel, ancient, 9, 28, 51, 67, 90, 114,
    147, 148, 176, 181
Italy, 7
Itelmen (Siberia), 134
Ivory Coast (Sub-Saharan Africa), 10

Japan, 51, 73, 81, 130, 138, 150, 169
Jewish, 51, 53, 54, 88, 93, 144, 165
Jicaque (Native American), 18
Judaeo-Christian, 51
Juruna (Native American), 43

Kabyle (North Africa), 43
Karnataka (India), 12
Karuk (Native American), 23, 104
Kathlamet Chinook (Native American),
    23, 187
Kato (Native American), 43
Kenya (Sub-Saharan Africa), 107
Kerala (India), 12
Kerek (Siberia), 134
Ket (Siberia), 134
Khanty (Siberia), 134
Kikuyu; Gikuyu (Sub-Saharan Africa), 50,
    107
Kiowa (Native American), 19, 159, 187
Klamath (Native American), 113
Kogi (Native American), 20
Kono (Sub-Saharan Africa), 67
Korea, 165
Koryak (Siberia), 134
Krachi (Sub-Saharan Africa), 67
Krio (Sub-Saharan Africa), 16
Krobo (Sub-Saharan Africa), 16
Kwakiutl (Native American), 19, 82

Laguna (Native American), 3
Lakota (Native American), 27, 82
Larteh (Sub-Saharan Africa), 16
Latvia, 165
Lenape; Delaware (Native American),
    19, 21, 59, 171, 172
Les Saintes, 10

Liberia (Sub-Saharan Africa), 10
Lozi (Sub-Saharan Africa), 67
Luiseno (Native American), 19, 113
Luo (Sub-Saharan Africa), 45

Madagascar (Sub-Saharan Africa), 150
Maidu (Native American), 67, 130
Mali (Sub-Saharan Africa), 10, 180
Malinke (Sub-Saharan Africa), 10
Maliseet (Native American), 27
Mandan (Native American), 130, 150, 158
Mandinka (Sub-Saharan Africa), 10
Manipur (India), 12
Mansi (Siberia), 134
Maori (New Zealand), 150, 162
Margi (Sub-Saharan Africa), 43
Marie Galante, 10
Martinique, 10
Mataco (Native American), 20
Maya (Native American), 17, 67, 99, 106, 117, 138, 150, 160, 161, 173
Mazatec; Mazateco (Native American), 18, 117
Mbala (Sub-Saharan Africa), 10
Mbya Guarani (Native American), 20
Melanesia, 67
Mende (Sub-Saharan Africa), 58
Mesopotamia, 40, 51, 67, 86, 107, 130, 138, 148, 150, 166, 189
Mexican American, 178
Mexico, 10, 117, 138, 150
Micmac (Native American), 27, 113, 150, 159, 187
Micronesia, 8, 67
Middle East, 4, 9, 28, 40, 51, 54, 67, 86, 90, 107, 114, 120, 121, 130, 138, 147, 148, 150, 166, 181, 189
Minyong (India), 67
Miskito (Native American), 18, 136
Miwok; Miowok (Native American), 43, 145
Mixe (Native American), 18
Mixtec (Native American), 106
Modoc (Native American), 130, 158
Mohawk (Native American), 3, 43, 52, 158, 159
Monache (Native American), 113

Mongolia, 43, 165
Mosi (Sub-Saharan Africa), 10
Mundurucu (Native American), 20

Nagaland (India), 12, 43
Namibia (Sub-Saharan Africa), 10
Nanai (Siberia), 134
Naskapi (Native American), 165
Natchez (Native American), 10
Native American, 2, 3, 10, 13, 15, 17, 18, 19, 20, 21, 22, 23, 24, 25, 27, 31, 33, 34, 36, 37, 41, 43, 44, 51, 52, 55, 59, 60, 62, 63, 65, 67, 68, 74, 76, 80, 81, 82, 83, 87, 91, 96, 97, 99, 102, 104, 105, 106, 107, 110, 113, 115, 116, 117, 118, 126, 127, 130, 132, 133, 135, 136, 137, 138, 140, 141, 145, 147, 149, 150, 151, 158, 159, 160, 161, 164, 165, 168, 170, 171, 172, 173, 176, 182, 184, 187, 188
Navajo; Navaho (Native American), 23, 24, 27, 43, 68, 74, 87, 113, 126, 127, 130, 138, 150
Ndabele (Sub-Saharan Africa), 58
Nenets (Siberia), 134
New Zealand, 150, 162
Nez Perce (Native American), 23, 171
Nganasan (Siberia), 134
Nigeria (Sub-Saharan Africa), 10, 16, 43, 58, 67, 116, 133, 138, 167
Nisqually; Nisqualli (Native American), 27, 68, 115
Nivakle (Native American), 43
Nivkh (Siberia), 134
Norse, 32, 64, 65, 67, 69, 70, 81, 84, 107, 124, 128, 130, 133, 138, 148, 150, 166
Northern Europe (unspecified), 164
Northern Paiute (Native American), 23
Northern Pueblo (Native American), 187
Nunivak (Native American), 19
Nyanga (Sub-Saharan Africa), 138

Ojibwa; Ojibway; Chippewa (Native American), 60, 76, 91, 97, 145, 150
Okanagan (Native American), 3
Omaha (Native American), 113
Oneida (Native American), 3, 159

Onondaga (Native American), 27, 113, 150
Osage (Native American), 158

Pacific Islands, 8, 43, 51, 67, 81, 107, 130, 133, 150, 176
Pacific Northwest (Native American), 41, 110, 176
Paiute, Northern (Native American), 23
Paiute, Southern (Native American), 23
Papago (Native American), 159
Paraguay (Native American), 20, 43
Passamaquoddy (Native American), 63, 151
Pawnee (Native American), 11, 27, 33, 68, 82, 113, 132
Persia, 107
Peru (Native American), 2, 20, 138
Phoenecia, 150
Phrygia, 6
Picuris Pueblo (Native American), 113
Pima (Native American), 19, 82
Pitahawirata Pawnee (Native American), 113
Plains Indians (unspecified), 170
Pokonoket (Native American), 105
Polynesia, 51, 67, 81, 107, 130, 133, 150
Pueblo (Native American), 23, 113, 132, 145, 187
Puerto Rico, 37
Pygmy (Sub-Saharan Africa), 58

Quechua (Native American), 2
Quiche (Native American), 160, 161
Quileute (Native American), 113

Ramkokamekra (Native American), 13
Rome, 107, 130, 138, 150, 166
Russia, 67, 134, 150, 177

Saami (Siberia), 134
Saint Lucia, 10
Salish (Native American), 19
San (Sub-Saharan Africa), 150
Santeria, 42, 56
Scotland, 125
Sefwi (Sub-Saharan Africa), 16
Selkam (Native American), 13

Selkup (Siberia), 134
Seminole (Native American), 10, 96
Seneca (Native American), 24, 27, 132, 171, 187
Serbia, 130
Shasta (Native American), 113
Shinto (Japan), 51
Siberia, 130, 134, 165
Sierra Leone (Sub-Saharan Africa), 10, 16, 150
Sikh (India), 51
Siksika (Native American), 27
Sioux (Native American), 27, 34, 43, 82
Skidi Pawnee (Native American), 82, 113
Slavey (Native American), 171
Snohomish (Native American), 113
Soninke (Sub-Saharan Africa), 138
South Africa (Sub-Saharan Africa), 10
South America (unspecified), 164
Spain, 95, 107, 148, 188
Sugpiaq (Eskimo), 145
Sulawesi (Indonesia), 150
Sumer (Middle East), 86, 130, 138, 148, 189
Swazi (Sub-Saharan Africa), 57
Switzerland, 48

Tachi Yokuts (Native American), 113
Tahiti (Pacific Islands), 43, 67, 150
Taino (Native American), 37, 188
Tamiladu (India), 43
Tapirape (Native American), 13
Tarahumara (Native American), 18
Tariana (Native American), 20
Tartar (Russia), 150
Teheulces (Native American), 13
Temne (Sub-Saharan Africa), 10
Tewa (Native American), 171
Tiahuanaco (Native American), 138
Tibet, 43
Ticuna (Native American), 137
Tlingit (Native American), 82, 138, 150, 171
Toba (Native American), 20
Togo (Sub-Saharan Africa), 67
Tohono O'Odhan (Native American), 159
Toltec (Native American), 106, 138
Trinidad, 10

Trio (Native American), 138
Tsimshian (Native American), 19, 27, 82, 150
Tswana (Sub-Saharan Africa), 45
Twi (Sub-Saharan Africa), 16
Tzotzil (Native American), 18

Udegei (Siberia), 134
United States, 11, 44, 92, 107, 122, 145, 146, 175, 186
Upper Volta (Sub-Saharan Africa), 10

Vane Avatime (Sub-Saharan Africa), 16
Venezuela (Native American), 10
Vietnam, 174

Waiwai (Native American), 20
Wakaranga (Sub-Saharan Africa), 43
Wales, 130, 139, 163
Wampanoag (Native American), 24, 105
Warao (Native American), 10
Wasco (Native American), 113

West Africa (unspecified), 14, 133
West Bengal (India), 12
West Indies, 10, 107
Winnebago (Native American), 19, 43
Wishosk (Native American), 171
Witoto (Native American), 20
Wobe (Sub-Saharan Africa), 10

Yamana (Native American), 20
Yana (Native American), 23
Yanomami (Native American), 36
Yoruba (Sub-Saharan Africa), 5, 10, 16, 42, 43, 67, 116, 138, 167
Yuchi (Native American), 96
Yuracare (Native American), 20
Yurok (Native American), 27

Zaire (Sub-Saharan Africa), 10, 138
Zambia (Sub-Saharan Africa), 67
Zimbabwe (Sub-Saharan Africa), 43
Zinacantec (Native American), 117
Zuni (Native American), 19, 27, 83, 138, 147, 158

Index of Characters, Places, and Other Significant Items

(Numerals after the names refer to the entries in the Guide; numerals in parentheses indicate the pages on which the items first appear in their stories.)

Aaron, 9 (47, 66), 28 (unp), 148 (104)
Abbot of St. Mary's, 101 (20)
Abel, 114 (11)
Able to Dry Up Rivers, 43 (198)
Able to See Trouble, 43 (198)
Abraham, 51 (80), 114 (20, 23)
A.B.S., 122 (49)
Accalon, Sir, 79 (17)
Achilles, 26 (33, 48), 108 (78), 138 (45, 93), 148 (51), 150 (66), 153 (14), 155 (171)
Acrisius (Akrisios), King, 26 (63), 133 (85), 148 (17), 155 (81)
Ad, 4 (37)
Adam, 9 (19), 51, (20), 67 (123), 114 (7, 9, 11), 120 (unp), 121 (unp)
Adapa, 40 (184), 107 (100), 130 (38)
Adene, 16 (27)
Adewu, 16 (89)
Adhiratha, 29 (68)
Adi, 4 (60)
Admetus, 26 (24)
Adonis, 147 (20), 155 (148)
Adyga, 134 (179)
Aeetes (Aetes), King, 26 (61), 47 (unp), 147 (42), 148 (47)
Aegean Sea, 108 (65), 155 (111)
Aegeus (Aigeus), King, 26 (25), 108 (62), 147 (48), 148 (38), 155 (102)

Aeneas, 26 (41), 130 (154), 138 (123), 155 (176), 166 (77)
Aeolus, 138 (87), 148 (58), 154 (18), 155 (194)
Ae-pungishimook (Epingishmook), 76 (46), 91 (17, 27, 37, 52)
Aesir, 124 (6), 128 (22, 25, 27, 43, 49, 67), 138 (223)
Aetes. See Aeetes
Aethra (Aithra), 26 (25), 148 (38)
Afeer, 4 (52)
Agamemnon, King, 26 (34), 138 (45, 92), 148 (51), 150 (64), 153 (14), 155 (168, 185)
Agni, 29 (32), 51 (52)
Agravain, Sir, 103 (66), 131 (2)
Ahab, King, 9 (159), 114 (120)
Ahaiyuta (Ahaiyute), 83 (unp), 138 (495)
Ahasuerus, King, 114 (124, 126), 147 (68), 181 (unp)
Ah Ling, 44 (326)
Ahriman, 130 (30, 176)
Ahura Mazda, 130 (30, 176)
Ahweyoh, Water Lily, 25 (146)
Aido-Hwedo, 130 (173)
Aidos, 26 (45)
Aigeus. See Aegeus
Ailbe, 139 (110)

Ailell (Ailill), King, 130 (128), 139 (44), 148 (149), 166 (20)

Aino, 148 (92)

Aiofe, 111 (4)

Aioga, 134 (68)

Aithra. *See* Aethra

Aja, 16 (21, 141)

Ajax, 150 (66), 153 (14), 155 (176)

Akainik, 13 (21)

Akanidi, 134 (33, 41)

Aklibimo, 187 (137)

Akrisios. *See* Acrisius

Alamo, 11 (151), 44 (59, 68)

Alan-a-Dale (Allan-a-Dale), 75 (45), 101 (11), 107 (23)

Alatangana (God), 67 (15)

Albatross (ship), 146 (18)

Alcyone, 123 (13)

Alda, 148 (162)

Alesha the Priest's Son, 177 (73)

Alfred Bulltop Stormalong, 122 (39), 146 (13)

Algon, 145 (5)

Aliquipiso, 3 (54)

Aliyu (Man), 12 (270)

Alkestis, 26 (24)

Alkmene, 26 (16)

Alkuntam (Creator), 19 (40)

Allah, 51 (48, 70, 77)

Allan-a-Dale. *See* Alan-a-Dale

Amaterasu (Ama-Terasu), 51 (17), 81 (211), 130 (27, 84), 138 (403, 406), 150 (33)

Amazons, 26 (20, 30), 47 (unp), 108 (56), 148 (32), 155 (96, 112)

Amergin, 139 (20)

Amliq, 4 (36)

Amr bin Zarib, 4 (57)

Amritsar, 51 (86)

Amulius, 150 (46)

Anaanu. *See* Ananse

Ananda, 112 (80)

Ananse (Anaanu; Anansi) the spider, 10 (48), 14 (11, 61, 71, 89), 16 (11, 64, 66, 77, 90, 101, 120, 163, 189), 43 (195, 198, 200), 58 (134), 67 (53), 96 (229), 98 (68, 71), 107 (110), 130 (70), 185 (76, 78, 81, 87, 93)

Anat, 150 (76)

Anchises, 138 (142), 147 (22), 166 (87)

Ancients, 43 (42)

Ancient Snake, 58 (14)

Andes Mts., 2 (10)

Andromache, 138 (55), 153 (38), 155 (177)

Andromeda, 26 (65), 64 (16), 85 (unp), 108 (46), 130 (148), 133 (91), 148 (20), 155 (88), 165 (80)

Andvari, 64 (74), 69 (11), 128 (68), 138 (249), 148 (83)

Anga, 134 (88)

angels, 120 (unp)

Angus, 139 (58)

Animal People, 176 (55)

Anishinaubaek (Anishinabeg), 76 (x), 91 (xvi, 9, 29, 77, 103)

Ankakumikaityn, 134 (132)

Annie Christmas, 66 (84), 145 (35), 185 (130)

Annie Oakley, 11 (479)

Antaios, 26 (23)

Antelope, 10 (52)

Antero Vipunen, 148 (96)

Antigone, 26 (69), 155 (132, 133)

Anu, 51 (27), 67 (79), 107 (101), 130 (38, 45)

Anutherwun, 23 (136)

Anzu, 40 (205)

Aoife, 139 (29)

Apatasok, 145 (117)

Aphrodite, 26 (14), 31 (unp), 130 (154), 138 (44), 147 (19), 153 (6), 155 (148, 169)

Apollo, 108 (36, 60), 123 (23), 130 (60, 96, 104, 154, 166), 155 (142, 147), 165 (118)

Apophis, 67 (111)

Apple of Discord, 26 (33)

Appleseed, Johnny, 11 (12), 122 (25)

apples of youth, 128 (25)

apsaras, 29 (82)

Apsu, 40 (233), 67 (79), 138 (160)

Apsyrtus, 147 (38, 43)

Arachne, 31 (5), 108 (32), 123 (19), 147 (16)

Ararat, 114 (17), 165 (138)

Arawn, King of Annwn, 139 (67), 163 (11)

Arcas, 165 (77)

Arcus, 123 (41)

Ares, 26 (14), 147 (22), 155 (177)

Argayu, 42 (42)

Argo (ship), 26 (59), 47 (unp), 108 (66), 155 (118)

Argonauts, 26 (59), 47 (unp), 108 (66), 147 (42), 148 (46), 155 (118)

Argus, 148 (47)

Ariadne, 26 (28), 108 (63), 130 (110), 148 (42), 155 (108), 183 (unp)

Arianrhod, 139 (80), 163 (71)

Arjuna, 12 (280), 29 (44, 71)

Artemis, 26 (19), 155 (172), 165 (118)

Arthur, King, 49 (7), 72 (6), 77 (1), 78 (unp), 79 (6, 13, 21, 31, 47, 53, 65, 75, 85), 81 (165), 103 (5), 130 (86, 89, 116, 156), 131 (5), 138 (314), 139 (82), 143 (unp), 148 (130), 156 (1), 157 (unp), 166 (135)

Aruru, 148 (66)

Asgard, 32 (5), 107 (103), 124 (9, 14, 24, 29, 36, 43, 53, 67, 77), 128 (14, 43, 49), 130 (21, 62, 64, 72, 118), 138 (221, 228), 150 (70), 166 (14)

Asiedua, 16 (182)

Aso Yoa, 16 (90)

Asuras, 51 (11, 14)

Ata, 16 (78)

Ataentsic, 165 (26)

Atalanta, 30 (unp), 108 (75), 123 (51), 147 (30)

Ate (Ata's brother), 16 (78)

Atendefianoma, the nightjar, 16 (66)

Athena (Athene), 26 (63), 108 (32, 42), 116 (104), 133 (87), 138 (44), 147 (14), 148 (19), 153 (6), 155 (85, 169, 190, 192), 165 (74, 122)

Athens, 26 (25, 72), 155 (101)

Atlantis, 130 (170)

Atlas, 26 (21), 67 (133), 85 (unp), 108 (57), 130 (134), 148 (34), 155 (97)

Atli, King, 69 (70), 128 (77)

Atrahasis, 40 (18)

Atreus, 155 (185)

Attis, 6 (38), 165 (119)

Atum, 61 (unp), 71 (11, 18)

Auberon, 49 (34)

Audumla, 124 (1), 128 (57)

Augean Stables, 26 (20), 148 (30), 155 (95)

Auilix, 161 (171)

Aurelius, King, 103 (14)

Autumn Bird, 168 (17)

Avalon, 79 (94), 130 (157), 138 (349)

Averiri, 13 (36)

Avraluk, 145 (112)

Awonawilona, 19 (84)

Ayar Cachi, 138 (462)

Ayodhya, 89 (48), 138 (365)

Azmun, 134 (71)

Azrail, 120 (unp)

Aztecs, 130 (140)

Aztlan, 106 (394)

Baakil, 113 (13)

Baal, 9 (159), 114 (120), 150 (76)

Babalu-Aye, 56 (21)

Babel, 114 (19)

Babe the Blue Ox, 11 (604, 611, 624, 629), 44 (154, 164), 122 (97), 146 (48), 175 (50)

Babylon, 9 (29)

Bacchus, 123 (9)

Badger, 23 (124)

Ba'dotlizhe, 23 (132)

Bagabornabou, 64 (90)

Baghdad, 1 (9)

Baiame (Biami; Baiamai), 51 (8), 119 (64, 67, 79)

Bailey, Mad Ann, 44 (49)

Bakola, 51 (86)

Balder (Baldr; Baldur), 70, (61), 124 (5, 44, 70, 77), 128 (48, 63, 67), 130 (162, 175), 133 (28), 138 (224, 230, 232), 166 (65)

Balla Fasseke, 180 (unp)

Bali, 29 (36)

Balor, 139 (21)

Balquis (Balqis; Bilqis), Queen, 4 (50), 147 (82)

Balshazzar, King, 114 (141)

Bamapama, 130 (69)

Bao Chu, 138 (396)

Barab, 9 (79)

Barabbas, 51 (91)

Barak, 9 (79)

Baramon, 169 (33, 34)

Barinthus, Father, 139 (112)

Basket Woman, 113 (59)

Bast, 130 (146)

Ba'ts'oosee, 23 (131)

Battle of Badr, 51 (70)

Battle of Uhud, 51 (70)

Baucis, 123 (67)

Baugi, 124 (12)

Bayart, 49 (38)

Baylon, 114 (141)

Bean, Judge Roy, 44 (323, 325, 328, 330, 332)

Bear, 25 (32, 37, 51, 55), 104 (19), 133 (15), 140 (16), 150 (23, 33), 164 (18), 187 (111)

Bear-Killer, 25 (86)

Bear People, 91 (20)

bears, 60 (29), 96 (69), 171 (24)

Bearskin-Woman, 132 (96)

Beaudricourt, Capt. Robert de, 147 (107)

Beautiful Star, 113 (101)

Beaver, 25 (47), 43 (34), 76 (88, 92, 95), 87 (unp), 171 (50, 95)

Beaver, Tony, 11 (626)

Beckwourth, Jim, 44 (128)

Be-deg-wad-zo, 24 (23)

Bedivere (Bedevere), Sir, 79 (90), 103 (93), 130 (157), 138 (346), 148 (140)

Beetle, 24 (11)

Begochiddy, 27 (31)

Belle Starr, 186 (21, 83, 148)

Benares, 43 (112)

Bendigeidfran, 163 (30)

Ben Hardin, 175 (17)

Bennadonner, 133 (77)

Benu Bird, 61 (unp)

Beowulf, 81 (161), 130 (106), 138 (289), 148 (120)

Bertik Khan, 165 (100)

Bertilak, Sir, 131 (32)

Bethlehem, 51 (50)

Bhagavan, 165 (105)

Bharata (Bharat), 89 (50), 138 (366)

Bhasmasura, 29 (28)

Bhima, 12 (280), 29 (55)

Biami. See Baiame

Big Dipper, 27 (117)

Big Earth, 25 (116)

Big Eater of the Forest, 122 (10)

Big Fish, 21 (47)

Big Mose, 175 (29)

Big Raven, 158 (13)

Big Reed, 27 (31)

Big Toolie, 175 (65)

Billy the Kid, 44 (235, 241, 244, 246)

Bilquis, Queen. See Balquis

Bishop Turpin, 49 (29)

blackbirds, 171 (68)

Black Duck, 76 (145)

Black Feather, 173 (24)

Black God, 113 (31)

Black Hills, 11 (239)

Black Knight, 72 (8), 77 (1), 166 (123)

Blanchfleur, Lady of the White Flower, 49 (15), 79 (55)

Blizzard, 134 (120)

Blodeuwedd, 163 (76)

the Bloodsucker, 187 (85)

Bluebird, 43 (238), 82 (33)

Blue Corn Maiden, 187 (51)

Blue Dawn, 74 (4)

Blue Jay (Bluejay), 43 (238), 74 (18), 187 (129)

boa, 43 (207)

Boadicea, 147 (97)

boar of Erymanthus, 148 (30)

Boaz, 114 (85)

Bobbi-bobbi, 150 (83)

Bobcat, 34 (50)

Bobd Deargh, 139 (29)

Bodvild, 81 (177)

Bon Homme Richard (ship), 146 (15)

Bonney, William H. See Billy the Kid

Boone, Daniel, 11 (51, 225), 44 (37, 42)

Boone, Rebecca Bryan, 11 (225), 44 (38)

Boriquen, 37 (unp)

Bors, Sir, 79 (78), 103 (66)

Botany Bay, 147 (141)

Botoque, 150 (51)

Bouki, 65 (102)

Bowie, Jim, 44 (63, 282)

boy-hero, 33 (unp)
Bra Antelope, 16 (123)
Bra Deer, 16 (123)
Brady, Sam, 44 (45)
Brady's Leap, 44 (46)
Brahma, 12 (72, 156), 29 (17), 51 (11, 14), 138 (354, 365)
Brahmaloka, 12 (156)
Branstock, 148 (76)
Bran the Blessed, 130 (159), 139 (69)
Branwen, 139 (69), 163 (30)
Bra Spider, 16 (122)
Brendan, Saint, 139 (112)
Br'er Bear, 43 (215), 116 (197)
Br'er Coon, 116 (197), 185 (66)
Br'er Fox, 11 (346, 348)
Br'er Possum, 116 (197)
Br'er Rabbit, 11 (346, 348), 43 (215), 46 (unp), 116 (197), 185 (66)
Br'er Tiger, 46 (unp)
Br'er Wolf, 116 (197)
Brian, 139 (25)
Bright Shining Old Man, 113 (5)
Bright Sunbeam, 134 (30)
Briseis, 153 (20)
Brok (Brokk), 124 (21), 128 (53)
Brolga, 100 (44)
Brother Alligator, 185 (103)
Brother Bear, 185 (60, 167)
Brother Coyote ('Mano Coyote), 178 (89)
Brother Lion, 185 (59)
Brother Man, 185 (167)
Brother Possum. See Possum
Brother Rabbit, 185 (60, 103, 163, 171)
Brother Snake, 185 (170)
Brother Trouble, 185 (104)
Bruno the bear, 44 (332)
Brynhild, 69 (46), 128 (73), 138 (244), 148 (87)
Buddha, 43 (112), 51 (37, 46, 74), 81 (208), 107 (49), 130 (147), 142 (unp), 165 (70)
Buddha RuLai, 129 (29)
Buffalo, 11 (343), 24 (17), 44 (209)
Buffalo Bill, 44 (247)
Buffalo Maiden, 132 (128)
Buffalo-Ones, 132 (128)
Buffalo-Woman, 132 (128)

Buh Rabby, 66 (3)
bull, Deacon's, 11 (101)
Bull of Heaven, 40 (80), 86 (37), 148 (71)
Bull of Marathon, 26 (27)
Bull of Ulster, 130 (128)
Bunyan, Paul. See Paul Bunyan
Bunyip, 119 (64)
Burd Ellen, 65 (65)
Buri, 150 (16)
Bush Pig, 16 (65)
Butler, Frank, 11 (479)
Buzzard, 25 (61), 96 (126), 132 (109), 187 (121)

Cadmus, 130 (96)
Caedmon, 115 (75)
Cagn, 150 (80)
Cain, 114 (11)
Cairbre, 139 (110)
Calamity Jane, 11 (478), 44 (261, 299, 302, 304, 305, 313), 186 (164, 190, 202)
Callisto, 123 (41), 165 (76)
Calypso, 26 (50), 138 (78), 154 (45), 155 (197)
camel of God, 4 (33)
Camelot, 79 (11, 13, 21, 47, 53, 65, 82), 103 (48)
Camillus, 107 (66)
Canaan, 114 (20)
Canaanites, 9 (77)
Candlefly, 185 (93)
Cannary, Martha Jane. See Calamity Jane
Cannibal Demon, 147 (119)
Cannonball, 185 (133)
Caoilte mac Ronan, 139 (64)
Captain Tommy, 175 (57)
Captain Walters, 146 (4)
Carbonek, 49 (16)
Carlos Robles, 44 (330)
Carson, Kit, 44 (95, 100)
Carthage, 138 (123)
Casey Jones, 185 (133)
Cassandra, 26 (40), 155 (173, 187)
Cassiopeia, 26 (65), 133 (91), 165 (77)
Cathbad the druid, 139 (36, 129), 148 (144)

Cattle of Geryon, 26 (20)

Cauldron of Plenty, 138 (285)

Cei, Sir. *See* Kay, Sir

Celebrated Seahouse, 161 (167)

Celestial Emperor, 129 (6)

centaurs, 26 (29), 107 (1), 155 (99)

Cepheus, 64 (16), 133 (91), 148 (20), 165 (77)

Cerberus, 26 (21), 108 (56, 72), 130 (135), 148 (34), 155 (39, 98), 166 (79)

Cercyon, 148 (39)

Ceres, 123 (35)

Cetus, 165 (80)

Ceyx, 123 (13)

Chac, 17 (66, 84)

Chalchihuitlicue, 62 (15)

Chameleon, 5 (23), 43 (80), 58 (15, 125, 126, 134), 67 (73)

Chandu, 51 (63)

Changing Woman, 27 (34), 130 (36), 149 (7)

Chango, 56 (37)

Chaos, 61 (unp), 67 (127), 138 (6), 155 (10)

Chapman, John, 11 (12), 122 (25)

Charlemagne, Emperor, 49 (28), 148 (160)

Charon, 130 (154, 166), 155 (40), 166 (79)

Charybdis, 26 (49), 108 (90), 155 (196)

Cheeby-aub-oozoo, 91 (30, 37)

Cheepii, 105 (62)

Cheetah, 57 (28)

Chelm, 53 (21), 144 (3)

Chernava, 177 (48)

Chickadee, 113 (19)

the Chief, 14 (94)

Chief Duck, 76 (113)

Chief Sage of Chelm, 53 (21)

Childe Rowland, 65 (65)

Child-of-the-Water, 68 (20)

Children of Nemed, 139 (15)

Children of the Morning Light, 105 (13, 40, 56)

Chimaera, 130 (149)

Chinook Wind, 113 (104)

Chipmunk, 3 (112), 25 (37)

Chiron the Centaur, 148 (46), 155 (116)

Christmas, Annie. *See* Annie Christmas

Chuc Nu, 174 (54)

Chuku, 43 (79), 130 (77)

Cian the Mighty, 139 (25)

Cid. *See* El Cid Campeador

Cigfa, 139 (72), 163 (46)

Circe, 26 (46), 108 (87), 138 (89), 147 (36), 148 (58), 154 (28), 155 (194)

Clam, 187 (131)

Clashing Cliffs, 108 (68)

the clashing rocks, 26 (60)

Clay Pot Woman, 187 (23)

Clear Sky, 173 (4)

Cleave, 69 (28)

Cloud Eater, 83 (unp), 138 (495)

Clytemnestra, 26 (35), 155 (172, 186)

Coatlicue, 106 (380)

Colchis, 47 (unp), 148 (47), 155 (120)

Cold Wind, 113 (104)

Conann, 139 (15)

Conchobar mac Nessa, King, 139 (32), 148 (142)

Connacht, 139 (17)

Coon, 11 (180)

Coot, 134 (102)

Corinth, 155 (124)

Cormac, King, 111 (14), 139 (109)

corn, 27 (137), 150 (51)

Corn Mountain, 83 (unp), 138 (495)

Corn Spirit, 165 (124)

Corynetes, 155 (104)

Cottontail, 23 (105)

Cougar, 34 (61)

Countess of the Fountain, 166 (129)

Count Palatine, 107 (78)

Count Potocki, 93 (24, 37)

Courser (ship), 175 (24)

Coyote, 3 (115), 11 (343), 17 (72, 81), 19 (86, 101, 142, 144), 23 (30, 38, 44, 49, 65, 84, 92, 105, 122, 124, 131, 135, 146, 152), 24 (19), 27 (31, 57), 31 (30), 34 (61), 41 (63), 43 (233, 235, 237), 44 (209), 67 (38), 74 (15, 22, 26), 82 (9, 33), 96 (126), 104 (2), 107 (120), 113 (7, 22, 40, 91, 101), 126 (unp), 130 (74), 138 (492), 164 (20), 170 (1, 11, 21, 29, 35, 41, 53), 171 (68), 176 (56), 178 (89, 91), 187 (114)

Crab, 14 (114), 16 (107, 170)

Crane, 113 (92), 164 (10)

Crane Woman, 113 (67)

Crazy Jack (Jack), 21 (79, 81)

Creator, 21 (21), 25 (61), 57 (14, 28, 47, 67, 89, 97, 104, 127, 134), 58 (14, 46, 100, 107, 121, 125, 136), 107 (114), 138 (470), 140 (19), 158 (6, 29), 165 (24, 100)

Creator (Kururumanni), 132 (21)

Creator of the Universe, 89 (71)

Creator Spirit, 187 (114)

Creon, King, 155 (129, 133)

Cretan Bull, 26 (20), 148 (31, 40), 155 (96)

Crete, 155 (107), 183 (unp)

Cricket, 140 (21)

Crockett, Davy, 11 (99, 151, 180, 224, 394), 44 (57, 60, 61, 75), 92 (unp), 122 (3, 17), 175 (15)

Crockett, Sally Ann Thunder Ann Whirl-wind, 92 (unp), 122 (15)

Crocodile, 16 (129), 45 (126)

Crocus, 165 (118)

Crom Dubh, 139 (124)

Cronus, 155 (10)

Crow, 164 (14), 172 (unp)

Crunnchu mac Agnoman, 139 (41)

Cuchulain (Cuchulainn; CuChulainn), 130 (125), 139 (32, 129), 148 (142), 150 (63)

Culann the Smith, 139 (33)

Cunnie Rabbit, 16 (75, 123)

Cuoi, 174 (38)

Cupid, 35 (unp), 108 (60), 123 (23, 57)

Curlew, 119 (79)

Cut-Nose, first man, 132 (128)

Cuzco, 51 (25), 138 (460, 463, 465)

Cybele, 6 (38), 165 (119)

Cyclops, 26 (43), 108 (85), 138 (82), 148 (54), 154 (11), 155 (193), 176 (36)

Cynan, 131 (17)

Cynon, 139 (92)

Dada, 42 (47)

Daedalus, 130 (112), 148 (40), 183 (unp)

Dagda the Good, 138 (279, 285), 139 (21)

Daijo Tenjin, 169 (146)

Danae, 26 (63), 85 (unp), 108 (41), 116 (106), 133 (85), 148 (17), 155 (81)

Dangling Nose, 138 (413)

Daniel, 114 (142)

Daniel Boone, 11 (51, 225), 44 (37, 42)

Daphne, 108 (60), 123 (23), 165 (119)

Dark Jaguar, 160 (3)

Dasa-ratha, 138 (365)

Daughters of Phorcus, 133 (88)

Daunni'si, 132 (88)

the Dauphin, Charles VIII, 147 (105)

David, King, 114 (94), 176 (64)

Davy Crockett, 11 (99, 151, 180, 224, 394), 44 (57, 60, 61, 75), 92 (unp), 122 (3, 17), 175 (15)

Dayamanti, 51 (52)

Deacon's Bull, 11 (101)

Deadwood, 11 (139)

Deadwood Dick, 44 (312, 317)

Death, 16 (141), 43 (79, 80), 58 (121), 65 (5), 67 (15, 105), 150 (77)

Death Hug, 175 (15)

Deborah, 9 (78)

Deer, 140 (29, 33)

De Fistycuff, 64 (89)

Deianeira, 26 (24), 148 (35), 155 (98)

Delilah, 9 (105), 114 (80), 148 (114)

Delphic oracle, 26 (69), 148 (26, 38)

Demeter, 26 (7), 108 (15), 130 (82), 133 (37), 138 (8, 16), 147 (25), 150 (39), 155 (11, 74)

Demne, 139 (53)

Deucalion, 138 (25)

Devaki, 51 (54), 89 (22, 26)

Devas, 51 (11, 14)

Devi, 130 (98, 144)

Devil, 66 (70), 165 (101, 130)

Dharma, 12 (71, 280), 29 (62)

Diana, 123 (51)

Diarmuid, 139 (57), 166 (28)

Diaz de Bivar, Rodrigo (El Cid), 95 (1), 107 (94), 148 (171), 188 (79, 88)

Dictys, 26 (63), 85 (unp), 133 (86), 148 (17), 155 (83)

Dido, 130 (154), 138 (123), 166 (81)

Dihi the jaguar, 36 (5)

Di Jun, 107 (7), 150 (28)

Dilmun, 86 (55), 138 (211)

Dilyehe, 113 (31)

Dinarzade, 147 (94)

Dine, 43 (30)

Dinewan the emu, 100 (44)

Diomedes, 155 (176)

Diomedes's horses, 26 (20), 148 (31)

Dionysus, 26 (68), 130 (102, 166), 133 (63), 148 (43), 155 (141)

Dirty Clothes, 25 (41)

divine woman, 67 (59)

Divyan, 12 (175)

Dobrynya Nikitich, 177 (37, 69)

Dog, 16 (136), 24 (17), 25 (85), 67 (29), 113 (117), 187 (108)

Donn, 139 (17)

the Donn of Cuailnge, 139 (43)

Dove Maidens, 113 (41)

doves, 43 (235)

Draco (the Dragon), 165 (74)

Dragon King, 75 (43), 129 (4)

dragons' teeth, 108 (68), 148 (47)

Draupadi, 29 (44)

Dreamtime, 51 (8), 130 (28, 69)

Drona, 29 (69)

Druids, 138 (278)

Duiker, 16 (181)

Dumuzi, 40 (160)

Dunai Ivanovich, 177 (37)

Dung Beetle, 58 (136)

Duni Chand, 51 (83)

Dunyazad, 1 (15), 4 (105)

Durandel, 49 (32), 148 (163)

Durga, 130 (98), 150 (93)

Duryodhana, 29 (45, 71)

dwarves (dwarfs), 124 (21), 128 (53)

Dyfed, 163 (10, 46)

Dyke of Ma'rib, 4 (57)

Ea, 40 (184), 51 (27), 67 (79), 107 (100), 130 (38, 45), 166 (61)

Eager-for-Life, 124 (80)

Eagle, 19 (144), 43 (109, 203), 45 (117), 104 (12), 116 (125, 195)

Eagle Man, 159 (10)

Eagle, Martial, 58 (107)

Earth, 16 (183), 40 (279), 67 (127), 120 (unp)

Earth God, 167 (10)

Earthmaker, 19 (103, 231), 130 (74)

Earthquake, 27 (93), 161 (99)

Earth Starter, 67 (35)

Earth-the-Mother, 170 (25, 33)

Earth Woman, 91 (9)

East Wind, 133 (17)

Echo, 108 (21), 123 (29), 150 (23), 155 (146), 165 (122)

Ector (Hector), Sir, 49 (6), 79 (7), 103 (29), 131 (8), 139 (84), 143 (unp), 148 (134), 157 (unp)

Eden, 9 (9), 67 (123), 114 (6), 120 (unp)

Efnisien, 139 (70), 163 (30)

Egypt, 9 (35, 47), 28 (unp), 51 (71), 114 (38, 46)

Eirik the Red, 84 (unp)

Elaine, 79 (33)

Elaine, the Fair Maid of Astolat, 79 (36)

Elayne, 103 (56). See also Elaine

El Capitan, 24 (9)

El Chivato, 44 (241)

El Cid Campeador (Diaz de Bivar, Rodrigo), 95 (1), 107 (94), 148 (171), 188 (79, 88)

Elder Brother, 19 (103)

Elder Duck, 187 (44)

Electra (Elektra), 26 (41), 155 (186)

Elegba, 116 (40)

Eleggua, 56 (31)

Elephant, 57 (53), 165 (105)

Eleusis, 26 (8)

Elijah, 9 (159), 114 (120)

Elisha, 9 (175)

Elk, 135 (18), 158 (18)

Ellen (King Arthur), 131 (48)

Ellen (Robin Hood), 75 (45)

Elli, 128 (54)

Elohim (God), 67 (149)

Emer, 139 (37), 148 (147)

Emir Musa, 4 (109)

Emperor of Heaven, 130 (52)

Emperor Yao, 107 (8)

Endekuma, 16 (91)

Enki, 40 (9)

Enkidu, 40 (53), 86 (4), 130 (44), 138 (185), 148 (64), 150 (58), 189 (5)

Enlil, 51 (27)

Ennead, 71 (13, 18)
En no Gyoja, 169 (127)
Eochaid Airem, 139 (105)
Eochaid Bres, 139 (21)
Epimetheus, 67 (133, 140), 108 (9), 130 (60), 150 (90), 155 (69)
Epingishmook. *See* Ae-pungishimook
Ereshkigal, 40 (155, 165), 166 (61)
Eris, 26 (33), 155 (169)
Eriu, 139 (18)
Erlang, 129 (22)
Erlik, 67 (29), 130 (34)
Eros, 165 (118)
Erymanthian Boar, 26 (19)
Esau, 114 (28, 30, 32)
Esclarmonde, 49 (34)
Eskimo Wolverine, 132 (121)
Esther, Queen, 114 (125, 126), 147 (68), 181 (unp)
Etain, 139 (105)
Etana, 40 (19)
Eteocles, 155 (134)
Ethiopia, 64 (16)
Etruscans, 107 (66)
Et-tetti, 145 (108)
Europa, 26 (66)
Euryclea, 154 (50)
Eurydice, 108 (71), 123 (45), 130 (166), 155 (20, 139)
Eurylochus, 147 (38), 154 (25)
Eurytheus, 26 (16), 108 (51), 148 (27), 155 (94)
Eve, 9 (19), 51 (20), 67 (123), 114 (11), 120 (unp), 121 (unp)
Evening Star, 43 (56), 187 (59)
Everything-Maker, 52 (unp)
Evil Kachina, 3 (182)
Evil Mind, 25 (20)
Evil Ones, 91 (xxi)
Evpraksiya, Princess, 177 (37)
Evva, 40 (285)
Excalibur, 79 (15, 92), 103 (44), 138 (326), 139 (89), 148 (138)

Fafnir, 64 (72), 69 (9), 128 (67), 138 (247), 148 (82)
The Fair Unknown, 131 (47)
Falcon, 24 (17)

False Face, 158 (28)
Farmer, 14 (72)
Fat Beetle, 45 (122)
Father Sky, 105 (16, 17), 158 (6)
Father Spider, 98 (69)
Faustulus, 150 (46)
Fawn, 133 (15), 135 (20)
Feathered Serpent, 67 (87), 188 (60)
Feboldson, Febold, 11 (585), 122 (63)
Fedelm, 139 (47)
Fenians, 139 (53)
Fenrir (Fenris), 65 (82), 124 (29, 77), 128 (63)
Ferdiad, 139 (47)
Fergus mac Roich, 139 (41)
Fer-li, 139 (60)
Fer-tai, 139 (60)
Fianna, 166 (28)
Fierabras, 49 (29)
Fifth World, 130 (36)
the Findbenmach, 139 (43)
Fink, Mike, 11 (99, 101), 44 (75, 77), 92 (unp), 122 (12, 21)
Fink, Sal, 44 (80, 81)
Finn MacCool (Finn Mac Cool), 125 (unp), 133 (77)
Finn Mac Cumal, 166 (105)
Fionn, 111 (14), 139 (53)
Fionnguala, 139 (29)
Fir Bolg, 138 (278), 139 (16)
Fire, 14 (77), 16 (158), 67 (134), 117 (75), 130 (58)
Fire Mistress, 134 (177)
First Angry, 74 (12)
First Creator, 130 (53)
First Man, 58 (99, 125), 74 (10), 87 (unp), 105 (25), 107 (120), 113 (29), 126 (unp), 138 (492)
First Woman, 23 (118), 58 (99), 87 (unp), 107 (120), 126 (unp), 138 (492)
Fir Tree, 135 (14)
Fisher, 27 (117), 168 (5)
Fisher-King, 49 (16), 103 (57)
Flies, Black, 58 (99)
Fling-A-Mile, 185 (88)
Flint, 19 (198), 22 (12), 140 (7), 158 (22), 165 (33)
Flint Bird, 187 (79)

Flint Coats, 25 (162)

Flying Head, 25 (184)

The Flying Head of the Forest, 159 (21)

Fomorians, 138 (277), 139 (14)

Forest of Cedars, 148 (68)

Forgall, 139 (37)

Four-Eyes, 25 (85)

the Four Hundred Boys, 161 (94)

Fox, 25 (32, 74, 80), 104 (16), 164 (18), 187 (111)

Frank Butler, 11 (479)

Frey (Freyr), 124 (6, 25, 53, 79), 128 (27, 54)

Freya (Freyia), 32 (12), 107 (104), 124 (6, 15, 34, 40), 128 (14, 27), 130 (64), 138 (238)

Friar Tuck, 39 (8), 75 (41), 101 (44), 107 (21)

Frigg (Frigga), 70 (61), 124 (1, 70), 128 (48), 130 (162), 133 (30), 138 (224, 232)

Frog, 19 (101), 87 (unp), 96 (110), 104 (23), 165 (32, 37), 185 (67)

Fuamnach, 139 (105)

Fu Hsi, 165 (21)

Furies, 155 (39, 190)

Gaan, 149 (17)

Gabriel, 51 (50), 54 (unp)

Gaea, 138 (6)

Gaels, 139 (21)

Gaheris (Gaherys), Sir, 103 (80), 131 (4)

Galahad, Sir, 79 (35, 68, 75, 85), 103 (70), 130 (89)

Galienne, 49 (28)

Galun'lati, 132 (109)

Game Master, 21 (67)

gandharvas, 29 (82)

Ganelon, 49 (32), 148 (160)

Ganesh, 29 (9), 51 (59), 89 (121), 130 (144)

Ga-oh, 82 (30), 133 (15)

Garcia, Three-Fingered Jack, 44 (225)

Garden of Gethsemane, 51 (91)

Gareth, Sir, 78 (unp), 103 (80), 131 (2)

Garrett, Sheriff Pat, 44 (236, 244)

Gassire, 138 (435)

Gaudisse, 49 (34)

Gauls, 107 (70)

Gau-wi-di-ne, 82 (26)

Gawain, Sir, 49 (9), 72 (17), 79 (35, 53, 86), 81 (167), 103 (51), 138 (332), 139 (96), 166 (135)

Geb, 61 (unp), 71 (14, 40)

Geirrod the giant, 70 (46), 166 (51)

George, Saint (George of Lydda), 7 (23), 107 (14), 109 (unp)

Gerd, 124 (53), 128 (29)

Geriguiaguiatugo, 81 (221)

Geryon, 148 (32)

Gessler, 48 (unp)

Ghede, Lord of Death, 130 (117)

Ghost country, 96 (62)

Giant, 19 (29)

Giant Arrogance, 49 (37)

Giant Beaver, 158 (10)

Giant Cannibals, 91 (xxi)

Giant Corsolt, 49 (42)

Giants, 67 (69), 107 (104), 138 (222), 165 (74)

Giant Sisters, 176 (56)

Giant Turtle, 91 (xv)

Gib Morgan, 11 (588, 593, 595, 596), 175 (62)

Gideon, 114 (76)

Giei, 169 (141)

Gifaethwy, 139 (77), 163 (64)

Gikuyu, 50 (8)

Gilgamesh, 40 (51), 86 (2), 130 (44), 138 (184), 148 (63), 150 (58), 189 (1)

Ginunngagap, 67 (69), 124 (1), 128 (57), 138 (221), 150 (16)

Giraffe, 57 (89)

girdle of Hippolyta, 148 (32), 155 (96)

the Girl with the Little Sleeves, 131 (69)

Gitche Gumee, 76 (178)

Gjoll, 166 (65)

Glastonbury, 79 (94)

Glauce (Glauke), 26 (59), 147 (46)

Glooskap (Gluscabi; Gluskabe), 27 (21, 67, 165), 43 (66), 116 (125), 130 (92). *See also* Koluscap

God, 9 (9, 19, 31, 47, 65, 96), 10 (44, 147), 16 (182, 189, 190), 43 (56, 80), 51 (18, 32, 71, 80, 88, 91), 54 (unp), 66 (69), 90 (unp), 107 (89, 110), 114

(1, 8, 13, 14, 18, 50, 62), 115 (75), 120 (unp), 121 (unp), 130 (17, 49), 144 (6), 165 (110, 130)

God (Alatangana), 67 (15)

God (Elohim), 67 (149)

God of the Animals, 117 (82)

God of Venus, 129 (6)

God (Ora), 12 (270)

Goewin, 139 (77), 163 (64)

Go-hay, 82 (31)

golden apple of discord, 148 (51)

Golden Apples of the Hesperides, 26 (21), 148 (33), 155 (97)

golden apples of youth, 124 (37)

golden bough, 166 (79)

Golden Fleece, 26 (59), 108 (66), 148 (47), 155 (114)

Golden Sunshine, 134 (30)

Goldfax, 124 (65)

Golgotha, 51 (91)

Goliath, 114 (94), 176 (63)

Golizhi the skunk, 23 (94)

Gomorrah, 114 (23)

Gong-gong, 138 (392)

Gonzalvo, 148 (179)

Good Mind, 25 (21)

Goo-goor-gaga (kookaburra), 100 (44)

Gorgons, 26 (63), 64 (19), 85 (unp)

Gorlois, Duke, 103 (18), 131 (6)

Gorm, King of Denmark, 166 (49)

Graeae (Graiai), 26 (63), 85 (unp), 108 (41), 148 (19), 155 (85)

Grainne, 139 (57)

Gram, 64 (73)

Grand Canyon, 122 (104)

Grandfather Spider, 41 (35)

Grandfather Sun, 105 (14, 49), 118 (2), 158 (18)

Grandma Wang, 129 (9)

Grand Medicine Society, 76 (107)

Grandmother, 83 (unp)

Grandmother Moon, 105 (14), 158 (17)

Grandmother Ocean, 105 (14)

Grandmother Spider, 24 (9), 27 (79), 187 (38)

Grandmother Turtle, 51 (24)

Grandmother Woodchuck, 27 (67, 165), 43 (66), 116 (125)

Grani, 64 (74)

Graybird, 82 (32)

Gray Man, 65 (5)

Gray Sisters (Grey Sisters), 85 (unp), 108 (41), 148 (19), 155 (85). *See also* Graeae

Gray Squirrel, 23 (105)

Gray Wolf, 159 (13)

Great Bear, 132 (96), 134 (89), 165 (74)

Great Beaver, 159 (30)

Great Buzzard, 24 (11)

Great Chief in the Sky, 135 (6)

Great Creator, 159 (7, 27)

Great Day, 187 (109)

Great Elk, 134 (82)

Great God, 67 (73), 150 (50)

Great-Grandmother Earth, 15 (unp)

Great Hare, 151 (unp)

Great King Bear of the Mud Forest, 122 (20)

Great Lakes, 11 (611), 105 (22), 122 (105)

Great Light, 13 (15)

Great Maker, 171 (60)

Great Mystery, 91 (xv)

Great Rabbit, 63 (4)

Great Sky Spirit, 172 (unp)

Great Smokies, 24 (11)

Great Spirit, 3 (54), 43 (109), 44 (162), 59 (unp), 60 (1), 96 (140), 171 (95)

Great Spirit of the Woods, 173 (29)

Great Turtle, 27 (26), 105 (19, 20)

Greenland, 84 (unp)

Grendel, 81 (160), 130 (106), 138 (289), 148 (120)

Grendel's mother, 130 (106), 138 (297)

Grimhild, 148 (89)

Grizzly Bear, 164 (20)

Gronw Bebr, 163 (76)

Guabancex, 37 (unp)

Guan Di, 150 (63)

Guanyin, 147 (50)

Guan Yu, 150 (63)

Guardian, 166 (129)

Gucamatz, 150 (17)

Gudmund the giant, 166 (51)

Gudrun, 69 (50), 128 (75), 138 (244), 148 (90)

Guinea Fowl, 16 (170), 58 (99)

Guinevere, Queen, 49 (7), 72 (10), 79 (21, 32, 43, 56, 65, 94), 103 (5), 130 (88, 90, 156), 131 (2), 138 (327), 139 (92), 148 (130), 156 (23)

Gulnara, 150 (62)

gum-man, 43 (201)

Gunderson, Shot, 11 (620), 44 (167)

Gunnar, 69 (50), 128 (75), 148 (90)

Guru Har Govind, 51 (63)

Guru Har Krishan, 51 (86)

Guru Nanak, 51 (82)

Gust of Wind, 158 (22)

Guy of Gisborne, Sir, 75 (10), 101 (61), 107 (20)

Gwawl, son of Clud, 163 (19)

Gwern, 163 (35)

Gwri Golden Hair, 163 (26)

Gwydion, 139 (77), 163 (64)

Gyogi, 169 (33)

Gyoja, 169 (127)

Hacauitz, 161 (171)

Hadding, Prince of Denmark, 166 (14)

Hades, 26 (7), 130 (135), 133 (37), 138 (8, 16, 91), 147 (25), 150 (39), 155 (11, 39, 74, 140, 148, 185, 195), 165 (119), 166 (77)

Hafgan, King, 139 (67), 163 (11)

hag, 165 (36)

Hahjanah, 25 (97)

Hahskwahot, 25 (12)

Haka-lani-leo, 176 (17)

Halibu, 43 (75)

Haman, 114 (126), 147 (70), 181 (unp)

hammer, 124 (25, 33), 138 (239)

Hanab Ku, 99 (unp)

Hang Nga, 174 (17)

Hanuman, 29 (59), 51 (43, 66), 89 (59), 138 (379)

Haran, 51 (80)

Hare, 10 (44, 147), 19 (218), 43 (81), 45 (108, 117), 134 (82), 151 (unp), 165 (70), 167 (16)

hare named Sasa, 107 (49)

Harmonia, 26 (66)

Harpies, 26 (60), 47 (unp), 108 (67), 155 (119)

Harva, 133 (18)

Hasanowane, 187 (139)

hastshin, 19 (84)

Hau Nghe, 174 (13)

Hawenio, the Creator, 25 (176)

Hawk, 135 (16)

Headless Harry, 44 (126)

Heart of Sky, 67 (87), 106 (107), 161 (73)

Heaven, 16 (183)

Heavenly Nectar of Immortality, 89 (71)

Hebrews, 9 (35, 47)

Hector, 26 (37), 138 (52), 150 (66), 153 (21), 155 (167)

Hector, Sir. See Ector, Sir

Hecuba, 26 (33)

Hefeydd the Old, 163 (18)

Heimdall, 124 (5, 34, 43, 79), 128 (65)

Hekeke, 145 (103)

Hel, 124 (29, 76, 77), 128 (49, 63), 130 (66, 162), 133 (35), 138 (224, 232), 166 (65)

Helen of Troy, 26 (30, 33), 108 (78), 138 (44), 148 (50), 150 (64), 153 (10), 154 (51), 155 (168, 185)

Helheim, 133 (28)

Heliopolis, 61 (unp), 71 (11)

Helios, 123 (1), 165 (41)

Helle, 26 (59)

Hell's Gate Gang, 122 (78)

Helluland, 84 (unp)

hen, 43 (203), 67 (21)

He-noh, 25 (149)

Henry, John, 11 (134), 122 (87), 146 (1), 175 (55), 185 (124)

Henry, Lucy, 122 (90)

Henry, Polly Ann, 11 (134), 175 (58), 185 (125)

Heorot, 81 (159), 148 (122)

Hephaestus (Hephaistos), 26 (14), 147 (20), 150 (40, 88), 155 (69)

Hera, 26 (16), 108 (21), 130 (58, 130), 138 (28, 44), 153 (6), 155 (11, 92, 146, 169), 165 (76, 118)

Heracles (Herakles; Hercules), 26 (16, 25, 48, 59), 47 (unp), 80 (138), 108 (51), 130 (61, 130), 138 (28, 80), 148 (25), 150 (62), 155 (91)

Hermes, 26 (8, 63), 65 (44), 85 (unp),

108 (18, 42), 133 (85), 148 (18), 155 (85, 195), 165 (38)

the Hermit King, 131 (60)

Hermod, 124 (72), 128 (49, 63), 133 (33), 166 (65)

Hermopolis, 71 (19)

Herod, King, 51 (50)

Heron Feather, 25 (81)

Hero Twins, 24 (9), 27 (79), 106 (316)

Hershel of Ostropol, 93 (9, 13, 16, 29, 32, 37, 44, 52, 61)

Hesperides, 108 (57), 148 (33)

Hestia, 155 (11)

He Who Gets Angry First, 74 (12)

He-Who-Kicks-Them-Over-the-Cliff, 24 (9)

He Who Minds Everybody's Business, 74 (12)

Hian, 130 (42)

Hickok, James Butler "Wild Bill," 44 (255), 186 (45)

Hiiaka, 145 (121)

hijira (flight), 51 (77)

Himalaya, 29 (24)

Hina, 67 (101), 107 (40), 176 (17)

Hind of Ceryneia (Keryneia), 26 (19), 148 (28)

Hiordis, Queen, 69 (25), 128 (72), 148 (79)

Hippo, 16 (158)

Hippolyta, 148 (32)

Hippolytus, 155 (112)

Hippomenes, 108 (75), 123 (52)

Hippo, 57 (67), 167 (21)

Hitokotonuski, 169 (128)

Hobomoko, 105 (14, 62)

Hodadenon: The Last One Left, 25 (169)

Hod (Hoder), 124 (5, 72, 79), 128 (49), 133 (28), 138 (233)

Hoenir (Honir), 69 (6), 128 (25, 27, 67)

Ho Hsien ku, 65 (75)

Holawaka, 107 (17)

Holofernes, 147 (74)

Holy Grail, 49 (9, 16), 79 (11, 29, 31, 63, 66, 76, 85), 103 (57), 130 (89), 139 (96)

Homer, 148 (50), 155 (167)

Honey Badger, 58 (46)

Honeyguide, 58 (107)

Honir. See Hoenir

hoopoe, 4 (52)

Horned Toad, 74 (26)

Horse with the Golden Horn, 98 (12)

Horus, 71 (30, 41)

Hossiadam, 134 (56)

Hou I, 150 (31)

Hreidmar, 69 (8), 128 (67)

Hrothgar, King, 81 (159), 138 (289), 148 (120)

Hrungnir, 124 (65), 128 (43)

Hud, 4 (37)

Hugi, 124 (50), 128 (54)

Huitzilopochtli, 106 (127, 380, 394)

Human People, 176 (56)

Humbaba, 40 (64), 86 (20), 138 (190), 148 (68), 150 (61)

Hummingbird House, 161 (167)

Humphries, Mose, 11 (141), 122 (51)

Hunahpu, 106 (316), 161 (89)

Huon de Bordeaux, 49 (29)

Hurakan (Hurricane), 106 (107), 150 (17)

Hutash, 182 (unp)

Hutu, 162 (105)

Hyacinth (Hyacinthus), 155 (147), 165 (119)

Hydra, Lernean, 26 (16), 108 (52), 148 (28), 150 (62), 155 (95)

Hymir, 124 (58), 128 (44)

Ibar mac Riangabra, 139 (36)

Iblis (Satan), 120 (unp), 121 (unp)

Icarus, 130 (112), 183 (unp)

Iceni, 147 (97)

Idun (Iduna; Idunna), 70 (52), 124 (37), 128 (25), 130 (72), 138 (228)

Ife (Ile-Ife), 5 (17), 56 (23), 67 (73), 138 (428)

Igraine (Igrayne), 49 (6), 103 (22), 131 (6), 139 (82), 148 (131)

Ijapa the tortoise, 43 (207, 209)

Ilf, 69 (22)

Ilmarinen, 43 (44), 130 (55), 148 (91)

Il'ya of Murom, 177 (76)

Imana, 150 (77)

Imir, 67 (69)

Inber-n-Ailbine, 139 (123)

Indra, 29 (16, 32, 38, 62), 51 (52), 138 (358), 150 (20), 165 (111)

Indraloka, 29 (38)

Inkslinger, Johnny, 11 (617, 625, 630), 122 (16), 146 (50)

Instantim, 167 (24)

Iolaus, 148 (28)

Iole, 155 (99)

Iphicles, 148 (25), 155 (92)

Iphigenia, 26 (35), 155 (172, 186)

Ironside, Sir, 78 (unp)

Iroquois Youth, 165 (124)

Isaac, 114 (26, 30)

Iseult, 49 (23, 24)

Ishtar, 40 (77, 155), 86 (33), 130 (44), 138 (198), 148 (70), 150 (61), 166 (61)

Ishum, 40 (285)

Isis, 71 (14, 29, 41), 130 (80), 138 (171), 150 (72)

Israelites, 9 (68), 28 (unp), 51 (71)

Israil, 120 (unp)

Ithaca, 26 (43), 108 (84), 138 (78), 148 (50), 155 (197)

Ivan, 93 (44)

Iwariwa, 36 (4)

Ix Chel, 150 (39)

Ixtaccihuatl, 188 (61)

Iyadola, 133 (11)

Izanagi, 51 (16), 130 (24 26, 84), 138 (402, 406), 150 (10)

Izanami, 51 (16), 130 (24, 26, 84), 138 (402, 406), 150 (10)

Jackal, 43 (203, 205), 57 (47), 58 (121)

Jack (Crazy Jack), 21 (79, 81)

Jack Garcia, Three-Fingered, 44 (225)

Jack Smithy, 75 (19)

Jacob, 114 (28, 30, 32, 36)

Jade Emperor, 174 (1, 54, 81)

Jadhima Al-Abrash, 4 (60)

Jadis, 4 (36)

Jael, 9 (83)

Jaguar, 150 (51)

Jaguar Cedar, 160 (3)

Jaguar Night, 160 (3), 161 (165)

Jaguar Quitze, 161 (165)

James, Frank, 186 (133)

James, Jesse, 186 (133)

Jasconius, 111 (14)

Jason, 26 (59), 47 (unp), 108 (66), 147 (36, 42), 148 (46), 155 (114)

Jatayu, 29 (2)

Jeggua, 42 (98)

Jehangir, 51 (63)

Jemmy Tell, 48 (unp)

Jericho, 9 (69), 114 (74)

Jerusalem, 51 (90)

Jesus, 51 (50, 90)

Jezebel, Queen, 9 (159)

Jibril, 51 (48, 77), 120 (unp)

Jilly Mosiro, 12 (270)

Jim Bridger, 175 (42)

Jimena, 107 (97), 148 (176)

Jiro Beppu, 73 (7)

Joan of Arc, 7 (41), 147 (105)

Jocasta, 26 (69), 155 (127)

Jochabed, 9 (41)

Joehgah, 25 (69)

Jo-Ge-Oh, the Little People, 25 (41)

John Barleycorn, 107 (74)

John Darling, 175 (37)

John Henry, 11 (134), 122 (87), 146 (1), 175 (55), 185 (124)

Johnny Appleseed, 11 (12), 122 (25)

Johnny Inkslinger, 11 (617, 625, 630), 122 (16), 146 (50)

John Paul Jones, 146 (13)

John, Prince, 75 (10)

John Rolfe, 147 (136)

Jonah, 114 (146)

Jones, Casey (John Luther), 185 (133)

Jones, John Paul, 146 (13)

Jordan River, 9 (69, 176)

Jormungandr, 150 (92)

Joseph (New Testament), 51 (50)

Joseph (Old Testament), 114 (36, 40)

Joshua, 9 (68), 114 (74), 147 (62)

Jotunheim, 124 (6, 10, 47, 53, 67), 128 (14), 138 (222)

Joukahainen, 148 (92)

Joyous Gard, 79 (50, 95)

Judas Iscariot, 51 (90)

Judith, 147 (74)

Juno, 107 (66), 123 (14, 29, 41), 138 (123)

Jupiter, 123 (4, 29, 37, 41, 68), 130 (139), 138 (147)
Jurgenson, Mother, 11 (239)
Juruna, 43 (52)

Kadmos, 26 (61, 66)
Kala Bhairav, 29 (25)
Kalchas, 26 (35)
Kalevala, 43 (44, 123), 148 (91)
Kali, 130 (98)
Kaliya, 89 (30)
Kal Pem, 165 (60)
Kamba, 107 (114)
Kamonu, 67 (65)
Kamui, 130 (24)
Kana, 176 (17)
Kanati the Hunter, 96 (148), 187 (117)
Kanoporiwa the bird, 36 (4)
Kans, 89 (22, 26, 32)
Karna, 29 (68)
Karora, 67 (47)
Kasuga, Lady, 73 (6)
Katholab, 8 (48)
Kauravas, 29 (44)
Kay (Cei), Sir, 49 (7), 78 (unp), 79 (7, 58, 68), 103 (30), 131 (8), 138 (316), 143 (unp), 148 (135), 157 (unp)
Kayura, 165 (94)
Kenos, 13 (42)
Kerkyon, 26 (26)
Kerynean Hind, 26 (19)
Khan Kuzlun, 150 (62)
Khlop, 8 (48)
Khnum, 71 (25)
Kiehtan the Creator, 105 (13)
Kikuyu, 107 (114)
Kililik, 13 (30)
Kilimanjaro, 179 (unp)
Kingfisher, 27 (93), 76 (85, 91)
King Lion, 150 (22)
King of the Air, 165 (9)
King of world of the dead, 43 (212)
Kishon River, 9 (79)
Kitche-Manitou, 76 (74), 91 (xv, 76)
Kixwet, 13 (30)
Knight of the Burning Dragon, 131 (73)
Knight of the Lion, 49 (21)
Kobo Daishi, 169 (35)

Kofi Babone, 16 (118)
Kokopilan, 27 (151)
Koluscap (Kuloskap), 27 (83), 187 (135). *See also* Glooskap
Konole, 16 (33, 56)
kookaburra (Goo-goor-gaga), 100 (44)
Korendo, 134 (141)
Kornorley, 16 (163)
Kotcimanyako, 113 (38)
Kotura, Lord of the Winds, 134 (59)
Kranyatz, 130 (49)
Kreon, 71 (26)
Krishna, 12 (155), 29 (43), 51 (54), 89 (22, 26, 30, 32)
Krommyonian Sow, 26 (26)
Kronos, 67 (127, 134)
Kuloskap. *See* Koluscap; Glooskap
Kumush, 130 (32)
Kunti, 29 (46, 65)
Kupe, 162 (27)
Kurent, 130 (49)
Kurroo the dove, 45 (123)
Kururumanni (Creator), 132 (21)
Kvasir, 128 (22, 27)
Kwaku Ananse (Kwaku Anansi), the spider, 16 (38, 165, 189), 43 (195, 198, 200), 96 (229), 130 (70). *See also* Ananse
Kwaku Nomo, 16 (148)
Kwanza, 179 (unp)

Laban, 114 (27, 32)
Labors of Heracles (Herakles; Hercules), 26 (16), 80 (138), 108 (51), 130 (130), 138 (28), 155 (94)
Labyrinth of Knossus, 26 (27), 108 (62), 148 (40), 155 (108)
Ladhra, 138 (277)
Lady Marian, 107 (26)
Lady of the Lake, 49 (10), 77 (9), 79 (16, 31, 85), 138 (326), 139 (89)
Lady of the Sea (ship), 175 (22)
Lady Washington Engine No. 40, 175 (29)
Laertes, 154 (46)
Lahore, 51 (83)
Laios (Laius), King, 26 (69), 155 (128)
Laistrygonians, 26 (46)

Lake Chapala, 15 (unp)

Lake Te Anau, 162 (85)

Lake Titiaca, 51 (25), 138 (459, 465)

Lakshan, 29 (1), 51 (66)

Lakshmi, 51 (15), 89 (83), 138 (366)

Lambard, Sir, 131 (50)

Lancelot, Sir, 49 (10), 78 (unp), 79 (32, 43, 66, 75, 86), 103 (37), 130 (89, 156), 131 (1), 138 (332), 139 (96), 148 (138)

Land of No Return, 166 (61)

Land of the Great Turtle, 91 (xvi)

Land of the Young, 166 (108)

Langtry, Lillie, 44 (324, 332, 335)

Lanka, 51 (43, 66), 89 (56), 138 (375)

Laocoon (Laokoon), 26 (40), 155 (181)

Laudine, Lady, 49 (19)

Lawe, 16 (78)

Laxshman, 89 (50)

Leah, 114 (32)

Legba, 107 (89)

Leif, 84 (61)

Lemmin Kainen, 148 (91)

Leodegrance (Lodegraunce), King, 79 (21), 103 (49), 156 (16)

Leopard, 16 (38, 89), 150 (22)

Lernean Hydra, 26 (16)

Lethe, 166 (89)

Leto, 165 (114)

Liban, 111 (14)

Lie on the Ground Like a Cushion, 43 (198)

Life, 67 (105), 124 (80)

Lightning, 96 (81), 145 (77), 167 (28), 187 (31)

Lijaba, 12 (273)

Lindu, 165 (72)

Linette, 78 (unp)

Lion, 14 (103), 43 (205)

Lion King of Mali, 180 (unp)

Lion of Nemea, 155 (94)

Lir, King, 111 (3), 139 (29)

Lisa, 67 (43)

Little Bear, 165 (74)

Little Beautiful One, 113 (57)

Little Bill, 146 (3)

Little Girl, 66 (3)

Little Jaguar Sun, 160 (31)

Little John, 38 (6), 39 (3), 75 (27), 101 (6)

Little Men, 96 (61)

Littlest Coyote, 113 (8)

Liu Chun, 138 (395)

Lizard, 16 (78, 120, 127, 130), 23 (105), 43 (80)

Lizard House, 99 (unp)

Lleu Llaw Gyffes, 139 (81), 163 (74)

Llwyd, 139 (76)

Loathly Lady, 72 (13)

Locust, 74 (9)

Lodegraunce. See Leodegrance

Lodge-Boy, 138 (497)

Logi, 124 (49), 128 (54)

Lohiau, 145 (121)

Loki, 32 (5), 69 (6), 70 (6, 18, 34, 46, 52, 61, 75), 107 (104), 124 (6, 14, 20, 27, 33, 36, 45, 47, 71, 77), 128 (13, 48, 67), 130 (64, 72, 118, 163, 174), 133 (30), 138 (224, 228, 239, 248), 148 (83), 166 (65)

Lololomai, 145 (79)

Lone Feather, 187 (155)

Lone Man, 130 (53), 150 (93)

Long Hair, 187 (79)

Long-Tooth, 25 (86)

Loon, 43 (35), 76 (88), 170 (2)

Loo-Wit, 27 (41)

Lord God, 9 (9, 19, 48, 65, 78, 145, 159), 66 (17), 67 (123), 114 (6, 8, 11, 13, 19, 20, 23, 28, 30, 73, 74, 76, 79, 80, 111, 146), 176 (66)

Lord of Mecca, 4 (38)

Lord of Rain, 12 (12)

Lord Sun, 17 (84)

Lord Thien Kim, 174 (74)

Lord Van Bao, 174 (42)

Lorelei, 107 (77)

Lot, 114 (20, 23)

Lot, King, 103 (28), 131 (10)

Lot's wife, 114 (23)

Lotus Eaters, 26 (43), 154 (10), 155 (192)

Louhi, 43 (123), 130 (55)

Louis, King, 49 (42)

Lowa, 67 (105)

Lucy Henry, 122 (90), 146 (5)

Lugh Long Arm, 138 (279, 286), 139 (21, 25, 33)
Luk, 8 (106)
Luned, 49 (19), 131 (22), 166 (129)
Lung Nu, 147 (57)
Lycaon, 138 (22)
Lydda, 107 (14)
Lynx, 27 (119)

The Mabinogion, 139 (65), 163 (5)
Mabon, 131 (52)
Macaw House, 160 (9), 161 (167)
Macha, 139 (41)
Mad Ann Bailey, 44 (49)
Madri, 112 (5)
Maeve, Queen, 111 (14), 130 (128), 148 (149), 166 (20)
Maghan Kon Fatta, King, 180 (unp)
Magic Hare, 151 (unp)
Magni, 124 (68), 128 (44)
Magpie, 74 (15)
Mahabharata, 12 (279), 29 (20)
Maha Yuga, 138 (354)
Mahdad, 4 (40)
Maheo, 51 (23)
Mahi, 12 (5)
Mahisha, 150 (93)
Mahtmi, 179 (unp)
Mahtoquehs, 151 (unp)
Mahucutah, 161 (165)
Mahuika, 133 (18)
Maidere, 67 (29)
Maid Marian, *See* Marian, Maid
the Maimed King, 131 (61)
Maize God, 99 (unp)
Maker, 67 (87), 107 (17)
Makhan Shah, 51 (88)
Maktini, 179 (unp)
Makunaima, 188 (96)
Makwa the bear, 76 (129)
Malagant, Sir (Sir Meleagant), 49 (12), 79 (43)
Malcandre, 150 (72)
Malice, 65 (102)
Mami, 15 (40)
Man, 66 (69), 185 (62)
Man (Aliyu), 12 (270)
Manabozho (Manabozo; Manibosho;

Menaboju), 27 (145), 60 (1, 15, 29), 65 (27), 76 (8, 57, 78, 124, 158, 181, 186, 188, 207, 217, 224). *See also* Nanabozhoo; Winabijou
Manannan Mac Lir, 139 (111, 126), 166 (108)
Manasa, 12 (75)
'Mana Sorra (Sister Fox), 178 (89)
Manawydan, 139 (69, 72), 163 (30, 46)
Manco Capac, 138 (464)
Maninga, 150 (93)
'Mano Coyote (Brother Coyote), 178 (89)
Man-of-Little, 107 (29)
Mantis, 57 (127)
Manu, 51 (29), 150 (34)
Mapana, 137 (42)
Mardana, 51 (82)
Marduk, 40 (235), 67 (79), 138 (161), 150 (92)
Mares of Diomedes, 155 (96)
Marian, Maid (Marian Fitzwalter), 39 (11), 75 (33), 101 (48)
Mark, King, 49 (22)
Markland, 84 (unp)
Marksman, 160 (31)
Mars, 150 (46)
Martha's Vineyard, 105 (24)
Marvelous Girl, 107 (29)
Mary, 51 (50)
Maryam, 51 (48)
Mary Bryant, 147 (141)
Mary Magdalene, 51 (90)
Masai, 107 (114)
Mason Wasp, 16 (147)
Masswaweinini, 76 (69)
Master Crow, 134 (150)
Master-of-Breath, 96 (118)
Master of Game, 21 (67)
Master of the Imperial Stables, 129 (6)
Matahdou, 105 (19, 20, 30, 35, 56)
Mataora, 162 (67)
Matchi-anwishuk, 91 (xxi)
Math, 139 (77), 163 (64)
Matholwch, King of Ireland, 139 (70)
Matsya, 150 (35)
Maudjee-kawiss, 91 (19, 27, 37, 51)
Maugantius, 103 (11)
Maugis, the Magician, 49 (38)

Maui, 81 (236), 107 (40), 130 (68), 133 (18), 150 (14), 162 (11, 17, 23, 117)

Maundau-meen, 91 (103)

Mau-shop (Maushop), 24 (5), 105 (19, 20, 25, 30, 35, 40, 49, 56, 64, 67)

Mawu, 67 (43)

Mayahuel, 106 (212)

McCarty, Henry, 44 (235, 247)

Mead of Poetry, 124 (11)

Measuring Worm, 104 (20)

Mecca, 51 (70, 77), 120 (unp)

Medb, Queen, 139 (43)

Medea, 26 (27, 59), 47 (unp), 108 (69), 147 (36, 42), 148 (39, 47), 155 (114)

Medicine Man, 159 (24), 187 (23)

Medina, 51 (70, 77), 120 (unp)

Medus, 147 (48)

Medusa, 26 (63), 65 (43), 85 (unp), 108 (42), 116 (104), 130 (148), 133 (87), 148 (18), 155 (84), 165 (81)

Megara, 148 (26)

Melanion, 30 (unp), 147 (34)

Meleagant, Sir. See Malagant, Sir

Meleager, 147 (31)

Meliant de Lis, Sir, 131 (68)

Melo, 67 (117)

Meme, 76 (147)

Memory, 124 (9)

Memphis, 71 (18, 30)

Menaboju. See Manabozho

Menelaus, King, 26 (34), 108 (78), 148 (50), 150 (64), 153 (10), 154 (51), 155 (170, 185)

Mengk, 134 (135)

Mercury, 123 (37, 68)

Meri, 13 (44)

Merlin, 49 (4), 65 (65), 77 (1), 79 (3, 14, 22, 31, 85), 103 (5), 130 (86, 89), 131 (6), 138 (315), 139 (84), 143 (unp), 148 (131), 156 (5), 157 (unp)

Messiah, 51 (48)

Methuselah the coyote, 44 (198)

Metis, 147 (14)

Miao Chuang, 147 (51)

Miao Shan, 147 (50)

Michabo, 68 (12)

Michael (angel), 54 (unp)

Mich-la-ne-qwe, 76 (94)

Mictlan, 106 (134)

Midas, King, 107 (1), 108 (36), 123 (9), 130 (102, 104), 133 (62), 155 (141)

Midgard, 32 (5), 67 (69), 124 (5), 128 (56), 130 (21, 62), 138 (222)

Midgard Serpent, 124 (29, 51, 62, 77)

Midianites, 114 (76)

Midir, 139 (105)

Midorimaru, 73 (6)

Mikail, 120 (unp)

Mike Fink, 11 (99, 101), 44 (75, 77), 92 (unp), 122 (12, 21)

Mikula Selyaninovich, 177 (21)

Milesians, 138 (283)

Milky Way, 165 (72), 187 (110)

Mimir, 124 (10), 128 (27, 65)

Mimir's Well, 124 (7, 10), 128 (58)

Minerva, 31 (7), 123 (19)

Mink, 19 (36)

Minos, King, 26 (27), 108 (62), 130 (96, 108, 112), 148 (40), 155 (96, 107), 183 (unp)

Minotaur, 26 (27), 108 (62), 130 (108), 148 (40), 155 (107), 183 (unp)

Miollnir. See Mjolnir

Miriam, 9 (41, 61, 66), 28 (unp), 148 (104)

Mirrabooka, 119 (67)

Mishi-bizheu, 91 (81)

Mister Lion, 185 (59)

Mistletoe, 124 (72), 128 (49)

Misty Shadow, 134 (30)

Miz Hattie, 66 (15)

Mjolnir (Miollnir), 32 (6), 128 (44), 150 (38, 92)

Mmoatia the fairy, 96 (229)

Mmoboro the hornet, 43 (195), 96 (229)

Moab, 114 (84)

Modgud, 166 (65)

Modred (Mordred), Sir, 79 (35, 86), 103 (68), 130 (156), 138 (325), 139 (96), 148 (138)

Mole, 25 (178), 83 (unp), 140 (30)

Moly, 26 (46)

Monad, 71 (11)

Monkey, 14 (23), 16 (178), 43 (220)

Monkey, King, 129 (3)

Monster-Slayer, 68 (20)

Moombi, 107 (115)

Moon, 10 (146)), 43 (56, 58, 65, 81, 198), 113 (66), 133 (25), 134 (150), 167 (4)

Moon Goddess, 99 (unp)

Moonlight, 173 (4)

Moon Man, 134 (94)

Moon Woman, 55 (15)

Moors, 107 (94)

Moose, 133 (16)

Moose Bird, 113 (18)

Mordecai, 147 (70), 114 (124, 126), 181 (unp)

Mordred, Sir. *See* Modred, Sir

Morgan, Gib, 11 (588, 593, 595, 596)

Morgan le Fay (Morgana le Fay), Queen, 49 (13), 79 (16), 81 (166), 103 (28), 131 (13)

Morgause, 103 (28), 131 (13)

Morholt, 49 (23)

Morning Star, 43 (56), 107 (34), 113 (66)

Morpheus, 123 (15)

the Morrigan, 139 (23), 150 (63)

Mose Humphries, 11 (141), 122 (51)

Moses, 9 (44, 47, 65), 28 (unp), 51 (71), 54 (unp), 114 (46, 50, 62, 73), 148 (104)

Mot, 150 (76)

Mother Bear, 113 (19)

Mother Deer, 74 (22)

Mother Earth, 33 (unp), 91 (xviii, 9, 100), 105 (17), 155 (11), 158 (6)

motherfathers, 160 (3, 18), 161 (164)

Mother Jurgenson, 11 (239)

Mother of Life, 119 (61, 64)

Mother of Water, 43 (46)

Mother Scorpion, 18 (117), 136 (18)

Mother Sun, 171 (80)

Mountain Lion, 104 (15)

Mountain Spirits, 149 (16)

Mount Carmel, 9 (165), 114 (120)

Mount Etna, 150 (40), 165 (38)

Mount Mandara, 51 (11, 14)

Mount Meru, 165 (90)

Mount Nebo, 114 (73)

Mount Olympus, 108 (9, 15, 21), 155 (11, 65, 69, 100, 169)

Mount Pisgah, 9 (66)

Mount Sinai, 9 (65, 173), 114 (62), 148 (110)

Mount Tabor, 9 (79)

Mouse, 164 (28), 167 (2)

Mr. Badger, 76 (95)

Mr. Frog, 76 (94)

Mr. Owl, 76 (122)

Much the Miller, 39 (3), 75 (18), 101 (11), 107 (23)

Muckachuck, 105 (67)

Mud Hen, 76 (95)

Mugai, 50 (6)

Muhammed, 51 (70, 77), 120 (unp)

Mukulu, 51 (22)

Multan, 51 (82)

Mumbi, 50 (13)

Murieta, Joaquin, 44 (225)

Musa bin Nusayr, 4 (109)

Mushrat, 76 (89)

Muskrat, 43 (35), 68 (13), 76 (92, 95), 91 (xv, 12), 132 (121), 150 (17), 171 (95)

Muspell, 67 (69), 124 (1), 128 (57)

Muspellheim, 138 (221), 150 (16)

Muwin, 151 (unp)

Muzzu-Kummik-Quae, 91 (9, 100)

Mwindo, 138 (441)

Mycenae, 26 (63)

Myoe, 169 (42)

Nainas, 134 (198)

Nakawe, 15 (unp)

Nala, King, 51 (52)

Nanabozhoo (Nana Bojou; Nana'b'oozoo; Nana-Bo-Zhoo; Nanabozsho; Nana-bush; Nanbush; Nanibozho; Ne-naw-bo-zhoo; Nenebojo; Nenebuc; Nenibush), 19 (222), 76 (29, 41, 45, 62, 66, 74, 83, 91, 94, 104, 107, 113, 119, 122, 129, 131, 137, 139, 141, 145, 147, 149, 151, 154, 156, 164, 168, 170, 172, 175, 178, 201, 210, 212, 221, 228), 91 (10, 32, 45, 51). *See also* Manabozho; Winabijou

Nana Buluku, 67 (43), 130 (173)

Nanabush (Nanbush). *See* Nanabozhoo

Nanahuatzin, 150 (32)

Nana Nyamee (Sky God), 16 (38)

Nanautzin, the Scabby-Pimply One, 62 (21)

Nanih Waya, 96 (111)

Nanoona, 145 (112)

Nanysaushet, 105 (14)

Naomi, 114 (84)

Na'pi (Old Man), 23 (117), 67 (25)

Narcissus, 108 (22), 123 (29), 150 (23), 155 (146), 165 (122)

Nastas'ya, Princess, 177 (37)

Natchez Bell (boat), 145 (37)

Nausicaa, Princess, 148 (52), 154 (63)

Nayenezgani, 150 (63)

Nazareth, 51 (50)

Nemean lion, 26 (16), 148 (27), 150 (62)

Nemed, 139 (14)

Nemedians, 138 (278)

Ne-naw-bo-zhoo. *See* Nanabozhoo.

Nenebojo. *See* Nanabozhoo.

Nenebuc. *See* Nanabozhoo

Nenibush. *See* Nanabozhoo

Nepausket, 105 (14)

Nephthys, 71 (14, 29)

Nera, 139 (44), 166 (20)

Nereids, 165 (79)

Nergal, 40 (167)

Nessos, 26 (24)

Net-Pos-Hu the Archer, 134 (134)

New Orleans, 66 (84)

Nezha, 129 (9)

Ngoc Hoang, 174 (1)

Ngoc Tho, 174 (18)

Ngo Cuong, 174 (21)

Ngutapa, 137 (42)

Nguu Lang, 174 (59)

Nguyet Tien, 174 (44)

Niagara Falls, 159 (6)

Niam of the Golden Hair, 166 (105)

Nichizo, 169 (144)

Nidud, King, 81 (174)

Niekia, 134 (199)

Niflheim, 67 (69), 124 (1, 29), 128 (57), 130 (18, 62, 66, 162), 138 (221), 150 (16), 166 (65)

Nightingale, 177 (77)

Night Jar, 98 (71)

Niheu, 176 (17)

Nikolai of Mozhaisk, 177 (48)

Nile, 9 (41, 49), 51 (71)

Nineveh, 114 (146)

Ninurta, 40 (211)

Niord (Njord), 124 (6, 44, 54), 128 (20, 27)

Nisien, 163 (30)

Niwareka, 162 (67)

Noah, 9 (20), 51 (32), 114 (13, 14, 18), 165 (130)

Nobody, 26 (43), 176 (40)

Nokomis (N'okomiss), 60 (1, 15, 29), 91 (40, 51)

No Man, 148 (55)

Nornagest, 81 (181)

Norns, 69 (6), 81 (181), 124 (27), 128 (58)

North Dakota, 11 (623)

Northern Lights, 165 (72, 82)

North Star, 113 (84)

North Wind, 27 (129), 82 (26), 133 (15)

Not-Coyote, 170 (60)

Not Right Now, 160 (3)

Ntikuma, 16 (165)

Nu, 71 (11, 20)

Nuada Silver Arm, 139 (21)

Nugua, 138 (391)

Nu Kua, 165 (18)

Numitor, 150 (46)

Nun, 4 (88), 61 (unp), 150 (16)

Nut, 61 (unp), 71 (14, 40)

Nyah-gwaheh, 25 (190)

Nyambi, 67 (65)

Nyame, 10 (50), 43 (195, 199), 133 (10)

Nya Nganas, 134 (107)

Nyankopon (Nyan-kon pon), the Sky God, 14 (73), 96 (229)

Nymo, 10 (45)

nymphs, 165 (92)

Nynyue, the Lady of the Lake, 103 (45)

Nyo-bog-ti, 13 (15)

Oadz, 134 (35, 46)

Oakley, Annie, 11 (479)

Oba, 10 (1)

Oba Nani, 42 (48)

Obatala, 5 (3), 56 (20), 138 (426)

Obba, 56 (31)

Obi Obi Gui, 116 (40)

Obleku the coucal, 16 (32)
O'Cealaigh, Tadg, 139 (126)
Ochosi, 56 (31)
Odaemin, 76 (74)
Oddua, 42 (39)
Odin, 32 (5), 64 (74), 65 (82), 67 (69), 69 (6), 70 (6, 43, 52, 61, 76), 107 (103), 124 (4, 9, 25, 29, 36, 43, 65, 70, 79), 128 (22, 25, 27, 43, 56, 67), 130 (18, 64, 162, 174), 133 (28), 138 (222, 228, 244), 148 (76), 150 (70), 166 (14, 65)
O'Donnell, Aodh Dubh, 139 (126)
Odysseus, 26 (34, 43), 108 (79, 84), 138 (44, 78), 147 (38), 148 (50), 150 (66), 153 (10), 154 (7), 155 (171, 191), 176 (35)
Od-zi-ho-zo, 24 (23)
Oedipus, 26 (66), 155 (126)
Ogdoad, 71 (19)
Oggun, 42 (42, 50, 78), 56 (56)
Ogier the Dane, 49 (30)
Ogloma, 134 (89)
ogres, 165 (92)
Oisin, 139 (59), 166 (105)
Ojola the boa, 43 (207)
Okhe (tiger), 12 (270)
Okteondon, 25 (104)
Okwapayikew, 118 (34)
Olaf Tryggvason, King, 81 (183)
Old Calam, 44 (301)
Older Sister, 138 (411)
Old Louhi, 148 (92)
Old Man (Napi), 23 (117), 34 (50), 67 (25), 187 (43)
Old-Man-Above, 31 (30), 171 (60)
Old Man Coyote, 27 (57)
Old Man Winter, 82 (26), 105 (42)
Old Spider, 51 (21)
Old Stormalong, 122 (37), 175 (22)
Old Woman, 41 (63), 117 (75)
Ole the Blacksmith, 11 (604)
Ol' Gabe, 175 (42)
Olifant, 148 (166)
Oliver, 49 (29), 148 (160)
Oloddumare, 42 (38), 56 (19)
Olofi, 56 (20), 116 (40)
Olokun, 56 (21)
Olorun, 5 (1), 67 (73), 138 (426)

Olosi, 56 (20)
Olsihpa, 8 (31)
Olsohpa, 8 (31)
Olukun, 138 (426)
Olympus, 130 (58, 167)
One, 132 (65)
One Death, 161 (106)
One Hunahpu, 161 (105)
Ong Dia, 174 (72)
Onini the python, 43 (196), 96 (229)
Onyame the Sky God, 98 (55)
Oonagh, 133 (78)
Oonyani, 134 (141)
Opossum, 18 (77), 117 (75)
Ops the armadillo, 36 (20)
Ora (God), 12 (270)
Oracle, 165 (79)
Orekeke, 13 (25)
Orestes, 26 (41), 155 (186)
Oriabel, Princess, 49 (42)
Orishas, 5 (1), 56 (21)
Orpheus, 26 (59), 108 (71), 123 (45), 130 (102, 166), 148 (47), 155 (139)
Orula, 42 (63), 56 (21)
Orunmila, 5 (7)
Osage Sky Seeing, 113 (49)
Osain, 42 (45), 56 (21)
Osai Tutu, 98 (52)
Osebo the leopard, 43 (196), 96 (229)
Oshun, 10 (1), 56 (46)
Osiris, 71 (14, 29, 41), 130 (80), 138 (171), 150 (72)
Ostrich, 57 (127)
Ostropol, 93 (9, 16, 25, 28, 52, 61)
Other World, 79 (93)
Otoonah, 145 (111)
Otr, 128 (67)
Otter, 27 (119), 64 (74), 69 (9), 76 (88, 92), 87 (unp), 140 (13, 43), 148 (83)
Our Mother, 113 (38, 40)
Owain, Sir, 131 (13)
Owein, Sir, 166 (121)
Owl, 52 (unp), 134 (48)
Owl Woman, 3 (112), 187 (158)
Oya, 56 (31)

Palamedes, 26 (34)
Pale-Faced Lightning, 145 (77)

Pallas Athena, 147 (15)

Pan, 108 (36), 155 (142)

Pana-ewa, 145 (122)

Pandavas, 29 (44, 55)

Pandora, 67 (140), 108 (9), 130 (60), 150 (90)

Pangolin, 58 (46)

Pan Ku (Pan Gu; Pangu; P'an-ku; Phan Ku), 51 (24), 67 (21), 130 (22), 138 (390), 165 (17)

Panther, 133 (16)

Pao Te, 147 (51)

Papa, 150 (18)

Papa Dios, 152 (unp)

Paponny (Old Man Winter), 105 (42)

Paradise, 120 (unp)

Paraparawa, 138 (466, 467)

Parasurama, 29 (69)

Pare, 162 (105)

Parikshit, 29 (61)

Paris, 26 (33), 108 (78), 138 (43), 148 (50), 150 (64), 153 (7), 155 (167, 185)

Parpara, 130 (42)

Parrot, 116 (194)

Partholon, 138 (277)

Paruksti, 132 (65)

Parvati, 12 (171, 175), 29 (10, 24), 51 (57), 89 (110, 115, 121), 130 (98, 144)

Passover, 51 (90)

Patal, 29 (36)

Patch, Sam, 11 (577)

Patrick, Saint, 139 (124)

Patroclus (Patroklos), 26 (36), 153 (15), 155 (178)

Paul Bunyan, 11 (603, 604, 611, 620, 623, 626), 44 (153, 157, 162, 167), 122 (97), 146 (47), 175 (49)

Paumpagusset, 105 (14)

Pau-o-palae, 145 (122)

peacock, 165 (111)

Pearl Feather, 76 (12)

Peboan (Pebon), 97 (19), 105 (42)

Pecos Bill, 11 (517), 44 (197, 203), 122 (73), 146 (25), 175 (69)

Pee-pauk-a-wis, 76 (201)

Pegasus, 130 (148), 165 (81)

Pegleg Smith, 44 (121)

Peivalke, 134 (30, 197)

Pele, 145 (121)

Peleus, 26 (33)

Pelias, King, 26 (59), 47 (unp), 147 (44), 148 (46), 155 (116)

Pellas, King, 103 (62)

Pellinore, Sir, 79 (14), 139 (89)

Penelope, 26 (43), 108 (88), 138 (92), 148 (50), 154 (46), 155 (197)

Pentheus, 26 (68)

Percival (Perceval), Sir, 49 (15), 79 (51, 78), 103 (68), 131 (55)

Periphetes the Clubman, 26 (25), 148 (39)

Persephone, 26 (7, 30), 108 (15, 72), 130 (82, 135, 166), 133 (37), 138 (16), 147 (25), 150 (39), 155 (39, 74, 148), 165 (119), 166 (77). *See also* Proserpina

Perseus, 26 (63), 64 (16), 65 (44), 108 (41), 130 (132, 148), 133 (85), 148 (17), 155 (83), 165 (81)

Persia, 114 (124)

Pe-ton-bowk, 24 (23)

Petrel, 150 (83)

Phaedra, 155 (110)

Phaethon (Phaeton), 123 (1), 165 (42)

Phaiacians, 26 (51)

Pham Vinh, 174 (72)

Phan Ku. *See* Pan Ku

Pharaoh, 9 (36, 47, 65), 28 (unp), 51 (71), 114 (20, 40, 46, 50)

Pharaoh's daughter, 9 (40), 28 (unp), 114 (46)

Philemon, 123 (67)

Philistines, 9 (95), 114 (79, 80, 94), 176 (63)

Phineus, 26 (60)

Phoenix, 130 (23, 151), 138 (396)

Phrixos, 26 (59)

Phung Mong, 174 (21)

Phyllis, 165 (122)

Pierithoos, 26 (29)

Pig, 150 (39)

Pillars of Hercules, 155 (97)

Pine Leaf, 44 (128)

Pine Tree, 135 (14), 171 (50)

plagues, 51 (71)

Pletun, 134 (71)

Plough, 40 (279)

Plumed Serpent, 106 (107), 130 (140), 161 (73)

Pluto, 108 (15, 42, 72), 123 (35, 46), 155 (39)

Pocahontas, 147 (131)

Pohaha, 145 (87)

Pohnpei, 8 (31, 106)

Polly Ann Henry, 11 (134), 175 (58), 185 (125)

Polydectes, King, 26 (63), 85 (unp), 108 (41), 116 (106), 133 (86), 148 (17), 155 (83)

Polynices, 155 (134)

Polyphemus, 26 (43), 108 (85), 138 (78, 137), 148 (54), 154 (16), 155 (193), 176 (36)

Pontius Pilate, 51 (91)

Pootana, 89 (26)

Popocate'petl, 188 (62)

Porcupine, 76 (154)

Poseidon, 26 (25), 108 (86), 116 (104), 147 (15), 148 (52), 154 (12), 155 (11, 39, 178, 192), 165 (80, 122), 176 (36)

Possum, 80 (90), 115 (135), 140 (19), 141 (unp), 171 (88), 185 (170), 187 (143)

Potiphar, 114 (38)

Powhatan, 147 (131)

Prawn House, 160 (9), 161 (167)

Priam, King of Troy, 26 (33), 138 (43), 148 (50), 153 (7), 155 (168)

Princess Glory, 169 (46)

Procrustes (Prokrustes), 26 (27), 148 (39)

Prometheus, 26 (31), 67 (134, 140), 108 (9), 130 (58), 138 (25), 148 (33), 150 (88), 155 (65, 68)

Promised Land, 28 (unp)

the Prophet, 51 (70, 77)

Proserpina, 123 (35, 46). See also Persephone

Pruwaheiyoma, 36 (4)

Pryderi, 139 (70, 72), 163 (28, 46, 65)

Psyche, 35 (unp), 123 (57)

Ptah, 71 (18)

Pud, 13 (10, 22)

Pudlere, 13 (10, 22)

Pukawiss, 91 (27, 38, 51)

Purim, 181 (unp)

Purralee, 66 (17)

Pururvas, Raja, 29 (81)

Putawai, 162 (91)

Pwyll, Lord of Dyfed, King of the Other World, 139 (65), 163 (10)

Pyrrha, 138 (25)

Python, 16 (39), 58 (122)

Qasir, 4 (60)

Quat, 67 (9)

Queen Maya, 51 (74)

Queen Mother of the West, 174 (9)

Queen of Lightning, 12 (12)

Queen of Sheba, 9 (151), 114 (116)

Queen of the Circle of Gold, 131 (72)

Quetzalcoatl, 62 (3), 102 (unp), 106 (127, 134, 212, 352), 107 (84), 130 (140), 136 (unp), 138 (476, 485), 150 (56), 188 (60)

Quick-Foot, 25 (86)

Ra. See Re

Rabbi Israel, 93 (28, 33, 52, 61)

Rabbit, 10 (53, 146), 17 (72, 77, 81), 25 (65, 74), 34 (43), 76 (149), 80 (90), 96 (68, 234), 117 (82), 140 (7, 13, 19, 29, 33, 43), 171 (82, 88, 98), 178 (91), 187 (143)

Rabbit Woman, 31 (31)

Raccoon, 25 (69), 113 (7, 86), 187 (138)

Rachel, 114 (32)

Ragnarok, 70 (75), 124 (7), 128 (63), 133 (28), 138 (223, 237), 150 (92)

Rahab (Rehab), 9 (69), 114 (74), 147 (62)

Rahu, 51 (13)

Rainbow Serpent, 130 (173)

Rainbow Snake (Rainbow Serpent), 107 (61), 119 (61, 64)

Rain God, 99 (unp)

Rain Spirit, 57 (53)

Rama (Ram), 29 (1), 51 (43, 66), 89 (48), 138 (365)

Rangi, 150 (18)

Rat, 16 (158)

Rattlesnake, 25 (57), 96 (61), 113 (84), 178 (91)

Ravana (Ravan), 29 (1), 51 (43, 66), 89 (48), 138 (365), 150 (20)

Raven, 19 (28, 61), 27 (103), 43 (223,

225, 226, 237), 67 (3), 74 (29), 82 (6, 20), 110 (unp), 134 (48), 138 (499, 500), 150 (83), 171 (40)

Rawennio, 43 (32)

Raweno, 52 (unp)

Re (Ra), 61 (unp), 67 (111), 130 (16, 146), 138 (170)

Rebecca Bryan Boone, 11 (225)

Rebekah, 114 (26, 28, 30)

Red Colobus Monkey, 58 (14)

Red Eagle, 158 (18)

Red Fox Woman, 31 (31)

Red Knight of the Red Plain, 78 (unp), 79 (51)

Red Plume, 76 (69)

Red Sea Turtle, 160 (9)

Regin, 64 (74), 69 (9), 128 (67), 138 (246), 148 (80)

Rehab. *See* Rahab

Remus, 130 (138), 138 (114), 150 (46)

Renaud, 49 (38)

repunkar, 138 (409)

Rhea, 30 (unp), 155 (11)

Rhea Silva, 150 (46)

Rhiannon (Riannon), 139 (72), 163 (18, 46)

Rhine River, 107 (77)

Rhodanthe, 165 (118)

Riach, 139 (128)

Riannon. *See* Rhiannon

rice, 150 (50)

Richard, King, 75 (10)

Richard of Lee, Sir, 38 (22), 39 (26), 101 (19)

Rimonah, 94 (unp)

Riverboat Charlie, 185 (131)

Road Builder, 43 (198)

Robin, 113 (19), 150 (22), 187 (155)

Robin Hood (Robert Locksley), 38 (1), 39 (1), 75 (9), 101 (4), 107 (21)

Rodrigo Diaz de Bivar, Don (El Cid), 95 (1), 107 (94), 148 (171), 188 (79, 88)

Roger, Sir, the Red Knight, 101 (54)

Roland, Count, 49 (29), 148 (160)

Rolfe, John, 147 (136)

Rolling Rio, 65 (5)

Rolling Skull, 113 (56)

Rome, 107 (66), 130 (138), 138 (125)

Romulus, 130 (138), 138 (114, 125), 150 (46)

Rona, 162 (101)

Roncesvalles, 148 (160)

rose, 60 (29)

Roskva, 124 (47)

Round Table, 79 (21, 31, 62, 66, 77, 85), 103 (49), 130 (88), 138 (327), 139 (92), 156 (16)

Ruad, 139 (123)

Rukmini, 12 (156)

runes, 124 (10)

Runs-Slender Buffalo, 187 (48)

Ruth, 114 (84)

Ryence, King of North Wales, 79 (24), 156 (16)

Ryon, Giant, 49 (8)

Sa (Death), 67 (15)

Sabra, 64 (91), 107 (13)

Sacred Pen, 4 (88)

Sadko, 177 (44, 45)

Sagbata, 138 (432)

Sagremor the Unruly, Sir, 49 (15)

Saint Francis of Assisi, 7 (24)

Saint George, 7 (23), 64 (89), 81 (153), 109 (unp)

Saint Joan of Arc, 7 (41)

Saint Patrick, 139 (64)

Sakti, 12 (71)

Sal Fink, the Mississippi Screamer, 44 (80, 81), 145 (51)

Salih, 4 (32)

Sally Ann Thunder Ann Whirlwind, 92 (unp), 122 (15)

Samain Eve, 166 (20)

Sammael (angel of death), 54 (unp)

Sam Patch, 11 (577)

Sampo, 43 (45), 130 (55)

Samson, 9 (95), 114 (79, 80), 148 (113)

Sankofa, 5 (17)

Sapling, 19 (198), 22 (12), 165 (33)

Sarah, 114 (20)

Sarjimoti-Amoa-Oplem-Dadja, 16 (107)

Sarras, 79 (79)

Sasa the hare, 107 (49)

Satan (Iblis), 120 (unp), 121 (unp)

Satawal, 8 (48)

Satwaras, 12 (85)

Satyabhama, 12 (156)

Satyaran, 81 (196)

Saul, King, 114 (94), 120 (unp), 176 (63)

Saunders, Wallace, 185 (133)

Savitri, 81 (195)

Scarface, 107 (29)

Schahriar, 147 (91)

Schahzaman, 147 (91)

Scheherazade. *See* Sheherezade

Sciron, 148 (39), 155 (104)

Scomalt, 3 (106)

Screech Owl Woman, 115 (210)

Scylla (Skylla) and Charybdis, 26 (49), 148 (58), 154 (38), 155 (196)

Sea Tsar, 177 (44, 45)

Sedi, 67 (117)

Sedna, 19 (64), 27 (95), 81 (227), 130 (168), 150 (78)

Seegwun (Sequan, Spring), 97 (19), 105 (45)

Selu, 96 (148)

Selu Cornwoman, 187 (117)

Semele, 26 (67)

Sequan (Spring). *See* Seegwun

Seriphos, 26 (63), 155 (83)

serpent, 9 (12), 114 (8)

Setanta, 139 (33), 148 (143)

Seth, 71 (14, 29, 41), 150 (72)

Seutonius Paulinus, 147 (97)

Seven Death, 161 (106)

Seven Macaw, 161 (86)

Seven Sisters, 187 (55)

Shachi, 29 (17)

Shaddad, 4 (44)

Shah Zaman, 1 (9), 4 (103)

Shahrayar, King (Shah Shahryar), 1 (9), 4 (103)

Shahrazad. *See* Sheherezade

Shaka, Buddha, 169 (144)

Shamash, 148 (68)

Shamat, 189 (7)

Shamus, 4 (36)

Shango, 42 (78)

Shan Ts'ai, 147 (57)

Shark, 14 (4)

Shar-pah the Moon, 96 (58)

Sheherezade (Scheherazade; Shahrazad), 1 (15), 4 (103), 147 (91)

Shell Man, 3 (186)

Shemwindo, 138 (441)

Shen Nung, 150 (52)

Sheriff of Nottingham, 38 (13), 39 (17), 75 (13), 101 (27)

Sherwood Forest, 38 (1), 39 (1), 75 (11), 101 (4)

Shibi, Raja, 29 (32)

Shi-pa-pu, 132 (51)

Shirley, Myra Maybelle, 186 (21)

Shiva, 29 (10, 24, 28), 51 (11, 14, 57), 89 (121), 130 (98, 144). *See also* Siva

Shiva-Rudra, 138 (355, 367)

Shot Gunderson, 11 (620), 44 (167), 122 (106)

Shu, 61 (unp), 71 (12)

Shukracharya, 29 (36)

Sibyl, 130 (154), 166 (77)

Siddhartha Gautama, 51 (74), 107 (49), 112 (18), 142 (unp)

Siege Perilous, 79 (29, 32, 66)

Sif, 70 (34), 124 (5, 20), 128 (53)

Siggeir, 128 (70), 148 (76)

Sigmund, 69 (21), 128 (70), 148 (76)

Signy, 128 (70), 148 (76)

Sigurd, 64 (72), 69 (27), 128 (72), 138 (244), 148 (76)

Silenus, 130 (102), 133 (63)

Simoon, 134 (89)

Sinadon, Lady of, 131 (48)

Sinai, 28 (unp)

Sindri, 124 (21)

Sinfiotli, 148 (78)

Singbonga, 165 (99)

Sinis the Pinebender, 26 (25), 148 (39), 155 (105)

Sinon, 26 (40), 150 (67), 155 (181)

Sirens, 26 (48), 108 (88), 138 (95), 154 (38), 155 (196)

Sisera, 9 (78)

Sister Fox ('Mana Sorra), 178 (89)

Sisyphus, 26 (48), 166 (85)

Sita, 29 (1), 51 (43, 66), 89 (52), 138 (367)

Siva, 12 (72, 86, 171, 175). *See also* Shiva

Skadi, 124 (43), 128 (20)

the Skinner of Game, 43 (198)

Skin Woman, 25 (179)

Skirnir, 124 (54)

Skiron, 26 (26), 128 (30)

Sklumyoa (female Creator), 19 (61)

Skrymir, 124 (48)

Skunk, 25 (56)

Skunnee Wundee (Skunny-Wundy), 25 (161), 187 (70)

Sky Chief, 110 (unp), 165 (26)

Sky God, 10 (47), 43 (195, 199), 98 (55), 130 (42), 167 (10)

Skylla. *See* Scylla

Sky Snake, 182 (unp)

Sky Woman, 25 (19), 43 (33), 91 (xv, 11), 105 (17), 158 (22)

Sky World, 25 (15)

Sleipner, 124 (19, 65, 72), 128 (21, 49), 133 (33)

Slue-Foot Sue, 11 (517), 44 (202, 207), 122 (83), 146 (23), 175 (73)

Smith, Captain John, 147 (131)

Smith, Pegleg, 44 (121)

Smoking Star, 55 (13)

Snaggletooth Charlie, 44 (206)

Snail, 87 (unp)

Snake, 14 (73), 107 (18)

Snake-Eye Sam, 44 (315)

snake, white, 43 (75)

Snowmaker, 159 (13)

Snow Woman, 134 (61)

Sodom, 114 (23)

Sogbo, 138 (432)

Sogolon, 180 (unp)

Solomon (Sulaiman; Sulayman), King, 4 (52), 9 (145), 51 (42), 53 (6), 88 (18), 114 (111, 112, 116), 147 (82)

Sons of Mil, 139 (17)

Sourdough Sam, 122 (106)

Southern Cross, 57 (89), 119 (67)

South Wind, 82 (30), 133 (15)

Sowbosom Sam, 44 (166)

Sphinx, 26 (68), 155 (128)

Spider, 10 (44), 16 (32, 56, 89, 128), 31 (3), 41 (107), 58 (126), 67 (65), 98 (36), 171 (60)

Spider Boy, 187 (80)

Spider Brothers, 31 (32)

Spider-Man Anansi, 107 (110)

Spider Woman, 3 (183, 186), 31 (30), 68 (21), 130 (36), 147 (4), 158 (16), 187 (80)

Spirit Son, 159 (16)

Spring, 27 (131), 82 (31)

Spring Bird, 168 (13)

Spring (Seegwun, Sequan), 97 (19), 105 (45)

Star Boy, 19 (158)

Stares-Them-in-the-Face, 170 (61)

Star Maiden, 145 (5)

Starr, Belle, 186 (21, 83, 148)

the Star That Does Not Walk Around, 113 (69)

Stick, 14 (76)

Stone Cloud, 159 (16)

Stone Coat Woman, 25 (136)

Stone Giants, 25 (137, 161)

Stonehenge, 103 (20)

Stone Thrower, 43 (198)

Stormalong, Old (Alfred Bulltop), 122 (37), 146 (13)

Stormy. *See* Stormalong

Strap Buckner, 146 (35)

Strickie, 175 (66)

Sturgeon, 23 (124)

Stygian Nymphs, 85 (unp)

Stymphalian Birds, 26 (19), 148 (31)

Styx, 166 (79)

Sualtaim, 139 (129)

Sudhodana, King, 51 (74)

Sukhman, 177 (41)

Sulaiman (Sulayman). *See* Solomon

Sumanguru the sorcerer, 180 (unp)

Sumedha, 112 (1)

Sumer, 148 (63)

Summer, 43 (66)

Summer Bird, 168 (15)

Summer Katsina, 187 (52)

Sun, 3 (186), 14 (78), 21 (52), 43 (52, 58, 65, 235), 67 (105), 68 (21), 96 (61), 107 (31, 40, 85), 113 (66), 116 (40, 74), 133 (25), 134 (150), 138 (464), 167 (4), 170 (11)

Sunbringer, 160 (31)

Sundiata, 180 (unp)

Sun God, 99 (unp)

Sungura the hare, 45 (117)

Sun Hou-tzu, 81 (207)

Sun Maiden, 134 (55)
Sun Man, 55 (15)
suns, 117 (66)
Sun's daughter, 96 (61)
Supreme Taoist Dignitary, 129 (17)
Surya, 29 (66)
Susanoo, 81 (211)
Susanowoo, 150 (33)
Sutting, 124 (11), 128 (22)
Swallower of Clouds, 27 (79)
Sweaty Hands, 25 (147)
Switzerland, 48 (unp)
Sykesy, 175 (31)
Symplegades, 47 (unp)

Ta'aroa, 67 (101), 150 (12)
Tablet of Destinies, 40 (207)
Tahil, 160 (16)
Tah-tah Kle-ah (Giant Sisters), 176 (61)
Tain Bo Cuailnge, 139 (32)
Tairnads, 134 (74)
Takako, 13 (15)
Talib, 4 (108)
Taliesin, 130 (114)
Talking God, 130 (36)
Talos, 147 (44)
Tama, 162 (13, 117)
Tammy, 166 (61)
Tane, 133 (19), 150 (14, 18)
Tangaroa, 43 (40)
Tangaro the Fool, 67 (9)
Tantalus, 26 (48), 155 (185), 166 (85)
Tapir, 164 (28)
T'appin (Terrapin), 43 (212)
Tara, 139 (20, 109)
Taranga, 162 (11)
Tar-Baby, 11 (346)
Taro Beppu, 73 (7)
Tartarus, 130 (154), 166 (83)
Tawis-karong, 67 (59)
Tayune, 134 (123)
Tay Vuong Mau, 174 (9)
T-cho the Sun, 96 (58)
Tecciztecal, God of the Snails (Teccizte-
    catl), 62 (21), 150 (32)
Tefnut, 61 (unp), 71 (12)
Teiresias of Thebes (Tiresias), 26 (47,
    71), 154 (32), 155 (92)

Telemachus, 26 (34, 43), 148 (51), 154
    (46), 155 (198)
Telepinu, 130 (94), 138 (178)
Tell, Jemmy, 48 (unp)
Tell, William, 48 (unp)
Tenjin, Daijo, 169 (146)
Tenochtitlan, 106 (394)
Tepe the anteater, 36 (12)
Terah, 51 (80)
Terrapin. See T'appin
Terror of the Mother Lode, 44 (231)
Tetteh Nomo, 16 (148)
Texas, 11 (596)
Teyrnon, 163 (24)
Tezcatlipoca, God of the Night, 62 (1),
    102 (unp), 106 (127, 133, 212, 371),
    107 (84), 130 (140), 138 (478, 484)
Thamud, 4 (32)
That-Nuong, 174 (72)
Thebes, 26 (66), 71 (27), 130 (96), 155
    (128, 133)
Theodelain, 131 (48)
Theseus, 26 (25, 72), 108 (62), 130 (108,
    132), 147 (48), 148 (38), 155 (94, 102,
    132), 183 (unp)
Thetis, 26 (33), 153 (6)
Thialfi, 124 (47, 68), 128 (44, 54)
Thiazi, 124 (37, 43), 128 (25)
Thor, 32 (6), 70 (18, 34, 46, 52, 75), 107
    (103), 124 (5, 14, 20, 29, 33, 47, 58,
    65, 79), 128 (13, 43, 53, 54), 130 (65,
    118, 174), 138 (224, 228, 239), 150
    (38, 92)
Thorkil, 166 (49)
Thoth, 71 (20, 40), 150 (16)
Thought, 124 (9)
Three-Fingered Jack Garcia, 44 (225)
three sons of Tuirenn, 139 (25)
Thrown-Away, 138 (497)
thrush, 43 (109)
Thrym, 32 (6), 124 (34), 128 (13)
Thrymheim, 128 (20)
Thunder, 27 (93), 82 (15), 107 (103), 167
    (28), 187 (31)
Thunder Beings, 24 (7)
Thunderbird (Thunder Bird), 82 (15),
    138 (499)
Thunderbolt, 107 (104)

Thunderer, 25 (146)

Thunderers, 168 (unp)

the Thunders, 76 (98)

Tiamat, 40 (233), 67 (79), 138 (160), 150 (92)

Tie-Snake, 96 (234), 171 (82)

Tiger, 185 (95)

Tiger (Okhe), 12 (270)

Ti-i, 67 (101)

Tijus-Reha, 67 (59)

Tintagel, 103 (23)

Tio Conejo (Uncle Rabbit), 152 (unp)

Tirawa, 68 (18)

Tiresias of Thebes. See Teiresias of Thebes

Titans, 67 (127, 138), 130 (58, 134), 138 (7), 165 (74)

Tiu, 65 (84)

Tlalloc, God of Rain, 62 (13)

Toad, 43 (79)

Tohil, 160 (16), 161 (171)

Tokwah, 20 (124)

Toltecs, 106 (353)

Tony Beaver, 11 (626)

Tornado, 13 (25)

Tortesca, 14 (24)

Tortie the tortoise, 14 (89)

Tortoise, 14 (23, 110), 16 (63, 69, 74, 120, 131, 135, 136, 170), 43 (207, 209), 57 (134), 164 (10), 167 (22). See also Turtle

Totori the tortoise, 36 (18)

Tracks in the Water, 113 (5)

Trickster, 43 (228)

Trojan Horse, 26 (38), 108 (79)

Trojan War, 26 (31), 148 (50), 153 (1), 165 (122), 176 (35)

Troy, 26 (43), 108 (78), 138 (43, 78, 123), 155 (167, 186, 192)

True Jaguar, 161 (165)

Tsessebe, 57 (104)

Tu, 67 (101)

Tuatha De Danann, 138 (278, 285), 139 (16, 21, 25, 29), 166 (20, 28, 105)

Tugarin, 177 (72)

Tungaks, 134 (161)

Tunka-shila, 27 (57)

Tuoni, 148 (95)

Turnus, 138 (147)

Turpin, Archbishop, 148 (165)

Turtle, 25 (47, 51, 55), 27 (157), 41 (107), 43 (35), 67 (35, 59), 80 (142), 87 (unp), 104 (21), 115 (135), 118 (9), 135 (16), 141 (unp), 165 (30), 171 (95), 185 (81), 187 (91). See also Tortoise

Turtle, Giant, 91 (xv)

Twelve Labors of Heracles. See Labors of Heracles

twins, 165 (56)

Two White-footed Mouse Boys, 31 (31)

Tybaut, 131 (68)

Typhon, 150 (40), 165 (38)

Tyr, 124 (30, 58), 128 (65)

Uitenegar, 8 (106)

Uko, King of the Heavens, 165 (72)

Uktena, 116 (75)

Ulgan, 130 (34)

Ulgen, 67 (29)

Ulli, 176 (17)

Ulster, 130 (125)

Ulysses, 138 (136). See also Odysseus

Uncle Zalman, 93 (19, 52)

Under-Wave, 166 (28)

Underworld, 26 (47)

Ungambikula, 130 (28)

Ur, 148 (63)

Uranus, 155 (11)

Urd's Well, 124 (7)

Urshanabi, 148 (71)

Uruk, 40 (50), 86 (2), 138 (184), 150 (58), 189 (1)

Urvashi, 29 (82)

Utgard, 124 (47)

Utgard-Loki, 128 (54)

Uther Pendragon, King, 49 (5), 79 (6, 21), 103 (5), 131 (6), 138 (315), 139 (82), 148 (131), 157 (unp)

Utnapishtim (Utnashapishtim), 40 (95), 86 (3), 130 (46), 138 (202), 148 (71)

Ut'set, 132 (51)

Uzume, 150 (33)

Uzziah, 147 (76)

Vagahe, 134 (39)

Vaida, 134 (88)

Vainamoinen, 43 (44, 123), 130 (54), 148 (91), 165 (16)

Valencia, 107 (94)

Valhalla (Valholl), 107 (103), 124 (5, 71), 128 (62), 130 (63), 138 (224), 150 (70)

Valkyries, 124 (5), 138 (257), 150 (70)

vampires, 165 (86)

Vanir, 124 (6), 128 (27)

Varuna, 51 (52)

Vasuder, 89 (22)

Vasudeva, 51 (54)

Vasuki 51 (12, 14)

Venerable Bede, 115 (75)

Venus, 35 (unp), 108 (75), 123 (53, 57), 130 (154), 138 (124)

Village Boy, 187 (27)

Vinland, 84 (unp)

Viracocha (Wirakocha), 20 (200), 51 (25), 138 (459, 463)

Vishnu, 12 (72, 155), 29 (2, 17, 31, 38, 43), 51 (11, 14, 31, 54), 89 (50, 89), 138 (354, 366)

Visvantara, 112 (5)

Vivien (Viviane), the Lady of the Lake, 49 (27), 79 (16, 31, 85)

Vladimir, Prince, 177 (37, 41, 69, 72, 76)

Vol'ga Svyatoslavovich, 177 (21)

Volsung, 128 (70), 148 (76)

Volund the Smith, 81 (174)

Volva, 133 (29)

Voodoo, 130 (117)

Vortigern, 49 (5), 103 (6)

Vritra, 138 (358)

Vulcan, 165 (38)

Vulture, 16 (185)

Vyasa, 29 (19)

Wagadu, 138 (435)

Wagnuka, 82 (39)

Wahine-omao, 145 (123)

Wahu, 82 (43)

Wakan-Tanka, 27 (57), 34 (43)

Wakatami, 15 (unp)

Walukaga, 130 (76)

Waraku, 138 (467)

the warlow, 103 (40)

Wasis, 130 (92)

Water, 14 (78), 133 (25), 167 (4)

Water Beetle, 132 (109)

Water Hummingbird, 160 (9)

Water-Mother, 165 (9)

Water Spirit, 159 (16)

Waub-oozoo, 91 (37, 51)

Weasel Man, 31 (31)

Webb, Simpson, 185 (133)

Weendigoes, 91 (xix, 91)

Wehixamukes, 21 (82, 85, 89)

West Wind, 25 (19), 105 (17), 133 (16)

Wetenga, 162 (91)

Whirlwind Man, 3 (186, 187)

White Buffalo Calf Woman, 27 (187)

White Dawn, 74 (4)

White Deer, 21 (67)

White Elk, 113 (60)

White Knight, 79 (73)

White Man's Island, 3 (106)

White Sparkstriker, 160 (38)

Widow Maker, 11 (517), 44 (200, 208), 122 (83), 146 (25), 175 (73)

Wiglaf, 138 (306), 148 (128)

Wild Bill Hickok, 44 (255, 300), 186 (45)

Wild Boy, 187 (26, 117)

Wildcat, 63 (4)

Wildcat of the Plains, 44 (302)

William of the Branch, Sir, 131 (49)

William Short-Nose, 49 (42)

Williams, Old Bill, 44 (109)

William Tell, 48 (unp)

Willka Qutu, 2 (21)

Will Scarlet, 39 (3), 38 (10), 75 (19), 101 (5), 107 (20)

Will Stutely, 38 (10), 101 (9)

Winabijou, 76 (98, 116). *See also* Manabozho; Nanabozhoo

Wind, 67 (105)

Wind Eagle, 27 (69), 116 (125)

Winonah, 91 (17, 27, 37, 51)

Winter, 27 (131), 43 (66)

Winter Katsina, 187 (51)

Wirakocha. *See* Viracocha

Wisagatcak (Wisahkecahk), 118 (13), 158 (10)

Wiyot, 19 (101)

Woden, 150 (70)

Wolf, 25 (56), 66 (5), 76 (104, 107), 91

(81), 113 (92), 135 (18), 158 (10), 168
  (3), 170 (1, 29), 171 (40)
Wolf Brothers, 113 (22)
Wolf Runner, 159 (21)
Wolf Star Spirit, 132 (65)
Wolverine, 27 (119)
Woman, 66 (69), 114 (7, 8)
Woman-Chief, 170 (60)
Woman from the Sky, 27 (25)
Woodchuck, Grandmother, 43 (66)
the Wooden Horse. *See* Trojan Horse
World Serpent, 128 (46, 54, 65)
World Tree, 124 (6, 10, 79)
Wuchowsen, 27 (67)
Wulbari, 67 (53)

Xbalanque, 106 (316), 161 (89, 105)
Xibalba, 106 (316), 161 (106)
Xi He, 107 (7), 150 (28)
Xmucane, 161 (105)
Xpiyacoc, 161 (105)
Xpuch, 161 (190)
Xtah, 161 (190)

Yafoor, 4 (52)
Yah-qua-whee, 59 (unp)
Yahweh (Lord God), 67 (123), 148 (104)
Yama, 51 (52), 65 (137), 81 (197)
Yama-Kumar, 65 (138)
Yamapur, 65 (137)
Yang, 51 (24), 165 (17)
Yarime the capuchin monkey, 36 (10)
Yatai, 165 (24)
Yatam, 165 (24)
Yatto, 134 (120)
Yaunkur, 138 (409)
Yayael, 37 (unp)
Yayali, 145 (104)
Yeitzo, 150 (63)
Yellow Dawn, 74 (4)

Yellow Jackets, 104 (2)
Yellow Woman, 3 (182, 186, 187)
Yemaya, 42 (64), 56 (27)
Yembo, 42 (41)
Yente, 93 (19, 32, 44)
Yewa, 56 (234)
Yggdrasil, 124 (6), 128 (58), 130 (21, 62,
  175), 138 (223), 150 (70)
Yin, 51 (24), 165 (17)
Yi the Archer, 138 (393)
Ymir, 124 (1), 128 (57), 130 (18), 138
  (222), 150 (16)
Yohah the Star, 96 (58)
Yonkon-pass-me-dollar-loss, 16 (175)
Younger Brother, 187 (117)
Younger Duck, 187 (43)
Young Tree, 158 (22)
Yucahu, 37 (unp)
Yudhishtira, 29 (60)
Yuriwaka, 73 (4)
Yvain, Sir, 49 (18)

Zabava, 177 (70)
Zabba, 4 (62)
Zabiba, 4 (62)
Zagzagle, 54 (unp)
Zao Gongen, 169 (128)
Zarifa, 4 (57)
Zarqa Al-Yamama, 4 (36)
Zebra, 57 (97)
Zeus, 26 (7, 16, 31, 63), 67 (127, 137,
  139), 108 (9), 116 (104), 130 (58, 83,
  96, 130, 148, 171), 133 (37), 138 (9,
  13, 16, 22, 78), 147 (14), 148 (17), 150
  (39, 40, 88), 155 (11, 65, 68, 76, 83,
  91, 148, 170, 194), 165 (38, 49, 74,
  118), 176 (38)
Zipacna, 161 (94)
Ziusdra, 51 (27)
Zuni maiden, 147 (115)

Index of Book Titles by Grade Levels

(Where titles of books do not indicate the culture from which the stories come, this information is provided in parentheses. If the stories come from a variety of cultures, the book is noted as an anthology. If a book contains stories from a single culture or group, it is termed a collection. If there is no such designation, it is a single story. Numerals at the end of each citation refer to entries in the Guide.)

Preschool–Grade 5:
  Thirty-Three Multicultural Tales to Tell (anthology), 41
  Saint George and the Dragon (British Isles), 109
  Raven: A Trickster Tale from the Pacific Northwest (Native American), 110

Preschool–Grade 6:
  Stolen Thunder: A Norse Myth (Norse), 32
  The Fifth and Final Sun: An Ancient Aztec Myth of the Sun's Origin (Native American), 62
  The Precious Gift: A Navaho Creation Myth (Native American), 87
  In a Circle Long Ago: A Treasury of Native Lore from North America (collection, Native American), 171
  Rainbow Crow: A Lenape Tale (Native American), 172

Preschool–Grade 9:
  How the Stars Fell into the Sky: A Navajo Legend (Native American), 126

Preschool up:
  Llama and the Great Flood: A Folktale from Peru (Native American), 2
  The Tree That Rains: The Flood Myth of the Huichol Indians of Mexico (Native American), 15
  Exodus (ancient Israel), 28
  Brer Tiger and the Big Wind (African American), 46
  Owl Eyes (Native American, Mohawk), 52
  The Kitchen Knight: A Tale of King Arthur (British Isles), 78
  The Creation (ancient Israel), 90
  Sally Ann Thunder Ann Whirlwind Crockett (United States), 92
  And the Earth Trembled: The Creation of Adam and Eve (Islam), 120
  The Illustrated Book of Myths (anthology), 130
  How Turtle's Back Was Cracked: A Traditional Cherokee Tale (Native American), 141
  Rabbit Wishes (Cuba), 152

Kindergarten–Grade 3:
  The Lost Children (Native American, Blackfeet), 55

Kindergarten–Grade 4:
   Song of the Chirimia: A Guatemalan Folktale (Native American, Maya), 173

Kindergarten–Grade 6:
   The Mud Pony (Native American, Pawnee), 33
   Leif's Saga: A Viking Tale (Norse), 84

Kindergarten–Grade 7:
   Keepers of the Earth: Native American Stories and Environmental Activities for Children (collection), 27
   How the World Was Saved & Other Native American Tales (collection), 68
   Why There Is No Arguing in Heaven: A Mayan Myth (Native American), 99
   Fire Race: A Karuk Coyote Tale (Native American), 104
   Muwin and the Magic Hare (Native American, Passamaquoddy), 151

Kindergarten–Grade 8:
   Ready-to-Tell Tales (anthology), 80

Kindergarten up:
   The Arabian Nights Or Tales Told by Sheherezade During a Thousand and One Nights (collection, Arabia), 1
   Lives and Legends of the Saints (anthology), 7
   The Woman Who Fell from the Sky: The Iroquois Story of Creation (Native American), 22
   Atalanta's Race (Greece), 30
   How Iwariwa the Cayman Learned to Share (Native American, Yanomami), 36
   Jason and the Golden Fleece (Greece), 47
   William Tell (Switzerland), 48
   The Shadow of a Flying Bird: A Legend from the Kurdistani Jews, 54
   Cry of the Benu Bird: An Egyptian Creation Story, 61
   Sir Gawain and the Loathly Lady (British Isles), 72

   Coyote Walks on Two Legs: A Book of Navajo Myths and Legends (collection, Native American), 74
   Ahaiyute and Cloud Eater (Native American, Zuni), 83
   Perseus (Greece), 85
   The Adventures of Hershel of Ostropol (collection, Jewish), 93
   Rimonah of the Flashing Sword: A North African Tale (Egypt), 94
   Peboan and Seegwun (Native American, Ojibwa), 97
   All of You Was Singing (Native American, Aztec), 102
   The Children of Lir (British Isles), 111
   The Fish Skin (Native American, Cree), 118
   Iblis (Islam), 121
   South and North, East and West: The Oxfam Book of Children's Stories (anthology), 137
   Buddha (Buddhist), 142
   Arthur and the Sword (British Isles), 143
   King Arthur and the Round Table (British Isles), 156
   King Arthur: The Sword in the Stone (British Isles), 157
   How the Seasons Came: A North American Indian Folk Tale (Native American, Algonquin), 168
   And in the Beginning . . . (Sub-Saharan Africa), 179
   Sundiata: Lion King of Mali (Sub-Saharan Africa), 180
   Wings (Greece), 183

Grades 1–5:
   Great Rabbit and the Long-Tailed Wildcat (Native American, Passamaquoddy), 63
   How We Saw the World: Nine Native Stories of the Way Things Began (collection, Native American), 159

Grades 1–6:
   How the Sea Began: A Taino Myth (Native American), 37
   The Legend of the Cranberry: A Paleo-Indian Tale (Native American, Delaware), 59

Grades 1–9:

Stories from the Days of Christopher Columbus: A Multicultural Collection for Young Readers (anthology), 188

Grades 1 up:

Nyumba ya Mumbi: The Gikuyu Creation Myth (Sub-Saharan Africa), 50

Her Stories: African American Folktales, Fairy Tales, and True Tales (collection), 66

Voices of the First Day: Awakening in the Aboriginal Dreamtime (collection, Australian Aboriginal), 100

How Rabbit Tricked Otter and Other Cherokee Trickster Stories (collection, Native American), 140

Bones in the Basket: Native Stories of the Origin of People (collection, Native American), 158

The Rainbow Bridge (Native American, Chumash), 182

Grades 2–6:

Robin Hood and His Merry Men (collection, British Isles), 38

Robin Hood in the Greenwood (collection, British Isles), 39

Manabozho's Gifts: Three Chippewa Tales (collection, Native American), 60

Favorite Greek Myths (collection, Graeco-Roman), 123

Grades 2–8:

Moses' Ark: Stories from the Bible (collection, ancient Israel), 9

Giants! Stories from Around the World (anthology), 176

Grades 2–9:

When Hippo Was Hairy and Other Tales from Africa (collection, Sub-Saharan Africa), 57

When Lion Could Fly and Other Tales from Africa (collection, Sub-Saharan Africa), 58

Grades 2 up:

Best-Loved Stories Told at the National Storytelling Festival (anthology), 115

More Best-Loved Stories Told at the National Storytelling Festival (anthology), 116

Favorite Norse Myths (collection), 124

Land of the Long White Cloud: Maori Myths, Tales and Legends (collection, New Zealand), 162

Esther's Story (ancient Israel), 181

Grades 3–7:

The Monkey's Haircut and Other Stories Told by the Maya (collection, Native American), 17

Iroquois Stories Heroes and Heroines Monsters and Magic (collection, Native American), 25

Larger Than Life: The Adventures of American Legendary Heroes (collection, United States), 146

Myths and Legends from Around the World (anthology), 150

Crow & Fox and Other Animal Legends (anthology), 164

How Stories Came into the World (collection, Sub-Saharan Africa), 167

Grades 3–8:

Bury My Bones But Keep My Words (collection, Sub-Saharan Africa), 45

My Grandmother's Stories: A Collection of Jewish Folk Tales (collection, Russian Jewish), 53

Greek Myths (collection), 108

Finn Mac Cool and the Small Men of Deeds (British Isles), 125

Grades 3–9:

The Golden Hoard: Myths and Legends of the World (anthology), 107

The Illustrated Children's Old Testament (collection, ancient Israel), 114

American Tall Tales (collection, United States), 122

Grades 3–10:

Out of the Ark: Stories from the World's Religions (anthology), 51

While Standing on One Foot: Puzzle Stories and Wisdom Tales from the Jewish Tradition (collection), 88

Grades 3 up:
The Origin of Life on Earth: An African Creation Myth (Sub-Saharan Africa), 5
Between Earth & Sky: Legends of Native American Sacred Places (collection), 24
Why the Possum's Tail Is Bare and Other North American Indian Nature Tales (collection, Native American), 34
Cupid and Psyche (Graeco-Roman), 35
The Book of Dragons (anthology), 64
The Curse of the Ring (collection, Norse), 69
The Doom of the Gods (collection, Norse), 70
Excalibur (British Isles), 77
Myths and Legends from Ghana for African-American Cultures (collection, Sub-Saharan Africa), 98
The Children of the Morning Light: Wampanoag Tales (collection, Native American), 105
The Tree Is Older Than You Are: A Bilingual Gathering of Poems & Stories from Mexico with Paintings by Mexican Artists (collection, Native American), 117
The Magic Weaver of Rugs: A Tale of the Navajo (Native American), 127
Monkey Creates Havoc in Heaven (collection, China), 129
White Wolf Woman and Other Native American Transformation Myths (collection), 132
Dance of the Sacred Circle: A Native American Tale (Blackfeet), 135
The Feather Merchants & Other Tales of the Fools of Chelm (collection, Jewish), 144
Black Ships Before Troy: The Story of THE ILIAD (single story, Greece), 153
The Wanderings of Odysseus: The Story of THE ODYSSEY (collection, Greece), 154
Big Men, Big Country: A Collection of American Tall Tales (collection, United States), 175
Moon Mother: A Native American Creation Tale, 184
Gilgamesh the King (Mesopotamia), 189

Grades 4–6:
Robin Hood (collection, British Isles), 75

Grades 4–7:
Someone Saw a Spider: Spider Facts and Folktales (anthology), 31
The Story of Yuriwaka (collection, Japan), 73

Grades 4–8:
Myths and Legends of The Age of Chivalry (anthology), 49
Realms of Gold: Myths & Legends from Around the World (anthology), 133

Grades 4–9:
Of Swords and Sorcerers: The Adventures of King Arthur and His Knights (collection, British Isles), 79
Myths and Legends (anthology), 81
The Legends of King Arthur (collection, British Isles), 103

Grades 4 up:
Never and Always: Micronesian Legends, Fables, and Folklore (collection), 8
Moon Was Tired of Walking on Air (collection, Native American), 13
West African Trickster Tales (collection, Sub-Saharan Africa), 14
The White Deer and Other Stories Told by the Lenape (collection, Native American), 21
The Elephant-Headed God and Other Hindu Tales (collection, India), 29
The Dark Way: Stories from the Spirit World (anthology), 65
In the Beginning: Creation Stories

from Around the World (anthology), 67

Seasons of Splendour: Tales, Myths and Legends of India (collection), 89

The Story of Robin Hood (collection, British Isles), 101

Dreamtime: Aboriginal Stories (collection, Australian Aboriginal), 119

The Great Deeds of Heroic Women (anthology), 147

The Great Deeds of Superheroes (anthology), 148

Maybe I Will Do Something (collection, Native American), 170

Sky Legends of Vietnam (collection), 174

African-American Folktales for Young Readers (collection), 185

Race with Buffalo and Other Native American Stories for Young Readers (collection), 187

Grades 5–9:

Native North American Stories (collection), 82

The Gift of Changing Woman (Native American, Apache), 149

Grades 5–12:

Mother Scorpion Country/La Tierra de la Madre Escorpion (Native American, Miskito), 136

Grades 5 up:

Fabled Cities, Princes & Jinn from Arab Myths and Legends (collection), 4

They Dance in the Sky: Native American Star Myths (collection), 113

The Tale of Sir Gawain (collection, British Isles), 131

Druids, Gods & Heroes from Celtic Mythology (collection, British Isles), 139

Cut From the Same Cloth: American Women of Myth, Legend, and Tall Tale (collection, United States), 145

Tales from the Mabinogion (collection, British Isles), 163

Heroes, Monsters and Other Worlds

from Russian Mythology (collection), 177

Grades 6 up:

Nanabozhoo, Giver of Life (collection, Native American, Ojibwa), 76

El Cid (collection, Spain), 95

The Book of Beginnings (anthology), 165

Fabled Lands (anthology), 166

Grades 7 up:

Spider Woman's Granddaughters: Traditional Tales and Contemporary Writing by Native American Women (collection), 3

Great American Folklore: Legends, Tales, Ballads and Superstitions from All Across America (collection, United States), 11

West African Folktales (collection, Sub-Saharan Africa), 16

Family of Earth and Sky: Indigenous Tales of Nature from Around the World (anthology), 43

Tales from the American Frontier (collection, United States), 44

The Buddha: His Life Retold (collection, India), 112

The Sun Maiden and the Crescent Moon: Siberian Folk Tales (collection), 134

Greek Myths: Gods, Heroes and Monsters (collection), 155

Japanese Tales (collection), 169

Mexican-American Folklore: Legends, Songs, Festivals, Proverbs, Crafts, Tales of Saints, of Revolutionaries, and More (collection), 178

Grades 8 up:

Legends of Santeria (collection, Cuba), 56

Grades 9 up:

Green Man: The Archetype of our Oneness with the Earth (anthology), 6

Folktales of India (collection), 12

The Mythology of Mexico and Central America (collection, Native American), 18

The Mythology of North America (collection, Native American), 19

The Mythology of South America (collection, Native American), 20

Egyptian Myths (collection), 71

The Epic of Gilgamesh (collection, Mesopotamia), 86

The Manitous: The Spiritual World of the Ojibway (collection, Native American), 91

Native American Legends: Southeastern Legends: Tales from the Natchez, Caddo, Biloxi, Chickasaw, and Other Nations (collection, Native American and Sub-Saharan Africa), 96

World Mythology: An Anthology of the World's Great Myths and Epics (anthology), 138

Outlaw Tales: Legends, Myths, and Folklore from America's Middle Border (collection, United States), 186

Grades 10 up:

African Folktales in the New World (anthology, Sub-Saharan Africa, African American, Native American), 10

A Coyote Reader (collection, Native American), 23

Greek Myths (collection), 26

Myths from Mesopotamia (collection), 40

Ita: Mythology of the Yoruba Religion (collection, Santeria stories from Sub-Saharan Africa later told in Brazil, Cuba, and Haiti), 42

The Flayed God: The Mesoamerican Mythological Tradition (collection, Native American), 106

Norse Myths (collection), 128

Breath on the Mirror: Mythic Voices & Visions of the Living Maya (collection, Native American), 160

Popol Vuh: The Definitive Edition of the Mayan Book of the Dawn of Life and the Glories of Gods and Kings (collection, Native American), 161

Index of Book Titles

(Numerals refer to entries in the Guide.)

The Adventures of Hershel of Ostropol (Kimmel, Eric A., ret.), 93

African-American Folktales for Young Readers (Young, Richard Alan, and Judy Dockrey Young, colls., eds., and rets.), 185

African Folktales in the New World (Bascom, William, coll. and ed.), 10

Ahaiyute and Cloud Eater (Hulpach, Vladimir, ret.), 83

All of You Was Singing (Lewis, Richard, ret.), 102

American Tall Tales (Osborne, Mary Pope, ret.), 122

And in the Beginning . . . (Williams, Sheron, ret.), 179

And the Earth Trembled: The Creation of Adam and Eve (Oppenheim, Shulamith Levey, ret.), 120

The Arabian Nights Or Tales Told by Sheherezade During a Thousand and One Nights (Alderson, Brian, ret.), 1

Arthur and the Sword (Sabuda, Robert, ret.), 143

Atalanta's Race (Climo, Shirley, ret.), 30

Best-Loved Stories Told at the National Storytelling Festival (The National Association for the Preservation and Perpetuation of Storytelling, coll.), 115

Between Earth & Sky: Legends of Native American Sacred Places (Bruchac, Joseph, ret.), 24

Big Men, Big Country: A Collection of American Tall Tales (Walker, Paul Robert, ret.), 175

Black Ships Before Troy: The Story of THE ILIAD (Sutcliff, Rosemary, ret.), 153

Bones in the Basket: Native Stories of the Origin of People (Taylor, C. J., ret.), 158

The Book of Beginnings (Time-Life Books Inc.), 165

The Book of Dragons (Hague, Michael, sel.), 64

Breath on the Mirror: Mythic Voices & Visions of the Living Maya (Tedlock, Dennis, ret.), 160

Brer Tiger and the Big Wind (Faulkner, William J., coll. and ret.), 46

Buddha (Roth, Susan L., ret.), 142

The Buddha: His Life Retold (Mitchell, Robert Allen, ret.), 112

Bury My Bones But Keep My Words (Fairman, Tony, ret.), 45

The Children of Lir (McGill-Callahan, Sheila, ret.), 111

The Children of the Morning Light: Wampanoag Tales (Manitonquat [Medicine Story], ret.), 105

A Coyote Reader (Bright, William, sel. and ed.), 23

Coyote Walks on Two Legs: A Book of Navajo Myths and Legends (Hausman, Gerald, ret.), 74

The Creation (Johnson, James Weldon, ret.), 90

Crow & Fox and Other Animal Legends (Thornhill, Jan, ret.), 164

Cry of the Benu Bird: An Egyptian Creation Story (Greger, C. Shana, ad.), 61

Cupid and Psyche (Craft, M. Charlotte, ret.), 35

The Curse of the Ring (Harrison, Michael, ret.), 69

Cut From the Same Cloth: American Women of Myth, Legend, and Tall Tale (San Souci, Robert D., ret.), 145

Dance of the Sacred Circle: A Native American Tale (Rodanas, Kristina, ad.), 135

The Dark Way: Stories from the Spirit World (Hamilton, Virginia, ret.), 65

The Doom of the Gods (Harrison, Michael, ret.), 70

Dreamtime: Aboriginal Stories (Oodgeroo [Kath Walker], ret.), 119

Druids, Gods & Heroes from Celtic Mythology (Ross, Anne, ret.), 139

Egyptian Myths (Hart, George, ed.), 71

El Cid (Koslow, Philip, ret.), 95

The Elephant-Headed God and Other Hindu Tales (Chatterjee, Debjani, ret.), 29

The Epic of Gilgamesh (Jackson, Danny P., trans.), 86

Esther's Story (Wolkstein, Diane, ret.), 181

Excalibur (Heyer, Carol, ret.), 77

Exodus (Chaikin, Miriam, ad.), 28

Fabled Cities, Princes & Jinn from Arab Myths and Legends (Al-Saleh, Khairat, ret.), 4

Fabled Lands (Time-Life Books Inc.), 166

Family of Earth and Sky: Indigenous Tales of Nature from Around the World (Elder, John, and Hertha D. Wong, eds.), 43

Favorite Greek Myths (Osborne, Mary Pope, ret.), 123

Favorite Norse Myths (Osborne, Mary Pope, ret.), 124

The Feather Merchants & Other Tales of the Fools of Chelm (Sanfield, Steve, coll. and ret.), 144

The Fifth and Final Sun: An Ancient Aztec Myth of the Sun's Origin (Greger, C. Shana, ret.), 62

Finn Mac Cool and the Small Men of Deeds (O'Shea, Pat, ret.), 125

Fire Race: A Karuk Coyote Tale (London, Jonathan, with Larry Pinola, rets.), 104

The Fish Skin (Oliviero, Jamie, ret.), 118

The Flayed God: The Mesoamerican Mythological Tradition (Markman, Roberta H., and Peter T. Markman, eds.), 106

Folktales of India (Beck, Brenda E. F., Peter J. Claus, Praphulladatta Goswami, and Jawaharlal Handoo, eds.), 12

Giants! Stories from Around the World (Walker, Paul Robert, ret.), 176

The Gift of Changing Woman (Seymour, Tryntje Van Ness, ret.), 149

Gilgamesh the King (Zeman, Ludmila, ret.), 189

The Golden Hoard: Myths and Legends of the World (McCaughrean, Geraldine, sel. and ret.), 107

Great American Folklore: Legends, Tales, Ballads and Superstitions from All Across America (Battle, Kemp P., comp.), 11

The Great Deeds of Heroic Women (Saxby, Maurice, ret.), 147

The Great Deeds of Superheroes (Saxby, Maurice, ret.), 148

Great Rabbit and the Long-Tailed Wildcat (Gregg, Andy, ret.), 63

Greek Myths (Burn, Lucilla, ret.), 26

Greek Myths (McCaughrean, Geraldine, ret.), 108

Greek Myths: Gods, Heroes and Monsters (Switzer, Ellen, and Costas, rets.), 155

Green Man: The Archetype of Our Oneness with the Earth (Anderson, William, coll. and ret.), 6

Heroes, Monsters and Other Worlds from Russian Mythology (Warner, Elizabeth, ret.), 177

Her Stories: African American Folktales, Fairy Tales, and True Tales (Hamilton, Virginia, sel. and ret.), 66

How Iwariwa the Cayman Learned to Share (Crespo, George, ret.), 36

How Rabbit Tricked Otter and Other Cherokee Trickster Stories (Ross, Gayle, ret.), 140

How Stories Came into the World (Troughton, Joanna, ret.), 167

How the Sea Began: A Taino Myth (Crespo, George, ret.), 37

How the Seasons Came: A North American Indian Folk Tale (Troughton, Joanna, ret.), 168

How the Stars Fell into the Sky: A Navajo Legend (Oughton, Jerrie, ret.), 126

How the World Was Saved & Other Native American Tales (Harper, Piers, ret.), 68

How Turtle's Back Was Cracked: A Traditional Cherokee Tale (Ross, Gayle, ret.), 141

How We Saw the World: Nine Native Stories of the Way Things Began (Taylor, C. J., ret.), 159

Iblis (Oppenheim, Shulamith Levey, ret.), 121

The Illustrated Book of Myths (Philip, Neil, ret.), 130

The Illustrated Children's Old Testament (Morris, Christopher, ed.), 114

In a Circle Long Ago: A Treasury of Native Lore from North America (Van Laan, Nancy, sel. and ret.), 171

In the Beginning: Creation Stories from Around the World (Hamilton, Virginia, ret.), 67

Iroquois Stories Heroes and Heroines Monsters and Magic (Bruchac, Joseph, ret.), 25

Ita: Mythology of the Yoruba Religion (Ecun, Oba [Cecilio Perez], coll. and ret.), 42

Japanese Tales (Tyler, Royall, ed. and trans.), 169

Jason and the Golden Fleece (Fisher, Leonard Everett, ret.), 47

Keepers of the Earth: Native American Stories and Environmental Activities for Children (Caduto, Michael J., and Joseph Bruchac, rets.), 27

King Arthur and the Round Table (Talbott, Hudson, ret.), 156

King Arthur: The Sword in the Stone (Talbott, Hudson, ret.), 157

The Kitchen Knight: A Tale of King Arthur (Hodges, Margaret, ret.), 78

Land of the Long White Cloud: Maori Myths, Tales and Legends (Te Kanawa, Kiri, ret.), 162

Larger Than Life: The Adventures of American Legendary Heroes (San Souci, Robert D., ret.), 146

The Legend of the Cranberry: A Paleo-Indian Tale (Greene, Ellin, ret.), 59

The Legends of King Arthur (Lister, Robin, ret.), 103

Legends of Santeria (Gonzalez-Wippler, Migene, ret.), 56

Leif's Saga: A Viking Tale (Hunt, Jonathan, ret.), 84

Lives and Legends of the Saints (Armstrong, Carole, ret.), 7

Llama and the Great Flood: A Folktale from Peru (Alexander, Ellen, ret.), 2

The Lost Children (Goble, Paul, ret.), 55

The Magic Weaver of Rugs: A Tale of the Navajo (Oughton, Jerrie, ret.), 127

Manabozho's Gifts: Three Chippewa Tales (Greene, Jacqueline Dembar, ret.), 60

The Manitous: The Spiritual World of the Ojibway (Johnston, Basil, coll., ed., and ret.), 91

Maybe I Will Do Something (Ude, Wayne, ret.), 170

Mexican-American Folklore: Legends, Songs, Festivals, Proverbs, Crafts, Tales of Saints, of Revolutionaries, and More (West, John O., comp. and ed.), 178

Monkey Creates Havoc in Heaven (Pan, Cai-Ying, ad.), 129

The Monkey's Haircut and Other Stories Told by the Maya (Bierhorst, John, ed.), 17

Moon Mother: A Native American Creation Tale (Young, Ed, ad.), 184

Moon Was Tired of Walking on Air (Belting, Natalia M., ret.), 13

More Best-Loved Stories Told at the National Storytelling Festival (The National Association for the Preservation and Perpetuation of Storytelling, coll.), 116

Moses' Ark: Stories from the Bible (Bach, Alice, and J. Cheryl Exum, rets.), 9

Mother Scorpion Country/La Tierra de la Madre Escorpión (Rohmer, Harriet, and Dorminster Wilson, rets.), 136

The Mud Pony (Cohen, Caron Lee, ret.), 33

Muwin and the Magic Hare (Shetterly, Susan Hand, ret.), 151

My Grandmother's Stories: A Collection of Jewish Folk Tales (Geras, Adele, ret.), 53

The Mythology of Mexico and Central America (Bierhorst, John, sel.), 18

The Mythology of North America (Bierhorst, John, sel. and ret.), 19

The Mythology of South America (Bierhorst, John, sel.), 20

Myths and Legends (Horowitz, Anthony, ret.), 81

Myths and Legends from Around the World (Shepherd, Sandy, ret.), 150

Myths and Legends from Ghana for African-American Cultures (Larungu, Rute, ret.), 98

Myths and Legends of The Age of Chivalry (Frost, Abigail, ret.), 49

Myths from Mesopotamia (Dalley, Stephanie, trans.), 40

Nanabozhoo, Giver of Life (Helbig, Alethea K., ed.), 76

Native American Legends: Southeastern Legends: Tales from the Natchez, Caddo, Biloxi, Chickasaw, and Other Nations (Lankford, George E., coll. and ed.), 96

Native North American Stories (Hull, Robert, ret.), 82

Never and Always: Micronesian Legends, Fables, and Folklore (Ashby, Gene, comp. and ed.), 8

Norse Myths (Page, R. I., ret. and ed.), 128

Nyumba ya Mumbi: The Gikuyu Creation Myth (Gakuo, Kariuki, ret.), 50

Of Swords and Sorcerers: The Adventures of King Arthur and His Knights (Hodges, Margaret, and Margery Evernden, rets.), 79

The Origin of Life on Earth: An African Creation Myth (Anderson, David A., ret.), 5

Outlaw Tales: Legends, Myths, and Folklore from America's Middle Border (Young, Richard Alan, and Judy Dockrey Young, colls. and eds.), 186

Out of the Ark: Stories from the World's Religions (Ganeri, Anita, ret.), 51

Owl Eyes (Gates, Frieda, ret.), 52

Peboan and Seegwun (Larry, Charles, ret.), 97

Perseus (Hutton, Warwick, ret.), 85

Popol Vuh: The Definitive Edition of the Mayan Book of the Dawn of Life and the Glories of Gods and Kings (Tedlock, Dennis, trans.), 161

The Precious Gift: A Navaho Creation Myth (Jackson, Ellen, ret.), 87

Rabbit Wishes (Shute, Linda, ret.), 152

Race with Buffalo and Other Native American Stories for Young Readers (Young, Richard, and Judy Dockrey Young, colls. and eds.), 187

The Rainbow Bridge (Wood, Audrey, ret.), 182

Rainbow Crow: A Lenape Tale (Van Laan, Nancy, ret.), 172

Raven: A Trickster Tale from the Pacific Northwest (McDermott, Gerald, ret.), 110

Ready-to-Tell Tales (Holt, David, and Bill Mooney, sels. and rets.), 80

Realms of Gold: Myths & Legends from Around the World (Pilling, Ann, ret.), 133

Rimonah of the Flashing Sword: A North African Tale (Kimmel, Eric A., ad.), 94

Robin Hood (Hayes, Sarah, ret.), 75

Robin Hood and His Merry Men (Curry, Jane Louise, ret.), 38

Robin Hood in the Greenwood (Curry, Jane Louise, ret.), 39

Saint George and the Dragon (McCaughrean, Geraldine, ret.), 109

Sally Ann Thunder Ann Whirlwind Crockett (Kellogg, Steven, ret.), 92

Seasons of Splendour: Tales, Myths and Legends of India (Jaffrey, Madhur, ret.), 89

The Shadow of a Flying Bird: A Legend from the Kurdistani Jews (Gerstein, Mordicai, ret.), 54

Sir Gawain and the Loathly Lady (Hastings, Selina, ret.), 72

Sky Legends of Vietnam (Vuong, Lynette Dyer, ret.), 174

Someone Saw a Spider: Spider Facts and Folktales (Climo, Shirley, ret.), 31

Song of the Chirimia: A Guatemalan Folktale (Volkmer, Jane Anne, ret.), 173

South and North, East and West: The Oxfam Book of Children's Stories (Rosen, Michael, ed.), 137

Spider Woman's Granddaughters: Traditional Tales and Contemporary Writing by Native American Women (Allen, Paula Gunn, ed.), 3

Stolen Thunder: A Norse Myth (Climo, Shirley, ret.), 32

Stories from the Days of Christopher Columbus: A Multicultural Collection for Young Readers (Young, Richard Alan, and Judy Dockrey Young, colls. and rets.), 188

The Story of Robin Hood (Leeson, Robert, ret.), 101

The Story of Yuriwaka (Haugaard, Erik, and Masako Haugaard, rets.), 73

Sundiata: Lion King of Mali (Wisniewski, David, ret.), 180

The Sun Maiden and the Crescent Moon: Siberian Folk Tales (Riordan, James, coll. and trans.), 134

The Tale of Sir Gawain (Philip, Neil, ret.), 131

Tales from the American Frontier (Erdoes, Richard, coll., ed., and ret.), 44

Tales from the Mabinogion (Thomas, Gwyn, and Kevin Crossley-Holland, rets.), 163

They Dance in the Sky: Native American Star Myths (Monroe, Jean Guard, and Roy A. Williamson, rets.), 113

Thirty-Three Multicultural Tales to Tell (DeSpain, Pleasant, coll. and ret.), 41

The Tree Is Older Than You Are: A Bilingual Gathering of Poems & Stories from Mexico with Paintings by Mexican Artists (Nye, Naomi Shihab, sel.), 117

The Tree That Rains: The Flood Myth of the Huichol Indians of Mexico (Bernhard, Emery, ret.), 15

Voices of the First Day: Awakening in the Aboriginal Dreamtime (Lawlor, Robert, ret.), 100

The Wanderings of Odysseus: The Story of THE ODYSSEY (Sutcliff, Rosemary, ret.), 154

West African Folktales (Berry, Jack, ret.), 16

West African Trickster Tales (Bennett, Martin, ret.), 14

When Hippo Was Hairy and Other Tales from Africa (Greaves, Nick, ret.), 57

When Lion Could Fly and Other Tales from Africa (Greaves, Nick, ret.), 58

While Standing on One Foot: Puzzle Stories and Wisdom Tales from the Jewish Tradition (Jaffe, Nina, and Steve Zeitlin, rets.), 88

The White Deer and Other Stories Told by the Lenape (Bierhorst, John, ed.), 21

White Wolf Woman and Other Native American Transformation Myths (Pijoan, Teresa, coll. and ret.), 132

Why the Possum's Tail Is Bare and Other North American Indian Nature Tales (Connolly, James E., ret.), 34

Why There Is No Arguing in Heaven: A Mayan Myth (Lattimore, Deborah Nourse, ret.), 99

William Tell (Fisher, Leonard Everett, ret.), 48

Wings (Yolen, Jane, ret.), 183

The Woman Who Fell from the Sky: The Iroquois Story of Creation (Bierhorst, John, ret.), 22

World Mythology: An Anthology of the World's Great Myths and Epics (Rosenberg, Donna, ret.), 138

Index of Illustrators

(Numerals refer to entries in the Guide.)

Adams, Andrea, 34
Alexander, Ellen, 2
Apache artists, various, 149
Arquette, Mary F., 105
Asare, Meshack, 45
Baker, Alan, 103
Bancroft, Bronwyn, 119
Battle, John M., 11
Begay, Shonto, 33
Benson, Patrick, 75
Bernardin, James, 175, 176
Bernhard, Durga, 15
Burgevin, Daniel, 25
Clark, Emma Chichester, 108
Clement, Rod, 57, 58
Cooper, Floyd, 74
Costas, 155
Craft, Kinuko Y., 35
Crespo, George, 36, 37
Davis, Lambert, 65
Denton, Kady MacDonald, 133
Desimini, Lisa, 126, 127, 171
Dillon, Diane, 9, 66
Dillon, Leo, 9, 66
Downing, Julie, 39
Erdoes, Richard, 44
Fadden, John Kahionhes, 27
Farnsworth, Bill, 114
Fei, Chang Fu, 129
Fisher, Leonard Everett, 47, 48

Florczak, Robert, 182
Foreman, Michael, 1, 89, 162
Frampton, David, 79
Garland, Roger, 139
Gerstein, Mordicai, 54
Glass, Andrew, 146
Goble, Paul, 55
Greger, C. Shana, 61, 62
Hague, Michael, 64, 166
Hall, Wendell E., 187
Harper, Piers, 68
Harris, Kenneth, 185
Hewitson, Jennifer, 60
Heyer, Carol, 77
Hicks, Clive, 6
Hillenbrand, Will, 13
Hook, Richard, 82
Howell, Troy, 123, 124
Hubbard, Woodleigh Marx, 87
Humphries, Tudor, 69, 70, 150
Hunt, Jonathan, 84
Hutton, Warwick, 85
Hyman, Trina Schart, 78, 93
Ingpen, Robert, 147, 148
Jacob, Murv, 140, 141
Joel, Thomas, 8
Johnson, David, 91
Jones, Margaret, 29, 163
Jordan, Jael, 53
Kapheim, Thom, 86

Keeping, Charles, 131
Kellogg, Steven, 92
Koshkin, Alexander, 30, 32, 177
Larry, Charles, 97
Lattimore, Deborah Nourse, 99
Lavis, Stephen, 125
Lee, Alan, 153, 154
Lin, Zheng, 129
Locker, Thomas, 24
Lofthouse, Barbara, 101
Long, Sylvia, 104
Lytle, John, 38
Mai, Vo-Dinh, 174
McCurdy, Michael, 122
McDermott, Gerald, 110
Mexican artists, various, 117
Mikolaycak, Charles, 28
Mistry, Nilesh, 130
Miyake, Yoshi, 52
Morris, Jackie, 51
Morrisseau, Brent, 118
Moser, Barry, 67
Mosley, Francis, 81
Ndekere, Mwaura, 50
Nolan, Dennis, 183
Palin, Nicki, 109
Parker, Robert Andrew, 17, 22
Phillips, Francis, 49
Pinkney, Brian, 145
Ransome, James E., 90
Rayyan, Omar, 94
Robinson, Claire, 82
Rodanas, Kristina, 135
Rorer, Abigail, 170
Roth, Robert, 179

Roth, Susan L., 142
Sabuda, Robert, 143
Saflund, Birgitta, 73
Salim, Rashad N., 4
Segal, John, 88
Shetterly, Robert, 151
Shlichta, Joe, 41
Shute, Linda, 152
Sibbick, John, 139, 165
Smith, Cat Bowman, 63
Sneed, Brad, 59
Spirin, Gennady, 111
Stearns, Virginia, 136
Stewart, Edgar, 113
Talbott, Hudson, 156, 157
Taylor, C. J., 158, 159
Thornhill, Jan, 164
Troughton, Joanna, 167, 168
Turechek, Lou, 98
Vidal, Beatriz, 172
Volkmer, Jane Anne, 173
Waldman, Neil, 120
Wijngaard, Juan, 72, 181
Willey, Bee, 107
Wilson, Kathleen Atkins, 5
Wilson, Roberta, 46
Wisniewski, David, 180
Wood, Carol, 27
Xin, Kuan Liang, 129
Young, Ed, 102, 121, 184
Zawadzki, Marek, 83
Zeman, Ludmila, 189
Zhang, Xiu Shi, 129
Zimmer, Dirk, 31

Standard Books of Myths and Hero Tales

Bertol, Roland. *Sundiata, the Epic of the Lion King*. Illus. Gregorio Prestopino. Crowell, 1970. (Mali; Sub-Saharan Africa)

Bryson, Bernarda. *Gilgamesh*. Illus. Bernarda Bryson. Holt, Rinehart & Winston, n.d. (1968?). (Mesopotamia)

Colum, Padraic. *The Children of Odin*. Illus. Willy Pogany. Macmillan, 1964 (1920). (Norse)

Colum, Padraic. *The Children's Homer: The Adventures of Odysseus and the Tale of Troy*. Illus. Willy Pogany. Macmillan, 1962 (1918). (Greece)

Colum, Padraic. *The Golden Fleece and the Heroes Who Lived Before Achilles*. Illus. Willy Pogany. Macmillan, 1964 (1921). (Greece)

Colum, Padraic. *Myths of the World*. Illus. Boris Artzbasheff. Grosset & Dunlap, n.d. (originally titled *Orpheus*. Macmillan, 1930).

Coolidge, Olivia. *Greek Myths*. Illus. Edouard Sandoz. Houghton Mifflin, 1949.

Coolidge, Olivia. *Legends of the North*. Illus. Edouard Sandoz. Houghton Mifflin, 1951. (Norse)

D'Aulaire, Ingri, and Edgar Parin D'Aulaire. *D'Aulaires' Book of Greek Myths*. Illus. Ingri and Edgar Parin D'Aulaire. Doubleday, 1962.

D'Aulaire, Ingri, and Edgar Parin D'Aulaire. *D'Aulaires' Norse Gods and Giants*. Illus. Ingri and Edgar Parin D'Aulaire. Doubleday, 1967.

Davidson, H. R. Ellis. *Scandinavian Mythology*. Paul Hamlyn, 1969. Hamlyn published an extensive set of mythologies, all profusely and tastefully illustrated, including volumes on Greece, Rome, China, Japan, the Middle East, India, North America, Central America, South America, and Africa.

Gaer, Joseph. *The Adventures of Rama*. Illus. Randy Monk. Little, Brown, 1954. (India)

Gates, Doris. *The Golden God: Apollo*. Illus. Constantinos CoConis. Viking, 1973. (Greece; others in series)

Hamilton, Edith. *Mythology*. Illus. Steele Savage. Little, Brown, 1942. (Greek and Norse)

Hieatt, Constance. *The Castle of Ladies*. Illus. Norman Laliberte. Crowell, 1973. (England; others in Arthurian series)

Hosford, Dorothy. *Sons of the Volsungs*. Illus. John Holder. Holt, 1932. (Norse)

Hosford, Dorothy. *Thunder of the Gods*. Illus. Claire and George Louden. Holt, 1952. (Norse)

Kingsley, Charles. *The Heroes*. Illus. Joan Kiddell-Monroe. Dutton, 1965 (1855). (Greece)

Lang, Andrew. *The Story of Robin Hood and Other Tales of Adventure and Battle*. Illus. H. J. Ford. Schocken, 1968 (1902). (England)

Malcolmson, Anne. *Song of Robin Hood*. Illus. Virginia Lee Burton. Houghton Mifflin, 1947. (England)

Marriott, Alice Lee, and Carol K. Rachlin. *American Indian Mythology*. Harper, 1968.

Picard, Barbara Leonie. *Stories of King Arthur and His Knights*. Illus. Roy Morgan. Oxford, 1955. (England)

Pyle, Howard. *The Merry Adventures of Robin Hood*. Illus. Howard Pyle. Scribner's, 1929. (England)

Sutcliff, Rosemary. *Beowulf*. Illus. Charles Keeping. Bodley Head, 1961; Dutton, 1962. (England; also titled *The Dragon Slayer*, English Puffin.)

Sutcliff, Rosemary. *The Hound of Ulster*. Illus. Victor Ambrus. Bodley Head, 1963; Dutton, 1963. (Ireland)

Watson, Jane Werner. *The Iliad and the Odyssey*. Illus. Alice and Martin Provensen. Golden Press, 1956. (Greece)

About the Authors

ALETHEA K. HELBIG, Professor, and AGNES REGAN PERKINS, Professor Emeritus, both of English Language and Literature at Eastern Michigan University, have taught and published in children's literature for many years and were instrumental in initiating master's and expanded undergraduate programs in children's literature at that school. They are authors of a series of encyclopedic works on fiction for children published by Greenwood Press: *Dictionary of American Children's Fiction* (four volumes), *Dictionary of British Children's Fiction* (two volumes), and *Dictionary of Children's Fiction from Australia, Canada, India, New Zealand, and Selected African Countries*. Also published by Greenwood is their work on multicultural literature for children and young adults, *This Land Is Our Land*.

They are compilers (with Helen Hill) of *Straight on Till Morning: Poems of the Imaginary World* and *Dusk to Dawn: Poems of Night* and editors of two volumes of articles on Phoenix Award books chosen by The Children's Literature Association. In addition, Perkins has compiled (with Hill) *New Coasts and Strange Harbors: Discovering Poems*. Helbig is also author of *Nanabozhoo, Giver of Life* and is a past president of The Children's Literature Association. Both have published numerous articles on literature for young people. They are currently working on the third supplement to the *Dictionary of American Children's Fiction*.